YOU MAY ALSO LIKE

YOU MAY ALSO LIKE

TASTE IN AN AGE OF ENDLESS CHOICE

TOM VANDERBILT

ALFRED A. KNOPF

NEW YORK   TORONTO

2016

THIS IS A BORZOI BOOK
PUBLISHED BY ALFRED A. KNOPF AND ALFRED A. KNOPF CANADA

Published in the United States by Alfred A. Knopf,
a division of Penguin Random House LLC, New York,
and in Canada by Alfred A. Knopf Canada, a division of
Penguin Random House Limited, Toronto.

www.aaknopf.com
www.penguinrandomhouse.ca

Portions of this book have appeared in slightly different form in
Nautilus, The New Yorker, Slate, Smithsonian, The Wilson Quarterly, and
Wired (U.K.).

Library of Congress Cataloging-in-Publication Data
Names: Vanderbilt, Tom, author.
Title: You may also like : taste in an age of endless choice /
by Tom Vanderbilt.
Description: First edition. | New York : Alfred A. Knopf, [2016] |
Includes bibliographical references.
Identifiers: LCCN 2015026997 | ISBN 9780307958242 (hardcover) |
ISBN 9780307958259 (eBook) | ISBN 9781101947661 (open market)
Subjects: LCSH: Choice (Psychology) | Consumers' preferences. |
Aesthetics—Psychological aspects.
Classification: LCC BF611 .V36 2016 | DDC 153.8/3—dc23 LC record
available at http://lccn.loc.gov/2015026997

Library and Archives Canada Cataloguing in Publication
Vanderbilt, Tom, author
You may also like : taste in an age of endless choice /
Tom Vanderbilt.
Includes bibliographical references and index.
Issued in print and electronic formats.
ISBN 978-0-307-40262-2
eBook ISBN 978-0-307-40264-6
1. Preferences (Philosophy). 2. Choice (Psychology). 3. Senses and
sensation. 4. Consumers' preferences. I. Title.
B105.P62V35 2016   128'.3 C2015-907332-4

Jacket design by Peter Mendelsund

Manufactured in the United States of America
First Edition

TO SYLVIE

FOR WONDERING WHY

Contents

YOU MAY ALSO LIKE

WHAT'S YOUR FAVORITE COLOR (AND WHY DO YOU EVEN HAVE ONE)?

And you say to me, friends, there is no disputing over tastes and tasting? But all of life is a dispute over taste and tasting!

—Friedrich Nietzsche, *Thus Spake Zarathustra*

"What's your favorite color?"

The question came, one morning on the walk to school, from my five-year-old daughter, lately obsessed with "favorites"—declaring hers, knowing mine.

"Blue," I said, feeling very much the Western male (the West loves blue, and men love it a bit more than women).

A pause. "Why isn't our car blue, then?"

"Well, I like blue, but I don't like it as much for cars."

She processes this. "My favorite color is red." This marks a change. Last week it was pink. On the horizon, green seems to be entering the picture.

"Is that why you wore red pants today?" I ask.

She smiles. "Do you have any red pants?"

"No," I say. When I lived in Spain, I bought and wore a pair of red pants, because I had noticed Spanish men wearing them. Once I got to New York, where hardly any men wore red pants, they stayed in the drawer. What was mainstream in Madrid was, to my eyes anyway, quite fashion forward in America circa 1991. But I do not explain any of this to her.

"You should get a pair of red pants."

"You think so?"

Nods. "What's your favorite number?"

This stops me. "Hmmm, I'm not sure I have a favorite number." Then I offer, "Maybe eight." As I say it, I try to fathom why. Perhaps because as a young child I always thought it was the most fun to write?

"Mine is six," she says.

"Why?"

Furrows brow, shrugs. "I don't know. I just like it."

Why do we like the things we like? In our brief conversation, my daughter and I had raised at least five important principles in the science of preferences. First, they tend be *categorical:* I like blue, just not for cars (and why ever not?). You may like orange juice, just not in cocktails. Second, they are usually *contextual.* The pants that charmed in Spain did not wear so well in New York. You have probably brought home some souvenir from your travels (espadrilles, a colorful blanket) that delighted in the place of its purchase but now sits in baleful exile in a closet. People buy fewer black cars when it gets hotter and pay more for houses with pools in the summertime. Third, they are often *constructed.* When asked for my favorite number, a digit swam into my head first, dragging in its wake possible explanations. Fourth, they are inherently *comparative.* Even before infants can talk, they seem more drawn to those who share their taste than those who do not. In one elegantly constructed (and no doubt fun to watch) study, infants first chose one of two foods. Then puppets were shown either "liking" or "disliking" those same foods. When the puppets were presented to the infants, the young research subjects tended to reach for the ones who "liked" the food they liked. Maddeningly, however, tastes are rarely *congenital:* However we may try to influence them, however much genetic material we share, children rarely match parental preferences in anything.

My daughter and I ended the conversation with the most familiar fact of all about tastes and preferences: They can be devilishly hard to explain. Nearly three centuries ago, the philosopher Edmund Burke, in one of the first thoroughgoing essays on taste, complained that "this delicate and aerial faculty, which seems too volatile to endure even the chains of a definition, cannot be properly tried by any test, nor regulated by any standard."

People struggling to understand taste have sometimes suggested there is nothing to explain. As the Nobel Prize–winning economists George Stigler and Gary Becker controversially argued, "No significant behavior has been illuminated by assumptions of differences in taste." Because any behavior—my daughter's fondness for the number six—could simply be attributed to a private preference, preferences could seem to "explain everything and therefore nothing." Arguing over tastes, Stigler and Becker suggested, would be like arguing over the Rocky Mountains: "Both are there, will be there next year, too, and are the same to all men."

But the Rocky Mountains *are* changing, as one economist noted, just not at a speed one can discern. As psychologists, increasingly aided by neuroscientists, have shown, in study after study, tastes change, often in the course of a single experiment: We like food more when a certain music is played; we like a certain music less when we learn some insalubrious fact about its composer.

Our tastes seem endlessly "adaptive," in the word favored by the influential Norwegian political theorist Jon Elster. Using the fable of sour grapes, in which the hapless fox, unable to reach a bunch of grapes he clearly desires, labels them "sour," Elster noted that rather than simply move on to his *next* preferred choice—as "rational choice" theorists might have it—the fox retroactively "downgrades" the grapes. The grapes were not sour, nor did the fox lose his overall taste for grapes. Preferences, Elster argued, may also be "counter-adaptive": Not being able to get the grapes, in a different situation, might have only increased the fox's desire to have them. In both cases, the preference seems shaped by the constraints of the moment, and the question looms: What is the fox's *true* preference for the grapes?

Where economists tend to think that a choice "reveals" a preference, psychologists often suspect a choice *creates* the preference. Imagine the fox making a "free choice" between grapes and cherries and then reporting he likes more what he has chosen; is he choosing what he wants or wanting what he chooses? Both may be right, for trying to fathom taste itself is a slippery process. Already you may be wondering, are we talking about the sensory experience of taste? Or one's taste in clothes? Or what society thinks is "good taste"? These are all subtly interrelated; the fox could have enjoyed the taste of the grapes, but he also could have liked the feeling of being the only animal able to enjoy the grapes.

For now, think of taste as the things one likes (for whatever reason). But one still has to identify the tastes; note who holds those tastes; try to account for why they do; then try to explain why other people (who might be quite similar across other variables) do *not*; try to figure out why tastes change; what tastes are for; and so on. As the design writer Stephen Bayley surmised, hoisting the flag of surrender, "An academic history of taste is not so much difficult as impossible." And yet, I think we can account for tastes. We can discern why and how we come to have tastes or what is going on when we express a preference for something out of a crowded field.

What is *your* favorite number? If you are like most people, you answered, "Seven." Seven—again, in the West—is the blue of numbers. The two were so often chosen together as favorites in a set of 1970s studies that psychologists began to talk of a "blue seven phenomenon," almost as if they were linked in some way. Leaving aside color for a moment, why should seven be preferred?

As with most preferences, the answer is a tangle of cultural learning, psychological biases, and internal qualities, influenced by the context of the choice. The simplest reason seven is a favorite is that it is culturally popular. It is the "lucky" number, probably because it is "the sacred number *par excellence*," as one scholar described it, making noteworthy appearances "in the Bible and the Rabbinic literature." Perhaps it is the way our ability to keep strings of things in working memory falls off at the "magical" seven (hence the digits in your phone number).

Or maybe there is something about seven itself. When asked to name the first number between one and ten that pops into their heads, people most often say seven (followed by three). They may want to make the choice that feels most "random," which seems, for obscure reasons of "mathiness," to be seven. We can imagine the thought process: "One or ten? Too obvious. Five? That's right in the middle. Two? Even numbers seem less random than odd ones, don't they? Zero? Is that a number?" As a prime, seven seems less related to other numbers, thus more random: It stands alone; it came unaccompanied by patterns. But for all its power, when you change the context—think of a number between six and twenty-two—suddenly seven is no longer the top choice. And yet its influence lives on; seventeen now comes out on top.

Each day, we are asked to decide, in many different ways, why we like one thing more than another. Why did you change the radio station when that song came on? Why did you "like" that Facebook post and not the other one? Why did you choose the lemonade over the Diet Coke? At one end, these choices are small and mundane ways we have of ordering our world, much as we "order" breakfast: "How would you like your eggs? White or whole wheat? Sausage or bacon?" As minor as those choices seem, you can surely appreciate the displeasure involved when they are gotten wrong. At the other end, these preferences might have morphed into broad, deep-seated tastes that help us define who we are: "I *love* country music." "I adore the sound of the French language." "I don't like sci-fi films."

As for why my daughter was so obsessed with favorites, there is actually scant research on the topic. With a touch of alarm, I noted that in one of the rare mentions of a "favorite number" I could find in the scientific literature, it was associated with obsessive-compulsive disorders. Without a grand theory, it is not hard to envision "favorites" as easily understood, cheaply acquired tokens of identity, ways of asserting yourself in the world and understanding others, of showing you are both like *and* unlike other people. Tellingly, one of the first items of information my daughter gives me about a new friend, after noting the child's birthday, is his or her favorite color.

One might presume that we grow out of this ever-shifting whirlwind of preferences and become rational holders of stable tastes. But this is not always the case. For example, we often, as if by superstition, seem to have a predilection for things that have no intrinsic superiority over another thing.

When you enter a public bathroom, for instance, do you have a preference for which stall to use? Assuming all are open, do you like to take one that is on the end of the row or in the middle? According to at least one study, conducted at a "public restroom at a California state beach" (and clearly reporting from the frontiers of social science), people preferred the middle stalls over the ends. The patrons were not queried, but one might imagine they had their reasons, just as with choosing a number. The first stall may seem too close to the door, while the stall on the end seems too far away. So the one in the middle is "just right." Is it the best choice? It depends on the criteria (ironically, these most preferred stalls may be the least clean, according to one microbiologist who measured bacteria counts).

To take another bathroom example, there is no strongly functional basis in a preference for the toilet paper being hung "over" or "under." Has paper mounted in either fashion ever failed to adequately dispatch? As inconsequential as either preference may seem, the advice columnist Ann Landers famously reported that it generated the highest volume of letters of any issue—abortion, gun control—she had tackled.

Perhaps the intimate nature of bathrooms brings out curiously strident convictions. But preferences can be so weak that they appear to be what psychologists call "unmotivated preferences," or preferences that seem to emerge for no real reason. Unmotivated preferences are, as one study described them, "a bit of experimental debris that tidy psychological theories have yet to sweep up." Perhaps we are employing some unseen, and barely expressed, rule in making such choices, a rule that helps us, in essence, choose without making a choice. Even then, the idea that most people settle on the same preference would hint that the most seemingly arbitrary choice might have some reasoning to it (and hence is not truly unmotivated).

But where does that preference *come* from? A classic exercise in linguistics is to ask people which of a series of words (for example, "blick" or "bnick") could most realistically be a word in English. You do not have to be a Scrabble champion to guess that "blick" is more likely, simply because there are English words that start with "bl" but none with "bn." But what happens, asks the MIT linguist Adam Albright, when you ask people to pick the word they prefer out of a series of words that are *all* unlikely to be real English words—"bnick," "bdick," "bzick"? How and why does one prefer something when there seems to be little solid basis for a preference, and yet one *must* choose among alternatives (in what is called a "forced choice" exercise)? If people seem to prefer "bnick," is it because it somehow seems most like other words in English (even if it is not)? Or is it because of some inherent "phonological bias"; that is, we like the way one "onset cluster"—what linguists term those first two consonants in the beginning of "bnick" or "bzick"—sounds more than the other when we say it? The answer seems to be in some ineffable combination of what we have learned and what we inherently favor. Because learning to like things usually happens beneath the level of conscious awareness, it can be hard to tell the two apart.

Which brings us back to blue. Not long after my daughter made her pronouncement, I traveled to Berkeley to visit Stephen Palmer, a professor of psychology at the University of California who directs the Visual Perception and Aesthetics Lab, usually just called the Palmer Lab. Palmer and his colleagues have come up with one of the more compelling theories for why we like the colors we do.

As we sat in his cluttered basement office, where his rendition of Van Gogh's *Starry Night* brought some relief to the institutional environment, Palmer told me that his interest in aesthetics came out of his own amateur photography (he painted the *Starry Night* for an art class he took to further understand artistic practice). As with all art, it involves discovering a series of preferences: What do I want to photograph? What angle would make the best photograph? Where to position the subject? Aspiring photographers like Palmer are typically taught to employ the famous "rule of thirds," placing the focal object of the work somewhere along the lines that divide the image, horizontally and vertically, into three parts. And yet, when he has asked subjects to rate their liking for photographs, or given them cameras and asked them to produce images that most pleased them, the overwhelming preference was to have images in the *center* of the composition.

Which raises another question: Why are artists being trained to produce images that people do not seem to prefer? Why would artists' preferences not match wider preferences? Palmer queried a range of art and music students (for a control, he added psychology students) on their "preference for harmony," as he called it; they would listen to different composers, see different color combinations, look at circles placed at different spots in rectangles. The participants all more or less agreed on what was harmonious (Maurice Ravel more so than the atonally inclined Arnold Schoenberg). But when it came to the art and music students, what they *liked* began to diverge from what they thought was harmonious.

Were they just being snobs? Does art training lower one's interest in harmony, or do people with lower preferences for harmony become artists? Palmer is not sure. It could be that the more one studies art, the more one requires a "stronger" stimulus to maintain interest. "I think some of it is just sort of overexposure," Palmer said. "I think you get bored with the same thing. You start out trying spatial compositions where the important stuff is in the middle of the frame, but it gets to be kind of boring. Moreover, the teachers reinforce novelty, and they actually tell you not to put things in the center of the frame."

Whether artist or layperson, we all have an aesthetic response. We cannot but help think—whether consciously or not—whether we like or dislike something. Days after being born, babies show a strong preference for looking at faces that are looking at them. So what would it be about blue, then, that would make so many people like it? Since the dawn of psychology, when the pioneering researcher Joseph Jastrow handed out color samples at the World's Columbian Exposition in 1893, querying thousands of visitors, people have generally been putting blue on top.

Does it just seem to hit some chromatic sweet spot? If we were born with this love of blue, however, one might expect most infants to prefer it. In one study, Palmer had infant subjects (at least those not dismissed for "general fussiness") look at pairs of colored circles. "Looking time" is used as a general indicator of infant (and, less so, adult) preference: The longer you look, the more you like. Adult subjects were given the same test. While blue, predictably, was the color that adults were most likely to spend time looking at, the infants not only did not show a decided preference for blue but seemed to possess a particular liking for "dark yellow." This happens to be one of the colors most typically *disliked* by adults (Palmer has his own scientific designation for this range of brownish yellows: "icky-poo colors").

What was going on? Palmer, and his colleague Karen Schloss, have an idea—called the ecological valence theory—that might explain both the adult and the infant preferences. The theory is that we like the colors of the *things* we most like. Their experimental procedure was elegantly simple. First, a group of subjects was asked to rate how much they liked thirty-two colors. Then another group was asked to name, in twenty seconds, as many things as they could that had that color. A final group was then asked to rate how much they liked these things. What they liked predicted, 80 percent of the time, what colors they liked. Blue, not surprisingly, came out on top, for think of what blue evokes: clear sky, clean water. Who does not like these things—indeed need them to survive? Might the predominance of blue shirts and khaki pants in men's wardrobes have something to do with nature? "It happens at the beach," the journalist Peter Kaplan once commented on his favored outfit of pale blue shirt and tan trousers. "The ocean meets the shore." Who does not like the seashore?

A color like a brownish yellow, by contrast, which did not do well in Palmer's test, can summon a host of unpleasant connotations: dark mucus, vomit, pus, the 1970s AMC Pacer. But then why did the infants seem so fond of the dark yellowish colors?

The beauty of the theory is that it encompasses the idea that color preference, like food preference, might be both evolutionarily hardwired (we like the things that are good for us) and a function of adaptive learning (we learn about things that make us feel good). Infants, after all, have not yet learned to associate things like feces with disgust—as any parent who has waged battle on the changing table can attest. It could also be, Palmer suggests, "to make up a story," of the sort that evolutionary accounts must in some sense be, that infant "liking" for the dark yellow-brownish spectrum has to do with some resemblance to the mother's nipple, which they eventually turn away from, or learn to dislike.

The ecological valence theory has been tested in other ways. When Palmer and his colleagues queried students at Berkeley and Stanford on a range of colors, they found that students at each college preferred their own school's colors to those of their rival school. The more they liked the school, the more they liked the colors. For Palmer, this hints that color preference comes more from association than from the colors themselves; it is unlikely, after all, that someone goes to Berkeley because he happens to like blue and gold. Show people images of positive things that are red (strawberries, tomatoes), and their reported liking of red goes up. Prime them with pictures of open wounds or a scab, their ardor for red dims a bit. Query Democrats and Republicans on Election Day, and their liking for blue or red, the colors that have of late become associated with each party, goes up slightly.

Talk to people in the color industry, and they will describe a version of adaptive learning quite similar to ecological valence. Leatrice Eiseman, the noted color consultant (she urged HP to come out with a teal-colored computer some months before Apple released its groundbreaking iMac), notes that people may have an initial aversion to a color like chartreuse—which occasionally goes through spells as a fashionable hue—but then they begin giving it a second look. "I call it your peripheral vision," she told me. "Oh, there's yellow-green there and yellow-green there. Hmmm, it's not such a bad color; it doesn't look bad in a shirt." And then suddenly you have forgotten why you disliked it. As Tom Mirabile, an executive at Lifetime Brands (the company that was on the cutting edge of bringing non-white appliances into the kitchen), described it to me, "You see it enough, and you start thinking it's something you want to see."

Some have argued, suggesting that the all-choices-are-constructed theory had gone too far, that preferences for things like consumer goods can be "inherent," in that they existed all along, buried like repressed memories, waiting to be unlocked. The iPhone, the argument goes, made us realize people actually did not prefer a mechanical keyboard on a smartphone (the way many insisted they did). And yet culture often lurks behind supposedly "natural" preferences. The idea that pink is "naturally" a color for girls is complicated by the fact that in the early part of the last century pink was thought of as the color for *boys*. It is most probable that girls like pink because they see other girls wearing pink. For even if females did slightly favor "reddish" hues, as some studies have found, this would hardly explain why pink is not deemed an appropriate color for boys' bicycles or red is so infrequent a color for girls' bikes—and indeed why one so rarely sees an adult woman's bike in pink.

And so begins a sort of feedback loop: The more chances one has to see a color, and the more that seeing that color is associated with positive experiences (a pink cake at a girl's birthday party, a man's purple shirt), the more one's liking for that color will increase. The more one likes the color, the more one will use it to help create other positive experiences: Red is great on a Ferrari, why not on a blender? As Palmer describes it, "We go through the world accumulating these statistics about the color associations of things that we like versus what we don't like; there's a sense in which we are constantly updating these things." Just as my daughter was constantly reassessing her favorites, we are, Palmer argues, "computing this stuff on the fly." A favorite color is like a chromatic record of everything that has ever made you feel good.

. . .

One day, a few years ago, I suddenly began noticing how much, in the course of an average day, I was asked whether I liked something or not (sometimes I was asking myself the question) and how muddled the answer often was. To wit,

"I saw that movie." "Did you like it?" "Yeah, sort of."

Or,

"We ate at that new Thai place." "Was it good?" "It was good, but not as good as I had hoped."

And, invariably,

Your opinion is important to us. Please tell us your thoughts on a scale from to 1 to 5 (1 = strongly dislike, 5 = strongly like).

But what did all this really mean? How many gradations could there be in a hedonic experience—were five enough? What did it mean when I thumbed a "like" on an Instagram post? That I liked the content of the image, the way it was shot, or the person posting it? Did my liking depend on how many others had or had not liked it? Was *not* "liking" it saying that I actually did not like it? Was I even aware of what was going on in my head as the electrical impulses traveled from brain to thumb? Just having a face in an Instagram photograph, as research has shown, drives up liking by some 30 percent (it does not matter how old or young, whether male or female, whether one person or ten—just a face). Did this fact consciously enter into my decision to move my thumb?

We are faced with an ever-increasing amount of things to figure out whether we like or dislike, and yet at the same time there are fewer overarching rules and standards to go by in helping one decide. Online, we swim in the streams of other people's opinions—the four-star Yelp review, the YouTube dislike—but whose opinion deserves attention? When you can listen to almost any song in the world, how do you decide what to play and whether you like it? The world is topsy-turvy: Foods and fashions that were once rarely attainable become commonplace, while things that were once commonplace are elevated into objects of connoisseurship. If it's "all good," is anything bad?

I want to ask the questions we rarely seem to as we ever more rapidly formulate our hedonic and aesthetic responses. Are liking and disliking merely opposite conditions on the same spectrum, or are they different things? How do we come to like things we once disliked? How much can liking be quantified? Why does the taste of experts and laypeople so often diverge? Can the pleasure of liking something that you think you are supposed to like be a sufficient substitute for liking something because you authentically like it? Do we know what we like or like what we know?

In 2000, a team of Italian neuroscientists reported an unusual case involving an older man suffering from frontotemporal dementia. He had suddenly acquired a liking for Italian pop music, a genre he had previously referred to as "mere noise" (he once liked mostly classical). It was not so much that he "forgot" his previous tastes; in Alzheimer's patients, for example, aesthetic preferences seem to survive, even as other memories fade. Rather, the researchers suggested, the neural effects of his treatment might have awakened in him a new desire for novelty.

This rapid, wholesale switch in tastes raises a number of questions. How open are we to changing our tastes? What happens in our brain when we discover that we no longer dislike something, when we decide that "mere noise" may actually be pleasurable music? Are some of us, by dint of our neural architecture, more open to novelty or more predisposed to like certain combinations of pitch and rhythm?

Let us imagine that the man's condition actually unlocked in him an existing—but repressed—preference for pop music. The idea seems far-fetched. But how much do we actually know about our own tastes, these collections of preferences and predispositions?

In an experiment conducted at a country fair in Germany, people were asked to sample two kinds of ketchup. They were both the same variety of Kraft, but a small amount of vanillin (a flavor compound of the vanilla bean) had been added to one. Why? In Germany, infant formula typically contains small amounts of the stuff. In a list of questions about food preference, the researchers rather slyly asked visitors if they had been bottle- or breast-fed as infants. People who were breast-fed overwhelmingly preferred the "natural" ketchup, while bottle-fed people liked the one with the hint of vanilla. It is unlikely they made any connection; they just liked what they liked.

One often hears, and says, with a shake of the head, "There's no accounting for taste." Typically, this comes as an incredulous response to someone *else's* taste. The person who says this rarely uses it to suggest that he might scarcely be able to explain his own tastes to himself. After all, what could be more authentic to us than the things we like? When preferences are actually tested, however, the results can be surprising, even unsettling, to those who hold them. The French social scientist Claudia Fritz has examined, in various settings, the preferences of accomplished violinists for instruments made by old Italian masters like Stradivari. Everyone knows, if only from hearing of these incredibly valuable instruments being left in the backs of taxicabs, how lush and resonant they must sound, as if bestowed with some ancient, now lost magic. Who would not want to play one? But the expert musicians she has tested tend to prefer, under blind conditions, the sound of new violins.

In his book *Strangers to Ourselves*, Timothy Wilson has argued that we are often unaware why we respond to things the way we do; much of this behavior occurs in what he calls the "adaptive unconscious." But we labor under a sort of illusion of authenticity, he argues, in which we think we know the reasons for our feelings because, well, they are *our* feelings. Following his example, how do you feel about the cover of this book? Do you like it? If you had a choice—and book buyers rarely do—which of the two covers did you prefer? Did you stop to think why you might have preferred one over another? Or is your preference only now swimming into view? Now try to imagine how a stranger feels about it. Unless the cover strikes some particular chord in you—perhaps it reminds you of another book you liked, or you are a student of graphic design—your own response to the cover will most likely be generated by a process that is not so different from how you would explain why a stranger likes it (for example, it gets your attention, the colors work together better). You will be making guesses.*

We are, in effect, strangers to our tastes. It is time we got acquainted. It seems only appropriate to begin with food, "the archetype of all taste."

---

* For added fun, now try to explain why the same book will typically have such different covers in different countries.

CHAPTER 1

WHAT WOULD YOU LIKE?

THINKING ABOUT OUR TASTE FOR FOOD

IT ALL SOUNDS SO GOOD;
OR, WHY THERE IS SO LITTLE WE SHOULD NOT LIKE

Nowhere do we encounter the question of what we like so broadly, so forcefully, so instinctively as in a restaurant meal. Sitting down to eat is not just a ritual of nourishment but a kind of story. Venturing through the "course of a meal," we encounter a narrative, with its prologues, its climaxes, its slow resolutions. But a meal is also a concentrated exercise in choice and pleasure, longing and regret, the satisfaction of wants and the creation of desires.

And so we begin our journey with the journey of a meal. It is a blustery winter day on the windy western reaches of Manhattan, but inside Del Posto, the Italian restaurant run by Mario Batali and Joe and Lidia Bastianich, the wood-paneled room is warmly lit, a pianist is deep into "Send in the Clowns," and the red wine is being poured by a waiter with a Continental accent and well-honed charm.

What's not to like?

Very little, really. One does not generally arrive at the white-clothed table of a restaurant accorded four stars by *The New York Times*, only to find a raft of unpalatable swill. The very fact that the food has made it onto the menu—the menu of a long-established culinary tradition—reflects that it is generally liked. We are not our evolutionary ancestors, forced to graze on the culinary savanna, scrounging for sustenance amid a host of unfamiliar plants and elusive prey, waiting for our bodies to tell us whether we like (or will survive) what we have chosen.

Nevertheless, the old tickle at the back of the brain—*eat this, not that!*—has hardly left us. We are born knowing two things: Sweet is good (caloric energy), bitter is bad (potential toxin). We also come into the world with a curious blend of full-spectrum liking and disliking. We are, on the one hand, omnivores. There is little we could not eat. As Paul Rozin, a psychologist at the University of Pennsylvania, has helpfully pointed out, we share this "generalist" status "with such other worthy species as rats and cockroaches." And yet, like rats, we are intensely "neophobic," afraid of trying new foods. Being dual omnivores/neophobes has its evolutionary advantages: The latter trait kept us from ingesting the wrong things; the former made sure we had plenty of access to the right things. But neophobia can go too far. In some experiments, rats, once mildly poisoned by new foods, became so afraid of subsequent new foods that they starved to death.

We actually seem predisposed to be more acutely aware of what we do not like than of what we like. We are particularly alert to even minor changes in what we *do* like, as if we had an internal alarm for when things go wrong. When I am served, by mistake, diet soda, which I do not like and thus do not drink, my response borders on the visceral: *Danger!* This alarm is most well tuned for the bitter, and we rate "aversive" tastes as being more intense than pleasurable ones. The worm found in the last bite of an otherwise delicious apple will pretty much wipe out the pleasure accumulated from eating the rest of it. Although this may be an occasional drag on our ability to enjoy life, being primed to spot the bad helps us have a life to enjoy.

And so, a few days out of the womb, we are already expressing preferences, picking sugary water over the plain variety, making faces at (some) bitter foods. This is pure survival, eating to live. We start getting *really* choosy at around age two, when we have figured out (a) we might be sticking around for a while and (b) we have the luxury of choice. The need for raw sustenance explains why for infants nothing can really be too sweet: It is the primordial liking. Even our desire for salt, which is so vital to the human endeavor that it informs town names like Salzburg and those English burghs with "wich" (brine pits were known as "wich houses") as their suffix, takes a few months to kick in.

Liking for sweetness is liking for life itself. As Gary Beauchamp, at the time the director of Philadelphia's Monell Chemical Senses Center—the country's preeminent taste and smell lab—had put it to me in his office one day, "I would say that *all* human pleasure derives from sugar. It's the prototypical thing—a single compound stimulating a very specific set of receptors." He told me this after first casually proffering a sample from a can of salted army ants (the ingredient label read, "Ants, salt"). Other kinds of substances—like salted ants—may have a more wayward trip upstream, he intimates, but with sugar "that pathway goes directly to the parts of the brain that are involved in emotion and pleasure." Even anencephalic babies, born missing parts of the brain that are central to consciousness, respond positively (through what's called a "gustofacial response") to sweetness. No one living really dislikes sweetness; they may only like it less than others do.

But few of our gustatory preferences are innate; that lump of sugar, a touch of salt, perhaps the feel of fat as it glides across our tongue, even those are not beyond change. Nor is much of what we do not like. Some people may be more biologically sensitive to certain substances, but often that is not taste per se. Cilantro, for some, brings out a "soapy" taste, but it has been argued that has to do with genetic variation in *olfactory* receptors. Meanwhile, only half the population, as it fries up pork chops or grills sausage, seems able to detect "boar taint." This is an unpleasant scent, to humans at least, often described as "off," evoking "urine," or, simply, being "pig like." Boar taint comes from androstenes, a steroid-driven musk that steams off male boars during mating to boost their desirability. The ability of humans to smell it is genetic, though people can be trained to detect it (for professional, not hobby, purposes).

But there is not a clear line between one's biological sensitivity to substances and one's food likes and dislikes. Beauchamp theorizes this may be some population-wide adaptive mechanism. One group liked a certain plant, and another group liked another; if one plant turned out to lack sufficient nutrition, it would not mean the end of the species. Just because you find a substance more bitter than someone else, however, does not mean you are going to like it any less. As one researcher puts it, "It is striking how little genetics predisposes humans to like or dislike food flavors."

And yet go to a restaurant, even a well-reviewed exemplar of a beloved cuisine, like Del Posto, and there will be things on the menu that you seem to prefer to others (this may even change from one day to another). The very array of choices that you are presented with—from the opening salvo of "Would you like fizzy or still water?"—speaks to this litany of tastes. But what actually goes on in the mind to make these decisions between seemingly inconsequential choices, of whether one prefers carbonation in one's water? An extra frisson of excitement to hydration? Or the desire for a more languorously silken mouthfeel? How passionate are you in your choice, or is it rather arbitrary? Let us imagine you opt for still. This earns you another choice: "Would you like tap or bottled?" Reasons though you may have for choosing one or the other, it almost certainly has nothing to do with sensory discernment: Studies show that most of us cannot distinguish the stuff.

As adamant as we are in our likes—"I *love ragù* Bolognese," one might say—we are even more adamant in our dislikes. "I can't *stand* eggplant," my wife has said, more than once. If pressed, though, we would find it hard to locate the precise origin of these preferences. Is there some ancient evolutionary fear at work here? Eggplant, after all, is part of the nightshade family, and its leaves, in high enough doses, can be toxic. Then again, tomatoes and potatoes are in the same *Solanum* genus, and my wife happily eats those.

She is certainly not alone in finding eggplant off-putting. Its mention in the culinary press often comes cloaked in cheerily conditional phrases like "love it or hate it" and "even if you dislike it," while one survey of Japanese schoolchildren found it to be the "most disliked" vegetable. It is probably a texture thing; done wrong, eggplant can feel a bit slimy, a trait we do not always prize. Indeed, texture, or mouthfeel, should not be underestimated: Not only can we literally "taste" texture, but as the food scientist Alina Surmacka Szczesniak has written, "People like to be in full control of the food placed in their mouth. Stringy, gummy, or slimy food or those with unexpected lumps or hard particles are rejected for fear of gagging or choking."

But our feelings about food are not often so clearly causal. Poison leaves aside, there is no biological aversion to eggplant itself or to most other foods. As the psychologist Paul Rozin—famously dubbed the King of Disgust for his work into aversions—once told me, over a meal in Philadelphia of sweet-and-sour shrimp, "Our explanations for why we like and dislike things are pretty lame. We have to invent accounts."

And yet where else but with food is liking and disliking so elemental? Our choices in food are directly related to our immediate or long-term well-being. Not to mention we are actually putting something in our mouths. "Since putting external things into the body can be thought of as a highly personal and risky act," Rozin has written, "the special emotion associated with ingestion is understandable." And then there is the simple fact that we eat so often. The Cornell University researcher Brian Wansink has estimated we make two hundred food decisions a day. We decide what to eat more than we decide what to wear or what to read or where to go on vacation—and what is a holiday but a whole new set of eating choices?

Not that eating is always driven by some unadulterated quest for pleasure. As Danielle Reed, a researcher at Monell, had suggested to me, there is more than one kind of food liking. There is liking in which you give someone food in a lab and ask her how much she likes it. This is relatively simple, more so than asking *why* she likes it. There is liking on the level of a person going into a store, and does she choose this or that? This is a bit more complicated. "And then there's what people habitually eat," Reed said. "As you can imagine, that's not a direct reflection of how much you like it." She gestured to some food carts across the street, visible through her office window. "I had God-knows-what something nasty for lunch. It's not what I *like*; it's just what happened to be convenient." It is sometimes difficult to distinguish between actual liking and simply choosing among the least disliked alternatives. An "interesting question," she suggested, and one that I will return to later in the book, is, how much do people differ in how much they respond to their own liking? For some, liking may be the key driver; others may lean more on other criteria.

Something besides sheer frequency makes liking so crucial in food: the idea that we bring all of our senses—and a whole lot more—to what we eat. Synesthetes aside, we do not like the sound of paintings or the smell of music. When you like something you eat, however, you are typically liking not only the way it tastes but also the way it smells, the way it feels, the way it looks (we like the same food less when we eat it in the dark). We even like the way it sounds. Research has shown that amping up just the high-frequency "crispiness" sounds of potato chips makes them seem crispier—and presumably more liked.

It can often be a bit hard to tell what is actually driving our liking: People have, for example, reported deeper-colored fruit juice—up to a point—as tasting better than lighter, but similarly flavored, varieties. On the other hand, toying with one of the "sensory inputs" can radically change things. When trained panelists cannot see the milk they are drinking, they suddenly find it hard to determine its fat content (as they lose the vital visual cue of "whiteness"). Flipping the switch on a special light in the course of one meal—so that a steak was suddenly bathed in a bluish tint—was enough, according to one marketing study, to virtually induce nausea.

We call our liking for all kinds of things—music, fashion, art—our "taste." It is interesting (and not accidental) that this word for our more general predilections coincides with our sense of taste. Carolyn Korsmeyer, a professor of philosophy at the University of Buffalo, notes that traditionally the notion of "bodily pleasure" did not discriminate between these two sorts of taste. The way we enjoyed art and music was not so dissimilar from the way we enjoyed food.

That began to change, at least to philosophers, in the eighteenth century. Gustatory taste (that "low," "physical" pleasure, which actually entails ingesting something) did not fit neatly into the philosopher Immanuel Kant's influential notion of "disinterested pleasure"—of coolly analyzing "free beauty" at a physical and intellectual remove—in terms of judging aesthetic quality. As Korsmeyer writes in *Making Sense of Taste: Food and Philosophy*, "In virtually all analyses of the senses in Western philosophy the distance between object and perceiver has been seen as a cognitive, moral, and aesthetic advantage." We look at paintings or watch movies without being *in* them, or them in us. But how could you ever divorce liking food from its host of "bodily sensations"? Ever since, taste, in terms of what we eat, has been judged as primal and instinctive, as well as hopelessly private and relative. "The all-important problem of Taste," writes Korsmeyer, "was not conceived to pertain to sensory taste."

. . .

It was bearing this heavy philosophical and scientific load that I sat down to lunch at Del Posto, joined by Debra Zellner, a professor of psychology at Montclair State University, who for several decades has studied the intersection of food and "positive affect," as they say in the field. A onetime student of Paul Rozin's—a disciple of disgust, if you will—in her work on liking, she has watched rats as they lapped at dripping tubes, and, more salubriously, she has conducted experiments with the Culinary Institute of America on how "plating" can influence how much food we eat.

With rats, the equation is fairly simple: If they eat it, they like it. The more they eat, the more they like (and vice versa). Rat eating behavior does not change according to who is watching or to feelings of guilt or virtuousness. Humans are trickier. Asking people what they like often does not reveal the full truth of what they eat, but neither does measuring what they eat always match up with what they like. In Zellner's plating study, the same restaurant meal, on different nights, was presented first rather conventionally and then with a bit more flair. People who got the latter treatment actually reported liking the food more. When plates were weighed, however, there was no difference between the "conventional" and "flair" groups in the amount of food consumed.

Zellner, who has spent decades thinking about liking, is herself a case study for the vagaries of it. As we sat down, she informed me that she is allergic to dairy. Does this mean she instinctively does not like it? Not at all. To acquire a "conditioned taste aversion," a visceral dislike of a food, one must generally vomit after consuming it. The reason for this is an ongoing mystery. As Paul Rozin wondered, "What is the adaptive value of endowing nausea with a qualitatively different (hedonic) change as opposed to other events, including gut pain?" Perhaps the simple intensity of dislike, the conscious removal of the food *from the stomach itself,* sears itself into memory.

The importance of the nauseous response may even go beyond food: Rozin notes that the "aversive gape"—that scrunching and slight opening of the mouth upon ingesting something gross—has the "function to promote egress of substances from the mouth." This particular face (and we use more facial muscles when we eat food we do not like) is what we also use to signal all kinds of disgust, from bad smells to unpleasant images to moral transgressions. Disgust *began*, he suggested, with disliked food: the mouth as gatekeeper, the gape as message. Instances of disgusting behavior, which leave a "bad taste in the mouth," may in some ancient or metaphoric sense be akin to an actual bad taste in the mouth that needs to be expelled.

Precisely because Zellner is allergic, she has never eaten enough of a dairy product to get severe nausea. So she dwells in a purgatory of pleasure—pitched somewhere between desire and revulsion. She admitted to not caring for the mouthfeel of many dairy products. "Maybe because I know that it means I have just consumed something that might make me feel bad. I don't know." To complicate matters, she occasionally "cheats" with cheese, eating tiny shards of especially alluring varieties.

The waiter appeared. "Is this your first time at Del Posto?" It is an innocent question but one that itself is important, as we shall see. As we study the menu, one of the principal liking questions looms. "What determines what you're selecting?" Zellner asked, as I wavered between the "Heritage Pork Trio" with "Ribollita alla Casella and Black Cabbage Stew" and the "Wild Striped Bass" with "Soft Sunchokes, Wilted Romaine & Warm Occelli Butter." "What I'm choosing, is that liking?" she continues. "It's not liking the taste, because I don't have it in my mouth." If I had been to this restaurant before and had a particular dish, I might remember liking it. One might argue that liking is entirely based on memory: The single biggest predictor for whether you will like a food is whether you have had it before (more on that in a while).

But let us say it is new to me. Perhaps I like the *idea* of it, because it reminds me of similar choices in the past. "Choices depend on tastes," as one economist wrote, "as tastes depend on past choices." Perhaps it is the way the entrée is described. Language is a seasoning that can make food seem even more palatable. Words like "warm" and "soft" and "heritage" are not idle; they are appetizers for the brain. In his book *The Omnivorous Mind*, the neuroscientist John S. Allen notes that simply hearing an onomatopoetic word like "crispy"—which the chef Mario Batali calls "innately appealing"—is "likely to evoke the sense of eating that type of food." The more tempting the language, the more strongly one rehearses the act of consumption. The economist Tyler Cowen argues one should resist such blandishments and order the thing that sounds *least* appetizing on a menu. "An item won't be on the menu unless there's a good reason for its presence," he writes. "If it sounds bad, it probably tastes especially good."

But it is hard to find anything that does not appetize on this menu. "It all sounds so good," says Zellner (a curious phrase because we are reading the menu to ourselves). At this point, all we can be sure of what we like is this: We like to choose. The mere fact of having a menu of items from which to choose, research has shown, lifts all our liking for *all* items on that menu. And while the anticipation of our choice excites us, our anticipation of being able to *make* a choice, as brain imaging work has shown, seems to result in more neural activity than simply looking forward to getting something without making a choice.

If language helps us "pre-eat" the food, something similar goes on as we merely consider the choice. "Prefeeling" is how the psychologists Timothy Wilson and Daniel Gilbert have described it. In their view, we "try out" different future scenarios, taking our hedonic response in the moment as a gauge of how we are going to feel about our choice in the future. Not surprisingly, *thinking* about rewards seems to prompt similar brain activity to actually *experiencing* rewards. Even thinking about the future calls upon memory, however. Amnesiacs often have trouble "prospecting," or looking ahead, because, as Wilson and Gilbert describe it, "memories are the building blocks of simulations." You will not really know if you are going to like something you have never had until you have had it.

Which raises the question: Are you better off ordering your favorite food off a menu or something you have never had? Rozin had suggested to me it might depend on where you want your pleasure to occur: before, during, or after the meal. "The anticipated pleasure is greater if it's your favorite food. You've had it, you're familiar with it, you know what it's like. The *experienced* pleasure is probably going to be higher for your favorite," he says. "On the other hand, for remembered pleasures, you're much better off ordering a new food. If you order your favorite food, it's not going to be a memory—you've had it already."

Liking is really about anticipation and memory. Even as you are looking forward to something, you are looking backward to the memory of the last time you enjoyed it. As Pascal once lamented, "The present is never our end." The past and the future seem to dominate our thoughts. Perhaps it is the simple fact that the past and the future *last* longer than the present. You can spend weeks waiting for the "meal of a lifetime," which will itself last a few hours. We can try to "live for the moment," but how long is that "moment," before we are already shuttling it off into our memory, encoding it with the gauzy Instagram filters of our own minds? That so many people photograph their "memorable" meals speaks not only to how fleeting the experience may be but to how photographing it helps actually *make* it memorable, if only in the moment. As the slogan for Field Notes, my favorite notebook brand, goes, "I'm not writing it down to remember it later, I'm writing it down to remember it now."

Unfortunately, neither memories *nor* anticipation is an entirely reliable guide to how much we will like or liked something. When people in one study were asked to predict how much they would like a favorite ice cream after eating it every day for a week, what they reported at the end of the week hardly looked like what they predicted. Tastes did change, in various ways, just not reliably. As Rozin notes, "The correlation between estimated and actual liking is close to zero."

We also seem to crave more variety at the point of decision than we will actually desire down the road. When I was young, for example, I was obsessed by the Kellogg's variety packs of cereal. Wooed by the sight of the Apple Jacks and Frosted Flakes jostling up against each other, I would clamor for my parents to buy the largest package on offer, a towering block of shrink-wrapped goodness. Having raced through my favorites, however, I would find my liking gradually diminishing, from dizzy Apple Jacks heights to the sad denouement of a few sparse clusters of Special K and All-Bran, which often went unconsumed, dying a slow death in a shroud of plastic. My parents would, of course, have been better off simply buying a few boxes of my favorites, which I would reliably eat every day.

Trying to look backward, to the last remembered experience of a meal—if only to make a new choice—invites its own distortions. In one experiment, psychologists were able to change how much people liked something (in this case, a "microwavable Heinz Weight Watchers Tomato & Basil Chicken ready meal") *after* they had eaten it—not, as has been done with rats, by physically manipulating their brains. Instead, researchers simply had subjects "rehearse" the "enjoyable aspects" of the meal. This, the idea goes, made those best moments more "accessible" in memory, and thus they popped out more easily when people were later thinking about the meal. Voilà! The food not only suddenly seemed better; the subjects wanted to eat more of it. If you want to like a meal you have just eaten more, talk about why you liked it so much.

At Del Posto, I finally made my choice. This might be the key to liking: the fact that I have chosen it. Where before I might have considered the choices equally valid, the one I have chosen is bathed in a new glow. Already the pork seems better than when it was just one of a number of enticing-sounding entrées. There are a couple of things going on. First, since Leon Festinger's 1957 theory of "cognitive dissonance," psychologists have argued that we try to avoid any post-decision choice malaise (*What if I really wanted the fish?*) by increasing our liking for what we have chosen (*Oh, this pasta is divine!*) and boosting our disliking for the unpicked alternative, a kind of built-in system to avoid perpetually experiencing buyer's remorse. This is not always successful: Many is the time I have looked at a companion's choice in a restaurant and said, "You won." Buyer's remorse, it has been argued, happens because we buy something in an "affective" frame of mind (*I really want this*) and reflect back in a more "cognitive" state (*What was I thinking?*).

As much as preferences influence choices, choices influence preferences. Even amnesiacs who could not remember making the choice seemed to like what they had chosen more. The same effect, interestingly, has been shown in non-amnesiacs, who might temporarily have forgotten their choices. Even when people were making purely *hypothetical* choices of vacation destinations, the neuroscientist Tali Sharot and colleagues found, there seemed to be more robust brain activity in subjects when they thought about what they had "chosen" versus what they had "rejected." In other words, they were already feeling better about the destination they picked and "deflating" that which they had not. In a follow-up study, the team had subjects pick "subliminally" presented vacation destinations. In fact, all they ever "saw" were nonsense phrases. When they next saw their "choice"—a randomly presented location they had actually not seen before—they rated it higher than the alternative they had "rejected." We seem to have a preference that we prefer our preferences.

You might argue that they were tricked. But consider what may really be going on when you hear the phrase "What would you like?" when asked to select among some range of options. What we are really being asked is, "What do you choose?" The liking often comes afterward. Some even suggest that we are already beginning the "reappraisal process" as we choose—as opposed to rationalizing ex post facto.

When I finally make my pick, something else is probably happening: I think more people would want to pick what I have chosen than actually do. This is the well-known "false consensus effect." In a study done at the University of Michigan, subjects were asked to rate various combinations of sundae flavors. When students were asked how many other people they thought shared their opinion, more people thought others would agree than disagree, particularly if they *liked* the flavors. I have my own ice cream example of this. My father-in-law, for years, has been offering me ice cream whenever we have pie at family gatherings, despite my loudly proclaimed aversion to pie à la mode. I have come to think that this is less about his forgetting my preference than his simply reasoning the following: I like pie with ice cream, so Tom probably does too. What's not to like?

At Del Posto, the waiter, doing double duty as sommelier, has asked us about the wine list. I mentioned the Friulian red, a 2004 Antico Broilo. He did not, of course, simply say, "It's good," or "You'll like it." I will talk about experts like sommeliers later. For now, let us simply hear what he had to say. "It's a bit fuller in body, some notes of pepper; it pairs well with the pork," he said. "It shows the geography of the place, because you've got the Dolomites, and so on the palate you have this minerality coming out. It's the same latitude as the Bordeaux region, so you have all this herbal quality as well, a little mint, a little sage." We ordered the Friulian red.

As I took a sip, another fact about liking came into play: What you like something *as* influences how much you like it. Is it a good wine? Is it a good red wine? Is it a good wine from the *refosco* grape? Is it a good red wine from Friulia? Is it good for the price? Experts, as we shall see, are able to more finely delineate categories than nonexperts. This categorization, says Zellner, works in several ways. Once you have had a really good wine, she says, "you can't go back. You wind up comparing all these lesser things to it." If a bottle of Château Margaux 1990 is your ideal benchmark for red wine, your liking of most other red wines will probably decrease.

Is there a way to still appreciate all of the other wine in the world? Can we find something to like in even the most bog-standard plonk? In studies Zellner has done with beer and coffee, she interviewed people about their drinking of, and liking for, "specialty beer" and "gourmet coffee" versus their "regular" equivalents (for example, Budweiser and Folgers). The ones who tended to put the drinks into categories actually liked the everyday beverages more than the people who simply lumped everything together as "beer" or "coffee." Their "hedonic contrast" was reduced. In other words, the more they could discriminate what was good about the very good, the more they could enjoy the less good (even if they were enjoying it *as the less good*). Almost instinctively, you have no doubt said something like "It's not bad, for fast food." You are not only limiting the scope of what you are judging it against; you have arguably freed yourself to enjoy the experience more—or at least to lessen your discontent.

It was on to the food itself. As has become standard in fine-dining restaurants, a meal at Del Posto begins with a set of *amuse-bouches*, French for "mouth amusers." The name is well chosen. "Just having a little something in your mouth releases insulin, which causes the glucose in your bloodstream to be taken up by cells," Zellner said. "That signals hunger. So if you just have one little thing, you become even more hungry than you were to begin with." It's been dubbed the "appetizer effect." A more palatable opening course, evidence suggests, might actually increase our appetite—even how fast we eat. We eat to remind ourselves how hungry we were.

There is, however, a flip side to this initial burst of joy. What many may overlook in the moment is the tragic irony of food pleasure: As we eat something, we begin to like it less. From a heady peak of lustful wanting ("Oh my God!"), we slide into a slow despond of dimming affection ("This is *good*," you say, half convincing yourself), hovering around a plateau of ambivalence ("save room for dessert!"), then into a slow, fraught decline ("I *really* shouldn't have another," you say, nervously laughing), before finally slouching into a bout of revulsion ("Get this away from me," you say, pushing away a once-loved plate).*

The peak of our sudden disliking seems to occur a few minutes

---

* And then the check arrives. As the comedian Jerry Seinfeld, arguing that we should pay restaurant checks *before* we eat, puts it, "We're not hungry now. Why are we buying all this food?"

after we have eaten something. In the phenomenon known as "sensory-specific satiety," the body in essence sends signals when it has had enough of a certain food. It is not simply that we are "getting full"; it is that we are getting full of that particular food. "The pleasantness of foods which have been eaten," as one seminal study noted, "declines more than the pleasantness of foods which have not been eaten." Simply having food in the mouth, without swallowing, lowers that pleasantness. In monkeys, the mere *sight* of a kind of food they had already consumed excited neurons less than food that had not been eaten.

The presence of variety stimulates not only minds but also appetites. Some studies have seen subjects eating up to 40 percent more food when there was variety. Scientists have speculated that "sensory-specific satiety" is a kind of evolutionary advantageous mechanism to help us eat a nutritionally varied diet. It lurks behind our choices. On weekend mornings, you may enjoy a leisurely family breakfast of carb-heavy, syrup-drenched pancakes. By lunch, you probably desire something more savory, less bread-like. In some abstract way, you still like pancakes as much as ever—just not in that moment. It is as if we have little hedonic thermostats inside us, always readjusting based on our bodies' needs. In the famous experiments of the food researcher Clara Davis in the 1920s and 1930s, postweaning infants in a state hospital were free to pick what they wanted ("a self-selective feeding method") from a tray of options that were generally healthy, if very much of their time ("brains," "bone jelly"). It was less "free range" parenting than trying to solve the common problem of infants not eating "doctor-prescribed diets." Her report, severely lacking data, was nonetheless emphatic: "There were no failures of infants to manage their own diets; all had hearty appetites; all throve."

Liking is stable but *temporal*, even as we eat. Do you savor the last few milk-sodden flakes you fish out of a bowl of once-crispy cereal as much as you enjoyed the first few bites? You may like the burst of intense cinnamon you get in an Altoids mint, but what if the taste still lingered a few minutes later? Sensory-specific satiety is one reason that we break meals into courses (and we seem to prefer some optimal mix of three food items and three colors on a plate): Once you have had the mixed greens, you are not going to like or want more mixed greens. But pork is a different story.

Curiously, sensory-specific satiety is not triggered simply by taste.

When people were offered differently colored Smarties candies, they said they liked the taste of the colors they had not consumed more than those they had eaten. In a potato chip study, Ruffles—with their prominent ridges—seemed to trigger satiety faster than other varieties. Along with similar findings for baguettes, this suggests we "tire" more quickly of things that are actually harder to eat. In the so-called ice cream effect, the food scientists Robert Hyde and Steven Witherly have argued that ice cream is so pleasurable because its texture, temperature, and other sensory properties change as we eat it. It thus ping-pongs among different sources of pleasure, in essence buying a bit more time in our mouth before satiety arrives to spoil the party.

Speaking of ice cream, it is suddenly time at Del Posto for dessert. Sated as we are, we are suddenly faced with a whole new range of flavors and sensations. So different are these from what has come before that we always seem to have "room for dessert." We are also falling under the spell of the so-called dessert effect. When we eat dessert—or whatever other flavors come at the very end of a meal—we are beginning to get the "post-ingestive" nutritional benefits of the food we have eaten earlier in the meal. Sure, that chocolate tastes good, but it may be the vegetables that are making you feel so satisfied (if we ate dessert at the *beginning* of a meal, it would not be nearly as exciting). Because things begin to taste less good to us the more full we are, Zellner suggests, "at the end, you really have to have something that tastes good, so you go for the desserts, which are over the top." Death by Chocolate never kills us.

In the end, memory blurs it all. Curiously, studies by Rozin suggest that the pleasure we remember from a meal has little to do with how much we consumed or how long we spent doing it. It is called "duration neglect." "A few bites of a favorite dish in a meal," he writes, "may do the full job for memory." Or, as he told me in Philadelphia, "when you double the size of the favorite food, it doesn't have any effect on how much you like the meal." Score one for the "small plates" movement. Our memory for meals, according to Rozin's research, seems less beholden to well-known phenomena like "end" or "peak" effects—in which people remember the most recent or intense moments of an experience. In other words, we do not necessarily like a meal more when we eat our favorite part of it last. Rozin thinks "beginnings" in general are underrated, and indeed studies of "dynamic liking" in food sometimes find pleasure to be higher in the first few bites than in the last. But I have had enough of this thinking ahead to my remembered pleasure, when so much is sitting on the plate in front of me.

BETTER THAN I EXPECTED IT TO BE,
BUT NOT AS GOOD AS I REMEMBER

We go to a good restaurant expecting to have a good meal. But another way to think about what food we like, and why, is to think about food that we are expected to *not* like.

I am talking here about the military rations arrayed before me on a camouflage tablecloth in the "Warfighter Café," located inside the U.S. Army's Soldier Systems Center in Natick, Massachusetts, where I have traveled to understand the challenges of making a much-disliked food—the MRE, or meals ready to eat—more likable. Natick, as it is generally dubbed, a sprawling collection of low-slung 1960s-era institutional buildings, is home to camouflage laboratories, wind and rain tunnels, and drop towers. It also hosts the Combat Feeding Directorate of the Department of Defense (DOD). "Coming soon to a theater near you!" announced the trademarked slogan above a list of menu items. My hosts, Gerald Darsch and Kathy Evangelos, spearhead the DOD's Combat Feeding Directorate. "You put diesel in to fuel a tank," Darsch said. "Our job is fueling the war fighter."

The most startling thing about the spread before me—from trans-fat-free vanilla pound cake to herb focaccia to "caffeinated meat sticks"—is that I could return to this room in three years and eat the same meal. I mean the *same* meal.

"The MRE requires a minimum shelf life of three years," Darsch told me. It has its own special constraints. "Kraft doesn't have to worry about air-dropping their food." An incredible amount of engineering goes into ensuring that the food, and its package, will survive rough handling; sandwiches get MRI scans at a local hospital to make sure too much moisture—and thus mold—isn't moving through them. It is an old challenge. One new technology pioneered at Natick—"pressure-assisted thermal sterilization"—has its origins in the "retorting" process developed by the Paris chef Nicolas Appert, who responded to a call from Napoleon to improve food preservation techniques. "Napoleon was losing more soldiers to malnutrition and food poisoning," Darsch said, "than to adversaries' bullets."

For all the technology that goes into ensuring the food's survivability—"this is like the Willy Wonka factory for combat feeding," Evangelos joked—an even more important issue is ensuring the food's palatability, or "acceptability," as it is called here. This is the barest threshold of liking: You agree to put it into your mouth. "We knew we could pack as many calories and nutrition into the smallest amount of space possible," Darsch said. "That's a good thing on paper. One tiny element of the formula we didn't pay as much attention to was whether war fighters would even find it acceptable—would they even eat it?" At the end of the day, that ration has "to look good, to taste good, *and* provide one-third the recommended military nutritional allowance."

One of the biggest ongoing campaigns the Combat Feeding Directorate wages is fighting expectation. This is a virtual law of liking: *There is a greater chance we will like something when we expect we are going to like it.* Military rations, unfortunately, have a long and broad history of low expectations. As the historian William C. Davis notes in *A Taste for War*, the U.S. Civil War produced a range of such novel foods as "desiccated vegetables"—large circular disks, compressed to about two inches, formed of everything from cabbage leaves to parsnips to "a large residue of insoluble and in*solvable* material." When later boiled, they expanded, reminding one soldier of a "dirty brook with all the dead leaves floating around promiscuously." Soldiers, not surprisingly, called them "desecrated vegetables."

While the food scientists work to make dishes more palatable, researchers like Armand Cardello, a senior research scientist at Natick, have for decades been trying to crack the psychology of how soldiers eat and what they like. This work, in turn, has been enormously influential in the commercial food industry. "No matter what kind of survey you do, looking at what it is that drives people's choice or consumption of food, whether it's price, or nutrition, you name it," Cardello tells me, from behind a cluttered desk in a small office, "taste always comes out as the most important factor. When we talk about taste, we're talking about the liking of the food."

With military food, there is often a lot more to dislike than to like. Soldiers receive a strange-looking package containing a just recognizable food that, as Cardello noted, "has been sitting in a warehouse in the desert at 120 degrees for the past three months." It might be better than they expect, but they might also start to wonder what strange alchemy has gone into keeping that food edible under the extreme conditions of combat. Which is why the team, when possible, tries to make food look as much like its referent in the real world. Or to just use the real thing.

Darsch handed me a plain-looking package labeled "Toaster Pastry, Brown Sugar." "It's a Pop-Tart!" he said. Not a military Pop-Tart, but a real Pop-Tart, albeit clad in military drab. The directorate knows, based on Cardello's research, that soldiers would like it more if it actually came packaged like the Pop-Tarts they know. Why not simply give them off-the-shelf Pop-Tarts? "The package the Pop-Tart comes in does not have the barrier properties that we need," Darsch told me, "to prevent the migration of moisture, oxygen, and light." Mil-spec shelf stable is not supermarket shelf stable. This Pop-Tart wears Kevlar.

Expectations drive liking. We spend almost as much time anticipating whether we will like something as we do actually liking it. When you are told how good a movie is, two things can happen when you see it. The first is "assimilation." This is when all those built-up expectations actually lead you to like it more than you might have otherwise. With "contrast," on the other hand, you end up being disappointed, more than if your expectations had not been lifted to such a lofty plateau.

With food, we tend toward assimilation. "The first taste is always with the eyes," as the saying goes, but even before that the food has been sampled by the mind. The problem at Natick is that expectations are often so poor. In one study, Cardello's team took Green Giant corn and put it in an MRE package, and vice versa. "People will like the corn significantly more when they think it's Green Giant," he says. Perhaps even more than an inherent liking for Green Giant, "that negative stereotype of military products drives the liking down."

Assimilation speaks to another virtual law of liking: The more a person's experience with a product matches his expectation, the more he will like it, and vice versa. This happens all the time with food, in ways that have little to do with our actual sensory reactions to a product. Tell people a coffee is bitter, and they will think it is more bitter than if you had not told them. The opposite can happen as well, with our brains, neuroscientists have suggested, actually "suppressing" our response to the bitter when we are not told to expect it. Tell subjects that an orange juice has vodka in it, and they will like it more than the one that does not—even when *neither* juice actually has alcohol (I need hardly mention these were college students).

Simply give people some kind of information about what they can expect from a food they have never eaten—in one Natick trial, Arctic cloudberries—and they will like it more. If it is "weird space food," call it weird space food! People will still like it more (the research was done on astronauts). A Natick study had soldiers eat in the dark, a not unlikely occurrence for soldiers. They liked things more when they were told what they were eating.

When our expectations are violated, interesting things happen. In one well-known study, people were given a salmon-flavored ice cream that was labeled simply as "ice cream" or "frozen savory mousse." People liked it more as mousse than ice cream. Their dislike for the ice cream was so intense, in fact, that, as the researchers noted with some concern, "many participants verbally described the food as disgusting." The idea of assimilation and contrast is why menus always announce the noticeable presence of salt in desserts with chocolate or caramel. As one prominent pastry chef noted, "If we say something is salted, it's to call out the salt so people aren't surprised. It gives them a chance to appreciate the contrast of salty against the sweet." In other words, to like it more. Remember, we are primed to notice—and not like—things that are "wrong" with our food.

But the salmon ice cream experiment shows that liking is not merely liking a thing in itself. What you like it *as* can be just as important. In one study Cardello conducted on "novel foods" ("The U.S. Armed Forces and N.A.S.A. frequently require the development of 'novel' foods for use in extreme environments"), subjects were given "soup" (Campbell's cream of mushroom from concentrate) and a "liquid diet" (a pulverized, viscous chicken cacciatore substance developed for jaw-surgery patients—which I believe my school cafeteria also once dished up for me). Both were served in a ceramic bowl and a glass with a straw. Everything was labeled "soup." Perhaps not surprisingly, people liked the actual soup more. But in a second trial, the substance in the glass was labeled "dental liquid diet." Suddenly people liked the *dental liquid* more than the soup, when it was in the glass. As the researchers noted, "The change in expectancy, caused by the change in label, made the soup more dissonant and resulted in a reduced affective response."

This expectations dissonance is not limited to strange foods in military labs. One afternoon, I went to visit Garrett Oliver, the stylish, urbane, and opinionated brewmaster of Brooklyn Brewery. As we sat over a few "ghost bottles" of a one-off beer aged in a bourbon barrel and containing yeast sediment from a Riesling fermentation, Oliver told me how, a few years prior, he had come up with a new limited-run beer. The brew was based on a popular cocktail called Penicillin, which blends the flavors of scotch, ginger, honey, and lemon. "It has some sourness, some sweetness," he said. "What I loved about it was these elements all hang together to make a harmonious whole." He wondered if he might bottle some of that same magic in a beer. And so he blended peat-smoked malt, organic lemon juice, wildflower honey, and minced ginger.

The response was incredibly polarized. "*Draft* magazine called it one of the top twenty-five beers of 2011," he said. "But some people wanted to punch us in the head." The problem, he suspected, was that not every bartender was presenting it in the way Oliver had imagined. "All the bartender had to tell somebody at the end of the day was that it's based on a cocktail that has scotch-ginger-honey-lemon. They didn't always do it." So some consumers drank a beer that they expected to be based on a cocktail, with maybe the original cocktail even served alongside as a cue. Others simply got, as Oliver described it, " 'Oh, here's a new beer from Brooklyn Brewery, probably a pale ale or something' that did not prepare them for this weird flavor experience. They got it in their mouth and were, like, 'bleh.' " They were not told *how* to like it.

ON A SCALE FROM ONE TO NINE:
THE PROBLEM OF MEASURING LIKING

As we have seen, one messes with consumer expectation at one's peril.

One of the most notorious cases of taste and violated expectations is with Crystal Pepsi, the clear soft drink released by the beverage company in the early 1990s. The drink was inspired by rising sales of bottled waters and an identified trend toward "clear" products, ranging from dishwashing liquid to deodorant. Crystal Pepsi was positioned as a "lighter," in both color and calorie content, more "natural" alternative to Pepsi-Cola itself. Early indications were positive. There was what the then Pepsi CEO, David Novak, described as a "hugely successful" test launch in Colorado. Three months after it was distributed nationally, Crystal Pepsi had grabbed a respectable 2.4 percent market share. It was even priced higher than Pepsi, hinting at its premium cachet.

Then the fizz went out. By 1994, Crystal Pepsi was gone, relegated to an inglorious footnote in the history of marketing mishaps. What went wrong? Aside from the obvious—that most new products fail—there were early stirrings of discontent. A blind taste test by one newspaper hinted at the problem: People preferred the taste of Crystal Pepsi, but only when their eyes were *closed*. Seeing Crystal Pepsi created expectations of what it should taste like, and these expectations were clearly violated. Pepsi bottlers, Novak recalls, raised a different kind of expectation issue: Crystal Pepsi did not "taste enough like Pepsi." The name Pepsi itself led consumers to believe it would be Pepsi-like. Calling it simply Crystal might have helped. But the episode raised a tricky question: If a food color's "principal use," as one study noted, is for "flavor identification," what flavor are you identifying when you take the color away?

Apart from the problem of violated expectations, the Crystal Pepsi debacle contains another important lesson: just how difficult it is to anticipate consumer liking. It seems a simple problem: If enough people like something in a taste test, why would they not like it in the real world? Pepsi certainly did not just chuck Crystal Pepsi into the marketplace on a whim. Some ninety people, it was said, worked fifteen months on the product, cycling through several thousand versions. And well before it even made it to a regional taste market, one can be sure it was tested in-house by any number of sensory and consumer panels, the bulk of which, one presumes, must have said that they liked it.

As it happens, this very thing—measuring people's liking for a product on a food company "consumer panel"—was developed and perfected at Natick. The program itself was founded in 1944 at Chicago's Quartermaster Food and Container Institute, in response to an ongoing problem of ration quality and its impact on troop morale. A team of psychologists, many of whom would go on to do seminal work in the food industry, was assembled. "One of the first issues that came up," Cardello told me, "was how do you measure how much someone likes something?"

Pioneering psychologists like Wilhelm Wundt had tried to quantify, through "psychophysics," the inexact ways our senses responded to various stimuli (for example, when you double the sweetness of something, and it does not taste twice as sweet).

But no one had been able, or had much tried, to quantify liking. And so the "nine-point hedonic scale" was born. First used on soldiers, it eventually found its way into the test kitchens of just about every major food manufacturer. Whatever is in your refrigerator at this moment, chances are that someone, somewhere has indicated his liking of it on a scale from one to nine. There was, according to one account, an early attempt to introduce an "11-point scale," but it would not fit on government-regulated paper. Humans have even been trotted out and asked to write down their scale-of-one-to-nine reaction on products like cat food. Why? Felines, as an accompanying report noted, are "clearly unable to verbalize their likes and dislikes." They may haughtily strut away from the bowl, their tail a flag of disdain, but this gesture does not easily translate into a numerical scale. "Perhaps surprisingly," the report concluded, "the grand mean of all hedonic scores was 4.7, placing it between the 'neither like nor dislike' and 'like slightly' scale adjectives." People thought cat food was not too bad, at least *as* cat food.

The simplicity, relative accuracy, and value of hedonic scores as an industry standard has overshadowed the ongoing methodological issues in trying to put a number on liking. Other methods, like polygraphs, have failed dismally. But issues abound. There are semantic problems. Does "like slightly" mean the same thing to one person as another? There are issues with the math. The number eight, Cardello noted, does not mean twice as much liking as the number four. Could liking and disliking be expressed on the same scale? As work by Timothy Wilson and colleagues at the University of Virginia has made clear, asking people to analyze why they chose something can lead them to change their original choice—and usually not for the better.

But merely asking consumers *what* they like is also not as simple as you might think. In one common tool, the "just about right" scale, people are given samples of a product. Each will have, say, a different gradation of sweetening. The consumer indicates which is "just about right." Sounds fine, no? There is just one problem: The level of sweet-ening a subject chooses is often different from what he says he likes.

Then there is the fact that most people do not pick the number one or nine. Those seem too artificial. People hedge. It becomes, by default, a seven-point scale. "You're never sure that you're not going to get a product in the next sample that's even better than one you just tasted," Cardello said.

Our confusion about our own tastes translates into trouble for people trying to measure those tastes. People in general tend toward a "regression to the mean" in terms of liking. Ask them ahead of time how much they like lasagna or liver, say, and then ask them again after they have actually consumed it, and subjects will mark their favorite foods a bit lower and their least favorite a bit higher. Expectations haunt our liking, but they confound us. Peer into the science of liking long enough, and you might begin to think this is something approach-ing a mantra: *The bad is never as bad as we think it is, the good never as good.*

One reason Natick has proven so influential is that, year after year, it has had an essentially captive audience of subjects to test. It is also a laboratory of pure liking, uncorrupted by the contexts of the outside world. Soldiers eating MREs do not see the price of food; they are not swayed by advertising. Nor do they have any choice. One of the research concerns has been food "monotony"—how long a soldier could be rea-sonably expected to eat nothing but MREs. The army's own analysis, Darsch tells me, targeted twenty-one days. This was probably "on the conservative side," he allowed. "You could probably go thirty-plus days and not have a statistical loss of body mass and muscle."

But more broadly, Natick has thought long and hard about how to plan menus that offer the most variety as is logistically feasible and that are most liked. Soldiers will not simply eat anything when they are hun-gry. Consumption, not to mention health and morale, drops off as food acceptability declines. Feeding an entire army means preferences must be broad and wide. As an early study observed, "Even foods that are extremely well-liked, but only by a small proportion of the consumers, are unsuited for military use." Dishes like New England clam chowder have failed because, as Darsch put it, "a lot of the folks eating it didn't really know what New England clam chowder was."

Howard Moskowitz, a prominent figure in the food industry, was working at Natick in the 1950s on mathematical models for "menu optimization." Over breakfast at the Harvard Club in New York City, he said his inquiry was simple: "How frequently can we serve something so it doesn't become tiring?" Menus, in his view, are driven by two dynamics: liking and time. There are things that we like, but how quickly will we tire of them? The thing most liked in a taste test, various studies have shown, often becomes the *least* liked after a number of samples. Crystal Pepsi might have seemed fresh and interesting in a taste test, but was it actually something consumers would restock the fridge with? That intense sugar rush or novel flavor may seem great the first time, "but you have to live with it," Moskowitz said.

"If you like something a lot more," he continued, "do you choose it more often?" Not necessarily. We begin to pick things we may like much less, perhaps as a way of protecting our liking for that loved thing. One wants to avoid "death by hamburger," as he dubbed it. Why *should* we even tire of a particular food? I asked. Is it, per sensory-specific satiety, that our nutritional needs are being met? Is there some innate desire for novelty? "I don't know," he said, sighing. "Why do we habituate to the smell of a fragrance? Why is it when we sit in a house next to the railroad tracks, we don't hear the railroad anymore?" Why should we need choice? "Go to a diner," he said. "Diners have menus with seven pages. But you order the same thing. You don't want choice. You want the illusion of choice."

Tyler Cowen, perhaps our most food-aware economist, noted that he is often puzzled to hear, as that day's lunch choice is being deliberated, someone utter something like "I don't want Thai food today; I just had that yesterday." This rather neglects the fact that Thais are eating Thai food *every day*. "Would it be so terrible," he wondered, "to eat only Indian food, whether at home or in restaurants, every day for a week?" Often, when we think we are tired of something, we may simply be forgetting how much variety we have actually had (in a phenomenon that has been called "variety amnesia"). Curiously, while one might expect people to tire less quickly of flavorful food, food monotony research at Natick has shown the opposite: The more bland it is, the less quickly soldiers grew tired of it. Bland food, after all, fades from memory more quickly than exciting food. The less you remember having it, the less tired of it you get.

Natick also had to grapple with *where* food was being consumed. The very same food will be rated higher when served in a restaurant versus an institutional cafeteria or a lab. Soldiers in the field face two challenges: Not only are they eating MREs, with their limited variety and entrées of approximate flavor and dubious texture, but they are often eating them in the far-flung, inhospitable environments for which they were designed. In a series of groundbreaking experiments, a group of soldiers (bivouacked on an island in Hawaii) and MIT students (on campus) ate nothing but MREs. The soldiers ate them for thirty-four days straight, the students for forty-five days. Both groups deemed the food "acceptable" (which did not speak well for MIT's canteen). Both groups lost weight. The students, however, ate more than the soldiers in the field. The experiments showed the importance of *context* on liking. For many reasons, it is more difficult to get people in the field to eat.

Context is no less important in the real world. People eating in an ethnic restaurant with appropriate decor rate the food higher; add some red-checkered tablecloths or a Sergio Leone poster, they eat more pasta. The loudness, and type, of music can affect the way we feel about our food. We eat more when we are in larger groups. The type of glassware, the weight of plates, whether the color of the food matches the color of the plate—even how long people have to wait for their meal—all have been shown to influence how much we like, and eat, food.

There is a poignant scene in the film *Sideways* in which Miles, the hapless protagonist, in a fit of pique and despair over his dismal life prospects, brings his treasured bottle of 1961 Cheval Blanc to a fast-food joint. Amid the harsh light and the smell of grease, to the accompaniment of a burger and onion rings, he surreptitiously quaffs his "special occasion wine" from a Styrofoam cup. The wine is still the same wine, and if consumption were always just about the thing being consumed, the level of enjoyment should theoretically be the same. But all the context factors are "off": He is alone, he is eating mediocre food, he does not have a proper glass, the decor is terrible. He is drinking with vengeance, not appreciation.

Context is not just place but time. Your love of breakfast cereals probably does not, in normal circumstances, extend to dinner. Breakfast itself is a rather strange meal, as the Dutch researcher E. P. Köster has observed. The most adventurous gourmands will eat the same thing for breakfast, day after day. They would hardly contemplate this at dinner. Sheer convenience explains much of it, to be sure, but research suggests there are whole classes of textures that are less liked at breakfast, varying by culture. By the time our after-dinner dessert rolls around, we are hungry for variety. It is as if we wake up less primed to desire novelty, our threshold for excitement slowly ramping up as the day progresses.

Back at the Warfighter Café, I contemplated the spread before me. How did the MREs of tomorrow stand up? Did they still deserve the unfortunate sobriquets such as "meals refusing to exit" or "meals rejected by Ethiopians"? I took a bite of "MATS Salmon," "MATS" standing for "microwave-assisted thermal sterilization." The name could use a little work and the fish was, admittedly, a bit tough. "It's a little chewier than we'd like," Darsch told me. Not surprisingly: The salmon had been bombarded with over 120,000 psi of pressure, literally rupturing the cell walls of any lingering bacteria with the ruthlessness of a bunker-busting bomb. But the taste was there, at least more than one would expect for a shrink-wrapped piece of room-temperature fish with no immediate sell-by date. Would it fly at Del Posto? No. But to a soldier faced with a long-range patrol in a hot desert, it might be just good enough.

I MAY KNOW WHAT I LIKE,
BUT I KNOW I DON'T LIKE WHAT I DON'T KNOW:
LIKING IS LEARNING

On the morning I went to Philadelphia to meet Marcia Pelchat, a long-time researcher at Monell, I was nursing a slight cold. When I arrived at her office, Pelchat, a petite, polite woman with a disarming sense of humor, offered me coffee. I asked if she had tea, explaining that whenever I have a cold, I prefer tea, which suddenly seems to taste better than coffee. She considered it for a moment, then said, "Coffee without the aroma would seem like ashes to me."

Here is that thing that is so easy to forget yet never fails to startle when we experience it firsthand: Most of the action when we are tasting something comes from the nose. Coffee is one of those curious things that smells better than it tastes, and to lose the smell of it is in essence to lose what we like about it. To remind yourself of this basic sensory fact, it is worth, every once in a while, administering to yourself what Pelchat does to me on this morning: the jelly-bean test. She handed me three jelly beans and asked me to hold my already stuffed nose. They each tasted, simply, sweet. When I released my nostrils on the last jelly bean, I suddenly experienced, even with my cold, a spreading flood of flavor, something like Häagen-Dazs coffee ice cream, through the back of my mouth and nose. I had, in fact, just eaten a coffee-flavored jelly bean, as well as its banana- and licorice-flavored cousins.

Our taste-bud-studded tongues do the basic sensory sorting: sweet, sour, bitter, salty, and, less officially, umami (and maybe fat). But all the finer distinctions—mango versus papaya, lamb versus pork—come "retronasally," from the mouth up through the nasal passage, as a smell. The things we know as strawberries or Coca-Cola or *sriracha* sauce are not tastes; they are flavors. There is, strictly speaking, no "taste of honey"; there is "retronasal olfaction of honey." Honey, to be honey, needs to waft on a gust of inhaled air into our nasopharynx. Even seemingly strong "tastes," like lemon, only read on the tongue as a collection of sours and bitters and sweets. Terpenes triggering receptors in the olfactory mucosa make lemon lemony.

How we perceive something, Paul Rozin has argued, influences how we feel about it. Even people who do not like the taste of coffee can no doubt appreciate the aroma. By contrast, on a plate, Limburger cheese may strike us, via our nose, as unpleasant. Once in the mouth, however, it undergoes a stunning change into something we may find pleasurable. It is as if the brain, sensing that food is in the mouth, and thus no longer represents some external hazard, shifts its whole outlook. Give someone who has a nose-blocking cold a cup of beef broth to which yellow food coloring has been added, Pelchat told me, and he will think he is eating chicken soup. Take away the retronasal passage, and it would be like going from a cable television package with an almost infinite number of channels down to a handful of networks playing the same old shows.

But I have come to Pelchat's office to talk about liking. Regardless of which part of my mouth and nasal cavities are telling me what the flavor is, what is telling me I like it? Virginia Woolf once wrote that "reading is a longer and more complicated process than seeing." So too is the question of whether we like something more than feeling a sensory response to something we have put in our mouths. What we like is sometimes corrupted by what we know we like. A study that had consumers test pineapple varieties found those who preferred pineapples labeled "organic" and "free trade" tended to be those who were more fond of organic and free trade produce itself. Those less keen on organics were less happy about the pineapple. As the researchers noted, "The same cognitive information evoked opposite affective reactions in different subjects."

Pelchat, it turned out, did have some tea for me. But first she wanted me to take a capsule, which would contain either sugar or, simply, noncaloric cellulose. She wanted to show me the taste mechanism known as "flavor-nutrient" conditioning—the idea that we like what makes us feel good, *even if we do not know it.*

The power of this conditioning has been shown in any number of studies on rats, our fellow neophobic omnivores. Typically, a rat will drink, ad libitum (as much as it wants), something like orange Kool-Aid. Rats, as a cursory glance at the scientific literature reveals, drink a *lot* of Kool-Aid. Meanwhile, sometime before, during, or after, a sweetener will be "infused," via "intragastric catheter," directly to its stomach. Later, the rat will sample grape Kool-Aid without getting the sugar drip to the stomach. When both flavors are later tested, rats will prefer the one that *was* sweetened, even when both flavors are now unsweetened. Sometimes they still cling to the old favorite when one of the *new* options actually tastes sweet in the moment.

Curiously, the way the rat came to like one flavor over another had nothing to do with a taste preference. How do researchers know? "In fact," Pelchat tells me, her voice lowering a bit, "the esophagus is externalized." With the gullet sitting outside its body, the rat cannot taste the glucose, nor could he belch it back up into his mouth. Infused into the stomach, however, that sweetness still provides a hedonic payoff. "Something in the gut or the metabolic system is making them like that flavor," Pelchat said.

Pelchat wondered if humans' sensory mechanisms could be similarly bypassed, without such extreme surgery. So she once swallowed a nasogastric tube for a day and tried to mainline glucose. "I thought, I know what I'm doing, I'll pretend it's food and I'll swallow it, it'll be fine. Instead, I was puking, tearing up." Finally, she hit upon pills, which would or would not release sweetness into the gut. A placebo cellulose pill has no calories, no benefit for the body. Well, almost no benefit. "Incidentally," she noted with a laugh as I inspected a pill, "that will keep you regular." In her study, people who downed the (tasteless) sugar pills ended up liking the flavor of tea more than the tea they drank with the unsweetened pills.

So without even knowing why, people preferred one tea over another (*we are strangers to our taste*). They were getting "post-ingestive" signals, in the form of a nutritional reward, that predisposed them toward a flavor. "I always make a point of telling people that reward and pleasure are not the same thing," she says. "Food can be rewarding without the conscious experience of pleasure." How we have all known this, eating in front of the television. The reverse can happen as well. Cancer patients who sampled a novel ice cream flavor prior to chemotherapy, with its attendant nausea, grew to dislike that flavor (more than the familiar flavors they liked). With liking for all foods diminished, patients were in little mood for novelty. One way to avoid the treatment from negatively interfering with normal appetites, interestingly, was to provide a new "scapegoat" flavor—like Life Savers candy—during patients' normal meals. The scapegoat flavor, rather than the usual foods, absorbed the brunt of disliking. This plays into our tendency to want to like familiar foods and to dislike the novel.

In Pelchat's study, sponsored by a tea company wanting to see if Americans could acquire a taste for unsweetened teas, people even grew to like the tea more that did not have the glucose hit. Why? Simply because they were drinking it more than once. In 1968, the psychologist Robert B. Zajonc, in a profoundly influential paper, termed what he called the "mere exposure" effect: "Mere repeated exposure of the individual to a stimulus is sufficient condition for the enhancement of his attitude toward it." He was not actually talking about food, but exposure has come to be a central idea in food liking. In one typical study, children as young as two sampled a collection of unfamiliar fruits and cheeses for twenty-six days in a row. When they were later given a choice between random pairs of the food objects they had tried, they chose the ones they had had more often—even when they had spat those out initially.

Try it, the old Alka-Seltzer ad (cheekily) promised, you'll like it. Parents do not usually have the patience of researchers (nor can they resort to gastric tubes). They often abandon efforts to give their children new foods after three or four tries. In an English study, one group was asked to repeatedly eat spinach, not a huge delicacy in England. Another group was asked to eat peas, which are more liked. People began to like spinach a bit more, particularly those who disliked it at first. But liking for peas started high and stayed high. People liked peas because they were already used to liking peas.

Exposure speaks to the idea that we like what we know. But to know it means we first have to eat it, even if we dislike it. In one study, people began to like an initially disliked low-salt soup after having it just a few times (the soup was not labeled "low salt," because this in itself could be enough to negatively sway liking). In another experiment, people ate canned ratatouille servings with successively higher levels of chili added. The hotter the burn, the more they grew to like it. George Orwell, in his 1946 essay "A Nice Cup of Tea," predicted this kind of taste adaptation: "Some people would answer that they don't like tea in itself, that they only drink it in order to be warmed and stimulated, and they need sugar to take the taste away. To those misguided people I would say: Try drinking tea without sugar for, say, a fortnight and it is very unlikely that you will ever want to ruin your tea by sweetening it again."

Liking is learning: This truism runs from entire cultures down to the individual. The exposure effects begin even before we are born. Like carrot juice as an infant? Chances are your mother did. The odors and tastes were all around you, in the atmosphere of amniotic fluid that was your earliest dining experience. Trained sensory panelists can even tell which women have consumed garlic pills based on the scent of their amniotic fluid alone. Out of the womb, we strain toward the things we prefer (that is, the familiar) and make "aversive gapes" at the things we dislike. Making faces is part of the social experience of liking and, especially, disliking: We send cues about what we are eating and look for information about what others are eating.

Simply seeing other people eating something seems to promote liking. In a classic study looking at the feeding of children in a women's prison in the 1930s, children's preferences seemed to be informed by whoever was feeding them: "Babies who refused tomato juice were found to be fed by adults who also expressed a dislike for tomato juice." In a study of preschoolers, a "target" child who preferred one vegetable to another was seated with three classmates who had the opposite preference. By the second day of the study, the target child had already switched preferences. Exposure to people, as much as food itself, influences our liking.

Mysteries still abound in our liking for food. Consider the simple question of why we should suddenly like something that we previously disliked. Very few of us "like" a substance like coffee or beer the first time we drink it, but many of us come to like it. All tastes are, in essence, "acquired tastes." Or, as Pelchat suggests, "an acquired *liking* is really what we should say."

And when we talk about "acquired tastes," we should really be talking about "acquired flavors," as Dana Small, an associate fellow in Yale University's John B. Pierce Laboratory who studies the neuropsychology of eating, suggested to me. We are not born knowing about flavors like coffee; we simply know the drink as bitter and thus bad. "The bitter is there as a sign that there is a potential toxin in whatever you're sampling," she said. "You just want to know that; you don't want to have to learn that."

But no one is born liking, or not liking, chicken feet. Those "gatekeeper" taste systems, after all, would not likely know feet from wing. It is all chicken. Before food even gets to us, culture has done that first big sort, sifting out the boundaries of what is acceptable to like. "The French eat horses and frogs but the British eat neither," notes Jared Diamond. As with any food, the French, during a discrete historical moment, had to be taught to "learn to like" horse as food. But what we like in *taste*, as opposed to flavor, is remarkably similar around the world. As John Prescott writes in *Taste Matters*, "The sweet taste of sucrose in water, is optimally pleasant at around 10–12 percent by weight (approximately the same as is found in many ripe fruits), regardless of whether you are from Japan, Taiwan, or Australia."

Flavor conditioning helps us to like or dislike flavors. The benefit of this is, as Small put it, that we can "learn to like the foods that are available to us, and avoid particular foods rather than entire classes of nutrients." When she was young, she went to a popular sailing event in her hometown of Victoria, British Columbia. With college friends, she partook of one too many drinks of Malibu and 7UP, an unholy and intensely cloying concoction of sweet, coconut-flavored rum and cit-rusy soda pop. "That was twenty years ago," she recalled. "I can't even wear coconut suntan lotion. It makes me ill."

Through a complex chain of activity in the brain, she said, we learn "flavor objects"—the "perceptual gestalt" of touch, taste, and smell in everything we eat. "Did this food make me sick? Did this food give me energy? You learn preferences based on the entire flavor object." The flavor object itself is "created" by a network of neural activity, described as "a distributed circuit including the neural representation of the odor object, unimodal taste cells, unimodal oral somatosensory cells, mul-timodal cells, and a 'binding mechanism.'" You do not just "taste" a strawberry; you virtually conjure it into being.

Coffee—the actual substance—becomes no less bitter the hun-dredth time we drink it than the first time we drank it. But something happens. "It *becomes* coffee," Small said. "The brain has learned that coffee is not a potentially harmful signal." Many of us, when first drink-ing coffee, add things that we like—milk and sugar. This not only weak-ens the bitterness but helps build positive associations with the coffee. The relationship is one-way, notes John Prescott: We do not learn to like sugar by drinking coffee; we learn to like coffee by drinking it with sugar. Add the post-ingestive signal of caffeine, and you have got a drink that we like, almost as if in spite of ourselves. You may be thinking the pleasures of caffeine or alcohol are enough to explain why we become conditioned to liking coffee or whiskey. But then why not just add those substances to what we already like? Why is it the things that are most disliked in the beginning go on to be the things we like the most?

There must be a moment when our disliking actually shifts to lik-ing. Small has been trying to locate it in neurologic time and space. In one experiment, she had subjects try novel-flavored beverages that had no calories. After a few weeks, she added caloric but tasteless maltodex-trin to one of the flavors. Even though they could not sense its presence, subjects liked the beverages with maltodextrin more. As with Pelchat's tea study, the "post-oral signal" coming from the gut—which is happily converting the maltodextrin into glucose—changed liking.

In Small's study, though, the beverages were all chosen to be "slightly liked." This still does not answer how we get from disliking to liking. What if you could take a food that is intensely disliked and, in the flick of a switch, suddenly generate an intense desire? Kent Berridge, a neuroscientist at the University of Michigan, did just that in a Pavlovian conditioning experiment with rats. First, rats got "pulses" of a pleasant sucrose solution, along with a sound. They also got a deeply unpleasant, three-times-as-strong-as-seawater solution of "Dead Sea salt," accompanied by a different sound.

The rats *hated* the salt—so much so that it had to be delivered into their mouths via an "implanted cannula." And when the rats subsequently heard the respective tones, they turned either away or toward the food source and made the appropriate facial expression. Next, the rats' brains were altered with injections that triggered a kind of simulated extreme salt craving. The following day, when the rats were again presented with the tones, they immediately moved toward the Dead Sea salt, making vigorous lip-licking "pleasure" faces (the same as seen in human infants)—*before they had even tasted it in its new, "pleasant" state.* In other words, without even knowing that they liked it, they suddenly wanted it.

This might help explain not just addictive behaviors but everyday liking. In one study, Berridge and colleagues asked student subjects to identify the gender of faces seen on a computer screen. They were also shown, rather surreptitiously—at one-sixtieth of a second—angry or sad faces. Afterward, they were given a fruit beverage, which they were told was in development by a soft-drink company, and asked how much they liked it. Subjects who saw the "happy" faces reported liking the drink 50 percent more than subjects who saw the sad faces. The happy faces triggered "mesolimbic circuits of 'wanting' in the brains of students who viewed them, which persisted for some minutes undetected as students evaluated their own mood," Berridge wrote. "The 'wanting' surfaced only when an appropriate target was finally presented in the form of a hedonically laden sweet stimulus they could taste and choose to ingest or not." It was as if they were, to paraphrase the old country song, "looking for like in all the wrong places," finally finding something in which to express their interest.

These kinds of mechanisms might help explain how disliking turns to liking. "Tastes" enter the brain far "downstream." Even babies possessing not much more than a brain stem are "making both a recognition and evaluation decision." But they are not, as Berridge suggested to me, forming that "flavor object." That happens somewhere "upstream." In a classic study by Ivan de Araújo and colleagues, people were given short whiffs of a mix of isovaleric acid and cheddar cheese and told it was cheese or body odor. Those in the "body odor" condition (so to speak) rated the compound lower than those who were told it was cheese. No surprise there. But the cheese people also had more activation in a wider network of brain regions, which reflects a common finding that "liking" seems to activate a larger chain of brain activity than disliking. It is as if we need to expend more energy to figure out why we like, rather than dislike, something.

Body odor and cheese read differently in the brain. But for the first steps of mental processing, "the signal is going to be the same," Berridge said. "That signal could be modified pretty early in the pathway, however, by expectation and anticipation. How long is that signal still the same by the time you get into various parts of the brain?" So strong are those expectation and anticipation overlays, of course, that in the de Araújo study, even people who were given a "clean smell," but were told it was cheese or body odor, had similar patterns of brain activity. They were readying themselves to like or dislike a smell that never came, a phantom pleasure or displeasure.

"In the end," Berridge told me, "we are aware of a final product, but we're not aware of the process that gave us that product." The bitter signal at the brain stem is the same, but somewhere in the higher cognitive processes "coffee" takes shape. Learning is interacting with taste to cause a pleasure. "Whatever pleasure we are getting is probably coming from the same basic pleasure circuits that the sweetness has a special privilege tapping into," Berridge said. The brain has sweetened your coffee.

The idea of finding some precise moment and place where disliking turns to liking is complicated by the fact that the same areas of the brain that are excited by liking are also activated by disliking. The amygdala, for example, seems to respond in equal measure to things we like and things we dislike. Perhaps someday scientists will discover a *meh* circuit—a discovery that suggests that at heart we are actually fairly ambivalent about most things and that it is some particular firing of synapses, or the person we had lunch with that day, or what song is on the radio, that eventually pushes us one way or the other.

It is striking to realize how strongly we stand by our likes and dislikes, given how open they are to distortion and manipulation, as much by our own brains as by outside influences. Perhaps we instinctively sense the fragility and arbitrariness of these preferences, and so cling to them even harder. What is clear is that food is where we find the most intensely personal relationship with our own taste, literally and metaphorically. As Beauchamp had told me, at Monell, "The most important decision every human being makes every day is whether to put something in their mouth or not." This was once a life-or-death decision; now it is just personal taste.

And yet that only seems to make the decisions that much more elaborate, bringing that much more insecurity to our choices. Back at the Chinese restaurant, Rozin described our "affective" relationship with food as "very fundamental, very basic, and it's frequent. Not as frequent as breathing, but breathing isn't a matter of taste." He paused to collect the last bit of sweet-and-sour shrimp, plucked it into his mouth, then added, "Same hole."

CHAPTER 2

THE FAULT IS NOT IN OUR STARS, BUT IN OURSELVES

LIKING IN A NETWORKED AGE

Of themselves, judgments of taste do not even set up any interest whatsoever. Only in society is it interesting to have taste.

—Immanuel Kant, *The Critique of Pure Reason*

IT'S NOT WHAT YOU SAY YOU LIKE; IT'S WHAT YOU DO

One night, as I trolled for something to watch on Netflix, a film called *The Rocking Horse Winner* popped up ("Because you enjoyed: *Psycho, Annie Hall, Fargo*"). I clicked through to find a 1949 British adaption of a D. H. Lawrence story about a boy who could predict the winners of actual horse races by riding his toy horse faster. The story, like the film, was new to me.

Here, I thought, was the genius of algorithmic recommendation systems: picking some obscure film out of the historical dustbin, based on some unseen alchemy that was beyond me. What linked *The Rocking Horse Winner* to Woody Allen's iconic comedy, Alfred Hitchcock's shocker, and the Coen brothers' dark midwestern gothic? And what in my own rating activity had summoned this cinematic *ménage à quatre*? What if I had *loved* the Hitchcock but not liked *Annie Hall*—would that have triggered some other recommendation?

Greg Linden, who helped create Amazon's pioneering algorithms, reminds us that we should not ascribe them too much power in finding some odd, uncannily prescient suggestion. "The computer," he said, "merely performs an analysis of what humans are doing." And yet their own creators have admitted that the ever more complex mathematical regimes can become, in effect, HAL-like "black boxes" whose precise behavior can no longer actually be determined or predicted (something we humans can at least identify with).

I have occasionally bristled at the recommendations of Netflix—*an Adam Sandler film? Are you kidding me?* But the flip side of having access to so many films is expending more time in deciding what to watch. And so I have come to accept that in an age of often bewildering choice in which I no longer have time to read back issues of *Cahiers du Cinéma* or flip through cutout bins at record shops, there might be some benefit to off-loading some of my decision making and discovery process to a computer, the way we have largely outsourced our memory lapses to Google.

For a time, anyway, I rigorously trained my Netflix algorithm. I rated each film I had seen and studied the predictions of what I might like with Talmudic intensity. I wanted the thing fine-tuned, able to handle the twisting contours of my taste profile. I wanted it to know that just because I loved *The Evil Dead* did not necessarily mean I liked most other horror films. I wanted it to know not just that I liked something but *why* I liked it. I wanted more than it could give.

And so when I found myself at Netflix's headquarters, in a red-tile-roofed building—half old Hollywood, half La Quinta Inn—in Los Gatos, California, I had rating stars in mind. They were a borderline obsession. I would spend strange amounts of time pondering whether the 2.9 predicted rating for me warranted seeing the film (the distance from 2.9 to 3.0 had a gnomic power). Watching a film in the 1 ratings seemed almost illicit. And when I came across a film I had not seen but that had a 4.7 predicted rating for me, I could feel the room move.

I knew I was not alone: The company had awarded a million dollars, in its famous "optimization prize," to the computer scientists who devised a 10 percent improvement to Netflix's predicted ratings. Many smart people had invested hours thinking about things like the so-called *Napoleon Dynamite* Problem—or what to do with movies that seem to polarize taste along less than predictable lines. Here, in Los Gatos, was, I imagined, a kind of benevolent Stasi of taste that knew everything about how people watched films, a massive repository of human predilection. I wanted to know things that I knew were proprietary and they would not tell me: How responsive was the algorithm to rating? If I gave a movie 2.7 stars that Netflix had predicted was for me 3.2, how quickly would this divergence ripple through my rating ecosystem? What film had the widest distribution of extremely negative and extremely positive ratings?

All this is why I could practically hear the needle scratching across the record when I sat down with Todd Yellin, the company's vice president of product innovation, in the *Top Gun* room (all of Netflix's rooms are named after films or television shows), and he proceeded to tell me, "My first job here was director for product personalization. I led the effort of how to get ratings, how to get better predictions out of those ratings, where to put them in the user interface." So far, so good. Then he said, "As we've broadened the scope of personalization, we deemphasized ratings predictions over the years."

I let it sink in. *Deemphasized.* I probably looked a bit crestfallen. I could tell Yellin sensed my disappointment. I had come here to understand the world's most sophisticated engine of predictive taste in movies, and I was being told that taste—at least as expressed through ratings—was being deemphasized. "We've gotten more people to hit stars than anyone in the universe on movies and TV shows," said Yellin. "And we've come up with many algorithmic recipes to improve the accuracy of that prediction." But that, he said, was state of the art circa "2005 or 2006." My geeky "stars" questions suddenly seemed like horribly out-of-style fashions. So after all that extensive time and effort toward building the perfect ratings-based recommendation system, Netflix walked away?

Not quite. "We still have people rate, we still find that very useful information," said Yellin. "It's just secondary." Two things happened to dim the usefulness of stars. The first, suggested Xavier Amatriain, the company's director of recommendation systems, is that the company was getting close to some kind of terminal velocity in taste prediction. "It's pretty much like many things in the algorithmic world," he told me. "It takes you 20 percent of your time to get to that 90 percent accuracy, then 80 percent of your time you're trying to get that final 10 percent accuracy." It was less than clear that the investment in getting that final 10 percent, and the complexity it would add—to a recommendation system already groaning with "Restricted Boltzmann Machines,"

"Random Forests," and "Latent Dirichlet Allocations"—would actually pay off.

Something else had changed. Since the Netflix Prize, Netflix had gone from a strictly DVD-by-mail company to, largely, a video-streaming service. "What people wanted to do when they were giving us a rating," Amatriain said, "was expressing a thought process. You added something to your queue; you watched it two days later. And then you were expressing an opinion you knew was going to have feedback in the long term." But with instant streaming, "it's a very different concept. You don't like it, it's okay. You just switch to something else. The cost of switching is much lower."

With streaming, Netflix might have had less explicit feedback, but it had more implicit *behavior.* "We're able to get real-time data play," Yellin said, "which is richer than what they say about what they want." Netflix knows infinitely more about what and *how* you watch: when you watch something, where you watch, the moment you stop in a movie, what you watch next, whether you watch something twice. What you *search* for—another taste signal. Yellin tells me all this with passionate intensity. With his jittery patter and angular, slightly drawn look, accentuated by a lack of hair, he comes across like a hyper-knowledgeable video store clerk, back in the days when they existed. But he is a video store clerk who has been given an omnipotent glimpse into what the people in this country have been sticking into their VCRs—and what parts they hit "rewind" on. If there is a violation of privacy here, its most salient feature is that you cannot hide from your own taste.

The arrival of companies like Netflix, with their petabytes of data on people's likes and dislikes, all those thumbs and favorites, offered unprecedented insight into what had long been an elusive field: the formation of judgments, the expression of preferences, the mechanics of taste. This vast range of online activity—"electronic word of mouth," as it is called—is where abstract, "unaccountable" notions of taste run into the empirical order of the Internet, with its collaborative filtering algorithms, its sprawling data sets, its seemingly perpetual record of activity. Any one review—or thumb or like—is essentially useless. It suffers from what Ray Fisman has called the "cheap talk" problem. The aggregate level is where, through sheer numbers, the noise can be filtered, the outliers marginalized, and statistical consensus achieved.

Sociologists like Pierre Bourdieu, who probably thought more about taste than anyone else (and whom we shall revisit later), had always faced the problem of self-reporting: Asking people what they like is not the same thing as observing what they do. The beauty of the Internet is that regardless of what people say, you can see, with increasing fidelity, their actual behavior. Almost every aspect of human taste that Bourdieu was interested in is, every day, being cataloged online, in numbers beyond any sociologist's dream. What music do you like? (Spotify, Pandora.) What is your ideal human face? (OkCupid, Match .com.) What is the ideal subject of a photograph? (Flickr, Instagram.)

So where Netflix once relied much more on what people *said* they liked—the itself rather novel bedrock upon which recommendation systems were founded—it was now focusing more on what people actually *watched*. "There are many advantages to this," says Amatriain. "One is the way people rate: They rate in an aspirational way—what they would like to be watching or how they would like to be watching." As Carlos Gómez Uribe, Netflix's director for product innovation, told me, "A relatively high fraction of people tell us that they often watch foreign movies or documentaries. But in practice that doesn't happen very much."

Netflix had always sensed this gap between people's aspirations and their behavior. It could, to cite one example, track how long a DVD sat at a user's house, presumably unplayed. "Al Gore's *Inconvenient Truth*," said Yellin, to nods around the table. "We noticed that movie would stay at people's houses forever. That was a great cup holder." But now the level of scrutiny was more real-time, more visceral: You quit that Bergman film for *Dodgeball*? You just created a data point.

People, Yellin suggested, "want to feel good about themselves. Or they could even be self-delusional about the image they have of themselves—what kinds of things they say they like, how many stars they'll give a particular title, and what they actually watch." You might give five stars to *Hotel Rwanda* and two stars to *Captain America*, he said, "but you're much more likely to watch *Captain America*."

There is nothing particularly new in this. Economists since Thorstein Veblen have talked about our conspicuous "signals" of taste, whether honest or not. They usually only flow upward: People do not rate *Captain America* five stars, *Hotel Rwanda* two stars, and then secretly watch the latter. The sociologist Erving Goffman famously described the way we present ourselves as a "dramaturgical" act: "We find that upward mobility involves the presentation of proper performances and that efforts to move upward and efforts to keep from moving downward are expressed in terms of sacrifices made for the maintenance of front."

We all have wanted, at one time or another, to appear as an idealized self. "I'm actually a quite different person," as the playwright Ödön von Horváth wrote, "I just never get around to being him." Think of the moment in *Play It Again, Sam* where Woody Allen's character is scrambling, ahead of a date, to array his coffee table with respectable books ("You can't leave books lying around if you're not reading them," his friend complains, to which he replies, "It creates an image"). What is curious about the Netflix data is that they were private; there is no one to see your tasteful choices or interesting queue. As Yellin suggested, the dramaturgy involved here is directed at one's *self*.

Which leads to the interesting question posed by the anthropologist Robert Trivers and his psychologist colleague William von Hippel: "Who is the audience for self-deception?" Goffman wrote that people are often compelled to maintain standards "because of a lively belief that an unseen audience is present who will punish deviations from these standards." Hence the guilt in "guilty pleasure," a subject I will treat later. If deception itself is an evolutionarily useful strategy, "fundamental in animal communication," self-deception too becomes "an offensive strategy evolved for deceiving others." Woody Allen's character, by displaying those books, is making himself feel better, as well as helping to convince *himself* that he is the sort of person who reads those books, which will thus help convince his date.

This does not mean it cannot be jarring when the mirror is held up to self-deception. A rather common complaint Netflix hears is "Why are you recommending all these two- or three-star movies to me?" In other words, why are you giving me stuff I will not like? Netflix, however, is not in business to turn you into a cineast. It wants to keep you signed up with Netflix. It is like a casino using clever math to keep you on the machines. It wants to recommend things you will watch. "Engagement," Netflix calls it. "When someone rates a movie like *Schindler's List*," says Gómez Uribe, "it tends to be pretty high—as opposed to one of the silly comedies I watch, like *Hot Tub Time Machine*." But if you give people nothing but four- or five-star films, "that doesn't mean that user will actually want to watch that video on a Wednesday night after a long day at work."

The star system itself is filled with biases. People avoid the ends of scales—"contraction bias," it is called. So you get many more two- or four-star reviews than one or five. Another statistical hiccup, Amatriain said, is that "we know the rating scale is not linear; you don't have the same distance from a one star to a two, as from a two to a three." That middle ground, the landscape of *meh*, gets pretty muddy in terms of what is watchable. Then there is "integer bias," or the idea that people seem predisposed to give whole-number ratings.

Assigning stars to a cultural product is itself a curious—and long contentious—enterprise. It seemed to kick off in books, actually, with Edward O'Brien's inaugural edited volume, *The Best Short Stories of 1915*. As he described in an introduction, the stories he selected "fell *naturally* into four groups" (my italics). These were denoted by asterisks, the more the better, all the way up to three (for stories that deserve "a position of some permanence in our literature"). With the vision of the disinterested critic, he declared, "I have permitted no personal preference or prejudice to influence my judgment consciously for or against a story" (later in the book we shall see just how difficult that is). O'Brien's star system—and indeed the very act of choosing the "best" stories of the year—itself came under some withering criticism.* Reviewing *The Best Short Stories of 1925*, a critic for *The New York Times*, chiding O'Brien's "dogmatic" valuation system, declared, "A great many people will believe almost anything that any one tells them positively enough." Star history gets a bit murky but seems to finally pop up in film in a review by Irene Thirer in the July 31, 1928, edition of the New York *Daily News*. She writes, "Judging movies via the star system, as we're going to do henceforth as a permanent thing"—implying it was already under way. She then pans *Port of Missing Girls* with a single star.†

People have been quibbling over stars ever since. One obvious problem is that because people's tastes are different, what one person thinks is a three-star movie may be for you a five-star flick. This is why Netflix distinguishes between the overall number of stars and the

---

* O'Brien's volume itself has a 3.75 out of 5 stars ranking on Goodreads.com.
† Time has been kinder to the movie. On IMDb.com, it has a 6.9 out of 10 rating.

metric "Our best guess for you." This lays taste right out on the table: You liked this movie o./ more than others. While we might take this to be some purer expression of "our" taste, one complication is that, as with all recommendation engines, that number is partially derived from what *other* people are doing. Another problem is that you may just rate differently—with a high or low bias—regardless of what you actually thought about the movie. "Some people I know are very selective on giving high ratings," says Amatriain. "So two or three stars for them is not necessarily a bad rating."

This points to something interesting about Netflix and its ratings. Perhaps as a holdover from the days when we received our opinions largely from reviewers, who had their own rating systems, we might think of a star rating as a kind of stable measure of quality, or at least of one's taste. At both the individual and the aggregate level, however, Netflix stars are far from fixed. Rather, they are like free markets: prone to corrections, bubbles, hedges, inflation, and other forms of statistical "noise."

In early 2004, to take one case, there was a "sudden rise in the average movie rating" on Netflix. Did Hollywood films suddenly get better? Actually, the recommendation system did. "Users are increasingly rating movies that are more suitable for their own taste," wrote Yehuda Koren, a researcher who participated in the Netflix Prize. In other words, the movies got better because they were chosen by more people who thought they were better. Depending on how you look at it, this could be thought of as a kind of selection bias—the people who were likely to like a movie were rating it more favorably—or as a kind of market equilibrium in taste: People were more accurately finding the movies (that is, the supply) they were more likely to like (that is, the demand).

Things are even messier at the individual level. Ask someone to re-rate a movie he has already seen, and more likely than not he will rate it differently. Simply by altering a user's initial rating, experiments have shown, you can affect how that same person re-rates it later. People seem to rate things differently when they rate a bunch of films en masse (training their algorithms) versus a single film. People rate television shows differently than films. "The average rating on a TV show tends to be much higher than on a movie," Yellin said. Has television gotten better than film? "My intuition is that there's selection," he said.

"Who's likely to rate *The Sopranos*? Not someone who watched five minutes and didn't like it because it wasn't really part of their life. It's the person who committed to it and spent a hundred hours of their life watching it." On the other hand, "who will rate *Paul Blart: Mall Cop*? It might not be a very good movie, but it's ninety minutes long. Your bar or criteria might be different."

Similarly, the same movie seen on streaming versus DVD might have different ratings. "Especially if a movie is much more visceral," Yellin said—like a "very emotional" Spielberg title. "It's going to have an impact on you, but that impact might be ephemeral. So if you rated it right at the credits, you might give it a higher rating. A week later, it might not have that effect on you." Watching a movie alone might yield a lower rating than watching a movie with enthusiastic friends.

And so on. "I was deep into the ratings game for years," Yellin said gravely, sounding like a jaded gangster reflecting on his unsavory past on the streets. I sensed he was striving for some purity in those ratings, a Platonic ideal of what we like. "You question how much hair I have? I tore my hair out trying to understand these kinds of things." Ratings, in the end, were not as potent a signal of what people would watch as one might think. Neither are things like gender and geography. "If you know nothing else, it will help a tiny bit," Yellin said. "But if they watch five things on Netflix, we will know magnitudes more about them than age, gender, where they live." You are what you watch.

All this talk of how ratings have been deemphasized does not mean that *recommendations* are any less important. They are indeed more central than ever to Netflix's algorithmic work, driving some 75 percent of all viewing.

Now, though, they are more *implicit*. Rather than tell you what you like, Netflix now in essence shows you what you like, in "personalized" rows whose architecture has essentially been created by your own behavior. "Everything is a recommendation," as Amatriain liked to say of the new, "beyond the five stars" thinking. Even searching for things—a sign that "we are not able to show them what to watch"—feeds into the recommendation engine. Knowing what you are looking for betrays what you might like. Doing *anything* on Netflix is itself a kind of meta-recommendation: The site, like much of the Internet, is one big constant experiment in preferences, a series of "A/B tests" you probably participated in without being aware. Did moving the search box to the left or the right of the online shoe retailer lead you to buy more products? Did putting a row on your splash page titled "Foreign Dramas from the 1980s" get you to watch more foreign dramas from the 1980s?

The rows reflect a kind of middle ground between two extremes of signals that in and of themselves are not wholly useful: The first is your stated likes. These can lead into a kind of taste cul-de-sac, full of obscure, interesting films that you rarely get around to watching. "Overfitting" is the algorithmic word: The engine makes recommendations that are, in a sense, *too* perfect—and perfectly sterile.

The second is popularity. This is the antithesis of "personalization," Amatriain told me; then again, if you are trying to optimize consumption, "a member is most likely to watch what most others are watching." This can lead to the *Shawshank Redemption* Problem, or the rather superfluous recommendation of something the whole world has seen. *The Shawshank Redemption* is Netflix's highest-ever-rated film, a film so universally lauded on the site it has almost no predictive power beyond its own seemingly inherent likability. "People love that film all over the frickin' place," Yellin marveled, shaking his head.

Perhaps as a concession to the inexorable noisiness of human taste, Netflix does not rely entirely on the behavior of users themselves to make recommendations. It also has a paid army of human "taggers" erecting a labyrinth of cinematic meta-data. Rather than trying to figure out what makes two people's taste similar, Netflix has found it is often easier to ascertain what makes two *films* similar. This can lead to curious discoveries. The presence of the director Pedro Almodóvar may forge a link between two films, no matter how different they may be, where nothing else would. But meta-data by themselves can mislead. Recommending *Dogville*—a film as polarizing as *Napoleon Dynamite*—to people who watched *The Hours* or *Moulin Rouge*, simply because Nicole Kidman was in both of them, could be disastrous.

But meta-data can also tease out things we might not have discovered ourselves. The often quirkily specific, human-generated genre rows remind us, as I have noted, of how categories can influence our preferences. We like things *as* something, even if, with a film like *The Big Lebowski*, it can take a while to figure out what "it" is. Netflix's quirky genres try to shape meaning from what might otherwise seem capricious suggestions. "Recommendations can be too out-there," Yellin said. "You're like, 'Wow, why would it say that just because I rated *Raise the Red Lantern* five stars that I'm going to really like this Japanese kids' movie?" Yellin pointed to his laptop. On his Netflix page was an array of recommendations: *Gomorrah*, *Valhalla Rising*, *Enter the Void*, and *Un Chien Andalou*. They were all contained in a genre dubbed Mind-Bending Foreign Dramas. "I got psyched looking at this," he said, "but if you had shown it to me without any context, it might not be as compelling." As the writer Alexis Madrigal described it, "It's not just that Netflix can show you things you might like, but that it can tell you *what* kinds of things those are."

That these two things can influence each other is not only one of the curious forms of quantum entanglement found in the Big Data of recommendation systems but a fact of human taste.

EVERYONE'S A CRITIC: LET A THOUSAND KVETCHES BLOOM

My husband and I found this "off-the-beaten-path" place one night while driving on a dark desert highway. Our room was a bit dated (mirrors on the ceiling LOL!) but we were pleasantly surprised to find that we had been upgraded—our room even had champagne on ice! But the place has a serious noise problem: we were woken up in the middle of the night by voices coming from somewhere down the hallway. While I would agree with the previous reviewer that it is "Such a Lovely Place!" I have very mixed feelings. The worst thing, however, were the checkout policies, which I found to be completely unacceptable.

You may recognize the above as my mashing up of two familiar narratives: the lyrics to the Eagles' "Hotel California" and a review on the travel Web site TripAdvisor.com. You know "Hotel California" because you have heard it to death on FM radio. And if you have spent any time on TripAdvisor.com, you will, after reading the twenty-eighth review of a hotel, have begun to absorb its gentle cadences: the casual, confessional tone; the banter with other reviewers; the personality that seems to come across at once as both the relatable everyman being wronged and the aggrieved diva with a heightened sense of entitlement. Then there is the "but"—a hallmark of the "speech act" known as a complaint. As the linguist Harvey Sacks once noted, complaints tend to follow a standard pattern: "a piece of praise plus 'but' plus something else." The praise typically comes first, as if to say, "This is not me being unreasonable."

Reading these sorts of reviews, I cannot help but wonder, where did people, previously, before the Internet and social media, channel this torrent of opinion? If the hotel shower's water pressure was not quite to one's liking, where was there, besides the captive audience at the front desk, to channel this disquietude? Then, as now, a person having a poor experience might simply have vowed never to visit the place again. He could have told friends and family about this experience, and this casual griping might have rippled out to a few people. But how could he warn that stranger, down the road, heading toward the proverbial Hotel California, that it might not be worth her money?

It may already seem difficult to remember, but in the days before the Internet, and then smartphones, to do something like eat at an unknown restaurant meant relying on a clutch of quick-and-dirty heuristics. The presence of a lot of truck drivers or cops at a lonely diner was a supposed claim to its quality (though it might simply have been the only option around). For "ethnic" food, there was the classic "We were the only non-[insert ethnicity] people in there." Or one spent anxious minutes on the sidewalk, under the watchful gaze of the host, reading curling, yellowed reviews from local weeklies, wondering if the opinion of a critic who passed by one afternoon in 1987 still held.

We lived in an information-poor environment. To choose a hotel in an unfamiliar city, we might have paged through a guidebook. But what if that guidebook only covered a few hotels and was not recently updated? We might have relied simply on brands: I stayed at this hotel in Akron, so I will stay at the one in Davenport. But what if the Akron one was much better run?

"The difficulty of distinguishing good quality from bad is inherent in the business world," wrote the economist George Akerlof. His famous "lemon problem" took the used-car market as the quintessential case of information asymmetry: The seller knew much more about the quality of the car than the buyer. This could lead to the buyer's being cheated. Because of that very danger, however, the price the seller was able to offer could be depressed. Brands, for Akerlof, were one way for consumers to "retaliate" in the face of a poor product, by not giving it their business, across the board, in the future. And chains, brands writ upon the landscape, could offer that same assurance. The customer knew what to expect. However modest that expectation was, it was *better than having an expectation violated.*

Eating at the chain restaurant on the highway posed its own information problem. "The customers are seldom local," Akerlof wrote. "The reason is that these well-known chains offer a better hamburger than the *average* local restaurant; at the same time, the local customer, who knows his area, can usually choose a place he prefers."

Let us call this the "lemon chicken problem." That local consumer, having more information than you, was always going to eat better. In an information-poor environment, you could settle for a series of blandly average experiences but never find that one transcendent place to which, as travel magazines like to say, "locals flock." Of course, by the time tourists began to flock, that business probably began caring less about what locals thought, and maybe the quality slipped—because how many would be back anyway? In a pinch, you could simply go with your gut. Sometimes you left clutching it.

The arrival of Web sites like Yelp and TripAdvisor and Amazon fundamentally altered things. That mold on the shower curtain in room 224? Tell the world about it! That hidden place on Route 51 that made the amazing doughnuts? A touch of GPS, an aggregate of "user-generated content," and you were suddenly privy to an experience you might have previously missed.

That "electronic word of mouth" can move markets is beyond question. On Amazon.com, a National Bureau of Economic Research study has found, an increase in the "average star" of a book gives that book a "higher relative share" of all books on the site. A group of researchers in Ireland, meanwhile, found a "TripAdvisor effect": After the service was introduced in Ireland, hotels' TripAdvisor aggregate ratings rose over a two-year period. Hotels were either responding to online feedback or indeed trying to earn higher ratings. Either way, guests got better rooms. Hotels in Las Vegas, meanwhile, where TripAdvisor was already known, saw no change. Like some version of the "efficient market" hypothesis, all information had already been "priced" into the Vegas hotels' reviews.

On Yelp, Michael Luca, an economist at Harvard University, found in the Seattle market that a one star increase in a restaurant's rating lifted its revenue as much as 9 percent. The effect was "being driven entirely from independent restaurants." This makes sense: Because chains, in essence, fill in the gaps in word of mouth, they do not depend on it for their business. What could you say about a chain that someone would not already know? Does the world care if you do not happen to like the secret sauce on a McDonald's Big Mac? No—because billions of others apparently do.

Luca also found that chains, after Yelp was introduced in the market he was studying, began to lose market share to independent restaurants. Picture Akerlof's prototypical customer in 1963, eating his slightly better-than-average hamburger at a roadside chain, magically granted a smartphone: Suddenly he could learn where to get a *great* hamburger. As Luca notes, the "utility" of going to an independent restaurant was higher. Eaters had nothing to lose but the chains. It was that "efficient market" again: When all "known information" has already been built into stock prices (or restaurant ratings), amateur investors (or amateur diners) can do as well as experts. One might even argue that Yelp, and the broader transmission of online taste, have helped drive the emergence of better chain restaurant options.

But electronic word of mouth introduces its own problems. Instead of a paucity of information, you may these days encounter the reverse problem: too much information. You wade into a Yelp entry for a simple diagnosis of whether a place is worth your money. You find zigzagging polarities of experience: A meal was "to die for"; the same meal was "pretty lame." Or you find yourself pulled into the narrow channels of people's proclivities—a dislike of the music, a digression into the flatware design. Having sifted through a morass of reviews, you may begin to feel a kind of hangover. Either you quit the place altogether, or by the time you arrive, you already feel weighted by a certain exhaustion of expectation, as if you had already consumed the experience and were now simply going through the motions.

Reading through the reviews of a restaurant, you may find yourself reviewing the reviewers. For as important as the question of whether they liked it is, *Are they like us?* One looks for signals of authority and a shared outlook. A red flag for me, for example, is the word "awesome." It is not simply that I think the word has lost most of its connotation.

It is that I place less trust in the opinion of someone who uses it (for example, "awesome margaritas"*—and you may trust me less for not trusting it. The word "anniversary" or "honeymoon" in a review portends people with inflated expectations for their special night. Their complaint with any perceived failure by the restaurant or hotel to rise to this solemn occasion is not necessarily ours. I reflexively downgrade reviewers writing with syrupy dross picked up from hotel brochures ("It was a vision of perfection") or employing such trite abominations as "sin-fully delicious!"

This idea that we are interested as much in what a person's review says about him as it does about the restaurant or hotel is, in one respect, not new. Our previous choices were informed either by friends we trusted or by critics whose voices seemed to carry authority. But suddenly the door has been opened to a multitude of voices, each bearing no preexisting authority or social trust. Critics have always been suspected of having their own preferences and biases, but on the Internet a thousand critics have bloomed. The messy, complicated, often hidden dynamics of taste and preference, and the battles over them, are suddenly laid out in front of us.

The rise of this crowd-sourced aggregate of amateur reviewers is generally seen as an egalitarian blossoming, freeing consumers from the tyranny of individual, elite mandarins, each harboring his own agenda and tastes. "The excising of the expert review is happening right across the board," declared the writer Suzanne Moore in *The Guardian*. "Who needs expertise when every Tom, Dick and Harriet reviews everything for free anyway. Isn't this truly democratic? The nature of criticism is changing, so this hierarchy of expertise is crumbling."

One can almost hear the anticipatory echoes of something like Yelp in the context of the Spanish philosopher José Ortega y Gasset's 1930 tract *The Revolt of the Masses*. The multitude, he wrote, once "scattered about the world in small groups," appears "as an agglomeration," it has "suddenly become visible," and where it once occupied the "back-

---

* Language inflation is another problem with online reviews. The creators of RevMiner, an information extraction app designed to streamline Yelp, note that a person searching for something like "good dim sum" does not really mean *good* dim sum, but "dim sum that others have described as 'great' or 'amazing.'" Good is no longer good enough. You need to be awesome.

ground of the social stage," it "now has advanced to the footlights and is the principal character." The disgruntled and disenfranchised diner is now able to make or break a restaurant through sheer collective will. Against this leveling of critical power, the old guard fulminates. Ruth Reichl, the former editor of *Gourmet*, raised the clarion: "Anybody who believes Yelp is an idiot. Most people on Yelp have no idea what they're talking about."

There are complications with this idea that the Internet has done away with the need for experts and for critical authority. For one, much reviewing energy on Yelp is precisely an effort to establish one's bona fides. A reviewer for an Indian restaurant in midtown Manhattan lays down a triple claim of authority: "I am a foodie and my love for Indian food (as an Indian) is tough to match. I eat at this restaurant at least once a week. Really innovative mix of ingredients, and yet extremely authentic." Not only is he a foodie; he is an Indian foodie who, like all true food critics, has eaten here more than once. And we will not unpack that thorny word "authentic." Slippery though it may be, the word "authentic," or synonyms thereof, seems to lead to higher ratings for Yelp restaurants.

Yelp is filled with this sort of signaling, as economists call it, subtle references conferring one's authority in an effort to rise above the masses of similar reviewers. ("I knew the chef from his previous stint at . . ." or, "Of all the Henan cuisine places I've eaten, this is one of the best.") It is "conventional signaling": There is nothing in the signal itself to verify what you are saying beyond the fact that you are saying it. If you wear a T-shirt saying, "I ♥ NYC," who are we to doubt your ardor? There is little "cost," in money or energy, involved in the signal; hence, there is little reliability. What is there, actually, to keep these signals from losing *all* reliability? As Judith Donath argues, their honesty may in essence come simply "because there is little motivation to produce them dishonestly." There is also little motivation to doubt their veracity. So online, where anonymity rules and, as Donath argues, "everything is a signal," how can you quickly assess the quality of a review?

Even as it aggregates its democratic horde, Yelp itself strives to reintroduce hierarchy, through its class of "elite" reviewers. They wear badges—a kind of signal—and are picked by a team known as the Council. "We don't share how it's done," a Yelp spokesperson declared, as if describing the covert hiring of Michelin inspectors. This is a bit of a paradox. We are said to live in a world where traditional expert authority—from the media to the government to the health-care establishment—is now suspect. But have the online review sites (with Amazon's "Top Reviewer" and TripAdvisor's "Top Contributor" designations) simply reconstituted a new form of expertise, the curious phenomenon of "lay expertise"?

How much trust do we put in this new class of experts? When you glance at a restaurant or hotel or book review online, do you simply look at the aggregate number of stars, or do you skim down into the thicket of individual opinions? If the power of online word of mouth comes from the ability to quantify a collective mass of opinion—liberating us from the narrowness of one person's perspective—what is the value of reading any one review?

In his Yelp study, Luca reported examples of "Bayesian learning." In other words, people reacted more strongly to reviews that seemed to have more information. Elite Yelp reviewers, he found, had twice the statistical impact as nonelites. Another group that had an outsized effect on Yelp were users of Groupon, the online coupon site. Groupon users, once on Yelp, write longer reviews that are better liked than those of the average Yelp user, as research has shown. This influence has real weight: They also seem to bring down the average review for a restaurant. Curiously, it is not that they are critical per se. In fact, Groupon users on Yelp, the authors pointed out, are more "moderate."

The idea of the masses liberating the objects of criticism from the tyranny of critics is clouded by the number of reviewers who seem to turn toward petty despotism. Reading Yelp or TripAdvisor reviews, particularly of the one-star variety, one quickly senses the particular axe being ground: the hostess who shot the "wrong" look to the "girls' night" group; the waiter who did not respond with enthusiasm to the cuteness of the diner's toddler; the "judgmental attitude" of a server; a greeting that is too effusive or insufficiently so; the waiter deemed "too uneasy with being a waiter"; or any number of episodes (these are all actual examples I have gleaned from the site) that have little to do with food. They are labor disputes: between patrons' capital and the endlessly subjective expectation of what they should receive.

As so much of the service economy now revolves around "affective labor"—the enforced smiles that organizations induce their employees to give "guests"—evaluations of the "product" turn increasingly sub-jective and interpersonal. The writer Paul Myerscough has observed, "Work increasingly isn't, or isn't only, a matter of producing things, but of supplying your energies, physical and emotional, in the service of others." For those who feel they did not receive the right kind of emotional energy, Yelp becomes a place to catalog these litanies of complaint. How are we to know the reviewer was not simply having a bad day?

At the extreme end of the trust problem with online reviews are those that are actually fake: planted by the rival restaurateur, the jealous author, the jilted hotel guest. Nearly one-fourth of Yelp reviews are rejected by the site's own authenticity filters. The frequency of these false ratings, as Luca and Georgios Zervas have found, tends to follow fairly predictable patterns. The more negative a restaurant's reputa-tion, or the fewer the reviews, the greater the chance for a false positive review. When restaurants are of a similar type (for example, "Thai" or "Vegan") and geographically *closer*, the odds goes up for a false negative review. Similar patterns are observed on TripAdvisor.

Sometimes the reasons for deception are rather unclear: A study by Eric Anderson and Duncan Simester of one online apparel site found that in 5 percent of all reviews customers had not actually purchased the item (but had purchased many other things at the site). These reviews tended to be more negative, and the authors hypothesized the custom-ers were acting as de facto "brand managers"—a form of that customer "retaliation" that Akerlof described.

But for whatever reason it is done, how does one know a review is false? Consider these snippets of two reviews:

I have stayed at many hotels traveling for both business and pleasure and I can honestly stay that The James is tops. The service at the hotel is first class. The rooms are modern and very comfortable.

My husband and I stayed at the James Chicago Hotel for our an-niversary. This place is fantastic! We knew as soon as we arrived we made the right choice! The rooms are BEAUTIFUL and the staff very attentive and wonderful!!

As it turns out, the second of these reviews is fake. A group of Cornell University researchers created a machine-learning system that can tell, with accuracy near 90 percent, whether a review is authentic or not. This is far better than trained humans typically achieve; among other problems, we tend to suffer from "truth bias"—a wish to assume people are not lying.

To create the algorithm, the Cornell team largely relied on decades of research into the way people talk when they are confabulating. In "invented accounts," people tend to be less accurate with contextual details, because they were not actually there. Fake hotel reviews, they found, had less detailed information about things like room size and location. Prevaricating reviewers used more superlatives (*the best! The worst!*). Because lying takes more mental work, false reviews are usually shorter. When people lie, they also seem to use more verbs than nouns, because it is easier to go on about things you *did* than to describe how things *were*. Liars also tend to use personal pronouns less than truth tellers do, presumably to put more "space" between themselves and the act of deception.

But doesn't the fake example above have plenty of personal pronouns? Indeed, the Cornell team found that people actually referred to themselves *more* in fake reviews, in hopes of making the review sound more credible. Curiously, the researchers noted that people used personal pronouns less in fake negative than in fake positive reviews, as if the distancing were more important when the lie was meant to sound nasty. Lying in general is arguably easier online, absent the interpersonal and time pressures of trying to make up something on the spot in front of someone. How easy? When I ran my imagined "Hotel California" review through Review Skeptic, a Web site created by a member of the Cornell team, it was declared "truthful."

Fake reviews do exist and undoubtedly have economic consequences. But the enormous amount of attention they have received in the media, and all the energy dedicated to automatically sniffing out deceptive reviews, may leave one with the comfortable assumption that all the other reviews are, simply, "true." While they may not be knowingly deceptive, there are any number of ways they are subject to distortion and biases, hidden or otherwise.

The first problem is that hardly anyone writes reviews. At one online retailer, it was less than 5 percent of customers—hardly democratic. And the first reviewers of a product are going to differ from people who chime in a year later; for one thing, there are existing reviews to influence the later ones. Merely buying something from a place may tilt you positive; people who rated but did not buy a book on Amazon, as Simester and Anderson discovered, were twice as likely to *not* like it. Finally, customers are often moved to write a review because of an inordinately positive or negative experience. So ratings tend to be "bimodal"—not evenly distributed across a range of stars, but clustered at the top and the bottom. This is known as a "J-shaped distribution" or, more colorfully, the "brag and moan phenomenon."

The curve is J-shaped, not reverse-candy-cane-shaped, because of another phenomenon in online ratings: a "positivity bias." On Goodreads.com, the average is 3.8 stars out of 5. On Yelp, one analysis found, the reviews suffer from an "artificially high baseline." The average of all reviews on TripAdvisor is 3.7 stars; when a similar property is listed on Airbnb, it does even better, because owners can review *guests*. Similarly, on eBay, hardly anyone leaves negative feedback, in part because, in a kind of variant of the famed "ultimatum game," both buyer and seller can rate each other. Positivity bias was so rampant that in 2009 eBay overhauled its system. Now vendors, rather than needing to reach a minimum threshold of stars to ensure they were meeting the site's "minimum service standard," needed to have a certain number of *negative* reviews. They had to be bad to be good.

A few years ago, YouTube had a problem: Everyone was leaving five-star reviews. "Seems like when it comes to ratings," the site's blog noted, "it's pretty much all or nothing." The ratings, the site's engineers reasoned, were primarily being used as a "seal of approval," a basic "like," not as some "editorial indicator" of overall quality (the next most popular rating was one star, for all the dislikers). Faced with this massively biased, nearly meaningless statistical regimen, they switched to a "thumbs up/thumbs down" rating regimen. Yet the binary system is hardly without flaws. The kitten video that has a mildly cute kitten—let us be honest, a fairly low bar—is endowed with the same sentiment as the world's cutest kitten video. But in the heuristic, lightning-fast world of the Internet, where information is cheap and the cost of switching virtually nil, people may not want an evaluation system that takes as much time as the consumption experience. And so all likes are alike.

And then there is the act of reviewing the review—or the reviewer.

The most helpful reviews actually make people more likely to buy something, particularly when it comes to "long tail" products. But these reviews suffer from their own kinds of curious dynamics. Early reviews get more helpfulness votes, and the more votes a review has, the more votes it tends to attract. On Amazon, reviews that themselves were judged more "helpful" helped drive more sales—regardless of how many stars were given to the product.

What makes a review helpful? A team of Cornell University and Google researchers, looking at reviewing behavior on Amazon.com, found that a review's "helpfulness" rating falls as the review's star rating deviates from the average number of stars. Defining "helpfulness" is itself tricky: Did a review help someone make a purchase, or was it being rewarded for conforming with what others were saying? To explore this, they identified reviews in which text had been plagiarized, a "rampant" practice on Amazon, they note, in which the very same review is used for different products. They found, with these pairs, that when one review was closer to the stars of *all* reviews, it was deemed more helpful than the other. In other words, regardless of its actual content, a review was better when it was more like what other people had said.

Taste *is* social comparison. As Todd Yellin had said to me at Netflix, "How many times have you seen someone in an unfamiliar situation—like 'I'm at an opera and I've never been before'—they'll look right, they'll look left, they'll look around. 'Is this a good one?'" When the performance is over, whether a person joins in a standing ovation may have as much to do with what the surrounding crowd is doing as with whether he actually liked it. By contrast, when we cannot see what someone has chosen, as studies have shown, odds are we will choose differently.

Small wonder, then, that on social media, where the opinion of many others is ubiquitous and rather inescapable, we should find what Sinan Aral, a professor of management at MIT, has called "social influence bias." Aral and his colleagues wanted to know if the widespread positivity bias in rating behavior was due to previous ratings. How much of that four-and-a-half-star restaurant rating is down to the restaurant itself, and how much to previous people voting it four and a half stars? Does that first Instagram "like" lead to more likes than a picture with no likes?

So Aral and his colleagues devised a clever experiment, using a Digg-style "social news aggregation" site where users post articles, make comments on articles, and then "thumb up" or "thumb down" those comments. They divided some 100,000 comments into three groups. There was a "positive" group, in which comments had been artificially seeded with an "up" vote. Then there was a "negative" group, where comments were seeded "down." A control group had no comments.

As with other sites, things kick off with an initial positivity bias. People were already 4.6 times more likely to vote up than down. When the first vote was artificially made "up," however, it led to an even greater cascade of positivity. Not only was the next vote more likely to be positive, but the ones *after* that were too. When a first comment was negative, the next comment was more likely to also be negative. But eventually, those negatives would be "neutralized" by a counterforce of positive reviewers, like some cavalry riding in to the rescue.

What was happening? The researchers argued that up or down votes per se were not bringing out the people who generally like to vote up or down. It was that the presence of a rating on a comment encouraged more people to rate—and to rate even more positively than might be expected. Even people who were *negative* on control comments (the ones that had no ratings) tended to be more positive on comments seeded with a "down" vote. As Aral describes it, "We tend to herd on positive opinions and remain skeptical of negative ones."

The stakes are higher than just a few clicks on Digg temporarily lifting an article above the tide. An early positive review, authentic or not, can send a subtle ripple through all later reviews. Aral's study found that seeding a review positively boosted overall opinion scores by 25 percent, a result that persisted. Early positive reviews can create path dependence. Even if one went through and removed false reviews, the damage would have been done; those reviews might have influenced "authentic" reviews. "These ratings systems are ostensibly designed to give you unbiased aggregate opinion of the crowd," Aral told me. But, as with that standing ovation, can we find our own opinion amid the roar of the crowd?

All this does not mean that ratings, having been pushed in a certain positive direction, always rise. In fact, on a site like Amazon, while "sequential bias" patterns have been found, there is a general tendency for book ratings to grow more negative over time. "The more ratings amassed on a product," one study noted, "the lower the ratings will be." What distinguishes Amazon from the one-click liking or disliking mechanisms seen in Aral's experiment is the higher cost of expression: You cannot just say how much you like or dislike something; you have to give some explanation as to *why*.

This seems to change behavior. As the HP Labs researchers Fang Wu and Bernardo Huberman found in a study of Amazon reviewers, in contrast to the "herding and polarization" effects seen at the Digg-style sites, Amazon reviewers seem to react to previous "extreme" raters. Someone rating on the heels of a one-star review may feel compelled to "balance it out" with a three-star, when in reality he was thinking of leaving a two-star review. This reaction to extremes can lead to an overall "softening" of opinion over time.

One reason, they suspect, is an inherent desire to stand out from the crowd, to actually affect the result or inflate one's sense of self-worth. "What is the point of leaving another 5-star review," Wu and Huberman ask, "when one hundred people have already done so?" Rationally, there is none, just as, in the "voter's paradox," there is little rational sense in voting in elections where one's individual vote will not affect the outcome (although, unlike with voting, there is evidence that recent reviews do affect sales). So the people who leave opinions, after time, tend to be those who disagree with previous opinions.

It is easy to imagine several stages in the evolution of a book's ratings life on Amazon. The earliest reviews tend to come from people who are most interested in the book (not to mention an author's friends and relatives, if not the author herself) and who are most likely to like it.

Taste is self-selection writ large. But once an author's fans and other motivated customers have weighed in, over time a book might attract a wider audience with "weaker preferences," as the researchers David Godes and José Silva suggest. Whether they are more clear-eyed and objective critics, or they do not "get" a book the way early reviewers did, their opinion begins to diverge. With many books, a pronounced "undershooting dynamic" kicks in: a period in which reviews are even *lower* than the eventual lower average, as readers, perhaps swayed by the previous "positive review bias," make essentially mistaken purchases. Then they weigh in, in what might be called the "don't-believe-the-hype effect." So begins a feedback loop. "The more reviews there are," Godes and Silva suggest, "the lower the quality of the information available, which leads to worse decisions which leads to lower ratings." It is not uncommon to find late, fairly flummoxed one-star reviews of only a sentence or two: "I just didn't like it."

As more reviews are posted, people spend less time talking about the contents—because so many other people already have—than about the content of the other *reviews*. When a review mentions a previous review, it is more likely to be negative. Context takes over.

Which leads us back to Aral. How can you actually *tell* if a review has been influenced by a previous review, or whether it is simply homophily: correlated *group* preference, or, more simply, the idea that "birds of a feather flock together"? He gives an example from the sociologist Max Weber: If you see a group of people in a field open umbrellas as it begins to drizzle, you would not say they are influencing one another. They are merely people reacting to *endogenous* conditions, with a correlated group preference to not get wet. If a person opening an umbrella when there was *no* rain could get others to do so, that would be social influence.

Teasing out what is going on in online reviews, as with taste generally, is a messy affair, one that Aral has grappled with for a decade. Do people in my Subaru-heavy neighborhood buy Subarus because they see lots of other Subarus, or do Subaru buyers tend to be a certain sort of person, who also happens to like neighborhoods like mine? Are there seemingly lots of slender people in my neighborhood because they are influenced by other slender people, or are people predisposed to being slender moving to my neighborhood? The only way to ever know is to pick random people from across the country, who do not necessarily want to go to Brooklyn, and put them there.

We shall return to this question in the next chapter, but for now let us consider something else that is happening at a site like Amazon as feedback accrues. Godes and Silva argue that as more reviews come in, "the more dissimilar a shopper is from the previous set of reviewers." In other words, *taste* is happening. People are expressing their own disappointed reaction to a book, but they are also writing about other people's enthusiastic reactions. As much as they are coming up against a thing they do not seem to like, the more unsettling occurrence is that they are coming up against *people* who do not seem to be like them.

As the French sociologist Pierre Bourdieu argued, "Tastes (i.e., manifested preferences) are the practical affirmation of an inevitable difference. It is no accident that, when they have to be justified, they are asserted purely negatively, by the refusal of other tastes."

When the taste stakes are higher, the dissonance can seem even sharper. When a book, particularly a novel, wins a big prize, its reception by readers on the Amazon-owned user-generated review site Goodreads actually gets worse. Balázs Kovács and Amanda Sharkey, who performed the analysis, call it the "paradox of publicity." It is not that judges are incapable of picking good books or that readers cannot recognize their merits. In fact, books that were only short-listed for an award had lower ratings than the award-winning books—*before* the prize was issued. Once the book was adorned with a sticker denoting the prize it had won, however, its ratings began to drop more precipitously than those for the short-listed books it had beat out.

Why the backlash against this ostensible mark of quality? Prizes can increase book sales, but this is a double-edged sword. The prize, the authors note, raises expectations; it goes from being a book you *might* like to being a book you *should* like. The prize may also attract readers whose tastes are more mismatched than those of readers who weighed in before the book got the prize. This is the *reverse* of what had happened to Netflix, in the early twenty-first century, when its movie ratings went up across the board: The films did not get better; the algorithmic matching did. With Goodreads, when books "got better" because of having prizes bestowed on them, new, potentially less well-matched readers were drawn to them, like moths to a brightly burning flame.

Not surprisingly, this often ends in dashed expectations. This might have been what happened with Groupon users on Yelp; they were more casual consumers drawn in for less than "natural" reasons. Unlike the more gently oscillating patterns of opinion the usual book on Amazon sees, the "shock" of the award triggered a spike in polarization: Not only did more one- and two-star reviews begin to enter the picture, but the number of "likes" on *those* reviews, as Kovács told me, "went up like crazy." Middle-ground reviews—the landscape of *meh*—hardly moved the needle. Haters gonna hate, as it were. But haters also gonna *rate*.

By analyzing some thirty thousand reviews, the study bore out a long-held truism: You can be well liked by critics or by the majority of readers but rarely by both. Longtime fans of the author in question may themselves balk at the newfound popularity bestowed on "their" previous favorite. The legendarily acerbic Chicago producer and punk musician Steve Albini once described the dynamic he was experiencing as Big Black, his small, obscure band, became more popular: "As the band gets bigger, you start having people show up to the shows who aren't really of the same mind-set, they're just there for a night out, you know?" They were people who were not only more indifferent to the band, he suggested, but indeed "people that would probably be hostile to you in a neutral setting."

There is a rather gloomy endgame looming here, though: the artist only producing art that people he likes will like, people only drawn to artists they think they will like. Does the world of online taste open us to new experience or simply channel us more efficiently into our little pods of predisposition?

We are looking for "signals of trust" in the noise. When reviewers use their real names, their reviews are judged more helpful. What else drives that positive review of the review? As mentioned before, reviews that hew closer to the average number of stars are judged more helpful. Interestingly, that study found, the bias is not symmetrical: "Slightly negative reviews are punished more strongly, with respect to helpfulness evaluation, than slightly positive reviews." When in doubt, we skew positive.

But not always. There is one crucial variable that determines whether we like, or trust, negative reviews: whether something is an *experience good* (like a book or a movie) or a *search good* (a camera or replacement windshield wipers). While negative reviews in general were seen as less helpful than "moderate" reviews, as Susan Mudambi and David Schuff found in analyzing Amazon reviews, they were judged particularly harshly when the product was a book or a movie. Why? "Taste plays a large role in many experience goods," they write, "and consumers are often highly confident about their own tastes and subjective evaluations, and skeptical about the extreme views of others." Unlike with windshield wipers, people might have already made up their minds about a book or a film as they scan the reviews and can filter out someone's one-star critique as a form of cognitive dissonance.

In one of my favorite one-star reviews for Cormac McCarthy's novel *The Road*, you can practically feel the reviewer trying to escape this trap with a defensive thrust:

> I know that many people love this book. Keep in mind that although you and I disagree, I am still providing information about the book that can be useful to people who have not yet decided whether to buy it. That is my purpose. I'm not trying to malign McCarthy or your personal taste, but to give a review from a different point of view.

The reviewer is tap-dancing around taste, as if even mentioning it were to utter something indelicate. "Taste is a merciless betrayer of social and cultural attitudes," observes Stephen Bayley, "more of a taboo subject than sex or money."

With *search goods*, people are looking for technical information, user tips, product flaws, and the like. They may have no biases or preferences, and a negative review may signal a tangible product flaw.

The most extreme reviews for, say, an OXO salad spinner generally involve a product failure. But the one-star reviews for Rachel Kushner's *Flamethrowers*, the (prizewinning) book I happened to be reading while working on this chapter, are filled with sentences like "I think my main issue is that I couldn't relate to any of the characters." Is that a flaw with the product or the reader? Books may fail or succeed, but not in the same way for every reader. To paraphrase Tolstoy, each unhappy reader is unhappy in his own way. On the other hand, people do not have trouble relating to their salad spinners. Then again, devices for drying lettuce are probably less personally reflective of people than the books they buy. As the business scholar Sheena Iyengar writes, "The less a choice serves some utilitarian function, the more it implies about identity."

Curiously, in the study of prizewinning books, the post-prize falloff in ratings was actually less for nonfiction books. Arguably, these are more utilitarian products, with fewer places for taste to intercede. It is as if we were almost instinctively wired to recognize the expression of other people's taste when we see it—particularly when it diverges from our own.

It makes one wonder whether all disliking is, however remotely, linked to the primal disgust mechanisms mentioned earlier with food. Indeed, when people in one study looked at negative reviews of different products—"utilitarian" and "hedonic" goods—they were more likely to attribute the reasons for negative reviews to something about the *thing* when the product was utilitarian and to something about the *person* when it was hedonic. "Taste classifies," wrote Bourdieu, "and it classifies the classifier." And then we classify the classification.

You might argue that reviewing restaurants at Yelp and books and salad spinners on Amazon and films on Netflix are all different things. And yet a curious meta-logic takes over online. People are generally not situating a work in its historical context or doing the other kinds of heavy lifting that critics were once paid to do but reflecting upon their own consumption experience.

A "content analysis" of movie reviews on one Web site, looking at differences between critics and online "word of mouth," found that critics talked more regularly about plot, direction, and acting than average moviegoers (when they refer to themselves, interestingly, their reviews deviate more from the average; nothing signals taste more than the word "I"). Amateur critics, meanwhile, talked more about the personal relevance of a movie (in 33 percent of films, versus *zero* for critics). In nearly half of moviegoer reviews, the reviews responded to film critics (quite naturally, no critics talked about average moviegoer reviews).

In short, critics talk about why something should (or should not) be liked; people talk about why *they* did like something. Curiously, critics are often criticized for trying to impose their own taste on the "rest of us," when actually it is the "rest of us" who are most guilty of this practice.

People are now so accustomed to the reviewing mind-set that one occasionally spies a flummoxed "review" of a simple product like paper clips: "What can I say? They're paperclips!" Four stars! That a site like Amazon sells virtually everything tends to blur and flatten things. Books are savaged because they are not available as an e-book or for their typeface. The lines of authority are made muzzy. What does the competent paper clip critic have to say about French Symbolist poetry? What are the criteria for reviewing something such as a noise machine, and from where does authority come? (One actual line: "The white noise is a little too deep for us.") The rise of online reviewing may be toppling the singular critical voice from its pedestal. But with its fall, taste has shattered into a thousand fragments. We are sifting through those shards, trying to make meaning of other people's attempts to say what something meant to them.

Next, we shall flip the question over: not what you say about your choices, but what your choices say about *you*.

CHAPTER 3

HOW PREDICTABLE IS OUR TASTE?

WHAT YOUR PLAYLIST SAYS ABOUT YOU
(AND WHAT YOU SAY ABOUT YOUR PLAYLIST)

He guessed at intense little preferences and sharp little exclusions, a deep suspicion of the vulgar and a personal view of the right.

—Henry James, *The Ambassadors*

LOST IN TASTE SPACE

Who does Google think you are?

There is an easy way to find out. Type "http://www.google.com/ads/preferences."

The search company believes that I am an English-speaking male, age twenty-five to thirty-four, with leading interests in "air travel" and "Action & Adventure films." "Well, now," I think, "how useful could this be? It thinks I'm more than ten years younger than I really am!" But then a darker realization sets in: It could be that I am simply *acting* ten years younger than my age. All my Google searches have boiled me down to a person who flies a lot and watches action flicks (often at the same time). "You don't know me," I want to protest, with an air of Ray Charles anguish, but perhaps I do not know myself as well as my idealized self. Having this portrait played back at you can be as unsettling as seeing your reflection in the screen of your smartphone; is that really who I am?

We are, of course, more than our search terms. How much can

be inferred about *me* by my search for printer toner replacement cartridges, other than that I am a person in need of a new printer cartridge?

As Hugo Liu, chief data scientist of the recommendation start-up Hunch.com, told me one afternoon over coffee in New York City's Chelsea neighborhood, "If someone happens to search for cats a lot on the Internet, or if someone's looking for a stroller part, how much of that is taste?" Liu, who, with thick black glasses and an artful pile of tousled hair, affects a mad data scientist look, has long puzzled over the question of how to extract, model, and predict patterns of people's behavior online. As a student of the MIT Media Lab's Pattie Maes—who, among many other things, developed the pioneering Firefly collaborative filtering recommendation systems—he was bothered by those systems' lack of dimensionality. "They hint at people but don't really represent them in any way. It's my behavior in a particular domain," he tells me. What I bought at Amazon, what I watched on Netflix. "But what if I could create a model of people that could work across domains?"

In other words, what if you could meld what you watched on Netflix with what you listened to on Pandora; marry that up with what you bought on Amazon and other online retailers; then overlay that with the people who interested you on Match.com and the food you bought last month; then mix in myriad personal details—the way you talked, the images you saw on a Rorschach test, your beliefs in science and God—and then take all *that* and correlate it with data from millions of other people. Might you just then begin to have a more robust way of understanding people as a tangible variable? At the heart of the question lay a larger one: Just how predictable is our taste?

This was the crux of what Liu was working on at Hunch, a site that had been formed, as its founder had described, as a "way to give you recommendations of any kind." Hunch* invited the user to answer a series of simple, sometimes playful, seemingly unconnected questions: Have you ever purchased anything from an infomercial? Which of these greens would you usually prefer in a salad (images of iceberg, romaine, red leaf, and arugula)? Do you like it when the cabin crew cracks jokes on an airplane?

Initially, Hunch was meant to be a personalized "decision engine," a way to answer all kinds of questions (for example, where should I go to

---

* When I met Liu, the site was on the verge of being bought by eBay and has since been closed.

college?). But the line from how you sliced your sandwich (diagonally or across the middle) to "what Blu-ray should I buy?" could be tenuous. And how could you ever truly validate whether Hunch's ultimate recommendation was correct? It also turned out that "people loved talking about themselves" via the quirky personal questions. So Hunch "took this taste component," Liu told me, and made it the entire site. The idea was a kind of meta recommendation engine.

Answering the Hunch questions fell, to my mind, somewhere between taking a magazine psychology quiz and playing the old artificial intelligence program ELIZA. You vaguely sensed you were being manipulated, but with a compulsive fascination you pressed on. Most questions were not indicative of anything in and of themselves; Hunch had no psychological theory about what kinds of people liked jocular cabin crews. Rather, Liu said, the questions were meant to be, above all, engaging. The average person, he noted, gave more than 110 responses. The questions were also designed to be occasionally jarring. "People have come up with baked answers for many things," he said. Maybe they could avoid the typical biases. "If I ask, 'Are you a good person?' it's just like asking someone if they're middle class. Everyone in America is going to say they're middle class!"

But what if you are asked, "Will you go out of your way to step on a crunchy leaf?" It is probably not something you have thought much about. Would its answer betray any greater understanding beyond itself? Rather than asking, "Are you a good person?" Liu suggests, why not ask, "Would you drink from a public drinking fountain?" Does your inclination to answer yes to this question happen to correlate with your answer to the question of whether you would ever risk your life to save someone?

The idea with Hunch was that if you asked enough of these questions—the slight ones and the seemingly meaningful ones and everything in between—and then correlated all the answers into a massive "taste graph," a mathematical depiction showing where people and their collective preferences were in relation to each other, you could get a robust two-dimensional understanding of human behavior. You could get the "who" and the "what" and leave the "why"—why the leaf crunchers preferred Toyotas—for the psychologists.

The correlations were striking. The magazine *Wired* described a few: "People who swat flies have a thing for *USA Today*. People who believe in alien abductions are more likely than nonbelievers to drink Pepsi. People who eat fresh fruit every day are more likely to desire Canon's pricey EOS 7D camera. And respondents who cut their sandwiches diagonally rather than vertically are more likely to prefer men's Ray-Ban sunglasses." Whether any of these made sense, or were actionable on their own, was almost beside the point; by simply fathoming the vast web of associations, Hunch could know you. "A quietly radical promise" is what *Wired* called it, "implying that our tastes are defined not only by what we buy or what we've liked in the past but who we are as people."

Except it was not so radical. It was not even particularly new. The sociologist Georg Simmel, writing in 1904, noted that fashion "signifies union with those in the same class," while demarcating the "exclusion of all other groups." It is little surprise that Simmel was writing in the Victorian period, obsessed as it was with social distinctions. Philosophers had begun wrestling with aesthetic taste in earnest in the salons of the eighteenth century, spurred by a rising bourgeois class in which, as the historian Jennifer Tsien suggested, "everyone felt that they had the right to make judgments about paintings and books."

In the nineteenth century, taste went from philosopher's rumination to social obsession. As more people had more money, signifying who you were, socially, became a kind of game. Social and cultural identity was increasingly defined less by long-established institutions (the church, the aristocracy) and more by money—how much you had and, more important, how you spent it.* What you wore helped define who you were. And the more open to interpretation who you *were* was, the more important what you *wore* became.

"The more nervous the age," Simmel wrote, "the more its fashions change." Consider the Victorian "extreme makeover." When one upper-middle-class client called on the famed London decorative arts firm Morris & Co., asking Dante Gabriel Rossetti what should be done with his home, Rossetti's answer was as swift and emphatic as any latter-

---

* This message exists today in organs like the *Financial Times*'s suggestively titled weekend supplement, *How to Spend It*.

day reality television host's: Begin by "burning everything you have got." The client later praised the firm for saving innumerable people from "sitting on shepherdesses, or birds and butterflies, from vulgar ornaments and other atrocities in taste."

In a novel like Elizabeth Gaskell's *North and South* (1855), the geographic divide is really a taste divide, polite London society versus the emergent merchant classes of the North. Nothing is too minor to broach the fault lines of taste—from the pattern of the wallpaper to the appropriate "number of delicacies" on the dinner table. The very phrases "good taste" and "bad taste" actually did not surface in earnest until the twentieth century (according to Google's book database Ngram). They seemed to plateau in the 1950s, when the "middlebrow" reached its ascendance (as one wag described the concept, "People who are hoping that some day they will get used to the stuff they ought to like").

But no one quite so thoroughly plumbed the taxonomy of taste— what it was, what it was *for*—as the French sociologist Pierre Bourdieu. *Distinction*, his landmark 1979 book, was dubbed a "Copernican revolution in the study of taste." Bourdieu created "taste profiles"—as today's Internet sites would call them—of some 1,217 French subjects. He combined ethnographic observation with an exhaustive and innovative survey, which asked scores of questions: "Which are your three favorites among the painters listed below?" "Where did you get your furniture?" He even wanted to know how people did their hair.

He tallied all that against people's demographics, rigorously and rigidly sorted into groups like "Executives, engineers" and "Clerical, junior executives" (he warned it was a very "French book"). He found, through statistical correlation, that "social subjects, classified by their classifications, distinguish themselves by the distinctions they make." This itself was not novel, but Bourdieu emphasized just how minute these taste distinctions could run, how firmly tied to one's place in society they seemed to be, and how often they were determined less by one's wealth than by one's education.

The correlations were strong: In music, the "dominant classes" preferred works like Ravel's *Concerto for the Left Hand*; the "middlebrows" liked *Hungarian Rhapsody* (so often used in mid-century cartoons); while the "popular" classes went for "lighter" fare like *The Blue Danube*. One's "cultural" capital was a stronger predictor of taste than one's actual capital. More than money, cultural capital bracketed people: Parisian architects liked Kandinsky; dentists preferred Renoir.

You expressed your taste not simply through the films you saw. The way you *talked* about them also served as a none-too-covert display—a "rank to be upheld or a distance to be kept"—of your cultural capital. Did you go see the latest "George Clooney movie," or did you go see the latest "Alexander Payne film"? Talking about directors becomes a signal that you belong to a certain place in the social hierarchy. It is a subtle badge allowing admission into a kind of club, like knowing that the American designer Ray Eames was a woman and that Ortega y Gasset were not two different people but one Spanish philosopher (two of my early mistakes).

Bourdieu insisted these "oppositions" were found not only in "cultural practices" but in more mundane things, like "eating habits." He wanted to tear down the old Kantian divide between "aesthetic consumption"—the art we liked—and "the world of ordinary consumption": the baser pleasures of what we ate and bought. He saw taste at work everywhere. "Taste is the basis of all that one has—people and things—and all that one is for others," wrote Bourdieu. "The science of taste has to abolish the sacred frontier which makes legitimate culture a separate universe, in order to discover the intelligible relations which unite apparently incommensurable 'choices,' such as preferences in music and food, painting and sport, literature and hairstyle."

Hunch, in its own way, was trying to discover those "intelligible relations." Hunch was like Bourdieu on steroids, with none of the sociological weight but with a vastly wider data set (some fifty-five million responses), spanning a ridiculous number of behaviors. It was no longer just Bourdieu's paintings and food but what kind of Christmas tree you preferred (real or fake), what sort of french fries you liked, and how you came down on the question, "Is it wrong to keep dolphins in captivity and teach them to do tricks?" Every time you answered a Hunch question, as Liu told me, "you add[ed] some kind of clarification to your coordinate on the taste graph." In the way that GPS uses triangulated latitude and longitude coordinates to map your location on earth, Hunch had a fifty-coordinate system to place you in society.

If Hunch.com had a pop Bourdieu feel, it is little surprise to learn that Liu, in his MIT days, was inspired by the Frenchman. But much of that research had come from 1960s France. Subsequent scholarship had cast doubt on Bourdieu's rigid hierarchies of class and taste; broadly speaking, many contended that taste was no longer an upper-class strategy to vertically dominate the lower classes but a horizontally dispersed system of coexisting communities of interest, of "taste worlds."

Traditional taste signifiers had gotten a bit slippery and, in theory, more democratized. At a place like Hunch, as with other Internet start-ups, where everyone looked the same age, no one had an office, and it appeared that everyone wore jeans and a T-shirt, there was no immediate way to discern social hierarchy. It seemed to reflect a new rule in America: As income inequality rises, people dress more alike. When an executive such as Google's Sergey Brin wears sandals, is this counter-signaling, dressing down to disguise his wealth? Or is it just more signaling? *My seeming disregard for my look is actually a powerful connotation of my power.* When everyone sets the same smartphone on the table, where does one discern socioeconomic difference? In the gigabytes, which are not visible? Is it the hand-tooled ostrich-skin case, with one's initials burnished in a provocative typeface, that sets one apart? Or is it that your phone has no case at all, an indicator that you care not for its fate because you will have the next version on its release date anyway? The ultimate social demarcation may be to have *no* phone.

Signaling, Liu argued, had blurred. The expensive-looking shirt was a bargain at H&M. Much of the world Bourdieu charted in *Distinction* had moved online. One's *habitus* could be expressed in the casual Instagram post of the vintage modernist chair passed down from one's grandparents or the richness of the *crema* (a word no one knew a few years ago) in one's single-origin espresso.

The anxious positioning Bourdieu had noted could be felt in a tweeted "humblebrag," an attempt to claim cultural capital without looking as if one were doing so. Thus the up-and-coming band tweets, "Our song has just come on the radio in our taxi. Awkward!" People's musical likes, among others, could be displayed in their Facebook profiles. And not idly: One university study of Facebook accounts found that only people who put "classical" and "jazz," and not "indie" or "dance," in their "likes" encouraged others to follow suit. Only the former categories had an aura of prestige.

Teasing explanation from all the Hunch data could breed questionable correlations and fanciful theories. Liu suggested that someone's propensity to walk out of a movie he did not like could be a psychological surrogate for being more predisposed toward divorce. "A bad marriage is like a bad movie," he told me. "Do you stick around?" At moments like this, it seemed hard to take Hunch as little more than a data-driven gimmick. But then, back in the Decision Lounge (that is, the only enclosed space) at Hunch's offices, Liu ran me through the site's "Twitter Predictor." Hunch took my Twitter followers, and the people I followed, mapped all their taste coordinates, and then generated one for me. "This is taste by association," he said.

The Twitter Predictor then asked me questions and guessed how I would answer them. "Given the name of a well-known foreign country, would you know whether their time zone is ahead or behind yours?" *Yes.* "Did you vote in your country's last major election?" *Yes.* "Do you watch documentaries?" *Yes.* So far, the Twitter Predictor had me figured out quite well. I felt as if I were on OkCupid and had found myself.* But were they obvious questions? Or was I simply falling for the so-called Forer effect, that tendency, in places like psychological tests or fortune-teller readings, to see ourselves sharply revealed in what are actually very broad assertions?

As the questions kept coming, they seemed to get more specific and less naturally aligned by factors like politics: "Do you think giving clean needles to addicts is a good idea?" "Do you play games on Facebook?" "Should doctors be able to assist a patient with suicide?" But it did not falter. Liu checked my score. "Hunch is up 19–0." He told me they have achieved roughly 90 percent accuracy on predicting answers. As Hunch's founder Chris Dixon put it, "People in our studies are actually only consistent with *themselves* about 90 percent of the time."

It was a curious and powerful moment. In an age of individualism, many of us have convinced ourselves that we are complex creatures marching to our own drummers, unable to be pinned down into safe assumptions. "My own taste reflects my specialness," summarizes the music

---

* This recalls the scene in *Ghost World* in which the protagonist Seymour declares, "Maybe I don't want to meet someone who shares my interests. I hate my interests."

critic Carl Wilson, where "it's always other people following crowds." But here I was, in the Decision Lounge, seemingly pinned like a butterfly to a fifty-coordinate wall, my preferences clearly outlined in a connect-the-dots pattern. "What's so fascinating is that we aren't capturing your answers to these questions directly," Liu said. "We're capturing you as a location in taste space."

Actually, it is even one step removed: Because I had not previously answered any of Hunch's questions, I was being captured simply by the aggregation of all the answers to these questions given by all the people I am following on Twitter. "Taste is a space on a graph," Liu said. "Someone can inhabit it without necessarily knowing the specifics of what they believe and their experiences." This underscores the social homophily—that tendency to cluster—discussed in the last chapter: I was not motivated to answer any of these questions a certain way because I was influenced by someone's individual tweet (though "a lot of users," notes Liu, "suspected we were reading tweets" to make the Twitter Predictor work). Rather, I was associating with a lot of people on Twitter who were like me to begin with: Birds of a feather tweet together.

Because people are often puzzled by *other* people's tastes, it is easy to accept the maxim "There's no accounting for taste." "People just assume that tastes are inexplicable," Liu told me. They will say, "I am unique, just like everyone else." "Of course there's accounting for taste," he added. "You have to look for the right features."

For Bourdieu, one thing stood, above all else, as a shortcut to cracking someone's taste. "Nothing more clearly affirms one's 'class,' nothing more infallibly classifies," he wrote, "than tastes in music."

MUSIC IN THE KEY OF YOU

What sort of music do you like?

Is there a question that at once seems so reductionist yet so open-ended, so banal yet so freighted with meaning?

But it comes up: In studies of "zero acquaintance," where people were meant to try to get to know one another, music was the first topic broached (granted, they were college students). It is not just small talk:

People's music preferences are potent in drawing accurate inferences about their personality, or at least the personality they are trying to project.

Likes seem easier to discuss than dislikes. Likes are public, Hugo Liu had told me. A person's clothes reveal his likes, but not necessarily his dislikes. Dislikes—even though they are so crucial to taste—tend to be private. Sites such as Facebook do not even offer a "dislike" option.* Talking about likes might be a good way to find out if someone could be a possible friend. But discussing dislikes is generally reserved for those already in your social network; Liu compared dislikes to gossip you exchange with friends, a way to groom relationships. Simply expressing your musical preferences depends on any number of factors: who's asking, what you've listened to lately, where you are, what you can remember.

These kinds of questions animate the Echo Nest, a "music intelligence" company in Cambridge, Massachusetts, that is a kind of mashup between the neighbors MIT and the Berklee College of Music, data geeks playing with music geeks. The essential job of the Echo Nest, owned by Spotify, is to help solve the dilemma of matching people to music in an age when the latter is in virtually inexhaustible supply.

When I arrived at its offices one afternoon, it probably should not have come as a surprise that the very first interaction I had was about musical taste. As I sat down with Glenn McDonald, the company's principal engineer, I asked what was playing on the stereo. In an office where everyone must be bristling with opinions, how could they decide *what* to play? "The rule is 'anything but Coldplay,'" he said sardonically. There it was, that line in the sand, delivered half in jest but still able, in one cutting thrust, to divide the population into those who liked Coldplay, those who did not, and those who did not feel strongly either way—but could still perhaps get the joke. Coldplay may be a particularly good litmus test for taste. Type in "Coldplay is," and Google autocompletes, in this order, "Coldplay is the best band ever" and "Coldplay is the worst band ever." Much of the venom for Coldplay is no doubt driven by that very adoration. Whatever the reason,

* Though in late 2015 there was talk, not without controversy, of adding one—but this was only meant to show empathy with others (that is, "disliking" someone's bad-news posting).

people are taking sides. Take enough of these sides, and you begin to locate "your music"—and *yourself*—on the taste graph.

De gustibus non est disputandum. There is no disputing taste. The philosopher Roger Scruton counters, "Clearly no one really believes the Latin maxim. It is precisely over matters of taste that men are most prone to argue." Music is an exemplar of what the anthropologist Mary Douglas called the "fences or bridges" quality of goods (or taste), unifying people even as it separates them. "It's like religion in a way," an inveterately hip record store owner in Greenwich Village once told me. "Why do people hate you so much because you like San Francisco psychedelic rock but you don't like Japanese psychedelia?"

Of course, most people not only do not hate people because they like Japanese psychedelia; they probably have no clue what Japanese psychedelia *is*. This points to a curious thing about taste that Bourdieu identified: The closer people are to each other socially, the more pronounced taste disputes become. The smaller the territory, the more pitched the battle. This is Freud's famous "narcissism of small differences"; those minor variances, "in people who are otherwise alike," form "the basis of feelings of hostility between them."

Part of this must simply be because taste depends on knowledge (or at least the display of it). Who but fans of the band Pavement actually care about the contrarian position that *Wowee Zowee* was their best album? One study, which plotted people's musical taste on a graph, found that the people who like Philip Glass's opera *Einstein on the Beach* were "located" quite close to those who dislike it. Why? Because with a relatively obscure work, disliking something entails actually knowing something about it, which puts you in a social space close to the people who like it. Take something that more people have heard, like Vivaldi's *Four Seasons*, and the social gulf between likers and dislikers grows (as do the *reasons* for disliking). When the gulf becomes large enough, one's dislike might even spill over into a studied kind of appreciation, which itself gains power, and a kind of safety, by its social distance from the things one normally likes. Wrote Bourdieu, "The horrors of popular kitsch are easier to 'recuperate' than those of petit-bourgeois imitation."

What does the music you like say about you? Before coming to the Echo Nest, I had partaken in one of its playful experiments called "What's Your Stereotype?" You enter a few of your favorite musical acts and are profiled as a "Manic Pixie Dream Girl" or "Vengeance Dad." ("Based upon your affinity for artists like: Iron Maiden.") I was dubbed a "Hipster Barista," which, given that much of my music listening these days occurs in Brooklyn coffee shops, seemed predictive enough. Brian Whitman, the bearded, laid-back co-founder of the Echo Nest, sounded like a latter-day Bourdieu when he told me nothing is more predictive of a person than his music preference. "If all I knew about you was the last five books you read, I probably wouldn't know much," he says. "But if I knew the last five songs you listened to on a streaming service, I'd probably know a lot about you."

Films, he suggested, are less predictive. There are fewer of them and fewer consumption opportunities. Genres matter, but there is not the same hairsplitting as with music. "They're more directly social things," he said. "Your wife will make you watch a movie." Music is what people do on their own: in the car, with their headphones, via their playlists and customized stations. Preferences for it are strongly personal, and people will talk about "my music" in a way they do not about "my movies." When people broadcast the bands they like on a social network like Facebook, research indicates they will not necessary influence someone else to like that band. They may in fact do the opposite.

In an age in which, as the Echo Nest engineer Paul Lamere described it, you can carry "almost all of recorded music in your pocket," the question of *what to play next* has grown increasingly complex. Many of the people who sign up for trials on music-streaming services, Whitman said, never actually listen to anything. "They see a blank search box. What do you do?" Some people, McDonald suggested, might "listen to that Dave Matthews album, the CD of which is in a box somewhere they haven't unpacked from the last move." They are happy for forty-two minutes.

And then what? Call it "Search Fright." You sign up for a service that has everything you could ever want to listen to, and suddenly the prospect of listening to any *one* thing becomes overwhelming. The goal of music "discovery," as it is called, is to steer listeners through the morass, navigating within the boundaries of the acceptable and through the shoals of disaffection. "How would you distinguish between the ten million songs you're never going to like, either because they're terrible or because they're something that has no context for you," McDonald said, "and one of the ten million songs that might be your favorite thing, if only you knew it existed?"

Located on the other side of the computer screen, the Echo Nest faces the "cold start problem" that bedevils all recommendation enterprises: What is the first song I should play for this person whom I do not really know much about? Figuring out what kind of listener you are, the Echo Nest believes—rather than simply knowing what you listened to—is the key to keeping you engaged. It models attributes like "mainstreamness"—how far out do your tastes go compared with those of other services' listeners? Is Radiohead thrillingly experimental for you or about as popular a band as you will listen to?

The Echo Nest began as an effort to understand, through data and machine learning, the vast world of music by merging its two central qualities: how it sounds, and how we talk about it. A few years prior, Whitman had been recording "intelligent dance music" ("the only genre," he joked, "happy enough to compliment itself in its name") under the name Blitter. Like many musicians, he was finding it hard to successfully do it "at scale." That is geek talk for *no one listened to it.* As he recalls, the audience "was out there but hard to find." How could those fans be discovered and connected? Returning to grad school, he began doing work in natural language processing and thinking back to his original problem. "All these people are writing about music on the Web. There must be some way to automatically figure out what they're saying about it."

The way we talk about music is, it turns out, fairly predictable. "We see people talking about its context related to everything else they know," he said. "That's exactly the kind of text you want." Musicological detail is relatively unimportant; knowing the key or pitch of a song does not help guide listeners to the next song, Whitman suggested. You want to know where a band is from, what its influences are.

The Echo Nest's other co-founder, Tristan Jehan, meanwhile, was toiling in the world of "Music Information Retrieval," a wide-ranging discipline that seeks to turn music into data so it can be better understood. Trying to assign an emotional valence to songs can baffle machines. Is a propulsively major-key, but vaguely somber, song like New Order's "Ceremony" happy or sad? Computers struggle with distinguishing the harpsichord from the guitar. "It's a plucked string at the end of the day," said Jehan, a stylish Frenchman who, with his long, lank hair, looks more like one who performs, rather than analyzes, music. "The difference is how you play it."

Computers are also not very good—sonically, at least—at understanding the human classificatory system known as genre. In a sprawling project called "Every Noise at Once," McDonald was using the Echo Nest's semantic engines to map the world's corpus of musical genres—everything from "Romanian pop" to "Finnish hip-hop" to "Polish reggae." Curiously, he does not rely at all on what the genres *sound* like to identify them as genres (where a computer might struggle, humans can recognize a genre faster than we can say the word "genre").

Genres, to paraphrase the music critic Simon Frith, are as much social distinctions as musical distinctions. To human ears, there may indeed be Polish reggae; McDonald described a "Polish polka-folk melody to some of it." And the lyrics are in Polish. To a computer, however, the distinction is murkier. There are reggae bands from Bulgaria to Omaha that would sound, in terms of audio signal, fairly similar. "But 'Polish reggae' is clearly a thing," McDonald said, "and bands from Bulgaria to Omaha aren't part of it, no matter what they sound like." The Echo Nest's computers help tell us something about music: We say we like the way it sounds, but, often as not, what we really like is what it means. And something else: Knowing what to *call* something helps us like it.

Lamere gave the example of Miley Cyrus, whom his then-fifteen-year-old daughter was into a few years back. Acoustically, he suggested, you could line Cyrus up with "a few indie singer-songwriters." On paper, they sounded pretty similar. But you would not want to play, on a music service, one of those indie singer-songwriters after you had played Miley Cyrus. "The cultural impedance mismatch would just be too bad," he said.

What he was talking about, of course, in the wonky language of a software engineer, was perhaps the greatest machine learning challenge of all: human taste. It is humans who decide that Miley Cyrus is not appropriate to play among a group of other similar-sounding singer-songwriters. It is humans who decide what genre an artist belongs in or whether something is a genre; those genres are endlessly shifting.

The singer Lucinda Williams tells the story that when she was shopping around an early demo tape, she was turned down by the record labels. "At Sony records here in L.A., it's too country for rock, and so we sent it to Nashville." In Nashville, they said, "It's too rock for country." As it happens, her album was eventually released by an English record company known more for punk, and it became a touchstone in the emerging "alt-country" genre, "whatever that is," in the famous refrain of the movement's chronicling magazine, *No Depression*. Her song "Passionate Kisses" eventually charted in Nashville, but only when sung by Mary Chapin Carpenter, in a version that the Echo Nest's computers would probably have trouble distinguishing.

Whitman confessed that while the company's algorithms had gotten pretty good at automatically making sense of music itself—based on more than a trillion data points covering over thirty-five million songs and over 2.5 million artists—they had less of a grip "on understanding how listeners relate to that music." So when I visited, the company was testing its "Taste Profile" technology. At its furthest horizon, this is about using music to understand people's other affinities. In one Bourdieu-style exercise, the Echo Nest correlated people's listening preferences in the United States with their political affiliations. As Whitman asked, "Can we tell if someone is a Republican just from his or her iTunes collection?" There were some obvious findings: Republicans more often liked country; Democrats more often liked rap.

But other correlations were more unexpected. Pink Floyd, it turns out, is one of the bands most liked primarily by Republicans (even if the band's members seem to be rather liberal in outlook). Whitman speculated this was mostly about the changing demographics of an aging fan base. But Pink Floyd itself changed with age, musically, and so Whitman was able to identify a split in which fans of the earlier, more psychedelic, Syd Barrett–helmed Pink Floyd tilted more Democratic. Data mining revealed other tendencies: Democrats liked more music genres (ten) than Republicans (seven); and liking for the Beatles pretty much predicted nothing in the way of political preference.

Curiously, the least predictive of all musical genres when it came to political affiliation was metal. Loud and rebellious apparently cuts all kinds of ways. "Think about all the different ways you can get into metal," Whitman said. The Every Noise at Once genre map lists nearly a dozen variants of "black metal" alone. Radio-friendly head-banging anthems on the one end to "church-burning metal," as Whitman jokingly called it, at the other. They all seem united by a fierce, if free-floating, sense of "independence," the English music sociologist Adrian North had suggested to me. Lurking down in the subgenre level of metal—"symphonic black metal," "neo-trad metal," "death core"—might lie more robust political correlations. Maybe there were untapped delegations of "mathcore libertarians" or "synth-pop social Dems." Music could tell you a lot about people—once you figured out what the music *was*.

Bourdieu had proposed that one reason music was so predictive of people's class, historically, was that it was hard to acquire, for example, the ability to play a "noble instrument." Easier, less costly "cultural capital" could be found in galleries or theaters. This argument collapsed with the arrival of the phonograph. "One can hear famous pieces of music," the composer Claude Debussy noted, not kindly, "as easily as one can buy a glass of beer."

Now the cost of reproduction has dwindled to virtually nothing. There is so much to listen to on Spotify that, as the Forgotify Web site illustrated, circa 2013, some four million of the service's twenty-million-odd tracks had *never been played* (whatever the virtues of Desperation Squad's "I Need a Girl [with a Car]," the world was deaf). What happens to taste in an age when most people have equal access to much of the music that has ever been recorded? As the sociologist Richard Peterson writes, "The appreciation of classical music, rock, techno, and country can hardly be expected to retain their status-making value if they are increasingly commodified and easy to acquire." Is there anything *less* scarce these days than access to music?

Of course, Bourdieu had always hinted that what you did *not* listen to said as much about you as what you did. Your love of opera precluded a liking of country and western. But in the early 1990s, Peterson and his colleague Albert Simkus, poring over Census Bureau data on the arts, discovered an interesting trend: From 1982 to 1992, so-called highbrows began listening to—and liking—more kinds of music, including "lowbrow" genres like country and blues.

They called it "omnivorousness." It was not as if all relations between music and class were vanishing. Listeners of classical were still likely to be older, wealthier, better educated. And listeners of less prestigious genres were not suddenly buying box seats at the opera. Rather, a new kind of "distinction" had emerged that was less about symbolic exclusion than about a wide-ranging, inclusionary appreciation. This might have seemed as though Bourdieu's old categories were crumbling. Or were they? The mass media, and the Internet, were making all kinds of culture available. As the music critic Nitsuh Abebe put it, "There's just too much music in the world to be all that sure the stuff crossing your path is officially more worthwhile than the rest."

The old highbrows, now under the flag of the omnivore, were redeploying their cultural capital, going wider rather than deeper, redrawing taste hierarchies with *horizontal*, rather than *vertical*, boundary lines. Being a snob could actually be socially counterproductive, lessening one's ability to move across different social networks. The culture of the MP3 playlist—where nothing was physically owned—was less about having the right music than having the most eclectic; less about rejecting music genres outright than having "interesting" reasons for adding them to the mix (as Bourdieu put it, "liking the same things differently").

Bourdieu had always emphasized that the *way* you consumed things was as representative of your taste as *what* you consumed. The omnivore, as some have argued, was just taking the old highbrow strategy—the ability, wrote Bourdieu, to confidently "constitute aesthetically objects that are ordinary or even common"—and bringing it to heretofore excluded musical genres. In places like the personals section of *The New York Review of Books*, a watering hole of upper-middle-class educated taste if ever there was one, omnivorousness is as reliably encountered as the love for nature walks and France. To take an example at random, from the issue (pardon my cultural capital) at my side: "Affinity for great food, independent film, intriguing travel, chamber music, jazz, rock . . ." Subtext: *My tastes are as wildly adventurous as I am, but they are still tastes.* One struggles to imagine a cardiganed and horn-rimmed reader of the 1950s announcing that he liked Bill Haley as much as hard bop and Brahms.

It was not, suggests the sociologist Omar Lizardo, that omnivores really *loved* all that new music but that they could maintain a weak, wide-ranging appreciation, a number of small pots on a low boil. After all, liking things takes time. Not only do people consume music, notes the sociologist Noah Mark, but "musical forms consume people." The more you like one genre, the less time and energy you have to like others. At the Echo Nest, Whitman found flickers of omnivorousness: "We modeled listeners where we have a rich taste profile, and then compared their behavior for a week to station profiles for the top 12 radio formats. In a given week, the average on-demand listener went across 5.6 listening formats." Of course, there is probably self-selection going on here: The most omnivorous people are going to want the huge variety offered by online services. Most people still seem to want the hits: By one analysis, 1 percent of artists accounted for 77 percent of all income from recorded music.

Even omnivores, however, need to leave room for their dislikes. When the sociologist Bethany Bryson looked through those same Census Bureau taste data in 1996 but focused on what people said they disliked, heavy metal and rap (per the bureau's rather crude classifications) were least favored by the most "tolerant" subjects. This should not have surprised: After all, those were the genres least liked by people in the entire survey.*

But she found that tolerant listeners also disliked country and gospel, which were two of the three favorite genres among the general population. Why? "The genres most disliked by tolerant people," she writes, "are those appreciated by people with the lowest levels of education." Even within their omnivorousness, omnivores were still drawing careful—and statistically predictable—lines around what was safe to like, arguably determined less by the music than by *who* liked it.

The flip side of the omnivore is the so-called univore, those people who listen to the fewest genres and express the most disliking for other music genres. Univores tend to be lower-educated people in groups with lesser cultural status; curiously, Peterson suggested there may be "highbrow univores," similarly restrictive but for different reasons. In

---

* In 1996, at least. Like every former "outside" genre, there are signs that metal has been brought into the mainstream fold; for example, the pianist Lang Lang performing with Metallica at the 2014 Grammy Awards (and, arguably, both genres were looking for some form of legitimacy in this pairing).

a neat symbiosis, univores tend to inhabit the very same genres that are liked least by the omnivores. The Echo Nest has found some evidence of this in a metric it has dubbed the "passion index." Which artists, they wanted to know, "dominate the playlists of their fans"? Metal bands, that scourge of the omnivore, made up much of the list. Metal fans want to hear metal—to the exclusion of other music—more than fans of other genres want to hear their own music. In their own way, univores are drawing their own, more powerful cultural lines of exclusion, perhaps, in some ways, as a reaction against the symbolic (and real) exclusion they face.

Consider one of the most despised of all musical acts, the "horrorcore"* rap-rock outfit known as the Insane Clown Posse. They were deemed by *Blender* and *Spin* magazines as the worst musical act of all time. They and their fans are scorned by the wider public, lambasted by critics, seemingly beyond even an ironic appreciation by coolly aestheticizing omnivores. And yet their albums, despite little airplay, as the magazine *n+1* points out, have enjoyed greater independent label chart success than the White Stripes, Arcade Fire, and the Arctic Monkeys. The only people who actually admit to liking them are, indeed, their fans, a loosely defined but strongly self-identified "family" known as the juggalos. What is interesting about this "proto-utopian carnival community," as one sociologist dubbed their "gatherings," is that it seems to draw much of its power from being symbolically excluded, what Bourdieu called "the refusal of what is refused." "They're kind of accepted for who they are," said one juggalo of his fellow "family" members. "It's being who you are. You don't have to dress in fancy clothes or drive a nice car."

Reading about the Posse's gatherings, one hears Bourdieu talking about the "spectacular delights" of working-class art forms: "They satisfy the taste for and sense of revelry, the plain speaking and hearty laughter which liberate by setting the social world head over heels, overturning conventions and proprieties." The music itself may be beside the point. This was like a return in a sense to older rituals of music—not as an isolated object of casual consumption on a massive playlist, but as a means of forging a group identity. That neither the music nor that so-

---

* For the record, Every Noise at Once does not include this as a genre, but it does have one called, simply, "juggalo."

cial group seems particularly loved only sharpened its cohesion. This was a refuge from taste, an oasis of tolerance in opposition to the mores of everyone else, including the supposedly tolerant omnivores. Bourdieu wrote, "People's image of the classification is a function of their position within it." Or, as the writer Kent Russell put it, "you can be a juggalo or you can be white trash—the first term is yours, the second is somebody else's."

People label music; music labels people. The way those labels match up or do not between particular people and music is interesting. As always, however, the more revealing action is in what people say they do not like, rather than in what they do.

THE PANDORA'S BOX OF TASTE:
HOW CAN WE LIKE WHAT WE DON'T KNOW?

On a Saturday evening in 1950, the Danish Broadcasting Service played a series of unidentified songs it labeled "popular gramophone music." On the following Saturday, the evening when listenership was typically at its peak, the service played a program of music it called "classical." As you might expect, the audience was larger—by a factor of two—for the first program.

There is an interesting twist to the story, however. On both Saturdays, the same set of recordings was played. Only in the second week were the titles (with key, opus number, and so on) mentioned. Danish listeners, unbeknownst to them, were being subjected to an experiment by Theodor Geiger, a sociologist at the University of Aarhus. The Danish Broadcasting Service had been concerned about the public's seeming lack of regard for classical and "the more serious kind of modern music." But Geiger wanted to know this: Did people not really like classical music? Or did they just think they were not supposed to like it, because they lacked musical expertise or it was not "appropriate" for their social class?

Curiously, during the first week's listening, the number of listeners actually increased during the program. It was not as if people were being lured in by the "popular" tag and then, encountering music that Geiger described as "by no means too ear-pleasing," abandoned the show. Listeners mostly stayed. Some people—presumably classical fans—even called in to crankily ask why the music was being called "popular."

For Geiger, the experiment had a singular lesson: "The public has a more refined musical taste than it likes to admit." Or, to say it with less of that tweedy whiff of 1950s "highbrow" thinking, what the music was labeled *as* influenced how many people would listen. There is no way to know what was going on in the minds of listeners. Did they *actually* like the music? Or perhaps the designation "popular" was a signal they should like it because, apparently, others did. Why would "classical" seem to put them off? Was it a problem with the music or the labeling?

The larger question is, how often does our "taste" get in the way of what we might actually like? What if someone like Bourdieu, the French philosopher Jacques Rancière asked, had presented music to his subjects without the trappings of socioeconomic classification, the way the Argentine composer Miguel Ángel Estrella hauled his piano to "a village on the Andean plateau" and simply played, to his peasant audience, by trial and error? The villagers, it turned out, seemed to prefer Bach. And the name Bach by itself, it seems, can sway liking. In one study, people liked the same piece of music more when it was described as being by Bach versus a fictitious composer named Buxtehude. Tell people that Hitler liked a certain music? They will like it less than if you simply call it "romantic." It recalls Paul Rozin's experiments on disgust and "sympathetic magic": He once served subjects chocolate fudge shaped like dog feces. The mere association was enough to put most people off. Hitler was not the *author* of the music in the experiment, any more than the dog feces were real. But it had been symbolically contaminated. In taste, the symbolic is real enough.

In the early days of Pandora, the popular online music service, one of its founders, Tim Westergren, proposed something radical: What if the listener were shown no information about what was playing?

"The idea," he told me, "was that our appreciation of music is so deeply affected by our preconceived notions of what an artist stands for, what a genre means. You don't listen to music objectively. People have a knee-jerk reaction to an artist based on something that's not musical." This had helped inspire Pandora's Music Genome Project, the vast web of hand-coded musicological attributes driving what it plays for you.

"The idea of the genome was to strip that down, to make choices based on musicology," he said. Like using DNA to locate distant relatives, the genome could point you to music that shared secret bloodlines. "Getting rid of the names and pictures of the artist would be a way of making the listener do the same." The idea, he said, "was deemed stupid."

Before starting Pandora, Westergren worked as a film composer. His job was to find the right musical style for a film but also to discern the director's taste. "I would play someone a bunch of songs and get their feedback," he said. "I was trying to map their preferences." He compares it to the children's game Battleship. "It is literally like that, feeling around for what the shape of their taste was." This was the spirit of Pandora: trying to codify that taste-mapping process by playing you a bunch of songs and registering your feedback.

Something else haunted him. He had read an article about the singer Aimee Mann and her struggles to get her music distributed. "This is a woman who has a fan base," he said. "There must be some way to more cost-effectively connect them with her." Perhaps there were people who might like Aimee Mann—because she shared certain musical attributes with other artists they already knew and liked—if they could only hear her. Think about how many times artists have been lifted from obscurity by their placement in a film soundtrack, such as the Proclaimers' song "I'm Gonna Be (500 Miles)." A movie is a place where, like Westergren's early idea, music comes at us rather blind, without preconceptions. You do not know what it is or who is singing it. You *have* to listen to it.

The most fundamental factor in liking a song is whether you have heard it before. Exposure, as with food, is key: The more you hear something, the more you will like it (there are exceptions I will return to). There is a huge body of literature about the effects of exposure. In one typical study, when groups of English children and college students were played samples of unfamiliar Pakistani folk music, they liked it more the more they heard it. This is how DJs help make hits. The Echo Nest's Whitman admitted he was jealous of radio in that it had no "skip button." "Maybe some DJ out there did have insight into the fact that if you heard 'Bohemian Rhapsody' twenty times," he said, "that operatic thing got wired in your brain and became something you liked."

Many psychologists argue that as we are repeatedly exposed to a stimulus—like music, or shapes, or Chinese ideograms—our "perceptual fluency" increases, and we learn to process that thing more easily. We translate this case of processing, which itself feels good, into feelings for the thing itself. As the psychologist Elizabeth Hellmuth Margulis puts it, we do not necessarily think, seeing a triangle for the fourth time, "I've seen that triangle before, that's why I know it." Instead, people think, "Gee, I like that triangle. It makes me feel clever." The more "prototypical" things are, the easier they are to process. People in studies have tended to find digitally morphed composites of faces (or birds or cars or shapes) more attractive than any single face or bird or car, because in that averageness lies a greater chance for the thing to look like what a person thinks that thing should look like.

Even the order in which we hear things seems to influence liking. In one study, radio listeners were played a series of original songs and cover versions. As you might expect, people liked the original version when they themselves were older and when a lot of time had passed between versions. Those fans had been "exposed" to the original more. But for listeners who were hearing both versions for the first time, which they preferred depended on which they had heard first. "A first encountered stimulus," the authors suggested, "leaves more of a mental mark, as a result of which it is processed more fluently than later encountered related stimuli."

Before it had a name, the exposure effect was talked about like a kind of tautology: We like things that are familiar because we like their familiarity. The problem with that analysis, as Robert Zajonc, the psychologist and author of the term, noted, was that things people were liking were not necessarily what they better remembered. In some cases, he said, we may actually like things more upon repeated exposure when we have *not* been aware we have been exposed to them.

Years ago, I was traveling through Mexico when I suddenly noticed a song on the radio: "Burbujas de Amor," by the Dominican singer Juan Luis Guerra. It was, that year, inescapable. Why did that song jump out at me? Sure, it was catchy, but so was everything else played on the radio. It was the sort of song, with my usual taste, I might even have deemed a little cheesy. I probably heard it several times before it actually seeped into my consciousness. I began to slowly recognize the beat, to anticipate his now-familiar "ay ay ay ay!" refrain. Then someone told me that the lyrics, which I was barely beginning to grasp in my fledgling Spanish—more perceptual fluency—were filled with saucy double entendres. My fluency increased. And suddenly, without my having gone out of my way to acquire an appreciation for *bachata* ballads, I *liked* the song, and only because I had the chance to be exposed to it, time after time, on Mexican buses and in Mexican bars.

Liking is learning, and learning is liking—even if we are not always aware of it. In music, the arc of liking can be incredibly fast, within a few listens. One night, in the summer of 1985, when the "house music" scene was in full fledge in Chicago, a clarinetist and aspiring DJ was experimenting, along with a few of his teenage friends, with a Roland TB-303 bass synthesizer. As they twiddled the knobs, strange sounds began to emerge. They particularly liked the machine's "live" bass guitar. Not because it seemed like a good live bass, but because, as one put it, "it sounded like something you can dance to." The music critic Bob Stanley dubbed it the sound of a "melting brain."

One night, the crew took a tape titled "In Your Mind" to a club called the Music Box and gave it to the DJ. "The first time he played it the crowd didn't know how to react," one of the crew recalled. "Then he played it a second time and the crowd started to dance. The third time he played it people started to scream. The fourth time he played it people were dancing on their hands. It took control over them." In virtually one night, a new genre was born, called acid house, after the idea there might have been something in the club's water that evening. How many music careers were stalled because a song never got that proverbial second listen?

Exposure contains a hidden peril: We begin to like some things *less* the more we are exposed to them—especially the things we disliked before. There is no exact formula to this, but one leading theory, offered by the psychologist Daniel Berlyne, is that our liking for things like music follows an inverted U-shaped graph, based on the factor of "complexity." We like things less the more simple or complex they are. The sweet spot, for most people, is somewhere in the middle.

Each time we listen to that music, however, it gets less complex. So the infectious pop song built around a simple beat that tears up the charts one summer might quickly fall off the liking cliff. Another song, more intricately arranged, full of deeper melodies and meanings, might slowly ascend in our estimation. Nick Drake's *Pink Moon*, with its densely poetic lyrics and complex chords, missed the 1972 English pop charts by a mile. Yet you are far more likely to have heard the album's title song in the past few years—in films, in commercials, on the radio—than one of the *top* songs of that year: Donny Osmond's "Puppy Love" or Chuck Berry's "My Ding-a-Ling." It is as if it took longer to like Nick Drake. When the Beatles' catalog is arranged by complexity, note the music scholars Adrian North and David Hargreaves, albums such as *Please Please Me*, chart toppers in their day, have enjoyed less lasting popularity than more musically and lyrically complex works such as *Abbey Road*.

It is much the same with food. Our liking for sweetness, for example, tends to follow a similar inverted U shape—too much or too little, and the liking goes down. The food researcher Howard Moskowitz, in a consumer test of a "garlic-flavored condiment," had people try different versions of the product, each with differing levels of particular flavors. "As the condiment becomes stronger, liking of taste increases," he wrote, which makes sense. He then noted another curious effect. "But so does potential boredom." What is exciting the first few times quickly becomes tiring. It may be a kind of perceptual fluency. "Oh, you can really taste the garlic!" you say the first time. "Hmmm, there's that garlic!" you say the second. By the third sample, all you taste is garlic. If, as Moskowitz argued, colas were popular because we cannot tell what is really in them, then a genre like jazz might be the cola of music; pop music, meanwhile, might be orange soda—fun the first few times, but quickly cloying. Music scholars have even used the word "satiation" to describe a phenomenon, observed in studying the old *Your Hit Parade*, that the faster a song had risen into the Top 10, the more quickly it left, as if we binged too quickly and were having a post-sugar-rush comedown.

Complexity aside, why do we seem to prefer what is familiar? With food, the familiar is evolutionarily adaptive: What did not kill you last time is good for you this time. We face Paul Rozin's "omnivore's dilemma": Like rats, we are not restrictive in our food choices, but as a consequence, writes Michael Pollan, "a vast amount of brain space and time must be devoted to figuring out which of all the many potential dishes nature lays on are safe to eat." In music, and with taste in general, we face a similar omnivore's dilemma: more songs than you can listen to in a lifetime. The early promise of the digital music revolution was, as the musician Peter Gabriel noted, freedom to choose. As hard drives overflowed and the cloud began to burst with music, we suddenly needed freedom *from* choice.

So we fall back on exposure: Why should we not like what we know (even if there might be something we would like more)? It saves us time and energy, versus foraging in the great musical wilderness for things that are difficult to process. This may be why people seem to most like the music that they heard during "a critical period of maximum sensitivity," as research by Morris Holbrook and Robert Schindler has shown—an age they peg at 23.5 years. This too could be familiarity. It would be strange for people in their 70s to *not* prefer the Mills Brothers' "Smoke Rings" to Peter Gabriel's "Sledgehammer," if only because they will be more familiar with the former.

There may be more than mere exposure and familiarity, however, to explain why we hold a special place in our hearts for the music of our early adult years. Holbrook and Schindler raise the idea of some kind of Lorenzian imprinting, a "biologically fixed" period in which we form parental attachments or learn language (although the long-held idea of an age-based "critical period" for language acquisition has been more recently challenged).

I think something simpler is also going on. The college-age years are when we typically have the most time to search out and consume music. I still feel a vestigial crick in my neck from hunching over record bins. Now I barely have time to scroll through a playlist.

During a period of life when most of us do not have fancy watches or cars, music becomes a cheap, socially important signal of distinction. We are trying on, like silk-screened T-shirts, various identities. My high-school notebooks were filled with band logos, while an old cigar box held countless concert ticket stubs, like fetish objects, clues to my soul. Arguments over bands were arguments over who we wanted (and did not want) to be. How could these fierce attachments survive the transition to adulthood? In the documentary film *Rush: Beyond the Lighted Stage*, Matt Stone, the creator of *South Park*, talks about being the sort of person who would try in vain to impress upon his skeptical peers—whose taste ran to more "critically accepted" acts like Elvis Costello—the virtues of the Canadian progressive rock trio. "Now it's like we're all so old," he said, "even if you hated Rush in the '70s and '80s, you've just got to give it up for them. You've just got to."

And indeed, when I now hear a song like Rush's "Spirit of Radio," damned if I do not derive a certain pleasure from it. Was I wrong about Rush all those years ago? Is my new appreciation itself unadulterated or leavened with a dash of ironic distance? Or is it that not only do I not have time to figure out what music to like (all over again), I do not *even have time to maintain my dislikes.** I am "losing my edge." I am suffering "taste freeze." What is the opportunity cost of hunting down the latest band when it sounds to your ears like some rough derivative of a band you heard in your youth? It is hard to escape what has been called the "reminiscence peak," described as follows: "The events and changes that have maximum impact in terms of memorableness occur during a cohort's adolescence and young adulthood."

By this analysis, one suspects the reason Woodstock loomed so large in the culture is not the music itself but an almost *statistical* outcome of the largest birth cohort in American history suddenly hitting that age bracket of maximum impact. But why do we all—and not just *The Big Chill* generation—seem to insist that the music of our youth was *better*? As Carnegie Mellon's Carey Morewedge points out, because everyone basically has this experience, it cannot be objectively true. He suggests that in the same way we tend to remember positive life events more strongly than negative events, only the "good" music from our past tends to survive in our memory. In the raw and unpolished present, meanwhile, we hear music we think we like *and* music we know we do not like. Memory, as he describes it, is like a radio station that only plays what we want to hear. Given that we had devoted so much time to thinking about the music, it is no surprise that it still so easily fills our memory and that we seem to have a hedonic soft spot for it.

So how do we move beyond the safe perimeter of our typical foraging ground into promising, if terrifying, new vistas, filled with new, unknown pleasures? We look for someone to take us there. As Westergren had joked to me, "We allow the lazy middle-age man to get back in the game."

---

* In the film *While We're Young*, Ben Stiller's highbrow Gen X character, upon being played, with seemingly pure appreciation, Survivor's "Eye of the Tiger" by a hip young omnivore, says with wonder, "I remember when this was just supposed to be bad."

.   .   .

Before coming to Pandora, I had a rather anguished back-and-forth with the people in its public relations department. The sticking point seemed to be the word "taste." They wanted me to know they were not "tastemakers in any sense of the word." Rather, they strove to "provide each and every listener with a unique experience." It seemed another hint of how much the notion of Taste with a capital *T* had fallen since mid-century, as if prescribing taste were some old, outmoded habit, like drinking martinis at lunch.

People now talk in softer terms, floating words like "discovery" and "curation." The Book-of-the-Month Club, upon its launch in 1926, promised that any title that survived the "differing tastes" and "good judgment" of its panelists was "bound to be an outstanding book." Nearly a century on, the club more demurely promises "our favorite new titles that we know you'll want to read" (note the shift in focus, from objective standards from above to playing upon your personal preference).

But is this not still imposing some kind of selective criteria? Westergren tried to sound wholly catholic about Pandora's playlists. "We don't want to be judgmental about any of this," he said. "Some people want to hear the same ten songs over and over again; that's what we should give them." That raises the question of whether they need an army of music analysts and fancy algorithms. A moment later, he added, "We curate our collection. We turn down an awful lot of music, because it makes the other side more satisfying."

I put the question to Michael Zapruder, for many years the company's head music curator. His job was to pick which recordings—most of which he was unfamiliar with—would enter the Music Genome. He had wrestled with the problem of democratic inclusion versus the elitism of curation, comparing it to being a judge at a baby beauty contest (a not uncomplicated problem I will return to later in the book).

He called it a "paradox" and paraphrased Orwell: Some songs are more equal than others. There was taste at work here, even if it was not Pandora's per se. But it seemed to be working: As Westergren told me, more than 95 percent of the service's million-plus songs were played every month.

Pandora had created a giant musical sandbox. There was a lot to play with, a lot to discover, but there were still boundaries. As Steve Hogan, the company's manager of music operations, told me, "That's the reason we have one million songs." Other services may have eighteen million songs, he said, "but we have human beings making judgments. If a label sends us a bunch of karaoke music, they're going to pass on it." Rather, says Hogan, Pandora analysts will "try to pick the songs they feel best represent the artist and have the best chance to succeed in their opinion."

But where radio could only play one song at a time, typically in a format that listeners expected, Pandora was trying to use math and musicology to create an army of invisible DJs, each serving up a mix of what you liked and what you might like. In one story I heard, Tim Westergren was at a town-hall-style meeting where someone told him he had no idea there were so many fans of marching band music in the world. Indeed, Pandora has a marching band music channel, and to that listener that was what Pandora was *for.* Tom Conrad, the company's chief technical officer, told me, "We want people to feel like it's really theirs, and for our musical taste—or other people's musical taste—to not impinge upon that."

The question of what music people might potentially play was only a small part of the problem. By trying to create stations tailored to individuals, Pandora was opening the Pandora's box of taste. For our liking of music, like food, is open to a staggering amount of influence. Heard too much of one thing in a row? Sensory-specific satiety can set in. What did you listen to beforehand? A sad song might seem less sad after a succession of happy songs. Where are you listening to the music? In college, I used to visit a well-regarded local record shop, a shrine of obscure erudition where you felt vaguely blessed if a clerk gave a nod of tacit approval to your purchase. I soon realized that no music could *ever* sound as good as what those reedy, severe sages had on the turntable behind the counter.

And there is the idea that like food, music may comprise basic "tastes"— instead of saltiness or sweetness, think of syncopation or vocal breathiness or drum snare—but it is the "flavors" we learn to like and discern. A few years ago, Pandora listeners seemed to be lodging particularly negative feedback in the electronic dance music genre. "We had analyzed about forty-five thousand tracks, and we realized a lot of the club dance music was indiscriminately mixing together," Hogan said. "To the genome, they all have the same 'boosh boosh boosh' beat." But fans were hearing techno on their trance stations. Techno, says Eric Bieschke, "means something very specific if you're into electronic music. If you're my dad, everything I've ever listened to is techno." So Pandora, Bieschke said, added a dozen or so new "attributes" into the genome. "How much reverb and ambience is on there? What sort of eq'ing effects or filter sweeps are being used?"

Even an individual band can represent many different pathways of taste. Sometimes it's the people who change, while the song remains the same. Take the hit song "We Are Young" by Fun. The year prior, Conrad told me, Fun was "just one of the countless kind of semi-faceless bands that put out a record and get a review on *Pitchfork* and no one in any mass scale hears about them." The song, he noted, had been on Pandora "for years," played by a "core of people who felt like they had discovered this band." Then, suddenly, the song appeared on the soundtrack to the popular television show *Glee*. "Overnight this song had a huge new audience, who I think had a different set of expectations when they came to listen to it on Pandora. They wanted to hear other songs that had been on *Glee*."

The whole world of recorded music, Zapruder had suggested to me, is like an ocean. "Every recording is an entry point. So you might get into the water at the Beatles, and once you're in the water, you can end up anywhere." Some people hug the shore; others brave the open ocean. At its most incisive, Pandora might make a serendipitous connection, the way a free-form DJ might, following the Beatles with, say, "Lemons Never Forget" by the Bee Gees. The sound is quite Beatles-esque. But for many people, their mental model of the Bee Gees as a disco act would not permit them this connection. Bieschke says the "holy trinity" at Pandora is "variety, discovery, familiarity." It has a mathematical model of where you sit on that axis—from "active" to "passive" listening. The stations you create are shorthand for the breadth of your taste. "If you've ever created a jazz station, you probably have stations all over the map," he said. "If you ever typed in 'Coltrane,' you're likely to have a very wide umbrella of interested listening habits."

In the end, the thumb rules. In early 2015, someone's up or down vote was the fifty billionth thumb on Pandora. The thumb is the clearest signal it has, stronger than the skip button. But even here there is room for ambiguity. Are you saying you do not want to hear that right now? Do you not like that band, or is it not quite right for this station? "We actually ran a test," Bieschke said. "We took half of a percent of people listening to Pandora. When they hit thumb up or thumb down, we'd ask why." Listeners could list reasons why in a text box. "The tricky part was that the things people wrote in were all over the map. They would write things like 'I thumbed this up because it was the first dance at my daughter's wedding.' As an algorithm guy, I was like, what the hell am I going to do with that?" The feature was scuttled, and that particular Pandora's box—trying to learn why people liked or disliked something—was closed.

"They say there's no accounting for taste," Hogan told me. "But we can account for it, en masse. We can say there's an 84 percent chance that this song is going to work for people listening to Rolling Stones radio. It's a good bet; we've accounted for the taste of this big group of people." He paused, looked briefly into space, then added, "Maybe there's no accounting for why they *didn't* like it."

CHAPTER 4

HOW DO WE KNOW WHAT WE LIKE?

THE ECSTASIES AND ANXIETIES OF ART

WE LIKE WHAT WE SEE; WE SEE WHAT WE LIKE:
WHAT PEOPLE GET UP TO IN MUSEUMS

On the morning of April 9, 2008, on a drab pedestrian corridor in the Belgian city of Antwerp, an image was quietly unveiled: a black, white, and gray painting, applied directly to concrete, that depicted monkeys copulating.*

The painting was by Luc Tuymans, a Flemish painter of considerable import and renown. It had been "commissioned" by a Belgian arts television channel as a subtle way of answering a simple question: Would people, especially those who were not already devoted consumers of contemporary art, know art if they saw it?

In the short film about the experiment, one sees, ahead of the painting's debut, a variety of curators from major museums, all grandly declaiming the importance of Tuymans, most confidently betting that people would notice the work—that they could virtually not help noticing. The unsuspecting people of Antwerp, one curator predicted, would

---

* An homage, apparently, to an image found at a Japanese fertility museum.

be "forced" to think "why that work had come into their life." "I think it will stop people," another said. "Make them think, wake them up."

In forty-eight hours of observation, despite the painting's arresting subject matter and its visual prominence, less than 4 percent of nearly three thousand passersby stopped to examine it. Whatever the artistic merit of that particular Tuymans work, it was escaping most of the populace of Antwerp. "Can experiments like this help people to take more interest in art?" the station had wondered. People voted with their feet—and kept walking.

There are many objections to be raised to the experiment's methodology, perhaps to its entire premise. The first is equating people's failure to stop at an unheralded image on a random street with some lack of aesthetic appreciation. The average urban pedestrian is assaulted by a huge range of sounds, smells, and, especially, sights. Is failing to notice a Tuymans on a wall any more a lack of appreciation than failing to notice a paving pattern on the sidewalk or the unusual bird perched on a wire overhead? As W. H. Auden once observed of Brueghel's famous painting of the fall of Icarus—in which no one, arguably even Brueghel himself, seems to pay much notice to the downed wingman—even suffering happens "while someone is eating or opening a window or just dully walking along."

So already, Tuymans's painting is dwelling in the cognitive shadows, relying on some scrap of neural surplus to even be seen. Then there is "expectancy." Images appear on city walls all the time—graffiti, wheat-pasted advertisements. The one thing we are generally not expecting to see are original paintings executed by eminent contemporary artists (with the exception, of course, of an artist like Banksy, whose work people actually look for on urban walls and still miss). The things we are not expecting to see, we are less likely to see.

What if you did, in the busy course of your day, cast a glance over to the painting? (It is unclear how many people who did *not* stop for the painting actually might have seen it.) What if you did register it as an interesting, provocative, or even beautiful image? So what—the world is filled with such images. Content swims lost without context. How would a person, even one who recognized the style of Tuymans, know it was an original? How would this single image, outside the gallery walls, lacking wall text, announce its importance to the viewer?

Surely, a row of Tuymans's work, advertised as being "real" works—for we get a measurable neural charge from originals—would net more viewers.

Last, some people might have seen the painting and decided they simply did not like it and thus did not stop. "Liking," particularly in contemporary art, is a rather discouraged word. It is not uncommon to read, for example, sentences like "The question of 'liking' Nauman or not seems impertinent" (note the deadly quotation marks).

The mistrust of pleasure has, of course, long pervaded aesthetic thinking. Kant, in *The Critique of Judgment*, termed the base-level hedonic response the "agreeable," or that "which the senses find pleasing in sensation." This was not to be trusted: To the hungry man, everything tastes more or less good. These were, furthermore, "private judgments," the sort of thing we talk about when we say, "There's no accounting for taste." Kant was after bigger fish: the "disinterested" aesthetic response. Not only would you *not* know it was a Tuymans; you would not even think of it in terms of its style, its technique. You would not think of it as a painting at all. You would just let your faculties freely range over the thing's ineffable beauty. The empiricist David Hume, the other member of the heavyweight tag team of Enlightenment aesthetics,* might counter that it did not really matter whether you liked Tuymans—whatever the reasons, you would be "blameless"—for this would just be one of a "thousand sentiments." He was interested in an enduring standard that would confirm that Tuymans was more than a mere pleasure.

Kant and Hume had in mind ideal critics, not busy passersby on an Antwerp street, who are more likely to follow the injunction of the art critic Clement Greenberg: "Art is first of all, and most of all, a question of liking and of not liking—just so." The power of liking or disliking, or what psychologists call "affect," should not be underestimated: It not only informs what we feel about something like art but influences how we *see* it.

.   .   .

---

* There were many other supporting players in this extravaganza of wrestling with aesthetics, of course, from Lord Shaftesbury to Edmund Burke to Nietzsche. But Kant's and Hume's theories have generated the most subsequent attention.

For all its flaws, the Tuymans experiment reminds us that more than we are sometimes aware of, we live in a "top down" world: We see what we expect or want to see, rather than noticing, "bottom up," things in and of themselves. Or, as the neuroscientist Eric Kandel puts it, "we live in two worlds at once"—the bottom-up and the top-down—"and our ongoing visual experience is a dialogue between the two." A bottom-up stimulus, like a Tuymans painting, might "force" us to notice it if it were sufficiently large, vivid, or seemed to present some threat to us. It is more likely, however, to attract our attention by means of top-down perception: Perhaps we just came from, or are going to, a Tuymans show at a nearby museum and have him, and art in general, on our brains.

As Lisa Feldman Barrett, who directs the Interdisciplinary Affective Science Laboratory at Northeastern University, described it to me, for a long time the brain was viewed as a largely bottom-up organ. The script ran something like this: Neurons lie dormant in the brain until they are roused by some outside stimulus (say, a random Tuymans painting). Then the brain perceives the stimulus, perhaps evaluating it for personal relevance (does this look like something I have seen before?) before deciding on an appropriate emotional or affective response (how do I feel about this?). The philosopher Karl Popper called it, not charitably, "the bucket theory of the mind": the brain as empty vessel, waiting passively to be filled.

"That's not how it works, really," said Barrett. "I'm not saying that bottom-up processing doesn't happen." But what is most often going on, she suggests, is that the brain is a "generative model of the world based on your past experience of the world." Like your own obsessive Instagram account, the brain has encoded every event in your life—every sunset walk you have ever had, every person you have met, every piece of art you have ever seen, and whether you "liked" it. Indeed, our memory of how we felt about something is often stronger, paradoxically, than our memory of actually having experienced it. "Based on the context," Barrett said, "your brain is making predictions about what stimuli you expect in that situation."

How you feel about something, she said, is there *before* you detect the stimulus; you may see the Tuymans and decide you like it, but chances are you like Tuymans and then decide to see it. "It's part of the prediction," she argued. "It's actually helping to influence what you're paying attention to as the stimulus in the first place." If you are feeling good (or bad) about the world, the brain, she says, will try to complete the pattern of things that for you are associated with pleasantness (or unpleasantness).

A slogan painted on a truck by the artist Banksy nicely evokes this idea: "The grumpier you are, the more assholes you meet." Similarly, if you like contemporary art, the brain is more likely to be directing attention toward things that seem like contemporary art, the way, for example, that people who are hungry are able to more quickly pick out food-related words. The brain likes to resolve randomness into a recognizable pattern. And for most of us, a busy city street is simply too noisy, too random, to contemplate art, at least *as* art. As the critic Edwin Denby once observed, "I make a distinction between seeing everyday life and seeing art." It is not that the looking itself is function- ally different. "But seeing art," wrote Denby, "is seeing an ordered and imaginary world, subjective and concentrated." The fact that art is not something we see every day, on the street, is what, he suggested, makes it so extraordinary.

This is why we head to museums, not just to look at things that have been recognized as art, but to actually see them. Rituals, as the anthropologist Mary Douglas observed, are a kind of frame, separating some experience from the everyday. A museum, like a painting's frame, calls attention to what is inside it and sets the boundaries for where the art ends. We go inside to look at special things, to breathe "empy- rean air" and feel the demonstrable hedonic aura of authentic pieces of art. Yet we also go to look at them in special ways, freed from normal concerns and limitations; museums have been called a "way of seeing," perhaps even a training ground for looking at the wider world.

Think of the oft-reported experience people have, in exhibitions of modern art, of mistaking a building fixture for a work of art (fire extinguishers seem among the most common objects reported). The joke is often made that after conceptual artists like Duchamp, Warhol, and Koons it can be hard to tell the difference. But another way to think about it is that we are so primed in that moment toward the visual con- sumption of images, the things that are normally beneath our radar are suddenly swept up into our rapacious gaze. In the same way we miss the Tuymans, we suddenly see the building fixture in a new light.

. . .

But what is actually going on when we look at paintings in a museum?

There are many accounts of what *should* go on. In his classic *Art as Experience*, the philosopher John Dewey argued that to perceive, the "beholder," as he termed the viewer, "must *create* his own experience." In other words, the beholder must try to approach in some way, with the same rigor, the process by which the artist created the work—how it was done, what was intended, what choices were made. The beholder who was too "lazy, idle, or indurated in convention to perform this work," Dewey scolded, "will not see or hear."

There are stories of heroic episodes of viewing, with attendant moments of rapture. "It fixed me like a statue for a quarter of an hour, or half an hour, I do not know which," wrote Thomas Jefferson upon seeing Drouais's masterpiece *Marius at Minturnae* at the Louvre. "I lost all ideas of time, even consciousness of my existence" (today it might only be people waiting in long lines to enter the Louvre who can report this temporal disassociation). The philosopher Richard Wollheim reported logging up to *two hours* in front of works. "I came to recognize that it often took the first hour or so in front of a painting for stray associations or motivated misperceptions to settle down," he wrote in *Painting as an Art*. "It was only then, with the same amount of time or more to spend looking at it, that the picture could be relied upon to disclose itself as it was."

No one really knows how long it takes to "appreciate" a painting or what that even means. Apart from these acts of aesthetic endurance, how do most people really behave when they are in a museum? They are actually an elusive quarry. "This casual visitor is in the main a mystery," observed a report in 1928. Years later, after decades of "visitor studies," one museum researcher lamented, "The fact is that we do not have a good sense of who our visitors are beyond the basics." What they were *doing* was an even larger enigma.

One thing that is known is that they do not look at paintings very long. When Jeffrey Smith, who for many years headed the Office of Research and Evaluation at New York's Metropolitan Museum of Art, analyzed the viewing times of Met visitors across a variety of paintings—including Rembrandt's *Aristotle with a Bust of Homer* and Leutze's *Wash-*

ington Crossing the Delaware—he found the median viewing time for a painting was seventeen seconds.

What to make of this? An age of diminished attention, or a sign that people are incapable of participating in the deep looking so prized by Dewey and others? A few caveats. First, that is a *median* figure, meaning some viewings were much longer (the average was twenty-seven seconds). In a less scientific study conducted by the art critic Philip Hensher at Tate Britain, for instance, visitors gave glances of five seconds to contemporary works by artists like Tracey Emin but several minutes' worth of looking to works by Turner and Constable.

The second issue is the sheer size of a museum like the Met. Have you ever noticed how looking at art in museums seems to bring about a kind of acute tiredness, beyond what one might find in other activities combining walking and looking? In the early twentieth century, researchers identified, with some alarm, a condition they dubbed "museum fatigue." Part of the problem was in the poor ergonomics of museums. A 1916 report in *The Scientific Monthly* shows a rather dapper, mustachioed gentleman (identified as "an intelligent man, with good eye-sight") engaging in an aesthetic decathlon: straining down to peer inside cases, crouching to reach labels on sculptures, straining upward to look at paintings arrayed floor to ceiling in the old "salon style." Of course, the "salon style" is now only referenced in historical paintings; museums, over the twentieth century, in acknowledgment of this ergonomic crisis, got far more minimal in their displays—with the exception of wall text, which was once a rarity, but has prospered, particularly with art that needs a lot of explaining. As they get sparser, museums keep growing: The walls get more blank, but there are more of them.

The fatigue is not just physical but cognitive. To compare looking at art with shopping, one does not generally pause to look at each piece of clothing in a store, read the label to learn where it came from and how it was made, wonder what it is trying to "say," what was going on in the mind of the designer, wonder why you do not seem to be seeing the same detail in the item that your neighbor appears to be fixating on, and so forth. You basically assess whether it will look good on you and move on. The density of sheer sensory input people absorb in art museums helps explain why they tend to overestimate the amount of time they have actually been in them.

Moreover, the conditions of the contemporary museum can make sustained viewing well-nigh impossible. Looking at art in crowds, after all, is a rather strange concept: Would you want to read a book with six people looking over your shoulder? Would you want to watch a movie while someone behind you keeps saying things like "That looks like Uncle Joe's dog"? It is also uncertain that the "walking past works of art" model is the best way to consume art: Do we not generally take things in better, as the museum critic Kenneth Hudson once asked, sitting down? Perhaps as some holdover of the austere aesthetic theories of the nineteenth century, looking at art has been equated with an almost penitential exercise, a severe act of self-contemplating in forbidding concrete rooms. More than one museum consultant has said the best way to increase patrons' appreciation for art is simple: more coffee and chairs.

Researchers, very early, identified a distinct pattern: The more paintings a museum housed, the less time patrons spent looking at any one of them. The larger museums reduced the chance a painting would be seen at all. "According to averages," a 1928 study by the Yale University psychology professor Edward S. Robinson found, "a given picture has about a one in twenty chance of being observed by a given visitor to the largest collection, whereas such a picture in the most effective of the small collections has about 1 in 3 chance of being observed." Perhaps Tuymans would be relieved: Even *inside* museums, paintings go unseen.

And so a visitor to the Met or any other big museum is rather like a deep-sea explorer: trying to see as much as he can before the oxygen runs out. At the Met, at least for the onetime visitor, assuredly nobody is singling out, per Wollheim, one work for two hours of viewing. The impulse is to see as much great art as possible, thus the nagging sensation of looking at a painting in one gallery and having your eyes already drawn toward the crowd that has gathered in front of Vermeer's *Study of a Young Woman*. Research suggests that even as we are looking at one work, we are already becoming "involved" with the next piece. People may look more in large museums, but arguably they see more in small museums.

According to the museum researcher Stephen Bitgood, everything we do in a museum is driven by a utility-maximizing impulse: getting the biggest bang for our buck. The moment we enter a gallery, we generally turn right, because we have been walking on the right side and it takes fewer steps to get to the nearest art.* Similarly, visitors tend not to walk back in exhibits to revisit previous rooms (some studies have shown that when people accidentally began an exhibition by taking the wrong direction, they actually looked less at exhibits, panicked with finding the right path).

Where paintings are hung can matter more than their inherent quality in attracting visitor attention. In an experiment in a Swiss museum, when a painting was moved from its position in the middle of one room to the corner, the number of times it was "visited" during the experiment plummeted from 207 to 17. People do not like to read long wall text; when a 150-word text was divided into three "chunks" of 50 words, it got twice the readership (and the closer the wall text to the object, the better).

Curiously, other studies have shown that average viewing times are similar whether or not viewers actually read labels, as if they had some internal budget allotted to each work. Even when people visit in groups, they tend to look at paintings alone, as if maximizing attention; the more people do talk to someone else in a museum visit, the less time they spend looking at art and the less they are moved by it. Video presentations in museums are sparsely visited, suggests Bitgood, because it is harder to tell in advance how much one is going to get out of them—particularly when there are "lower cost" alternatives visible nearby. "Don't make large down payments," one museum researcher counsels.

When one is faced with the storehouse of visual treasures that is the Met, or any other big museum, seventeen seconds might begin to seem like a rational average viewing time. And when I began to research what actually happens when we stop to look, it seemed as if we could probably spend a lot *less* time.

One day, at the Met, I met with Paul Locher, a psychology profes-

---

* It depends, of course, on what side you were walking on prior to entering the gallery; people in the U.K. tend to walk more on the left, and so they turn more toward the left when entering galleries.

sor at Montclair State University who has shown subjects, via a device called a tachistoscope, images of paintings in bursts as short as fifty milliseconds. "Masking" occurs afterward to ensure the afterimage does not linger longer on the eye. At these speeds, notes Locher, paintings are "happening" on the retina in a precognitive way. Even before we know it, this "gist" response has told us a lot about a painting (despite the fact we have actually seen, in raw percentage terms, very little of its real estate).

In as little as fifty or a hundred milliseconds of looking at, say, Vermeer's *Study of a Young Woman*, we could tell what colors we are viewing, whether we are seeing a woman or a man, and the overall form (for example, if it's symmetrical). Because it is a person, our eyes are going to be drawn, virtually instinctively, just as in life, to the young woman's face (in landscape paintings, our eyes rove more freely). Judged by eye tracking, most of our looking takes place right in the center. "We never look at outer areas," Locher told me. "Artists seem to have known that foveal vision is very limited and to put the important stuff in the middle of the composition." As for the frame, while it may, as the philosopher José Ortega y Gasset once noted, "convert whatever happens to be visible within it into a picture," we do not seem to notice it much.

As the viewer keeps looking at the image, a "dual process" kicks in, a kind of conversation between our bottom-up sensory organs and our top-down cognitive machinery, moving from sheer object recognition to things like artistic style or semantic meanings. We can imagine the dialogue: *Bottom: Look! Here's eyes, nose, a mouth. Top: Hmmm . . . looks like a woman. But it's not real; it's a portrait of a young woman. Bottom: Hey, these colors are quite beautiful too! Top: That could be Dutch.* (Runs over to the memory room.) *Could be that guy Vermeer. Why don't you check out the quality of light? Bottom: I'll be right back!*

Of course, the more developed the "top," the better the "bottom," and the richer the conversation between the two. Art experts are said to have a "good eye." What they really have is a good brain. It is less that they spot things that others do not; it is that they know where to look; indeed, studies routinely demonstrate how the visual scan paths of experts differ from those of novices.

One of the most important things we glean in that first fifty-millisecond burst is whether or not we like it. "The appreciation of the aesthetic worth of a picture," argued the psychologist Hans Eysenck, "may be as instantaneous as the perception of the picture itself." In one of Locher's studies, when subjects were asked, after the second hundred-millisecond exposure to a painting, how "pleasing" they thought it was, the results roughly correlated with how pleasing they thought it was after almost thirty seconds of "exploration" (though the longer they had to look, the more they liked). "When you watch people in a gallery," Locher told me, "they know very quickly what they don't want to spend time with."

At these speeds, people are not necessarily asking themselves *why* they might like or dislike something. They are still in what the noted arts educator Abigail Housen calls "stage one" of aesthetic processing: simply gleaning the basic details and making a liking judgment (based largely on what they already know). Getting to stage two, starting to think about *ways* to look at it, she says, requires a question like "What do you see that makes you say that?" That requires looking again.

But most of us, she says, do not get past this second stage, to the third and fourth looks. This is the point at which a painting becomes an "old friend," when we begin to realize what was first pleasing may not be what is ultimately compelling. Perhaps not surprisingly, the painter Brueghel fared the worst in Locher's study; on the surface, his work might not seem, to echo Kant, "agreeable." The figures are often grotesque, the colors earthy and ocher tinged. As many art historians have noted, it can be difficult to even figure out the focal center of his works.

But the point is that we often know we like (or dislike) something before we know what *it* is. The psychologist Robert Zajonc argued that the way we feel about something, rather than coming on the heels of cognition—that is, "before I can like something, I must have some knowledge about it"—actually accompanies and may even *precede* it. "For most decisions," writes Zajonc, "it is extremely difficult to demonstrate that there has actually been *any* prior cognitive process whatsoever." How could there have been, for example, in the hundred-millisecond judgments of paintings? Affect is, suggested Zajonc, like a powerful, primal, independent early warning system. "The rabbit," he wrote, "cannot stop to contemplate the length of the snake's fangs or the geometry of its markings." It has to know how it feels about the snake even before it is fully aware it is a snake. And so we write off things before they ever get a second look.

. . .

Because this response feels so valid, Zajonc argued, it can be hard to overturn. Certainly, there is something valid in relying on gut feelings to help us sort out how we feel toward a work of art. Art critics do it all the time. Gut feelings help us filter the world, and what is taste, really, but a kind of cognitive mechanism for managing sensory overload? But there is reason to be cautious. We may not always be reading those gut feelings correctly.

We can be strangers to our taste. Have you ever brought something home from a trip—a bottle of Italian wine, a piece of Balinese art—that seemed fantastic when you first encountered it in Italy or Bali but no longer seems to excite you? Perhaps what you *really* liked was being in Italy or Bali. "Because affective judgments are inescapable," Zajonc observed, "they cannot be focused as easily as perceptual and cognitive processes." They are more open to influence, less easily controlled. Our own liking for something is affected not only by whether someone else is looking at something but by *how* they are looking at it. You are more likely to like the Vermeer if you see someone smiling at it rather than frowning. Even that creepy look from the overzealous guard might throw you off.

Changing your mind—or, more accurately, your feelings—takes effort. "Affect often persists after a complete invalidation of its original cognitive basis," wrote Zajonc. Another problem is that the brain, as a pattern-matching engine, is less likely to respond positively to things it has not encountered before. As the critic Clement Greenberg quipped, "All original art looks ugly at first." We may not even see what we do not like. "I think you need to give yourself a chance with art," the art historian Linda Nochlin has argued. "I don't think love at first sight is always what you're going to love at second, third, fourth and fifth." Our ability to so quickly get the "gist" of a painting affords the illusion that we have seen it all. The art critic Kenneth Clark, meanwhile, declared that he could spot a great picture in a shopwindow from a bus moving at thirty miles an hour—only to jump off the bus, go back, and "find my first impression betrayed by a lack of skill or curiosity in the execution."

But how does the way most people look at art in a museum influence what they like? One museum study found that its visitors reported wandering until something caught their eye. It sounds like a good strategy: Why waste time with things you do not like? But what catches your eye may have little to do with what you might really want to see; that first involuntary glance might have been triggered by a painting that is large, particularly garish, or in the center of the wall, where curators like to put "important" paintings and where we tend to look. What catches your eye may also be what you already had in mind to see.

These top-down influences are rather like the labels on paintings (which, as research has shown, influence where nonexpert viewers look in a painting). In the brilliant film *Museum Hours*, set at Vienna's Kunsthistorisches Museum, a tour guide leads a group through the astonishing gallery of works by Brueghel. Stopping by *The Conversion of St. Paul*, the guide notes how hard it is to locate the focus of the work (as already mentioned with the Icarus painting, this is a not-uncommon effect in Brueghel). Is it the figure of Saul? Yes, insists one viewer; consider the title of the painting. But then why is he barely visible, on the ground, fallen off his horse? Why is a "horse's ass" rendered so much more prominently? The guide suggests, not without controversy, that the painting's focus is a small boy, "a soldier too young for any war," his helmet dropping over his head, lurking beneath a "fine tree." It is just my interpretation, the guide cautions. But now that this intriguing, formerly invisible boy has been pointed out to me, he is one of the first things I look for when I see the painting. Would he otherwise have caught my eye?

With art, the critic Philip Hensher notes, unlike theater or a concert, you as the viewer "decide how much time you're going to give it." Viewing time, he suggests, is a "good measure of how interested you are by it." But it is a flawed measure. You may really like something but are feeling pressed to move on by the thought of how much there is to see. There may be things that would interest you, if only you knew. That abstract by de Kooning—did you know he used ordinary household paints to do it, hard up as he was for cash? We get caught in a feedback loop: We spend time with a painting to try to understand it, but how much time we spend with a painting is *driven* by how much we understand of it.

Certainly, some works need little interpretation. "We do not know what it means," writes Robert Hughes of Goya's *Dog*, with its lone forlorn canine head peering into the unknown, "but its pathos moves us on a level below narrative."* On the other hand, there are things that no one will ever really see—or feel—in a painting. Elsewhere in the Prado, Velázquez's *Las Meninas* has lost the meaning it must have had when hanging in Philip IV's private office. The art historian Michael Baxandall speaks of the "period eye," ways of looking that have been lost to us; even after being told, for example, that the ultramarine used in certain fifteenth-century Italian paintings was incredibly costly, we will not be able to look upon it with sheer fifteenth-century hunger, to feel its "exotic and dangerous character."

We may miss things even when we think we are paying attention: In a study of visitors to the Whitney Museum, viewers who listened to the museum's audio tour tended to linger longer in front of paintings, but when they were later asked questions about the work that were *not* covered in the audio text, they actually did worse than people who just looked. Any viewers who think they have "got the picture," that they have seen what they like or dislike, can be caught in a vicious circle: They are not looking in the ways that would bring out the "rewards" that would stimulate paying more attention, which itself would bring more things to see and thus more rewards.

In those same surveys, the idea of an emotional response to art looms large. People *want* to be moved; they want to feel something like a Stendhal syndrome—being lifted to ecstasy by sheer aesthetic bliss. They seem suspicious of a more "intellectual" response, of delving too deeply into why they might like something. This all accords with Zajonc's theories. As instinctive as feelings are, they are hard to talk about. Perhaps, he suggested, this is because humans, before we had language, had effective ways to express emotions nonverbally (your face reveals your dislike of food before words do). We reach for inexact terms like "cool" or "awesome" or even "beautiful."

The philosopher Ludwig Wittgenstein, who was particularly bothered by the word "lovely"—"a lot of people, of course, who can't express themselves properly use the word very frequently"—hit upon this when he suggested that emoticon-like faces (the sort that many decades later

---

* Curiously, the provenance of this work has recently been called into question, which raises an interesting philosophical quibble: Can pleasure for the inauthentic be thought of as an authentic pleasure?

would populate social media) would be more expressive of our aesthetic responses than adjectives. "Even when contemplating extremely
celebrated and much-loved images," notes Alain de Botton, "we are
liable to feel painfully silenced by the basic question of why we like
them."

Hence the anxieties of art: Not only am I not sure whether I do (or
should) like this work, but I cannot explain why. (What may often be
driving our liking, it has been suggested, is how easily we can verbalize
the things about a painting we like or dislike.) I wonder whether the
inherent hostility so many people have toward critics is less about the
idea of being told what they should like and more a frustration at someone being able to so eloquently say *why* he likes something.

But it would be wrong to presume, as some seem to, that thinking about
art is somehow at odds with having an emotional response to it. "Feeling
is not free of thought," wrote Zajonc, "nor is thought free of feelings."
As one museum consultant told me, part of the disappointment people
might have felt at Tate Britain as they wandered from the galleries of
historical paintings and into rooms containing contemporary art is that
they came from galleries rich not only with art but with interpretation
and stories about that art, and then they were plunged into spare rooms
of spare art with spare ways to think about it. "They were angry—all
the classic comments, 'my four-year-old could do this.' It was because
they'd been left in free fall. There was no hand-holding, no context."

Jeffrey Smith tells a story of one day hearing a curator at the Met
wax rhapsodic about a newly acquired painting by Delacroix. The work,
which now hangs in gallery 801, is a portrait of Félicité Longrois. As
Smith learned, she was close to Delacroix, a maternal figure to the artist, and, much earlier, was briefly a mistress of Napoleon's. Suddenly,
armed with this new information, as Smith puts it, he found that this
"nice painting of an old woman" captured his attention in a new way.
He had to "look closer." Who was this woman who had so touched
Delacroix (her death, he wrote to George Sand, augured the loss of "a
whole world of feelings that no other relationship can revive")? What in
the painting might reveal the depth of the painter's regard? The painting had not changed at all, and yet it was no longer the same work, nor
was he the same person in front of it. The more he knew about it, the

more he could feel toward it. Not only would it capture his eye where it would not before, but it had, in some measure, captured his heart. But first the painting had to get into his head.

LOOKING AT THE BRAIN LOOKING AT ART

But how does art strike us, lodge in our brains, change us? What happens to us when we have a "response" to art? Does it look different, biologically or neurologically, than a response to a great meal? And if our propensity to notice, much less be moved by, art is so tenuous, it raises the question: Amid the flurry of impressions of the gallery (or of daily life), are there things we are more *instinctively* drawn to?

One afternoon, I found myself inside the offices of a company called NeuroFocus, across from a skate park in Berkeley, California. I was watching a promo for the Discovery Channel's *Planet Earth* on a flat-screen monitor. The images were lushly beautiful (a time-lapse mushroom slowly unfolding itself to the world), striking (underwater footage of elephants swimming), and violent (a cheetah-targeted zebra at the point of the kill). Accompanied by a rousing score, which triumphantly swelled to the image of a jumping shark, it felt epic and sublime. But a question arose: The shark might have jumped, but did it register on my brain?

"Surprisingly, you're one of few people where the shark doesn't grab your attention," Andrew Pohlmann, the company's marketing director, later told me. We had before us a scrolling printout of thin jittery lines, each tied to some flicker of electrophysiological activity in the brain, as measured by the hive of EEG sensors dotting my head, enmeshed in a cafeteria-worker-style cap. Leave-in hair conditioner provided the conductance that electroencephalography requires.

"There are sixty-four sensors," A. K. Pradeep, the company's CEO, told me. "Each sensor measures the brain two thousand times a second—that's 128,000 data points every second." The plot marked "EX02" generated one of the largest spikes. "That's a blink," added Robert Knight, director of the Helen Wills Neuroscience Institute at the University of California, Berkeley and NeuroFocus's chief science adviser. "It's a huge artifact. When your eyes roll up, they sweep an electrical potential across the brain."

Such "artifacts" aside, what NeuroFocus, a subsidiary of the ratings giant Nielsen, was looking for in the jagged peaks of the EEG plot were harbingers of engagement. It wanted to know not only that I was doing more than gazing blankly at the images on the flat screen before me but, as indicated by the torrent of electrical activity, that I had noticed, remembered, and perhaps even been moved by what I had seen.

This has long been a holy grail of advertising. In the late nineteenth century, Harlow Gale, an instructor of "physiological psychology" at the University of Minnesota, set out to study what he called a "problem of involuntary attention." He was talking about advertising.

In a simple yet clever test, Gale sat participants at a table in a dark room and briefly flashed an electric light on a collection of magazine pages mounted to the wall, each containing different combinations of words and images of brands. He then asked them to recall what they had seen. He was interested in not only what subjects saw but "the conscious as against the unconscious effects of advertising." He found a "decided advantage for the left side of the page," based on reading patterns. Or that against a white background, black text captured men's attention most, while women seemed drawn to red text. The fledgling field of psychology had met the emerging discipline of mass advertising.

Gale wanted to know not only what advertisements people saw but why they reacted more to some than others. He was left with a lasting impression, one that speaks to the question of our liking for art: "how unconsciously many people reason and cannot indeed give the real reason when they try."

In 1871, people in the city of Dresden flocked to an exhibition of paintings by Hans Holbein the Younger. As much as for sheer appreciation of the old master, they were drawn by what *The Art-Journal* of London called "one of the most interesting Art-controversies that can be recalled." At the exhibition's center were two versions of what was widely considered the artist's supreme achievement: *The Madonna with the Family of Mayor Meyer.* The problem was that no one knew which was authentic: the "Dresden" version or the "Darmstadt" version. For years, art historians and critics had been probing the provenance and peering into the brushwork, and a surprising consensus was emerging that the Darmstadt painting—long assumed to be the fake—was actually authentic. "Certainly, compared with its rival," wrote *The New York Times* of the Darmstadt Madonna, "the execution is found to possess singular evenness and unity."

Into the fray came Gustav Fechner, a onetime professor of physics who had pioneered the study of "psychophysics"—the science of trying to quantify how much we perceive things. The distant influence of Fechner can be felt today on any consumer test panel. Under the auspices of a study on the painting's authenticity, Fechner distributed surveys to more than eleven thousand visitors of the Holbein exhibition. What he really wanted to know, as he probed them for their thoughts on which composition more beautifully depicted the Madonna, was which they *preferred.*

The study was a bit of a bust: Hardly anyone replied. Those who did said they liked the Darmstadt version more.* This surprised Fechner, who thought viewers would find the older-looking, darker Darmstadt version less pleasing; perhaps, he suggested, they simply equated the "antique appearance" with the more authentic, thus more liked, work. Later psychologists grumbled about the methodology. Who knows what confounding factors might have swayed the visitors' judgment (many press accounts, for example, favored the Darmstadt version).

As an idea, however, Fechner's study was strikingly novel: putting two pieces of art, almost identical, side by side, and asking everyday people what they thought. Fechner's work, which became known as "experimental aesthetics," was trying to unpack, using scientific means, people's aesthetic preferences "from below."

He wanted to know not what nineteenth-century aesthetic philosophy suggested the cultivated mind was supposed to like but what people actually did like when it was presented to them under controlled conditions. Fechner did not ignore the idea that we might like art for social reasons. "Everybody knows that he has to like Raphael, Michael Angelo [*sic*], Titian, Albrecht Dürer and Dutch genre paintings," he wrote. But what happened as people stood in front of paintings by new or unknown artists?

He took this all the way down to the most basic stimuli, probing

---

* The Darmstadt version became generally accepted as the real work, so score one for the aesthetic wisdom of crowds. It was purchased in early 2014 for seventy million dollars.

subjects with batteries of geometric shapes, emerging with the famous "golden section rectangle"—that precise ratio of length to width that seemed to hit the aesthetic sweet spot of the most people. He was accounting for taste: There was something inherent in that rectangle (or in people, per Hume) that made it rise above the other rectangles. But how accurate was his accounting? Critics noted that his studies actually showed preferences for rectangles to be fairly all over the place. And how did you know people were not simply choosing rectangles that looked like the rectangles they were used to seeing? Perhaps preference was just tradition. Who could ever disentangle the difference?

After Fechner, many have objected to the idea of reducing the complexity of people's reaction to art to a single variable (beauty, pleasantness, and so forth) on a sliding scale. But the arrival of modern neuroscience brought new promise—could the study of the brain help explain our reactions to art?—as well as revised versions of an old critique: How could our response to art be reduced to an electrical signal?

With this lingering question on my mind—what might our neural activity tell us about our feelings about art that we could not discern ourselves—I went to meet Semir Zeki, a professor of neuroscience at University College London who is credited with coining the term "neuroaesthetics." As the word entails, it is an empirical aesthetics updated for an age of fMRI, a search for the "neural laws" that might underlie our aesthetic experiences. Artists, Zeki has argued, not without controversy, *are* neuroscientists, "exploring the potential and capacities" of the brain, sometimes almost preternaturally anticipating in their work what seems to stimulate the "visual brain," as Zeki calls it.

So Mondrian, for example, might trigger, suggested Zeki in his book *Inner Vision*, neuronal cells that have a preference for the orientation of the lines he has painted. Is a liking for Mondrian then a preference that our art-viewing *cells* were having? Would they not respond, like an eager dog, to *any* set of lines in the world? If we did *not* care for Mondrian, was the problem with our line-orienting cells? Could we retrain them to appreciate what Mondrian was doing? It is not unthinkable: When people have received pulses of transcranial direct current stimulation to the left dorsolateral prefrontal cortex, they seem to like the images they are looking at more.

When I find Zeki in his office—strewn with Mondrian coffee mugs and other paraphernalia—I encounter not a raving rationalist ideologue bent on stripping the pleasure and mystery from artistic encounters but rather a courtly man with an intense twinkle in his eye, someone with a passionate interest in the workings of the human mind, an almost equally intense love of art, and what seems an entirely sensible desire to see what each might have to do with the other. "They say that neuroscience will never explain beauty and art," he said. "First of all, we never conflate beauty and art. Second of all, we do not seek to explain either art or beauty. The most detailed knowledge of the brain would not improve Beethoven's symphonies." I felt I was hearing a defensive echo of past slights, someone who had been politely told by fellow neuroscientists that art was beneath him and by artists that art was beyond the ken of neuroscience.

What might be going on in the brain of the average person as he looks at a painting? Whether the response has anything to do with why it is considered art, it seems churlish, even antiscientific, not to consider that knowledge as a part of the appreciation of that work. Consider Francis Bacon, with his portraits of notoriously misaligned faces. "Nobody ever describes Francis Bacon's work as beautiful," Zeki said. "They may ascribe lots of other qualities to it, painterly qualities, and attribute savage truth to it and so forth, but nobody calls it beautiful. They call it a chamber of horrors." Part of the reason, Zeki has suggested, may lie in the brain's instinctual response to severely disfigured faces. There is little the brain responds to more readily than human faces, particularly ones it deems attractive. Weeks out of the womb, infants are already voting with their eyes, staring longer at more visually pleasing faces. We even seem able to judge the attractiveness of a face before we have recognized it *as* a face (it may be *so* instinctive that to even think about it, as research has suggested, seems to reduce the pleasure). When people look at painted portraits, their liking of the paintings has correlated with the perceived attractiveness of their subjects.

Over time and over multiple exposures, sadly, the hedonic glow of looking at a lovely face begins to subside, at least as a neural signal. But there is one facial register, Zeki told me, to which the brain response never flags: severe disfigurement. "If you expose subjects to images of disfigured faces and images of disfigured objects, they soon get used to the objects. The activity in the frontal cortex soon dies out," Zeki said. "It never does so with disfigured faces. You can never accommodate to a disfigured face." And so Bacon's "visual shock," as the artist called it, seems to tap into this innate response in a way that, for example, the Cubists do not (perhaps because, Zeki suggests, the disfigurations are less violent). As Bacon's biographer Michael Peppiatt perceptively notes, the effect of a work like *Head I* is to alert the nerves "to *something unusual,* something sinisterly unpleasant, before the image has spelled itself out in the brain."

The neuroscience view supports that. The visual shock may be something acutely felt, much the same way it can be when looking at disfigured images of another sort: perfectly symmetrical faces. "Symmetry" has been taken, in a just-so kind of way, as "equating" with facial beauty. Actually, all human faces have some kind of asymmetry. "It is unnatural to have a perfectly symmetrical face," as Dahlia Zaidel, a professor of neuroscience at UCLA, told me. There is no "golden ratio," a universally preferred ratio of asymmetry. As the other famous Francis Bacon put it, "All beauty hath some strangeness in its proportion." The left side of the face, for example, is often more expressive—which is why it has more wrinkles—and "the fact that these facial asymmetries are present," Zaidel noted, "tells us that the brain of the observer has to pick them up." Artists, indeed, might have sensed these imbalances in expressiveness, because European portrait painters from the Renaissance onward have shown a preference for the left profile, particularly among women.

Look at computer-generated portraits of perfectly symmetrical faces, and you feel a tickle in the brain, not unlike when you make the "flip" on an ambiguous figure reversal, like the Necker cube. "The symmetry is monster-like," Zaidel suggested. "It does not exist in the real world." The fusiform gyrus, that right-hemispheric area largely devoted to processing human faces, is finding its hypothesis about the world violated. "The brain is very specific about what it considers to be a face," she said. "Your brain has to do a double take." Probably, as with Bacon's work, before you even know what you are looking at. None of this explains why we might think of Bacon as a great artist—or an artist at all. We could simply look at severely disfigured faces in an obscure medical journal. But does the knowledge that his work may affect us, at an irrevocably fundamental level, not add something to its appreciation, the way Smith began to like his Delacroix more by learning the life story of its subject? The pleasure of art and the pleasure of ice cream were different, the philosopher Rudolf Arnheim once protested. Might neuroscience not provide some way of demonstrating that was not merely a comforting fiction told by art lovers?

Later that day, Semir Zeki and I went out walking, to look at paintings. At the National Gallery, we looked at what is reputed to be Titian's self-portrait. "He uses the technique where his face was partly turned away," Zeki said. "There was a way in Venice in that time of showing some contempt, haughtiness, for everyone else. And the fact that the kind of half-turned-away face is a sign of contempt—and still is—tells you that our brains are similar in interpreting these sorts of things."

Later, over lunch at the Garrick Club—a ridiculously genteel place where members, instead of sending each other text messages, leave notes in creamy white envelopes in the lobby—Zeki told me, "I believe there's a basic skeleton in the brain that allows you to experience beauty. What the characteristics of the objects are, I would leave that to the art historian."

Art, rather than responding to or reflecting innate preferences, may actually succeed by tweaking them. Humans seem to overwhelmingly favor fractal patterns—those geometrically recurring forms seen in snowflakes and tree branches. The painter Jackson Pollock, as analysis revealed, generated fractal patterns in his monumental works of Abstract Expressionism. This alone would hardly explain his success as an artist, given the initial hostility to his work.

What is more interesting, however, as the physicist Richard Taylor and colleagues have found, is that Pollock's later, most developed, and eventually most famous work actually *departed* from the rather narrow bandwidth of the most preferred fractal patterns. As if, they suggested, he were trying to challenge or even confound viewers, pushing the limits of what they might like. After all, if the brain is primed for symmetry, what better way to capture attention than to violate it? With typefaces, we prefer fonts that are easier to read. No surprise there—we like fluency. But research has shown that when you make fonts more *disfluent*, harder to read, people seem to better remember the information conveyed by the words. Similarly, art that goes down too easy may be art that is easier to forget.

One critique of neuroaesthetics is that it is of little use if one could not, neurologically, distinguish between the urinal that Duchamp famously rendered as art and that same urinal in a hardware store. Of course, no one *else* could until Duchamp went ahead and claimed the distinction; he later admitted to being "horrified" that his readymades had come to be admired for "their aesthetic beauty." Art itself has not been very good at deciding what is art or what is good art. When Andy Warhol created his famous *Brillo Boxes* sculptures, as the critic Arthur Danto has noted, the more interesting question than whether they were art was why the actual Brillo box they faithfully replicated (designed by the artist James Harvey) was *not*. Those reasons, Danto notes, were "nothing that meets the eye." But they were certainly met somewhere in the brain. Perhaps, Danto averred, we could call them "commercial art."

You can parse the validity of that distinction, but at least one experiment has found that when you ask people to look at images with an aesthetic goal in mind, versus simply to look at them, different brain activity is observed with each exercise. This implies that even if not everything is art, we can try to *look* at everything as if it were. (Warhol, after all, said, "I just paint things I always thought were beautiful.") What would make it art? Danto, famously, summed it up: Art is what the art world says is art. This flip tautology raises the question, returning to the Tuymans experiment: How much of our response to art is being told that something *is* art? (Answer: A *lot*.)

Most people, even devoted lovers of visual arts, do not visit galleries and museums as philosophers of art. They are not trying to place works in a tradition, to confirm that these works embody meaning, or to tick some box of whatever the reigning art discourse may be. They look at what catches their eye—metaphorically or actually. And they look longer at what they like.

Looking can be a pleasure in itself. As Edward Vessel, a neuroscientist who directs New York University's ArtLab, told me in his office in lower Manhattan, he was surprised, during a study a few years ago with his colleague Irving Biederman, to find that there seemed to be opioid receptors in the brain's ventral visual pathway. The region is normally involved in the recognition of forms. Opioids, up to that point, had been associated with synthetic opiates (like heroin) in "reward" or "pain" pathways. So what were they doing in this "visual" area? He wondered if they might "mediate" some connection between the way we form visual representations and meaning in the brain and the way we get pleasure. As you moved up in the brain's sensory processing hierarchies, he theorized, the rewards began to kick in.

From here, it seemed a natural progression to ask, what is it about a scene that we find pleasing? "If you and I share a preference," he told me, "maybe it's because there's something out there in the world that is driving both of our preferences. Or maybe it's because our internal representations of the world are quite similar and it's those internal simulations that are really driving our preferences."

In one study, Vessel and a colleague asked people to rate their preferences for real-world scenes and a set of "abstract stimuli." People's preferences for real-world scenes were quite stable: Almost everyone liked an image of nature over an image of a parking lot. But when they were asked to describe how they felt about the abstract images, hardly anyone liked the same thing. Vessel suggests that with representational images, we are able to extract more "semantic meaning." That meaning is what subjects agreed upon. With the abstract images, subjects (and their brains) had to sort it out for themselves—much like the hapless viewer in front of an unlabeled piece of nonrepresentational art—and so preferences diverged.

At the height of mid-century Abstract Expressionism, it was suggested that nonrepresentational art could function as a kind of "universal language," typically stripped as it was of cultural references. A number of studies have shown, however, that abstract art is a much tougher sell. People seem to prefer things with meaning, and if you give them some context to the abstraction—even a title—they seem to like it more.

Neuroscience, far from reducing the mystery and power of our response to art, may only affirm them. After people are shown photographs of faces, algorithms can now predict, at a level higher than chance, which face someone saw, purely based on the subject's neural signature. But such neural "decoders" only work for *that person*. Similarly, the pattern of your neural response to a work of art will not be the same as mine; it may not even be the same as yours was a moment ago.

And yet, while our preferences may radically diverge, some of our brain activity may be strikingly similar, even while we are looking at different works. Vessel and his colleagues have done some tantalizingly suggestive research about what art—the art that we like—seems to do to us. In one study, while subjects were lying in a scanner (admittedly, not the way most of us view art), they were asked to rate, on a scale of one to four, how strongly they felt a painting moved them. As with any single scale, being "moved" may not be the appropriate measure, but it is a *response*. Subjects saw a wide range of artworks: new, old, familiar, unfamiliar. There was little similarity across what people rated. But something interesting happened to those people when they looked at paintings they rated a four. Those highest-rated paintings alone activated a set of regions, including the medial frontal cortex, known as the default mode network (DMN).

The DMN was discovered, more or less accidentally, in early brain-imaging studies. People were asked to do some task, and the brain's response was observed. In between tasks, however, researchers observed a number of regions that flickered to life as people, in essence, did nothing. The exact role of the DMN is unclear. It could be some sort of background monitoring system; it could be mind wandering. When people are asked to do things, the DMN is suppressed.

So is art that moves us sending us into a zoned-out aesthetic reverie? Where are the jagged peaks of neural sublimity? The DMN, it turns out, also whirs into life under conditions that Vessel terms "internally focused cognition"—or thinking about yourself. Seeing this work of art somehow generates a burst of neural activity not dissimilar to thinking about oneself. "I immediately thought of Kant," Vessel told me, "when he talks about beauty, how when you see an external object, that object is resonating with the shape of your mind."

Curiously, when one is merely looking, the DMN is normally inactive. At the same time, when we are at rest, visually oriented brain regions are less active. "You're not really letting things in," as Vessel put it. But when people looked at art that they judged most moving, *both* networks seemed to be active. It could be, he suggested, a "hallmark of what you might call an aesthetic experience"—"an immersion so complete," as John Dewey once described it, "that the qualities of the object and the emotions it arouses have no separate existence." We are, Vessel suggested, looking outward and inward at the same time, "an aha moment where you can learn something about yourself as well as the world around you."

HOW DO WE KNOW WHAT'S GOOD?

Have you ever gone to a museum and fallen in love with some obscure painting in a dark corner and wondered why no one else seemed to notice it? If only more people could see this unknown masterpiece, you surmised, it would become more well-known. The flip side of this, you might have suspected, is that some famous works, the ones that always draw crowds in museums, may not be as good as those more lonely paintings displayed elsewhere.

In the early 1990s, James Cutting, a professor of psychology, began to wonder if artistic canons were a form of mere exposure writ large. As you may recall from chapter 1, the theory goes that the more we encounter something—from a novel cuisine to a new song—the greater the chance that we will like it (perhaps, an evolution of the theory goes, because it becomes easier for us to process and our brains like "fluency"). But as Cutting told me, much of the mere exposure work was done with images with little relevance to people's normal lives: random geometric shapes or Chinese characters (when the subjects did not read Chinese).

Experiments had been done with paintings, but they tended to be with unfamiliar works of nonrepresentational art. But what about the canon—those paintings we were more likely to have been exposed to before, in real life? To do that, you would need to know what art people had actually been exposed to. Simply asking them could be problematic because, as it has been shown, mere exposure seems to work even when we do not *know* we have seen something before.

Cutting seized upon an interesting solution. For his "sample," he chose the collection of Gustave Caillebotte, the French Impressionist painter whose 1877 *Paris Street; Rainy Day* you have probably seen (in reproduction, if not in the original at the Art Institute of Chicago). Caillebotte was an enthusiastic Impressionist collector as well, amassing a monumental trove of works by Cézanne, Monet, and Renoir. At least it seems monumental today, housed proudly at the Musée d'Orsay. In his day, he had trouble unloading it, as a gift, to the French state.

Cutting chose 66 images from Caillebotte's collection. Then he matched each of those with another painting: by the same artist, in the same style, roughly the same subject and period. The ones, as Cutting suggests, that got away from Caillebotte. To figure out how often each image had actually been seen, Cutting embarked on an almost insanely dogged research quest: Like a character from a Borges story, he (and some tireless graduate students) haunted Cornell's libraries, counting *every* instance in which one of the 132 images had been reproduced among Cornell's considerable corpus of art books.

This seemed as true a measure as any—a visual arts version of Google's Ngram index—of the extent the paintings had rippled through the culture. "I was in pretty bad shape," Cutting told me, describing the period after his first wife's death. Throwing himself into something so "mechanical" had appeal, and, as he said, "I was tired of all the slipshod research I saw a lot of people doing. I wanted to do something really intensive."

The data collected, Cutting gathered a group of students and showed them the paired images, asking them which image "they liked best." Subjects preferred, by a slight but "significant" margin, the paintings that, it turned out, had been reproduced more frequently (even if there was little difference in how much subjects claimed to recognize each image). Cutting found the same result with a group of older subjects. None of this, of course, meant that mere exposure *caused* people's liking. It could be that they were reproduced more because they were better pictures. If there was a feedback loop, it did not mean it was not there for a good reason. The canon, in other words, had done its work of allowing the artistic cream to rise to the top.

In a final experiment, though, Cutting wondered if a more concentrated exposure to random paintings might change that equation. And so, over the course of a year in an introductory perception class— sometimes in the beginning, sometimes in the midst of a lecture—he would show, for about two seconds and without comment, the paintings from the earlier studies. But to this class, he more often showed the images that appeared *less* in the outside world. And that was what students, in most cases, now preferred. For Cutting, the idea was not so much to question what paintings were in the canon as to wonder about those paintings that were *not*. Were they actually any less good, or had they simply, through whim or accident or politics, been over-looked and thus "underliked"?

Was that the whole story, though? Was the question of judgments of quality now moot? Did people's liking of art as strongly depend on having seen it, as Cutting had suggested? Not that quality judgments and familiarity had to be at odds: Perhaps it takes many viewings to realize whether and why something was good (Caillebotte himself was "rediscovered" nearly a century later). But if this repeated exposure was helping people to discover what was good about a painting—rather than compelling them to like it through sheer familiarity—then it should only work for paintings that are actually *good*. That was the idea of a group of researchers at the University of Leeds as they undertook an exposure study inspired by Cutting's.

This time, the subject was not a group of all more or less good Impressionist paintings but one painter firmly in the canon, the nineteenth-century English painter John Everett Millais, and a painter who is decidedly not—the American Thomas Kinkade. The "painter of light," as Kinkade was known to his legion of fans, was, for a time, sold widely—not in mainstream galleries, but in his own shopping mall bou-tiques. He is, to date, the only artist who ever lent his name to a La-Z-Boy recliner. The work by Millais was lesser-known landscapes, chosen to at least "roughly match Kinkade's subject matter and palette."

As in Cutting's study, students saw brief glimpses of images, inci-dentally, in lectures. Of sixty images, most were by Kinkade, a dozen by Millais. For the Millais paintings, the results were in line with Cutting: The more they saw them, the more they reported liking them. But for Kinkade, the more they saw it, the less they liked it (as soon as the second exposure). Could it simply be that to English students the work of Millais just *looks* more like art that belongs in museums and thus art they should like? Whereas Kinkade, say what you will about his style or technique, is simply less reminiscent of what anyone who has been to a museum knows as art. Is there not an air of apples and oranges here?

I put this question to Matthew Kieran, a philosophy professor at Leeds and one of the study's authors, over coffee at Tate Britain, where a statue of John Millais himself stands outside the entrance. "It actually shouldn't matter," he told me. "If you rated the Millais nine, and the

Kinkade three, the exposure hypothesis says the liking will go up for both." He allowed that subjects might be predisposed toward a certain style of painting, which exposure would only intensify.

Lest you think the result was just a matter of Kinkade's not being as popular to begin with in England, curiously, Kinkade, on first viewing, was liked *more* than Millais. It could be that viewers were initially hedging their bets: Who knew if this was the best or the worst of each painter I have seen? It could be, per the fluency argument, that where Millais's subtle work did not precisely blow you away on first glance, over repeated viewings you found new reasons to like it. As Italo Calvino described it for literature, a "classic is a book that has never finished what it wants to say."

Kinkade's paintings, however, while first going down as easily as a sugary drink on a hot day—who does not like a candlelit cottage on a snowy lane?—could have come to seem limited in range or execution, perhaps even cloying. In his novel *The Unbearable Lightness of Being*, Milan Kundera defined kitsch as "two tears." "The first tear says: How nice to see children running on the grass! The second tear says: How nice to be moved, together with all mankind, by children running on the grass!" As the art historian Alexis Boylan described Kinkade, he does not so much paint things as he paints the "desire to feel," his glowing windows virtually blinding the viewer with sentiment. That "second tear" might be too much, just as the second viewing of Kinkade was already too much for the Leeds students.

What about people who like Kinkade?* Is their pleasure not authentic? Were we to put them in a brain scanner, might the neural response be just as strong as it would be for, say, a Raphael? "The meaning of a great work of art," wrote the critic Kenneth Clark, "must be related to our own life in such a way as to increase our energy of spirit." Kinkade's work, to read testimony from Kinkade's fans, certainly seems to do this. But Clark also insists that "art must do something more than give pleasure."

---

* They are out there, given the estimate that he was presumed to be found in one in twenty American homes.

Precisely *why*, he does not say, but it brings us back to Kant and Hume, whose thoughts still hover over how we think about what we like and, perhaps more important, what we *should* like. In an age of anxious social mobility and new forms of cultural authority, when judgments over art or literature or fashion were becoming more personal and subjective—more indicative of one's own character and thus ever more anxiously freighted with meaning—Kant and Hume were trying to rescue disputes over taste from the muddle of sheer relativism and the corruption of petty proclivities.

Kant, whose "notoriously difficult" 1790 work, *The Critique of Judgment*, has long been *the* text on how to think about aesthetics, set out a rather austere vision for the ideal way to judge beauty: You had to be "disinterested." This did not mean *uninterested*, but rather that you could not have any personal stake or desire in the thing under consideration. You needed to be engaged in an act of "mere contemplation." For something to be beautiful, it needed "free beauty"; it could not be tied to any concept, label, purpose, preconception. Something of Kant arguably lurks in neuroaesthetics, the idea that one might be able to find "innate" responses to aesthetic objects, like Pollock's fractals—as long as you did not know it was Pollock!

This studied disinterestedness, of course, pretty much runs counter to how we actually do judge beauty. Kant argues that things like flowers and seashells are free beauties, but it would seemingly take an alien who had just descended from an unknown planet (lacking flowers or seashells) to appreciate them according to the Kantian ideal. As the philosopher Denis Dutton describes it, you find a shell, and you admire it for certain reasons. Then you find another—*ooh, even nicer still!* Maybe you get a book on shells and learn the names, see how yours rate. "All of this activity—this seeking out, identifying, comparing, admiring," wrote Dutton, "involves concepts." Even knowing it was a shell is a concept.

Perhaps realizing the near impossibility of clearing this high aesthetic bar, Kant allowed for the "merely agreeable," those things that were tainted by our taste. Just because we liked them—in fact, *because* we liked them—we should not expect anyone else to; that was our "private" taste speaking. The paintings of Kinkade, I suspect, would fall under Kant's instructions that "a pure judgment of taste is one that is not influenced by charm or emotion"; not that beauty could not have charm or emotion, but it could not be *determined* by them.

After dwelling in Kant's shadow for a few centuries when it came to taste, David Hume, in the last few decades, has been rising steadily on the aesthetic charts. Whereas he was once "underrated," philosophy journals have noted a "surge" of interest in Hume. This may be because we are living in an age when absolute aesthetic judgments seem passé or perhaps because his theories seem to more capably account for the realities of being human.

Although he was said to have had questionable taste himself, Hume's essay "Of the Standard of Taste" seems strikingly relevant today. Ever the empiricist, he dwells more on how things are than on how things should be; human beings cannot seem to help being Humean. "The great variety of taste," he notes, "is too obvious not to fall under everyone's observation." It is not simply a matter of one's class, as Bourdieu would later try to document. "Men of the most confined knowledge," Hume wrote, "are able to remark a difference of taste in the narrow circle of their acquaintance, even where persons have been educated under the same government, and have early imbibed the same prejudices." Hume sensed that when we said "there's no accounting for taste," what we really meant was that there was no accounting for other people's taste.

But Hume was okay with this and thought you should be too. "It is almost impossible not to feel a predilection for that which suits our particular turn and disposition." *Of course* you liked Van Halen when you were a teenager, he said (to update his Ovid and Tacitus references a touch), and the Pixies when you were twenty-three, and you now favor Leonard Cohen at fifty. We are not here to judge you personally. But we do *need*, he implied, to judge. In spite—or because—of this multiplicity of opinions, "we seek in vain for a standard, by which we reconcile the contrary sentiments."

But who would make the judgment? For this, we needed good critics. These were rare: "Few are qualified to give judgment on any work of art, or establish their own sentiment as the standard of beauty." A good critic needed many things, including a "delicacy of taste," for which

Hume invoked not just the eye but the palate, for it was only recently that "taste" as a sensory act and as a synonym for refined discernment more generally had been separated.

The good critic also needed time, to avoid the "flutter or hurry of thought" that "confounds the genuine sentiment of beauty." In a comment that seems to explain the Kinkade study, Hume noted that good critics needed to take another look. "There is a species of beauty," he wrote, "which, as it is florid and superficial, pleases at first; but being found incompatible with a just expression either of reason or passion, soon palls upon the taste, and is then rejected with disdain, at least rated at a much lower value."

By now, you might have raised some of the questions that modern philosophers have of Hume. Did he, in saying that the standard of good art would be decided by good critics, merely punt the ball down the field? What if two critics, judged of equally good sense, still came to violent disagreement over a work? Hume insisted that critics preserve their minds "free from all prejudice" yet said a critic judging the work of another time or culture needs to allow for "the peculiar views or prejudices" of that time or culture. Was Hume, as the professor of philosophy Michelle Mason wondered, simply asking judges to "abandon their own prejudices in preparation for taking up others"?

Hume anticipated what an immemorial swamp he was wandering into. He was raising "embarrassing" questions that might circle back to the same despond of "uncertainty" from which he was trying to extricate himself. A contemporary critic of Hume's complained that "instead of fixing and ascertaining the standard of taste, as we expected, our author leaves us in the same uncertainty as he found us."

Centuries on, however, the essay seems fascinating and alive, if only because we seem no closer to any answers ourselves (and perhaps, as with the Bible, there is so much room for interpretation). As the professor of philosophy James Shelley suggested, Hume speaks so strongly to us because, whether we can ever achieve a standard, we want to *believe* we can. The best Hume hoped for was that the judgments of those who were judged the best judges would be paid attention to; the results of those "joint" decisions would then prove justified by the test of time. "Authority or prejudice may give a temporary vogue to a bad poet or orator," Hume wrote, "but his reputation will never be durable."

Exposure, in other words, could never be enough. Kinkade may be in one in twenty American homes now, but the work of Maxfield Parrish was once said to be in one in *five* homes. Good luck finding him there today.

"When you are in the grip of what you might think of as the cultural atmosphere," Matthew Kieran told me, "it's much harder to distinguish between something that's really good or just a quite good version of that thing which is really popular." Curiously, I only later realized we were standing in a gallery whose exhibit was titled *Forgotten Faces*. It featured works such as Charles Wellington Furse's *Diana of the Uplands*, a portrait that was, the wall text noted, once as popular as John Everett Millais's *Ophelia* (the work that one informal survey found people looked at longest at Tate). These paintings, the museum noted, were once "stars" of the collection, but they had "fallen out of fashion." Hume had it that the best work endures, that "the same Homer who pleased at Athens and Rome two thousand years ago, is still admired at Paris and at London." But without "exposure," how would anyone know a particular work *was* good or come to like it? What if changes in fashion swept away the good with the bad? But something else haunts the edges of Hume's inquiry: Why, exactly, did tastes *change*?

This question will be examined in the next chapter. But there is one unresolved complication of Hume's theory that deserves a deeper look. In his essay, appreciation and liking are more or less intertwined: It is assumed that what you (or ideal critics, anyway) like is what is good. But what about when things are a bit more mixed up?

IT'S NOT WHAT YOU LIKE; IT'S HOW YOU LIKE

When researchers want to investigate how people respond to art that they judge favorably—and the stuff they hate—they face a problem: How do you find art that most people are reliably going to think is *bad*? A number of scholars have solved this problem by heading to the Museum of Bad Art (MOBA), a decades-old institution near Boston that collects cultural castoffs under the mantra "Art too bad to be ignored."

Typically, they will gather a portfolio of paintings and then show them to subjects, contrasted with work from the Museum of Modern Art (MoMA). Usually—but not always—the MoMA trumps the MOBA.

The tenor of the collection is perhaps best summed up by a transcript of my conversation with Michael Frank, the MOBA's curator, as he tried to steer me, over the phone, to an image on the museum's Web site. "Have you gone past the Liza Minnelli with jazz hands? Do you see the eye with the tongue through it? The penis with teeth?" Finally, the object of our search swims into view: *Swamp Picnic*, by Ted Cate Jr., which depicts a couple wearing what look like chartreuse Lilly Pulitzer versions of the bodysuits worn in George Lucas's dystopian parable *THX 1138* and lounging in the eponymous swamp. It is a curious hybrid, as if two characters from a pulp sci-fi paperback cover had been airlifted from the future and settled into a hotel lobby landscape painting. "Whoever painted that had some technique," Frank told me. "But the image is kind of—you scratch your head and say, 'What was this person thinking?'"

This is one of the most striking things about the MOBA: not that it unabashedly uses the word "bad"—quality judgments being a bit taboo these days—but that it has a set of discriminating, if eclectic, standards about what is to be so dubbed. Nonrepresentational art tends to not make the MOBA because, as Frank told me, it is "hard to judge." The MOBA accepts only about half of what is donated; the rest is, presumably, too bad to be bad. "We don't collect kitsch," Frank told me. No velvet Elvis, no Bob Ross. What he looks for is someone who has tried to make an "artistic statement" but who, either in technique or in subject matter, has gone wrong. And yet, despite that failure—or precisely because of it—there is something about the image that captures the eye or the imagination.

Looking through the collection, occasionally, lurking beneath the knowing laugh, one feels the same gnawing anxiety one might feel in the auction house or at any showing of contemporary art: *Is this good or bad?* Hume had described how our first hurried glance at a work might cloud our true sentiment. As he put it, "perfections and dislikes" might together be "wrapped up in a species of confusion."

What is less important than *how* you first feel about a work of art is *that* you feel—a spark that keeps you coming back. Art critics often talk about how they first "resented" some of the works they have come to love the most. As the critic Linda Nochlin put it, "You can hate something, but maybe that powerful feeling unconsciously is igniting the flames of love somewhere."

Semir Zeki, in a study looking at the "neural correlates of hate," found that when people looked at photographs of people they hated, the brain networks that fired included several regions "that are almost identical to the ones activated by passionate, romantic love." It is something like the way a word such as "terrific" contains two strong, but contradictory, meanings. It means both "very bad" and "unusually fine." The context decides the meaning.

In his book *Love*, Stendhal noted how "even little facial blemishes" in a person might begin to "touch the heart" of someone in love. "*Ugliness*," he wrote, "even begins to be loved and given preference, because in this case it has become beauty." But there is a moment where judgment hangs in the balance, where flaws become charming or harden into indictments.

This happens as much in our feelings about art as in our feelings toward people. If you develop a "love" for, say, science fiction films, you no longer see them as you do other films; it becomes difficult to consider them outside your own love for the larger genre. A friend asks, "Should I see this sci-fi film?" You say, "Well, if you like science fiction films you will like it, otherwise . . ." When our love is too great, our taste blinds us. The designer Jason Kottke once described on his popular Web site a new viral video as "so perfectly in the kottke.org wheelhouse that I can't even tell if it's any good or not."

The point is that what you think about something *as* affects how you feel about it. Just as our liking for a scent varies wildly if we are told it is good cheese versus dirty socks, our aesthetic and liking judgments are influenced by the category under which something has been placed. As the art historian Kendall Walton observed, when we first encounter a Cubist painting or Chinese music (for those of us who are not Chinese), we might find it "formless, incoherent, or disturbing" because, he suggested, we are not perceiving the work by those categories. What animates a new art form, or really any new cultural trend, is being able to categorize it, to have a way to think about it. There is a bit of a causal loop here: While knowing the category of something can help us to like it, research suggests that when we like something, we *want* to categorize it.

My favorite record store, when it still existed, did not simply lump records into "rock" or "jazz" but lovingly curated the most arcane categories: "freakbeat," "acid folk," "soft psych." These were all probably indistinguishable to the average person but glaringly distinct to the store's clientele. Thinking of some obscure record as part of a larger *thing* no doubt made me appreciate it more.

When we do not like something, on the other hand, we tend to dismiss it quickly, with sweeping generality: "I don't like Spanish food." Not "I don't really care for that rare variety of Valencian paella in which the rice is braised in oil." Liking seems to require finer gradients on a hedonic scale than disliking, as if, once someone had decided he did not like something, he needed fewer ways to express that disliking, or it was not worth the mental energy.

In an argument that virtually anticipates the Museum of Bad Art, Walton suggested that if we took a "tenth-rate" artwork and perceived it by "some far-fetched set of categories that someone might dream up," it might begin to "appear to be first-rate, a masterpiece." An "offending feature" might become a virtue, a cliché in one category might be fresh in another. As the music critic Simon Frith argues, when 1970s disco songs are said to sound the same, it is a negative feature. They are "formulaic." When folk songs collected from a specific time and place are also said to "sound the same," this time it is viewed as a good thing (for example, they display "collective roots"). Some of the MOBA's work would not warrant a raised eyebrow at an "outsider art" show, or at least few would deign to call it "bad." Sometimes people call the MOBA, Frank told me, and say that "something doesn't belong here, it's too good, I like it." To which he replies, "*I* like it. If I didn't like it, I wouldn't collect it."

The idea that one might take pleasure in the avowedly *bad* is not something that Hume (or any other notable philosopher of aesthetics) was prepared to deal with. We might have our own tastes, our judgment might first be clouded, but eventually good critics would come around to the truth of a work's quality. If "irregular" art (poetry was Hume's example) did please, it pleased not by "transgressions of rule or order, but in spite of these transgressions."

The work at the MOBA falls into the curious category of "camp." This is viewing through quotation marks, as Susan Sontag put it, celebrating works—sometimes kitsch, sometimes not—that attempt "to do something extraordinary," exhibiting a "seriousness that fails." It is laughing *with* rather than laughing *at*. Camp, she wrote, "doesn't argue that the good is bad, or the bad is good." Instead, it provides a new set of standards: "It's good *because* it's awful." This raises the question, per Hume, of whether there can be "good critics" of "bad art." Frank's gut-level criteria at the MOBA is that a work be interesting. Merely being bad is not interesting. It needs, to dust off an old category invoked by George Orwell (quoting G. K. Chesterton), to be "good bad." This is harder than you might think. Frank rejects a lot of works that he says are trying to be "self-consciously silly." Sontag warned of works that were "bad to the point of being laughable, but not bad to the point of being enjoyable."

Something like camp, which did not become familiar until the twentieth century, could only flourish, Sontag argued, in "affluent societies," where we had grown bored with all the good taste on display and were looking for a new kind of high, a liberation from the endless worrying over what was good. As a curator described some works of the cult filmmaker Ed Wood (who directed the famously awful *Plan 9 from Outer Space*), the films "are rough and tumble and ugly, and if you can accept them on that level, then good or bad stops being a question." Of course, like cultural "omnivorousness," camp appreciation could also be a new way of proving one's cultural authority, by knowing what good camp is—a "good taste of bad taste," as Sontag describes.

Camp is now only one of the many complicated ways we have of interacting with taste objects. Were David Hume to return and draft a new "Standard of Taste," he would surely be flummoxed by the complex taxonomy that now prevails among our "contest of sentiment." He would have to, for example, understand the difference that can exist between camp sensibility and the "ironic" consumption of a bad painting or television show. Irony is all about protective distance and derision; one watches "serious" (but bad) television for laughs. Camp too can be "frivolous about the serious," as Sontag said, but it is a way of celebrating, of getting closer, to the failed work. Irony is an emotional dead end; you cannot ever love ironically.

Hume, too, would have had to grapple with the notion of "hate-watching," a term popularized by the television critic Emily Nussbaum to signify the act of watching a show that one actively dislikes: "Why would I go out of my way to watch a show that makes me so mad?" She must, "on some level," have been enjoying it, even though it "was bad in a truly spectacular way." Hate-watching may be the inverse of camp: not loving a work because it tried something grand and failed, but hating it because it did not try hard enough and seemed annoyingly, not charmingly, unaware that it was not good (or, per Orwell, "bad good"). Or, perhaps, as Stendhal hinted, the things that once seemed so hateful may come to signify love.

Lastly, Hume might have wanted to spend some time with the concept of the guilty pleasure. This is a term he would have known, though not in today's context. Samuel Johnson, writing in *The Rambler* in 1750, talks about a man who is rather self-satisfactorily "dwelling with delight upon a stratagem of successful fraud, a night of licentious riot, or an intrigue of guilty pleasure." In Johnson's day, of course, a guilty pleasure really *was* a guilty pleasure. It was not having a second piece of chocolate cake; it was visiting a brothel or some other actual transgression against established moral codes (the pleasure would wane, Johnson warned, but the guilt would not).

Only in the last few decades, however, as a survey of Google Ngram reveals, has the phrase "guilty pleasure" gained any real currency. We use it now to primarily talk about two things (often particularly implicating women): consuming culture and food—here again that slippage of the word "taste"—that we know is not "good for us" but we like anyway. The composer Nicholas McGegan compares his love of Strauss's waltzes to a high-cholesterol dessert, things he is not *supposed* to like: "I listen to it in secret much as one might eat a large portion of chocolate cake behind closed doors."

"Guilty pleasure" is a curious concept. There is a question of causality: Does the pleasure cause the guilt, or does it in fact stem from it? Would guilty pleasures be pleasurable without guilt? Or does the guilt come because we are *not* feeling any guilt for indulging in the pleasure?

Indeed, if we truly felt remorseful in having indulged in the guilty pleasure, we would not speak of it. The act of saying it out loud declares we are merely tourists in this temporary departure lounge of bad taste. By labeling something a guilty pleasure, we give ourselves license to consume it. In one study, subjects were offered a piece of chocolate cake (apparently, the benchmark for guilty pleasures!). While they were pre-empted by feelings of anticipated guilt, most were no less likely to want to consume it. The only people who were put off the cake by the prospect of guilt were those who least wanted it in the first place. Merely triggering feelings of guilt, the researchers speculated, might forge a mental pathway to pleasure—as if we were primed to think that something which makes us feel guilty will also make us feel good. It probably will, after all, at least *before* the fact. As Samuel Johnson observed, "In futurity events and chances are yet floating at large, without apparent connexion with their causes, we therefore indulge the liberty of gratifying ourselves with a pleasing choice."

If we *really* felt bad about a book we had read and liked—some abominable, morally repugnant tract—we would feel shame, not guilt. The two words may be conflated in your mind, but psychologists have made a convincing case that they are distinct phenomena.

One proposed difference is that shame is a "pure affective state"; you know it when you feel it (or see it upon a person's face). Guilt, on the other hand, is an "affective-cognitive hybrid"; one often has to think about *why* one feels guilty. Shame, it has been argued, more often indicts the self, while guilt indicts a particular act. One says you are a bad person; the other says you did a bad thing. Guilt offers the promise of atonement, hence "confessing" that we watched bad reality television. The only punishment will come from ourselves. To assuage guilt when we "transgress" against someone, the thinking goes, we may try to become more helpful, or we may in fact channel our negative feelings onto the victim (particularly if he is in an "out group"). This, I would argue, is what we do with "guilty pleasures": We consume some bit of culture that we feel is beneath us and then label *it* trash (not ourselves!).

The guilty pleasure is not only a "license to consume" but a signaling device: You and I both know this is beneath us, or, perhaps, we are above thinking it is beneath us. By calling it a guilty pleasure, we can assure ourselves (and others) this is actually the case. You would only call something a guilty pleasure in the presence of someone who would also find it a guilty pleasure. To the person who considers eating at a fast-food restaurant a relative luxury (as I did when I was young), you do not speak of eating there as a guilty pleasure. The whole construct of the guilty pleasure is oriented, culturally, downward. If the guy who every night watches mixed martial arts while eating atomic wings on his La-Z-Boy recliner (whether the Thomas Kinkade model or not) is tempted by a box at the Metropolitan Opera for the matinee of *Rigoletto*, he is probably not thinking of it as a guilty pleasure.

But to argue the opposite, that guilty pleasures should not exist, smacks of condescension even as it flaunts its democratic inclusiveness. For to declare what should *not* be considered a guilty pleasure is as judgmental a move as to declare what should be. To go further and declare that *nothing* we eat, watch, listen to, or read should be done without a twinge that something better lies out there is the chauvinism of one who knows there is and has already been there. In a way, this catholic, nonjudgmental omnivorousness might be the new snobbery, and you can almost feel the mix of pity and raised-eyebrow disdain as someone asks, "Oh, you feel weird about liking this?" Even as the idea of overarching standards is dismissed, a thousand new ones are invented, and it is now not so much what you like or should like as why or how you like. That contested terrain between you and what you like, on the one hand, and what you (or others) *should* like, on the other, so vexatious to Hume, now resembles a hopelessly booby-trapped minefield in a DMZ of taste, that thing we try not to mention but say much about in our silences.

CHAPTER 5

WHY (AND HOW) TASTES CHANGE

I liked liking things before they were cool before it was cool.

—Joss Whedon

WILL YOU STILL LOVE ME TOMORROW?

In 1882, at a Christie's auction in London, the record was set for the highest price ever paid (six thousand pounds) for a painting by a living artist. The work? *The Babylonian Marriage Market*, by Edwin Longsden Long. If the crickets are chirping as you ransack your memory, do not worry: Neither Long nor his monumental canvas is a household name today.

But both certainly were in 1882, when Thomas Holloway, the famed English vendor of patently iffy patent medicines (Queen Victoria herself was said to have consumed Holloway's Pills), paid his colossal sum. The painting, a large, dramatic, exquisitely detailed study of an ancient market where women without dowries were subsidized via the trade in more desirable brides (as described in a "far-fetched" tale by Herodotus), was a sensation, both popular and critical. No less an eminence than John Ruskin deemed it a "painting of great merit."

Despite its ancient subject, it was very much of its day. Its eroticized Orientalist imagery and none-too-subtle commentary on the pecuniary nature of marriage in contemporary London were Victorian catnip.

As the magazine of the Royal Academy suggested, the painting had it all: "richness and archaeology, scenic drama and amusement, much beauty and some grotesque by-play, antique fact and modern innuendo." It even spoke slyly to the ascendant—some said inflated—art market, roiled by men of money like Holloway. Indeed, the auctioneer in the picture was reputedly modeled on Christie's own auctioneer, the would-be bride buyers a subtle play on art dealers.

Long, a prolific and popular painter in his day, completed his blockbuster in 1875. The date stands out, for it was the year another noteworthy, though very different, art auction was held, at the Parisian house Drouot. The artists included Monet, Sisley, and Renoir. Instead of historical and painterly accuracy and big social themes, these works took on mundane subjects in a style one French critic—hardly out of touch with prevailing taste—described as what happens when a monkey "might have got hold of a box of paints." Far from commanding record-setting sums, the prices realized at the auction, as the onetime Christie's director Philip Hook notes, "were dispiritingly low."

We know how the story turned out. Long, while largely maintaining critical respect as an artist, gradually faded from view, while the much-scorned Impressionists, whose work could often not be *given* away, went on to become the equivalent of rock stars playing to sold-out arenas—the kinds of artists who are familiar to people who are not into art. Renoir's *La Loge*, which sold for a then paltry 220 francs at the 1875 auction, sold for $14.8 million in 2008.

What changed? Not the paintings themselves, but tastes: the way the paintings were seen, what they seemed to say, the rules they adhered to (or broke). Long's painting, however much it tapped into a kind of Victorian zeitgeist, did not seem to speak as much to succeeding generations, nor did its scrupulous academic style seem to excite subsequent critics. Photography captured the ground of realism. The Impressionists, meanwhile, saw all their faults turn into virtues. Writes Hook, "The garish color started looking exciting; the lack of finish was increasingly perceived as an exhilarating freedom of brush stroke; and the banality of subject matter took on the reassurance of the everyday, a confirmation of the universality of bourgeois experience."

There is always the chance, however unlikely, that the story may yet change again, with Long and his fellow Victorians propelled to some new esteem, the Impressionists pushed into some dark dustbin. Hume was well aware of the volatile, market-like shifts in taste. "Authority or prejudice may give a temporary vogue to a bad poet or orator," he wrote, "but his reputation will never be durable or general." He had enduring faith in the test of time: "On the contrary, a real genius, the longer his works endure, and the more wide they are spread, the more sincere is the admiration he meets with." Yet this hardly reassures. Are the Impressionists as qualitatively better than Long as the swing in valuation would imply, or is popular taste at work? And consider how many "lost masterpieces" have been revived. If they were so great to begin with, how did they go missing? Perhaps this only reaffirms Hume: that they fell out of favor because of "temporary vogue," but then, having been rediscovered and championed by one of his qualified critics, they are there, as good as ever, waiting to rejoin their deserved place in the canon.

The point is that we have little guarantee that those things most celebrated and esteemed today will be celebrated and esteemed tomorrow. But why are tastes, such an anchor in our daily lives, also so fleeting?

If you had asked me, when I was ten, to forecast my life as a situated adult, I would probably have sketched out something like this: I would be driving a Trans Am, a Corvette, or some other muscle car. My house would boast a mammoth collection of pinball machines. I would sip sophisticated drinks (like Baileys Irish Cream), read Robert Ludlum novels, and blast Van Halen while sitting in an easy chair wearing sunglasses, Maxell-ad style. Now that I am at a point to actually be able to realize *every one* of these feverishly envisioned tastes, they hold zero interest (well, perhaps the pinball machines in a weak moment).

It was not just that my ten-year-old self could not predict whom I would become but that I was incapable of imagining that my tastes could undergo such wholesale change. How could I know what I would want if I did not know who I would be? The psychologist George Loewenstein has called this "projection bias." "People behave as if their future preferences will be more like their current preferences than they actually will be," he writes, "as if they project their current preferences onto their future selves."

One problem, raised in earlier chapters with food or music, is that we often do not anticipate the effect of experiencing things themselves. We may instinctively realize we will tire of our favorite food if we eat too much of it, but we might underestimate how much more we could like something—if only we ate it more often. Another issue, notes Loewenstein, is psychological "salience," or the things we pay attention to. In the moment we buy a consumer good that offers a rebate, the rebate is hugely salient; it might even have influenced the purchase. By the time we get home, the salience fades; the rebate goes unclaimed. When I was ten, what was salient in a car to me was that it be "cool" and fast. *Not* salient to me were monthly payments, side-impact crash protection, being able to fit a stroller in the back, and wanting to avoid the appearance of being in a midlife crisis.

Even when we look back and see how much our tastes have changed, the idea that we will change equally in the future seems to confound us. It is what keeps tattoo removal practitioners in business. The psychologist Timothy Wilson and colleagues have called this the "end of history illusion," the idea that the present is a "watershed moment at which they have finally become the person they will be for the rest of their lives."

In one experiment, they found that people were willing to pay more money to see their favorite band perform ten years from now than they were willing to pay to see their favorite band from ten years ago play *now*. It is reminiscent of the moment, looking through an old photo album, when you see an earlier picture of yourself and exclaim something like "Oh my God, that hair!" Or "Those corduroy pants!" Just as pictures of ourselves can look jarring because we do not normally see ourselves as others see us, our previous tastes, viewed from "outside," from the perspective of what looks good now, come as a surprise. And yet your hairstyle per se was probably not good or bad, simply a reflection of contemporary taste. We say, with condescension, "I can't believe people actually dressed like that," without realizing we ourselves are currently living in what will be considered bad taste *in the future*.

The people in the auction room in 1882 in London, gathered before Long's painting, might well have thought that they were gazing upon the pinnacle of artistic achievement—and financial outlay—one that would continue to speak to them, and their successors, throughout the years. An important, popular artist, painting in a familiar style, with an epic work that spoke to current obsessions. The Impressionists? They were social misfits with weird ideas and few discernible skills. They were going nowhere.

This evokes what I call the High School Popularity Problem. We are all aware of the radiant prom king, who excels at various sports, an alpha surrounded by his retinue of friends and would-be romantic partners. He seems poised for big things but eventually settles into a life of quiet inconsequence. Meanwhile, there is the terminally shy geek, prone to be picked on or aggressively ignored, a seemingly unaccomplished sort who goes on to change the world.

There is a salience issue here. The things that the majority may tend to pay attention to in high school, the qualities that constitute popularity (contrived contests, cruel conformity, a small and captive audience), turn out to be poor predictors of success in the future. Someone who could see through those contextual blinders—the blinders that told us high school was some "end of history" moment—might be able to spot the "underachievers," often so dubbed because they did not meet the narrow normative standards of high school. Perhaps they could sense some nascent spark, which simply needed the right outlet and audience, much the way a few shrewd art dealers saw there might be something, if only financial gain, in the Impressionists' work, something that did not speak to a wide current audience but *might* speak to an audience in the future.

One of the reasons we cannot often predict our future preferences is, curiously, one of the things that makes those very preferences change: novelty. In the science of taste and preferences, novelty is a rather elusive phenomenon. On the one hand, we crave novelty, which virtually defines a field like fashion ("a field of ugliness so absolutely unbearable," quipped Oscar Wilde, "that we have to alter it every six months"). As Ronald Frasch, the dapper president of Saks Fifth Avenue, once told me, on the women's designer floor of the flagship store, "The first thing the customer asks when they come into the store is, 'What's new?' They don't want to know what was; they want to know what is." How strong is this impulse? "We will sell 60 percent of what we're going to sell the first four weeks the goods are on the floor."

We also, as we have seen, adore familiarity. "We like what we are used to," wrote Charlotte Perkins Gilman. And yet if this were strictly true, nothing would ever change. There would be no new art styles, no new musical genres, no new products. The economist Joseph Schumpeter argued that capitalism's role was in teaching people to like (and buy) new things. Producers drive economic change, he wrote, and consumers "are taught to want new things, or things which differ in some respect or other from those which they have been in the habit of using."

Or, as Steve Jobs put it, "a lot of times, people don't know what they want until you show it to them." And even then, they still might not want it. Apple's ill-fated Newton PDA device, as quaint as it now looks in this age of smartphone as human prosthesis, was arguably *too* new at the time of its release, anticipating needs and behaviors that were not yet fully realized. As *Wired* described it, it was "a completely new category of device running an entirely new architecture housed in a form factor that represented a completely new and bold design language."

So, novelty or familiarity? As is often the case, the answer lies somewhere in between, on the midway point of some optimal U-shaped curve plotting the new and the known. The noted industrial designer Raymond Loewy sensed this optimum in what he termed the "MAYA stage," for "most advanced, yet acceptable." This was the moment in a product design cycle when, Loewy argued, "resistance to the unfamiliar reaches the threshold of a shock-zone and resistance to buying sets in." We like the new as long as it reminds us in some way of the old.

Anticipating how much our tastes will change is hard because we cannot see past this inherent resistance. Or how much *we* will change when we do and how each change will open the door to another change. We forget just how fleeting even the most jarring novelty can be. Think back to the discussion of how we come to like foods we did not initially like. When you had your first sip of beer (or whiskey), you probably did not slap your knee and exclaim, "Where has this been all my life?" It was, "People *like* this?"

We come to like beer, but it is arguably wrong to call beer an "acquired taste," as the philosopher Daniel Dennett argues, because it is not that first taste that people are coming to like. "If beer went on tasting to me the way the first sip tasted," he writes, "I would never have gone on drinking beer!" Part of the problem is that alcohol is a shock to the system: It tastes like nothing that has come before, or at least nothing pleasant. New music or art can have the same effect. In a *New Yorker* profile, the music producer Rick Rubin recounted that when he first heard *Pretty Hate Machine*, the album by Nine Inch Nails, he did not care for it. But it soon became his favorite. Faced with something discordantly novel, "we don't always have the reference points to absorb and digest it," Rubin said. "It's a bit like learning a new language." The album, like the beer, was not an acquired taste, because he was not hearing the same album.

Looking back, we can find it hard to believe we did not like something we now do. Current popularity gets projected backward: We forget that a now ubiquitous song like the Romantics' "What I Like About You" was never a hit or that recently in vogue "antique" baby names like Isabella or Chloe, which seem to speak to some once-flourishing tradition, were never popular (Mittie or Virgie were more consistently liked names of the early twentieth century).

It now seems impossible to imagine, a few decades ago, the scandal provoked by the now widely cherished Sydney Opera House. The Danish architect, Jørn Utzon, was practically driven from the country, his name went unuttered at the opening ceremony, the sense of national scandal was palpable toward this harborside monstrosity. Not only did the building not fit the traditional form of an opera house; it did not fit the traditional form of a *building*. It was most advanced and *un*acceptable. It was as foreign as its architect.

The truth is, most people probably did not know what to make of it, and our default setting, faced with an insecure unknown, is disliking. Frank Gehry, talking about his iconic, widely admired Guggenheim Museum in Bilbao, admitted that "it took a couple of years for me to start to like it, actually." The architect Mark Wigley suggests that "maybe we only ever learn something when some form we think of as foreign provokes us—and we resist. But sometimes, many times, in the middle of the resistance, we end up loving this thing that has provoked us"—even if it is no longer the same "thing" it was when it first provoked us.

Fluency begets liking. When shown images of buildings, architects have rated them as "less complex" than laypersons did; in other words, they "read" them more fluently, and the buildings seem less "foreign." The role of the architect, suggests Wigley, is not to "give the client exactly what he was asking for"—in other words, to cater to current taste—but to "change the idea of what one can ask for," or to project future tastes no one knew they had. No one said an opera house could look like the Sydney Opera House until Utzon, taking his idea from a peeled orange, said it could. The world changed around the building, in response to it, which is why, in the curious words of one architecture critic, "Utzon's breathtaking building looks better today than ever."

A few decades from now, someone will inevitably look with dread upon a new building and say, "The Sydney Opera House, now there's a building. Why can't we build things like that anymore?" This argument—for example, "Why isn't music as good as it used to be?"—reflects a historical selection bias, one colorfully described by the designer Frank Chimero. "Let me let you in on a little secret," he writes. "If you are hearing about something old, it is almost certainly good. Why? Because nobody wants to talk about shitty old stuff, but lots of people still talk about shitty new stuff, because they are still trying to figure out if it is shitty or not. The past wasn't better, we just forgot about all the shitty shit."

The only guarantee we have of taste is that it will change. Now let us look a bit more closely at exactly how.

CONFORMIST DISTINCTION: ON WANTING TO BE DIFFERENTLY ALIKE

In a 2011 sketch on the show *Portlandia*, the obsessive satirical catalog of the hipster mores of the Oregon city, an exaggeratedly posturing character known as Spyke—replete with "chin beard," lobe-stretching disk earrings, and a fixed-gear bike—is shown walking past a bar. He sees some people inside, equally adorned with the trappings of a certain kind of cool, and gives an affirming nod. A few days later, he spies a clean-shaven guy wearing khakis and a dress shirt at the bar. "Aw, c'mon!" he hollers. "Guy like that is hanging out here? That bar is so *over!*" It only gets worse: He sees his straight-man nemesis astride a fixed-gear bicycle, partaking in "shell art," and wearing a chin beard—all of which, he churlishly admonishes, is "over." A year later, we see Spyke, freshly shorn of beard, wearing business casual, and having a banal conversation, perched in the very same bar that led off the whole cycle. The nemesis? He loiters outside, scornfully declaring the bar to be "over."

The sketch wonderfully encapsulates the idea of taste as a kind of

perpetual motion machine. This machine is driven in part by the oscil-
lations of novelty and familiarity, of hunger and satiation, that curious
internal psychophysical calculus that causes us to tire of food, music,
the color orange. But it is also driven in part by the subtle movements
of people trying to be like each other and people trying to be different
from each other. There is a second-guessing kind of struggle here, not
unknown to strategists of Cold War–era game theory (in which players are rarely acting on "perfect information"). Or, indeed, to readers
familiar with Dr. Seuss's Sneetches, the mythical star-adorned creatures
who suddenly ditch their decorations when they discover their rival
plain-bellied counterparts "have stars upon thars."

That taste might move in the kind of ouroboros-like cycle that
Portlandia hypothesized is not so far-fetched. A French mathematician
named Jonathan Touboul identified a "non-concerted emergent collective phenomenon of looking alike trying to look different," or what
he called the "hipster effect." Unlike "cooperative systems," in which
everyone might agree in a coordinated fashion on what decisions to
make, the hipster effect occurs, he suggests, when people try to make
decisions in opposition to the majority.

Because no one knows exactly what other people are going to do
next, and information can be noisy or delayed, there can also be peri-
ods of brief "synchronization," in which nonconformists fail to be
"disaligned with the majority." Spyke, in reality, might have had to see
several people doing shell art—maybe it even suddenly appeared at a
store in the mall—before quickly packing it in. And because there are
varying degrees of hipness, one person may choose to wade into a trend
later than another, that person is followed by another, and so on, until,
like an astronomical explorer chasing a dead star, there is nothing really
there anymore.* As another modeling analysis put it, "The quest for
distinctiveness can also generate conformity."

The *Portlandia* sketch actually goes well beyond taste and illumi-
nates two central, if seemingly contradictory, strands of human behavior. The first is that we want to be like other people. "The social being,

---

* There are also just those episodes of sheer randomness, such as the "accidental hipster," as a
friend once dubbed it, the old guy at the bus stop wearing the thrift store clothes—for him an
economic necessity—that happen to be the same ones currently fetishized by distinctiveness-
seeking hipsters.

in the degree that he is social, is essentially imitative," wrote the rather overlooked French sociologist Gabriel Tarde in his 1890 book *The Laws of Imitation*. Imitating others, what is known as "social learning," is an evolutionary adaptive strategy; that is, it helps you survive, even prosper. While it is seen in other species, there are no better social learners than humans, none that take that knowledge and *continue* to build upon it, through successive generations.

The sum of this social learning—culture—is what makes humans so unique, and so uniquely successful in spreading throughout the globe. As the anthropologist Joseph Henrich notes, humans, despite being more genetically alike than other primates, have foraged in the Arctic, harvested crops in the tropics, and lived pastorally in deserts—a wider range than all the other primates put together. This is not because we were meant to but because we learned to.

In their book *Not by Genes Alone*, the anthropologists Robert Boyd and Peter Richerson use the example of a bitter plant that turns out to have medicinal value. Our sensory system would interpret the bitter as potentially harmful and thus inedible. Instinctively, there is no reason we should *want* to eat it. But someone eats it anyway and sees some curiously beneficial result. Someone else sees this and gives it a try. "We take our medicine in spite of its bitter taste," they write, "not because our sensory psychology has evolved to make it less bitter, but because the idea that it has therapeutical value has spread through the population." It is like the primordial "first sip of beer" for an entire culture.

People imitate, and culture becomes adaptive, they argue, because learning from others is more efficient than trying everything out on your own through costly and time-consuming trial and error. The same is as true for people now reading Netflix or TripAdvisor reviews as it was for primitive foragers trying to figure out which foods were poisonous or where to find water. When there are too many choices, or the answer does not seem obvious, it seems better to go with the flow; after all, you might miss out on something good.

My favorite example of this comes from a study of Ugandan chimpanzees conducted by a pair of Scottish researchers. One chimp, an adult male they named Tinka, had almost completely paralyzed hands after he was caught in a hunter's snare. He also had a chronic skin condition. Because he was not a high-ranking chimp, he could not rely on others to scratch him. So Tinka improvised: He grasped a vine with his foot and pulled it across his back, the way one would dry oneself with a towel.

Clever stuff. Apparently, some juvenile chimpanzees thought so too: They began scratching themselves in the Tinka way, even though *they had no need to*. One of the researchers, Richard Byrne, told me the suggestion had been made that the chimps were mocking Tinka in some way, which he discounts: "That seems to imply a lot more theory of mind than I'm inclined to grant chimpanzees." More likely, they did it simply to see what the point of it was, to see what they were missing. "Of course, there was no point," Byrne said, "so they gave up that way of scratching in time." Curiously, even the most arbitrary, non-functional behavior can spread. One day in 2010, at a chimp refuge in Zambia, researchers at the Max Planck Institute observed that a chimp they'd named Julie had started putting a single blade of grass in her ear. Unlike Tinka's scratching mechanism, this seemed to have no purpose, even to Julie. And yet, not long after, most of the chimps of the group were seen also sporting ear grass.

This sort of imitative behavior has often been seen as crude and a bit slavish, hence the negative connotation in English of the verb "to ape." But no ape likes to ape more than humans do. In one compelling study, the researchers Victoria Horner and Andrew Whiten had a human subject demonstrate, to chimps, the proper way to open a box containing a food reward. In some conditions, the box was opaque; in others, transparent. Some of the moves the human guide performed were necessary to open the box, while some were not. When the clear box was used first, and chimps had a better sense of what was going on, they discarded the irrelevant steps the human model was showing them. They did this even when they tried to open the opaque box; they had transferred the learning.

When a similar experiment was performed with preschool children, however, the kids "tended to re-create the actions they observed without appearing to consider the causal efficiency of their behaviour." It is not as if the kids could not figure out cause and effect or that opening the box was too complex (for they seemed to imitate closely even when the task was made easier). Rather, suggested Horner and Whiten, the children seemed to focus more on the *model* than the task, even when that model was not showing them the easiest way to open the box. To ape is to be human.

If you are the parent of a small child, as I am, you probably do not need an experiment to inform you of children's tendency to imitate. One day, I asked my daughter why her pant legs were pushed up slightly. Because her friend Madeline's were, she told me. "Did you like the way it looked, or is it because you like your friend?" I asked. The question seemed to confuse her, and I sensed she wanted to say, "Both," without being able to disentangle the causes. It just seemed something worth copying, for whatever reason.

Ironically, the things that are often the *least* functional—like small variations in fashion—are the ones we seem to most want to copy. This is precisely because, the sociologist Georg Simmel suggested over a century ago, "they are independent of the vital motives of human action." Minor fashion gradations acquire such great power in their very lack of meaning, as well as the relatively low costs of switching. As noted by Adam Smith, "The modes of furniture change less rapidly than those of dress; because furniture is commonly more durable."

But imitation is going on everywhere. Recall the preschool experiments mentioned in chapter 1; children's food choices depended on what the other kids at their table were eating. Humans seem programmed to learn socially, as if in the face of uncertainty we instinctively rely on what others are doing. So powerful is this instinct that we not only look to others to see what to do but choose to do the things that others are *looking* at. In a study conducted by Henrich and other researchers at the University of British Columbia, children watched videos of adult "models" consuming food. Some models had bystanders watching them; others had bystanders looking away. When later asked what food they would prefer, children were more likely to choose the food eaten by the model who was watched by others. "When environmental cues are not of sufficiently high quality," write Henrich and Robert Boyd, "individuals imitate."

Think of the psychologist Stanley Milgram's famous New York City street corner experiment in which he had people look up toward a building—at nothing. The more people who were doing it, the more

others stopped to look. And why not? How could there not be something valuable in what so many others were doing?*

But if social learning is so easy and efficient, if all this imitation is such
a good way to ensure the survival of our genes, it raises the question
of why anyone does anything different to begin with. Or indeed why
someone, like Spyke, might abandon an innovation. It is a question
asked of evolution itself: Why is there so much *stuff* for natural selection to sift through? Survival of the fittest, as the biologist Hugo de
Vries pointed out, does not explain "arrival of the fittest." Jørn Utzon
could have turned in a more traditional opera house design; the Impressionists could have played more to the tastes of the current market. The
artist or innovator who was attacked in his day seems like some kind of
genetic altruist, sacrificing his own immediate fitness for some future
payoff at the level of the group.

Boyd and Richerson suggest there is an optimal balance between
social and individual learning in any group. Too many social learners,
and the ability to innovate is lost: People know how to catch that one
fish because they learned it from the smart elder, but what happens
when that fish dies out? Too few social learners, and people might be so
busy trying to learn things on their own that the society does not thrive;
while people were busily inventing their own better bow and arrow,
someone forgot to actually get food.

Perhaps some ingrained sense of the evolutionary utility of this dif-
ferentiation explains why humans—particularly the "WEIRD" ones†—
are so torn between wanting to belong to a group and wanting to be
distinct individuals. Let us call it conformist distinction. People want
to feel that their tastes are not unique, yet they feel an "anxiety" when
told they are exactly like another person. Think of the giddy discom-
fort you feel when a co-worker shows up wearing a similar outfit. The
inevitable joke: "Did you guys coordinate your wardrobe this morning?" We seek some happy medium, like the Miss America contestant in Woody Allen's *Bananas* who responds to a reporter's question,

---

* Social learning can, of course, be maladaptive. Everyone "learned" to smoke from someone
else; some even learned to smoke on the advice of health professionals.
† Namely, "Western, Educated, Industrialized, Rich, and Democratic" countries, a construction
made popular by Henrich.

"Differences of opinion should be tolerated, but not when they're too different."

Under a theory called optimal distinctiveness, people affiliate with groups in ways that let them feel as if they belong and yet are apart (this can be felt in something as simple as ordering food at a group dinner). If all we did was conform, there would be no taste; nor would there be taste if no one conformed. We conform locally and differentiate globally. The psychologists Matthew Hornsey and Jolanda Jetten have identified the ways we try to do that. One is to select the right-sized group or, if the group is too large, choose a subgroup. Be not just a Democrat but a centrist Democrat. Do not like just the Beatles; be a fan of John's.

Another strategy of conformist distinction is dubbed superior conformity of the self. You can show your individuality by, paradoxically, showing how much more you conform to the norms of a group than someone else: for example, "I'm more punk/country/Republican/vegan [insert your group here] than you." In a study of people with body piercings, the ones who identified most with the group—the most conformist—were precisely those who wanted to be as distinct as they could be from the mainstream.

When distinguishing yourself from the mainstream becomes too exhausting, you can always just ape some perceived version of the mainstream. This was the premise behind the "normcore" antifashion trend, in which once energetically fashionable people were said to be downshifting, out of sheer fatigue, into humdrum New Balance sneakers and unremarkable denim. Normcore was more conceptual art project than business case study, but one whose premise—"the most different thing to do is to reject being different altogether," ran the manifesto—seemed so plausible it was practically wish fulfilled into existence by a media that feasts upon novelty as Saturn did his son. As new as normcore seemed, Georg Simmel was talking about it a century ago: "If obedience to fashion consists in imitation of an example, conscious neglect of fashion represents similar imitation, but under an inverse sign."

And so back to Spyke. When he felt his drive for individuality (which he shared with others who were like him) threatened by someone from outside the group, he moved on. All the things he felt were threatened—the chin beard, the shell art—and that he was willing to walk away from were, of course, nonfunctional. As Jonah Berger and Chip Heath point out, we signal our identity only in certain domains:

Spyke is not likely to change his brand of toilet paper or toothbrush just because he learns it is shared by his nemesis. When everyone listened to records on vinyl, they were a commodity material that allowed one to listen to music; it was not until they were nearly driven to extinction as a technology that they became a way to signal one's identity—and as I write, there are stirrings of a "cassette revival."

In a revealing experiment conducted at Stanford University, Berger and Heath sold Lance Armstrong Foundation Livestrong wristbands (at a time when they were becoming increasingly popular) in a "target" dorm. The next week, they sold them in a dorm known for being some-what "geeky." A week later, the number of target dorm band wearers dropped by 32 percent. It was not that people from the target dorm disliked the geeks—or so they said—it was that they thought they were not *like* them. And so the yellow piece of rubber, worn for a good cause, became a vessel of identity signaling, of taste. The only way the tar-get group could avoid being symbolically linked with the geeks was to "abandon" the taste and move on to something else. As much a search for novelty, new tastes can be a conscious rejection of what has come before—and a distancing from those now enjoying that taste. "I liked that band before they got big," goes the common refrain.

The anthropologist Richard Wilk notes that because it is much easier to signal likes in public than dislikes, "this might help explain why consumption is often conspicuous, while avoidance and taboo is usually more subtle and subdued." When you see someone coming out of a butcher's, Wilk notes, you can be sure she likes meat. When you see someone buying vegetables, however, she is not necessarily signaling she does not like meat.

Disliking is arguably more of a force in forming social cohesion than liking. As the historian John Mullan noted, one of the first refer-ences to "good taste" (not of the food kind) in England, William Con-greve's 1693 play *The Double-Dealer*, "is saying someone hasn't got it." Shared group dislikes have hugely influenced the history of art, as E. H. Gombrich pointed out: "Most movements in art erect some new taboo, some negative principle," based on the "principle of exclusion." From Impressionism to punk rock, artists have set themselves against some prior artistic status quo. The Dadaists simply took this to its extreme, declaring themselves "against everything."

What our tastes "say about us" is mostly that we want to be like

other people whom we like and who have those tastes—up to a point—
and unlike others who have other tastes. This is where the idea of "conformist transmission," of simply socially learning what everyone else
is doing, gets complicated. Sometimes we learn what others are doing
and then stop doing that thing ourselves. Like Dr. Seuss's Sneetches,
we "counter-imitate."

Then there is the question of whether we are actually *conscious* of
picking up a behavior from someone else. When someone knows he is
being influenced by another and that other person knows it too, that is
persuasion; when someone is unaware he is being influenced, and the
influencer is unaware of his influence, that is contagion. In taste, we are
rarely presumed to be picking up things randomly. Through "prestige
bias," for example, we learn from people who are deemed socially significant. The classic explanation in sociology was always trickle-down:
Upper-class people embraced some taste, people lower down followed,
then upper-class people rejected the taste and embraced some new
taste. "Naturally the lower classes look and strive towards the upper,"
wrote Simmel, as if citing a biological law.

But it does not always work so neatly. Consider the use in English
of the "quotative 'like,'" that now ubiquitous tendency to say something along the lines of "I was like, 'No way.'" This conquered the language via young middle-class girls (hardly Bourdieu's cultural elite). In
culture, the omnivores, as discussed in chapter 3, routinely go "down"
in their listening. A food like lobster has ping-ponged multiple times
in history, between aspirational upper-class treat and a sign of "poverty and degradation." Then there is the nettlesome problem Bourdieu
left off the table: Even among similar social classes, tastes will diverge.
What drives that?

Tastes can change when people aspire to be different from other
people; they can change when we are trying to be like other people.
Groups "transmit" tastes to other groups, but tastes themselves can
help *create* groups. Small, seemingly trivial differences—what sort of
coffee one drinks—become "real" points of cultural contention. The
more people who have access to what is said to be proper taste, the finer
those gradations become. Witness the varieties of "distinction" now
available in things that were once rather homogeneous commodities,
like coffee and blue jeans; who knew what "single origin" or "selvage"
was a few decades ago? There is an ebb and flow of conformity and dif-

ferentiation and an almost paradoxical cycle: An individual, like Spyke in Portland, wants to be different. But in wanting to express that difference, he seeks out others who share those differences. He conforms to the group, but the conformists of that group, in being alike, increase their sense of difference from *other* groups, just as the Livestrong bracelet wearers took them off when they saw another group wearing them. The adoption of tastes is driven in part by this social jockeying, this learning and avoidance. But this is not the whole picture. Sometimes tastes change simply because of errors and randomness.

ACCIDENTALLY FAMOUS:
ON THE RANDOMNESS AND THE UNPREDICTABILITY OF TASTE

In a small patch of clearing where power lines snake through a forest in the Berkshires, a team of researchers from the University of Massachusetts has been recording, over several decades, the songs of the chestnut-sided warbler, a small New World warbler with a jaunty yellow crown. The songs, as judged by Audubon's *Guide to North American Birds*, are "rich and musical with an emphatic ending." There are two general types of songs the birds sing: "accented" and "unaccented" (the former has a "loud and distinctive terminal downsweep syllable"; the latter does not). Accented songs are generally used to attract mates; indeed, male warblers, like husbands who "give up" on their appearance after courtship is concluded, largely eschew singing them once they have shacked up. Unaccented songs, meanwhile, are often deployed in male-on-male conflict.

Looking over the course of their warbler song recordings, the researchers found that the unaccented songs that seemed most popular with the warblers in 1988 were almost entirely gone by 1995, replaced by a whole new repertoire. Rather like the *Billboard* Hot 100 charts, the chestnut-sided warbler culture had in a rather short span moved on, musically, to a whole new set of "tastes." What was going on? Why would novelty arise when the adaptive fitness of a species or an individual bird, the ability to pass on genes to the next generation, so often favors conformity in communication—singing the songs everyone knows, the way everyone knows them? Were male warblers engaging in impromptu song battles, like New York hip-hop DJs in the 1980s, trying to slay their opponent with their virtuosity, their clever turns of musical phrase?

Bruce Byers, a biologist at the University of Massachusetts and the lead researcher on the study, thinks there is something more prosaic at work: The birds are simply getting the songs *wrong*. "Individuals within a species vary in the precision with which they can imitate," he told me. "Just like people." And perfect imitation, he noted, "presumably has some costs. You have to maintain the brainpower necessary to do precise imitations. So unless there is some huge benefit to offset those costs, you expect some slack, some slight discrepancies in the copy, as compared to the model the birds imitate." As with a game of telephone, as the songs get passed down the line, "these slight variations accumulate rapidly enough so that songs turn over completely within a decade or so."

The accented, mate-attracting songs, by contrast, hardly changed at all. Byers suspects these are the songs where getting it right really counts. Females, as he has found, seem to prefer male birds who, like some avian Marvin Gaye, sang "more consistently and at higher pitch." Having males singing the same songs makes it easier to tell who is doing it best; if you are a male (and you want your genes passed on), it makes sense spending the extra energy to really *nail* that song.

With the evolving, unaccented songs, it was not as if the birds were craving novelty or that some creative bird set out to invent a new style. Nor were they slavishly imitating the new song variants of some prestigious warbler. And it was not as if the songs changed overnight. In the fashion of Raymond Loewy's "most advanced, yet acceptable" principle, it is likely that each new set of songs was recognizably similar to those that had come before, with a small twist. Because many of the unaccented songs are used less frequently, only dusted off against rivals, the birds are probably a bit rusty with them.

The songs that disappear first, as you might imagine, are the ones that were rare to begin with. Birdsongs are rather like the aptly named tweets of Twitter: Memes that thrive among bird populations, just like the spread of hashtags on Twitter, require, as a base condition for survival, wider sharing (that is, more "followers") and more frequent expression (that is, retweeting). Otherwise, they are likely to suffer "extinction by chance."

So error, and random copying, were driving changes in bird culture (while other elements stayed the same). In humans, we might think of the unchanging, accented songs as things like "core" beliefs: religion, morals, one's sense of self. Because these are more important in the long-term evolutionary sense, we invest more energy in them. The unaccented songs, by contrast, are like fashion or preferences, subject to change precisely because it is not so important they stay the same, being generally less useful to our evolutionary success (think of the low success rate of online dating, which often relies heavily on pure statistical matching of easily conveyed information like favorite music or hobbies).

For a tangible human example of what was happening with the birdsong, consider irregular verbs in English. Why have some been converted, over time, into "regularized" verbs? And why have some stayed irregular? As the data scientists Erez Aiden and Jean-Baptiste Michel note, we no longer say that something "throve" but that it "thrived." Using a database of English texts, they found that the more often an irregular verb was used, the more likely it was to stay irregular. Why? Because the irregular verbs we hardly ever encounter are the ones whose irregular forms we are least likely to remember; hence we convert them, through error, into regular verbs.

It is, they suggest, a process of cultural selection: "The more frequent a verb is, the more fit it is to survive." No conspiracy sought to kill off "throve," nor is "thrived" any more inherently appealing. "Thrived" thrived because people simply had trouble remembering the rarely used irregular form. People made mistakes, "thrived" got copied, more or less randomly, and, presto, over a few hundred years the past tense of "thrive" got changed into something new, much as the warblers' songs did.

This raises the question of how much our tastes evolve, on the wider social level, due to more or less accidental, random processes, cultural "mutations" that are not necessarily better, just different. Music is filled with moments where mistakes became innovations (for example, the rise of hip-hop "scratching," Cher's exaggerated use of Auto-Tune in "Believe"), innovations that ultimately shifted taste. The first use of guitar distortion on a record is, like many creation stories, a matter of historical debate. Some guitarist no doubt had a piece of equipment that malfunctioned—or maybe he simply turned it up too loud—and found some pleasure in the resulting imperfection. Then someone else likes what he has heard and decides to imitate it, while putting his own gloss on it, pushing the effect further along.

And so in a couple of decades you have gone from the slight (though certainly edgy at the time) buzz in a forgotten, proto-rock song like Goree Carter's 1949 "Rock Awhile," to the meatier growl of the Kinks' "You Really Got Me" (fashioned by Dave Davies's taking a razor blade to the amp), to the full-blown howl of Jimi Hendrix (now electronically engineered via a custom fuzz box and big Marshall amps). No guitarist really knew he would like it until it happened; otherwise, he would already have been playing that way. Even Pete Townshend's act of smashing his guitar began as a "complete accident." As Bourdieu once wrote, "To discover something is to one's taste is to discover oneself, to discover what . . . [o]ne had to say and didn't know how to say, and, consequently, didn't know."

Taste change is like Wall Street's "random walk," or the idea that the past is a shaky guide to the future. We expect convulsive change on the pop charts, but think of something like the most common colors in home furnishings, the most popular dog breeds, or the top baby names. In any given year, there would be a certain order. But this would almost certainly have been different five years earlier, just as it is sure to be different five years down the road. Could this turnover be explained, even *predicted*? I do not mean in the sense of which breeds or names or colors would rise and which would fall (because, per Wall Street's "efficient market" hypothesis, if we knew what was going to be popular, it already should be). But could the *rate* of change be predicted? That is the promise of what has been called the "neutral model" of cultural change.

The idea comes from a theory in genetics, revolutionary when it was introduced in 1968, which "predicted that the vast majority of evolutionary changes at the molecular level are caused not by selection but by random drift of selectively neutral mutants." In other words, most changes in genes just *happened*. They were driven not by external, functional selection pressures (for example, some factor of the local environment) but on their own, as if guided by some internal logic, one whose probabilities could be estimated.

When applied to culture, the "neutral model" says that something like a list of breed popularity will regularly shift. Some dogs will suddenly become popular—not because some breed is inherently better than another or the upper classes suddenly favor one over another. Rather, popularity shifts through "random copying," or one person wanting a dog because she saw another person with one. This was what R. Alexander Bentley, an anthropologist at England's University of Durham, and his co-researchers found after they sifted through many years of breed registration data. Statistically, the dog breed popularity index follows a power law: A dozen or so top dogs command a majority of the registrations in each year. But *what* those dogs are is subject to change, and that change seems entirely random. A dog can rise from obscurity to popularity with no dedicated promotional campaign behind it; similarly, it can fall from popularity with no apparent explanation.

It is not as if the top dogs became popular, for instance, because they were intrinsically *better* dogs. A study that looked at positive breed characteristics (good behavior, breed life, fewer genetic disorders) and breed popularity found no link between the two. Sometimes, those bred to be least healthy rise most in popularity (call it "unnatural selection"). Humans often do not even seem to pick dogs that are functionally adaptive for *humans.* Harold Herzog, a co-author of Bentley's and a professor of psychology at Western Carolina University, notes that Rottweilers surged from twenty-fifth place to the United States' most popular in a decade. What followed, Herzog notes, was a steep rise in the number of people killed by Rottweilers and then, not surprisingly, a sharp subsequent decline in Rottweiler registrations.

There are certainly cases of selective pressure on dog breed popularity. One of the strongest is movies for children: After Disney's *101 Dalmatians* and *The Shaggy Dog*, dalmatian and sheepdog registrations rose. The bigger the box office, the bigger the breed boost (though, in certain cases, the tail might have been wagging the dog, because the breed was already on the rise, which might be why it was chosen for the film). Movie tie-in breed fads, however, notes Herzog, are "the exception, not the rule," and they have been losing strength. After Taco Bell's famous Chihuahua ad campaign ran, he points out, Chihuahua registrations actually *plummeted;* what was at least initially good for Taco Bell sales was apparently bad for the breed. What about winning the Westminster Dog Show? This, after all, was said to explain the "fabulous rise in poodle popularity" in the 1950s. If it did then, it apparently does not anymore: Westminster winners do not seem to move the needle, breed-wise, in the years after their win.

As with Edwin Long's *Babylonian Market*, whatever breeds are currently top dogs—and however much we would like to think they are there because they are somehow best—the only thing that can be predicted of future taste is that it will change. Once, in a top-floor conference room in an art college in London, I witnessed a top secret annual meeting held by Pantone, the color company, surrounded by color experts. These are people who do not just see the color black, but can amiably chat about the "family of black." Their goal was to try to forecast what colors would be big the next year. Like movie producers in search of an ideal dog—one starting to show up at the margins but not overexposed—the colorists were attuned to what was already gaining some steam or being employed in a new way (for example, "a good navy is going to fulfill the role that black used to play"). Having found the spark, the company's color "forecasters" piled on the fuel.

When, for example, the company predicted orange for the summer of 2011, I was later told by an executive at Firmenich, the flavor and fragrance company, "you can look at what's out in the marketplace—this red orange, or flame orange." It lurked on the new Camaro, the Sony Vaio computer, Hugo Boss's new Orange line. "You're connecting dots here that are traceable," the executive told me. Like surfers, the forecasters were catching a wave that had already begun, and as with the complicated physics that explain those "rogue waves," which just surge "out of nowhere," orange, in all likelihood, was just coughed up from an ocean of color possibility. Like rogue waves, popularity tends to be nonlinear: Once it gets going, it gets bigger than you would have been able to predict from its initial condition (rogue waves "steal" energy from surrounding waves; popular dogs "steal" momentum from other dogs).

What makes the neutral model so compelling, suggests Bentley, is that it provides a way of thinking, at the wider "population level," about why things like tastes just seem to come and go. Statistically, the rate of turnover, on quite distinct indices of popularity—ranging from the *Billboard* Hot 100 to baby names to which "keywords" appear in academic papers in a given year—seems to look the same, as if there was some natural law of churn.

With baby names, Bentley argues that even as the population of countries grows, new names are created (and others disappear), and specific names rise and fall in popularity, the overall statistical shape of name popularity changes little, because of the way people randomly copy names from each other. Remember that from its origin in genetics, the neutral model says that genes cannot be under selection. They cannot be chosen for an "adaptive" reason, where one is "intrinsically" better than another. Are baby names, as Bentley argues, really "value-neutral cultural traits chosen proportionally from the population of existing names, created by 'mutation' and lost through sampling"?

Baby names have long fascinated taste researchers. As Stanley Lieberson, a sociologist at Harvard University, has pointed out, names, unlike many other fashions, are generally for life. No advertisers are cajoling you into a particular name, and they are "value-neutral," in terms of actual money. "It costs no more in dollars and cents to name a daughter *Lauren* or *Elizabeth*," he writes, "than it does to name her *Crystal* or *Tammy*." Names, notes Lieberson, were once largely bound up in tradition and social strictures; one took a family name or a name inspired by one's religion—sometimes to the point where the naming pool was beginning to get a bit small. In the genetic model, they were strongly selected, particularly for boys (in nineteenth-century England, for example, a consistent flurry of Williams and Johns and Henrys). But in the late nineteenth century, names, like so many aspects of culture, were becoming increasingly based on individual choice: "on whether parents like or dislike the name."

Names went from tradition to fashion. And fashion, argues Lieberson, is driven by two large and distinct forces. The first are external factors, big societal ripple effects, like the way the name Jacqueline began to rise in the United States in 1961, thanks to the prominence of the famous First Lady. These large external correlations often do not work, however. A rise in biblical names, Lieberson has found, corresponded to a *decline* in church attendance; what's more, the least religious people were using the names.

More important, he suggests, are the "internal mechanisms" that drive taste changes even "in the absence of external shifts." In what he calls the "ratchet effect," some new, small taste change is introduced (like a simple change of letter in a name, from Jenny to Jenna). A mutation, as the genetic model would have it. Another taste change subtly expands on that, typically in a similar direction. So skirt lengths or hair get a bit longer and then a bit longer, until reaching some point of disutility—or just ridiculousness. It echoes Loewy: most advanced, yet acceptable.

The attempt may be made to pin a taste change, after the fact, on some social factor (X became popular because Y). But it is often hard to escape the sense of sheer randomness and copying. Lieberson notes that boys' names ending in *n* became popular in the second half of the twentieth century (possibly hitting their zenith in 1975, when Jason, dramatically less popular decades earlier, hit number 2). They then began to decline. What happened? It is not as if an *n* sound confers any more intrinsic worth or that we are biologically programmed to prefer *n* names—for why would its ascent have stopped? Rather, it is as if people, like those warblers, were hearing a sound, presumably liked the way it sounded, and so took it on themselves. One statistical analysis, of a century's worth of names, found that names, even after taking their past popularity into account, were more likely to be used when a sound contained in the name was popular the previous year.

Once a sound is introduced to the naming picture, it opens the doors to "errors," imitations that are slightly off: The popular 1970s moniker Jennifer, writes Lieberson, "generates interest" in a number of similar-sounding names (like Jessica). The event that kick-starts a popular sound can literally be a matter of chance: A study of naming patterns in the wake of hurricanes—whose names are randomly drawn from a list—found an increase in names sharing the first letter of the named hurricane. The bigger the hurricane, the bigger the increase (up to a point), simply because the "phoneme" was thrust in the air. This is not so different from the way a "genre" book that hits the *New York Times* best-seller list can boost sales for non-best-selling books of the same genre, as if once people had read one, they were subtly influenced to read others.

You are probably protesting by now that this makes it sound as if we are all mindless drones marching in lockstep, naming our kids based on something we overheard at the grocery store or on the Weather Channel, doing things without any conscious thought. Indeed, critics of the neutral model insist there is almost *always* some kind of biased selection going on. Most common is popularity itself; what is popular gets reproduced because it is popular.

But there is an opposing selection force as well: when people begin to *not* do something (choose a name, retweet a tweet) because they sense too many other people are doing it. Economists call this "nonfunctional demand," or everything driving (or reducing) demand that has nothing to do with "the qualities inherent in the commodity."

While neutral drift says one choice is not somehow better than another, names often do have some intrinsic value. As one study showed, certain so-called racial names (for example, Latonya or Tremayne) were less likely to get callbacks on job interviews; another analysis found that having a German name after World War I made it harder to get a seat on the New York Stock Exchange (and fewer kids were named Wilhelm and Otto). Or they have perceived intrinsic value, like social cachet.* Names that appear to be neutrally distributed throughout the culture could be under some kind of "weak" selection pressure. Perhaps one parent, having read the novel *We Need to Talk About Kevin*, a mother's tale of a violent son, decides not to give her child that name (thus reducing the chance someone else will copy her) because of a negative connotation that only a few may be aware of.

When I raised this subject with Bentley, he insisted that this was precisely the value of the neutral model: If culture change viewed at the big, population-wide level looks as if random copying were driving everything, then that noisy statistical wallpaper makes an easier backdrop against which to see when selection pressures really *are* at work. When one looks at a crowded, rush-hour highway from above, it seems as if every driver were essentially copying the other; the highway seems to drift along neutrally. But look more closely, and one driver may be following another too closely, applying "selective pressure" that then influences the driver ahead. Taste is like traffic, actually—a large complex system with basic parameters and rules, a noisy feedback chamber where one does what others do and vice versa, in a way that is almost impossible to predict beyond that at the end of the day a certain number of cars will travel down a stretch of road, just as a certain number of new songs will be in the Hot 100.

---

* In my own Brooklyn neighborhood, I often have the sense parents are rather overbrandishing their children's names, like product placements in their own lifestyle marketing campaign.

All this leads to one last question. If taste moves along via imitative social learning, whether random or not, whether "biased" or not, what happens when people—thanks to the Internet—have ever more opportunity to see, in ever finer detail, what other people are doing?

When I was a teenager in the 1980s, I tuned one day, by accident, to a station on the far left of the dial and discovered a show playing punk rock and other eclectic forms of music. I felt as if I had walked into a private conversation being spoken in another language: Here were songs I had never heard before (my tastes were admittedly quite conventional) that sounded little like anything I had heard before.

As I quickly became a fan of this strange cacophony, I realized how time-consuming the pursuit was: long hours spent tracking down obscure albums in obscure record stores in obscure parts of town, driving to sweaty all-ages shows in not-quite-up-to-code social halls, talking to the few other kids in my school who knew what I was even talking about, never having a sense of how many people in other towns might like this same music. The whole time, I nursed a conviction that if only more people knew about this music, it would become more popular (leaving aside the awkward question, per optimal distinctiveness, of if my own liking for it would decline *because* more people liked it).

Things are now incredibly different. The Internet means that one click can access most of the world's music; via chat rooms and other forums, fans of the most rarefied genres can find each other; technology has blown open distribution bottlenecks, making it cheaper and easier for anyone to put a recording out into the world. As the Echo Nest showed, entire genres could spring up virtually overnight and find fans. In theory, my teenage hope had come alive: There was little, physically, preventing anyone from listening to anything. Music was *horizontal*: It took no more effort to listen to something obscure than to something popular. Perhaps, as I had imagined, the formerly less popular would become more popular, at the expense of the already popular, which would decline in importance as more people found more things on the "long tail" to listen to. At the very least, the hits on the radio, the ones you quickly grew tired of hearing so often, would turn over faster because of the sheer increase in new material.

This is not necessarily how it turned out, as I learned in speaking to

Chris Molanphy, a music critic and obsessive analyst of the pop charts. "There was this big theory that all this sort of democracy in action, this capturing of people's taste, was going to lead to more turnover, not less," he said. "In fact, if you watch the chart, it's totally the opposite. The big have gotten bigger." It is true that music sales as a whole declined in the new digital environment, but it was the albums further down the charts—from 200 to 800—that fared worst. Hit songs, meanwhile, gobbled up even more of the overall music market than they did before the Internet. The curving long tail chart, as he put it, looks more like a right angle. "It's kind of like once the nation has decided that we're all interested in 'Fancy' by Iggy Azalea or 'Happy' by Pharrell"—to name two pop hits of 2014—"we're *all* listening to it."

He calls these "snowball smashes": They gather momentum and pick up everything in their wake. With more momentum comes more staying power. The song "Radioactive" by Imagine Dragons lingered on the Hot 100, "*Billboard*'s flagship pop chart," for two years. By contrast, a song like the Beatles' "Yesterday"—as Molanphy notes, "the most covered song of all time"—lasted a mere eleven weeks on the charts.

It is not just that popularity can be self-fulfilling; it is that *not* being popular is even more so. In his classic 1963 book, *Formal Theories of Mass Behavior*, the social scientist William McPhee introduced a theory he called "double jeopardy." He was struck, looking at things like polls of movie star appeal and the popularity of radio shows, that when some cultural product was less popular, it was not only less well known (and thus less likely to be chosen) but less *chosen* by those who actually knew it—hence the double jeopardy. Did this mean the pop charts worked, that the best rose to the top? Not necessarily. McPhee speculated that the "lesser known alternative is known to people who know too many *competitive* alternatives." The favorites, by contrast, "become known to the kind of people who, in making choices, know little *else* to choose from." In other words, the sorts of people who listen to more obscure music probably like a *lot* of music a little, whereas the most devoted listeners of the Top 10 tend to concentrate their love. Through sheer statistical distribution, McPhee suggested, a "natural" monopoly emerged.

If this was already the case decades ago, why have things gotten so much more top-heavy, so much more sticky? It could be, as I discussed in chapter 3, that having the world's music in your pocket is too overwhelming, the blank search box of what to play next too terrifying, and so people take refuge in the exceedingly familiar. Or it could be that the more we know about what people are listening to—via new routes of social media—the more we are also listening.

This was what the network scientist Duncan Watts and colleagues found in a famous 2006 experiment. Groups of people were given the chance to download songs for free from a Web site after they had listened to and ranked the songs. When the participants could see what previous downloaders had chosen, they were more likely to follow that behavior—so "popular" songs became more popular, less popular songs became less so. These socially influenced choices were more *unpredictable*; it became harder to tell how a song would fare in popularity from its reported quality. When people made choices on their own, the choices were less unequal and more predictable; people were more likely to simply choose the songs they said were best. Knowing what other listeners did was not enough to completely reorder people's musical taste. As Watts and his co-author Matthew Salganik wrote, "The 'best' songs never do very badly, and the 'worst' songs never do extremely well." But when others' choices were visible, there was greater chance for the less good to do better, and vice versa. "When individual decisions are subject to social influence," they write, "markets do not simply aggregate pre-existing individual preference." The pop chart, in other words, just like taste itself, does not operate in a vacuum.

The route to the top of the charts has in theory gotten more democratic, less top-down, more unpredictable: It took a viral video to help make Pharrell's "Happy" a hit a year after the fact. But the hierarchy of popularity at the top, once established, is steeper than ever. In 2013, it was estimated that the top 1 percent of music acts took home 77 percent of *all* music income.

While record companies still try to engineer popularity, Molanphy argues it is "the general public infecting each other who now decide if something is a hit." The inescapable viral sensation "Gangnam Style," he notes, was virtually *forced* onto radio, where it became the number 12 song in the United States (without even factoring in YouTube, where it was mostly played). "Nobody manipulated that into being; that was clearly the general public being charmed by this goofy video and telling each other, 'You've got to watch this video.'" The snowball effect, he suggests, is reflected in radio. "Blurred Lines," the most played song of

2013 in the United States, was played *twice* as much as the most played song of 2003.

This is in sharp contrast to the 1970s, the period in which I did my most obsessive Top 40 listening, when it was an industry truism that, as the veteran radio consultant Sean Ross put it to me, after what could seem an unendurably long wait, "you heard your favorite song and you turned off the radio—your mission was accomplished." Molanphy suggests that if radio then had the access to sales and listening data that it does now, it would have played those favorite songs much more than it actually did, and a song like "Yesterday" would have spent more time on the charts. What ever-sharper, real-time data about people's actual listening behavior do is more strongly reinforce the feedback loop. "We always knew that people liked the familiar," he says. "Now we know exactly when they flip the station and, wow, if they don't already know a song, they *really* flip the station." There is an almost desperate attempt to convert, as fast as possible, the new into the familiar.

Pop songs have always been fleeting affairs. What about baby names, which are presumably more organic and enduring? Here, popularity *has* become more evenly distributed. As the researchers Todd Gureckis and Robert Goldstone point out, the name Robert was the "snowball smash" of 1880: Nearly one in ten baby boys was named Robert. By contrast, Jacob, 2007's top name, only reached 1.1 percent of boys. The most popular names, they note, have lost "market share." But something else changed over those years. At the turn of the twentieth century, the names at the top rather randomly fluctuated, because, one might imagine, more families with fathers named Robert had boys that year.

In the last few decades, however, a statistical pattern emerged in which the direction a name was headed in one year tended to predict—at a level greater than chance—where it was going the next year. If Tom was falling this year, Tom was likely to keep falling next year. Names acquired *momentum*. As naming lost the weight of cultural tradition, where did people look when making their choice? To each other. In 1880, even if names were freely chosen, it would have taken a while for name popularity to spread. But now, as parents-to-be visit data-heavy baby name Web sites or try out suggestive names on Facebook, they seem to be able to mystically divine where a name is headed and can latch on to a rising name (as long as it is not rising too quickly, for that is taken as a negative signal of faddishness) and stray from one that is falling. It is like trying to buy long-term stocks amid the noise of short-term volatility.

Something similar is happening in both pop music and naming. Things have at once become more horizontal—there are ever more songs to hear, ever more possible names to choose from—and more "spiky," as if, in the face of all that choice, people gravitate toward what others seem to be doing. Social learning has become hyper-social learning. In his famous 1930 tract, *The Revolt of the Masses*, the Spanish philosopher José Ortega y Gasset described how "the world had suddenly grown larger." Thanks to modern media, he noted, "each individual habitually lives the life of the whole world." People in Seville could follow, as he described, "what was happening to a few men near the North Pole." We also had vastly increased access to things: "The range of possibilities opened out before the present-day purchaser has become practically limitless." There was a "leveling" among social classes, which opened up "vital possibilities," but also a "strange combination of power and insecurity which [had] taken up its abode in the soul of modern man." He feels, he wrote, "lost in his own abundance."

Ortega's vision seems quaint now. Simply to live in a large city like New York is to dwell among a maelstrom of options: There are said to be—by many orders of magnitude—more choices of things to buy in New York than there are recorded species on the planet. As Bentley put it to me, "By my recent count there were 3,500 different laptops on the market. How does anyone make a 'utility-maximizing' choice among all those?" The cost of learning which one is truly best is almost beyond the individual; there may, in fact, actually be little that separates them in terms of quality, so any one purchase over another might simply reflect random copying (here is the "neutral drift" at work again, he argues). It is better to say—here he borrows the line from *When Harry Met Sally*—"I'll have what she's having."

And boy do we know what she's having. If, for Ortega, journalistic dispatches from explorers seemed to thrust one into a vertiginous global gyre, what would he make of the current situation, where a flurry of tweets comes even before the breaking news announcements, which then turn into wall-to-wall coverage, followed by a think piece in the next day's newspaper? He would have to factor in social media, in which it often seems as if we were really living "the life of the whole world"; one has a peripheral, real-time awareness of any number of people's whereabouts, achievements, status updates, via any number of platforms.

Ortega called this "the increase of life," even if it often seems to come with the cost of time in one's own life, or indeed our happiness (studies suggest social media can be bad for one's self-esteem). If media (large broadcasters creating audiences) helped define his age of mass society, social media (audiences creating ever more audiences) help define our age of mass individualism. The Internet is exponential social learning: You have ever more ways to learn what other people are doing; how many of the more than thirteen thousand reviews of the Bellagio in Las Vegas do you need to read on TripAdvisor before making a decision? There are ever more ways to learn that what you are doing is not good enough or was already done last week by someone else, that what you like or even *who* you like is also liked by some random person you have never met. It is social learning by proxy. Remotely seeing the perfect Instagram post of an artisanal pastry in San Francisco engenders a "frenzy" in others to consume it, not unlike Julie's grass-in-the-ear trick.

People have always wanted to be around other people and to learn from them. Cities have long been dynamos of social possibility, foundries of art, music, and fashion. Slang, or, if you prefer, "lexical innovation," has always started in cities—an outgrowth of all those different, densely packed people so frequently exposed to one another. It spreads outward, in a manner not unlike infectious disease, which itself typically "takes off" in cities. If, as the noted linguist Leonard Bloomfield contended, the way a person talks is a "composite result of what he has heard before," then language innovation would happen where the most people heard and talked to the most other people. Cities drive taste change because they offer the greatest exposure to other people, who not surprisingly are often the creative people cities seem to attract. Media, ever more global, ever more penetrating, spread language faster to more people (to cite just one example, the number of entries in Japanese "loanword" dictionaries—words "borrowed" from English—more than doubled from the 1970s to 2000).

With the Internet, we have a kind of city of the mind, a medium that people do not just consume but *inhabit*, even if it often seems to replicate and extend existing cities (New Yorkers, already physically exposed to so many other people, use Twitter the most). As Bentley has argued, "Living and working online, people have perhaps never copied each other so profusely (since it usually costs nothing), so accurately, and so indiscriminately." Things spread faster and more cheaply; more people can copy from more people.

But how do we know what to copy and from whom? The old ways of knowing what we should like—everything from radio station programmers to restaurant guides to book critics to brands themselves—have been supplanted by Ortega's "multitudes," acting not en masse but as a mass of individuals, connected but apart, unified but disparate. Whom to follow? What to choose? Whom can you trust?

This is why things have become both flatter and spikier: In an infinite realm of choice, our choices often seem to cluster by default toward those we can see others making (or *away* from those we sense too many are choosing). Whatever the direction, experimental work has shown that when "wise crowds" can see what others in the crowd are thinking, when there is too much "social influence," people start to think more like one another (and not like the "ideal judges" with whom we are about to visit in the next chapter). They take less information into account to make their decisions yet are *more* confident that what they are thinking is the truth—because more people seem to think that way. As in a high-frequency trading market, social imitation has gotten easier, faster, and more volatile; all those micro-motives of trying to be like others and yet different can intensify into explosive bursts of macro-behavior. The big waves have gotten bigger, and we know that they will come, but it is harder to tell from where in the vast and random ocean surface they will swell.

CHAPTER 6

BEER, CATS, AND DIRT

HOW DO EXPERTS DECIDE WHAT'S GOOD?

UP TO STANDARD: WHAT MAKES THE IDEAL IDEAL

I have been describing to you, over the last several hundred pages, how our tastes are so elusive, even to us; how they are inevitably malleable to social influence; what a fleeting grasp we have of the things we put in our mouths or before our eyes. If all this was really so messy, I began to think, it seemed worth spending some time with people who need to reasonably think about, and compellingly articulate, why they like things—or, at least, explain why certain things are not only good (and I would argue one does not generally like what one does not think is good), but better than *other* things. I am talking about judges in competitions. Surely they would be able to cut steely-eyed through our fog of proclivities and bring crystalline neutrality to the murky thickets of taste. What might we learn from them to bring more clarity to our own liking?

Let us begin with a simple inquiry, about something with which most of us have at least a passing familiarity: What makes a good cat? To find out, I have traveled to Paris, where, in a small conference center in the twelfth arrondissement, the Salon International du Chat is under way. Despite its grandiose title, it seems a pretty regional affair, a medium-sized hall's worth of blue-eyed Ragdolls and fluffy woolen Selkirk Rexes and sleekly poised European Burmese. Perhaps sensing it is getting away with something, a Seeing Eye dog leads its owner through the show aisles, but even the presence of this large hound does not measurably stir these unperturbed show cats.

I am not here because this is a particularly important cat show, and cat shows, it must be said, are, like their owners, more low-key than dog shows. Rather, I am here because one of the judges, a Dutchman named Peter Moormann, happens to be not only a cat judge but a professor of psychology at the University of Leiden in the Netherlands. To bring it full circle, he has investigated the psychology of judges in competitions.

Moormann, whose swept-back, flowing silver hair and sympathetic eyes give him an air of elegant Continental authority, got into cats around the same time he got into psychology. Born in colonial Indonesia to parents who were survivors of the Burma railroad and Japanese prisoner-of-war camps, he fled with his family to Holland. There, some old friends from Indonesia were raising Persian cats. Because he seemed to have an affinity for handling animals, they asked him along to a show. He steadily climbed through the cat show ranks: steward, pupil judge, judge. Meanwhile, he was a psychology student and a champion skater; first roller, then ice. ("I have always tried to combine things in life," he said.) His dissertation was on the psychology of figure skating performance, not a hard sell in the skating-mad Netherlands. It included a chapter on "involuntary bias when judging figure skating performance," which presumably he tried to rein in during the multiple times he was a judge on the television program *Sterren Dansen op het Ijs*, the Dutch version of *Dancing on Ice*.

As I sat next to Moormann at a folding table in the judge's area, a procession of owners, smiling and expectant, presented their cats to him. The first thing that became apparent was that as soon as the cats were on the table, the dynamics of just who was being judged were called into question. The cats seemed to pull off an astonishing double axel of casual haughtiness: They at once looked as if they owned the place and appeared vaguely annoyed for having been deposited here, in front of this cheery Dutchman waving a feather at them. The feather is a common judge's ploy to get the cats to, in essence, be cats. As one judge had described it to me, "You get the toy out, you want to see expression, the ears up."

One is hesitant to assign national characteristics to man or animal, but it is difficult to resist seeing in these French cats something of the famous and colossal disregard exhibited by French waiters, who will look upon you with an almost sympathetic glance as you wait for service, as if they were watching the playing out of an existential drama over which they have no control. Some cats glance at Moormann's feather with the world-weary pity the garçon exhibits toward a patron trying to signal for the check.

Moormann poked and prodded, feeling for skull deformations, scanning for "tail faults" or indistinct markings, probing for missing testicles. As with a used car, looks can be deceiving. Some breeds are even dismissed as being a "paint job," simply daubed up with a new coat color or pattern. A lot of the judging is done by feel: the length of the cat, the muscle tone, or whether, as one judge told me, "they have a funky front end." As he examined, Moormann occasionally issued a word of encouragement like "bonne" or "très expressif." "All cats," he declared, "have something you can penalize. No cat is perfect." But neither is any judge a robot. Sitting across from him is a human owner, who has paid money, some of which has gone to bringing the judges to this show. "You almost want to make the person feel . . ." He searched for the word. "Happy."

As Moormann studied the cats, I would study the owners. The woman with cat paw prints painted on her fingernails. The one who apologized as she struggled to restrain her charge. "I was once bit through the fingernail by a Persian," Moormann said wearily. I cannot help thinking there is some truth in the old cliché of owners taking on the appearance of their pets. The woman clutching an Oriental short-hair, when seen in profile, turned out to have a similarly long, sloping nose. As Moormann stroked the tail of one Persian, I caught its owner absently running her hand through her own hair.

For Moormann, there are two ways of judging cats. There is the "analytic style," in which "the whole is the sum of its parts." Each cat breed has a range of "points" that are assigned for certain attributes: eyes, color, tail. The best cat has the most points across these categories. This seems objective, but the judge, Moormann has written, "forgets that there is no objective measuring device available other than his/her own brain." In the "holistic style," by contrast, "the whole can be more than the sum of its parts." The judge in this case begins with "an ideal mental image of the cat," and the closer that cat seems to be to that image, the more the judge will like it. "The whole should have something special, something charismatic," he says. "Something that feels good, but you cannot describe it completely. All the parts fit together and make something additional which is very beautiful." The danger here, Moormann warns, is that the judge may lose the trees for the forest, overlooking flaws because of the "halo effect" of some larger impression.

As each cat was hoisted off the table, Moormann would scrawl a number of stars next to each cat's name. Sometimes he would write "BV," for "best variety." The stars are his own scaled system, meant less as some Michelin-style indication of quality than simply as a way to distinguish, and remember, individual cats in what can be a long succession of fur, claws, and arched backs. "If I have too many cats in one day, I am not able to do this; there's too much interference. Cats are cats." Judging them is no simpler than herding them.

Memory may be the most important skill for any judge. A "trained eye" may tell someone where to look. To make a quality judgment, however, means not only remembering what the judge has seen that day but measuring that against all the other cats or figure skaters he has *ever* seen. We remember what we like, but perhaps even more accurately *we like what we remember.*

There are many ways a judge in a competition might be biased. The gymnastics judge who shares a language with a competitor might give that gymnast a higher ranking (and this is why a Dutch judge is at a French cat show). The judge in an *American Idol*–style show who favors pop might be less enthusiastic about the heavy metal group. Or a judge with a strong personality at a table might sway the group. A Belgian study—and I must note here a distinct Low Countries bias in expert judging research—looked at competitive rope jumping (yes, it exists!). The researchers found that when judges were shown video clips of performances whose scores had been artificially manipulated upward, they voted higher. When the scores were falsely set lower, they followed suit. Judges, it seems, want to be judged well by their fellow judges.

One of the simplest and most innocent forms of bias, however, is memory itself. It has been found, for example, in various types of competitions, that people who performed later seemed to do better. You might think, as you headed to a job interview or some other competition with a number of candidates, that going later might be a liability. The judges, you would reason, may be tired. They might have already, in effect, decided. And yet, in studies that have looked at everything from classical music competitions to synchronized swim meets, researchers have found a clear and compelling pattern: The later contestants appeared, the higher they scored.

The Belgian (!) researcher Wändi Bruine de Bruin analyzed several decades' worth of voting data from the Eurovision Song Contest—an arguably more palatable task than actually listening to all the songs. She first controlled for potential "home advantage." Not only do German judges, for example, like German acts a bit more; they also like the acts from countries that *border* Germany a bit more than others. She emerged with another strong, linear relationship: Performers who appeared later were judged higher. "Judges," she concluded, "may base their final rating of a performance on how well they remember it."

In competitions where judges watch all of the contestants before finally issuing scores, this makes intuitive sense. It echoes findings of "primacy bias" and "recency bias" in so-called list memory: We seem to remember the first and last entrants in any kind of list or series. This is either because we shift those items into short- and long-term memory or because the first and last things are themselves distinctive: Nothing comes before or after. There is a reason the "first" of a thing (a car, a pet, and so on) is used as a prompt in computer security questions: It stands out more in your memory than your third. Poets and songwriters do not reminisce over fourth loves.

What happens when judges make their judgments just after each contestant has made an appearance, when the performance will still be clear in their memory? Curiously, the "later is better" effect seems to show up here as well. In looking at data from the World and European Figure Skating Championships, which are judged on a "step by step" basis, Bruine de Bruin again found an upward, linear pattern of scores, even when the appearance order of contestants was randomly drawn. What was going on? Bruine de Bruin suggests that judges may consider the first performance as its own discrete thing. With each successive performance, however, judges began to look for what was *better* and *different* from the previous performance.

This has been called, after work by the psychologist Amos Tversky, the "direction of comparison effect." Later performances are compared only with earlier ones; the earlier ones, as they are happening, cannot be compared with later performances. So the scores tend to travel in one direction, with one important qualifier, which I will shortly return to: Judges need to be looking for instances of *positive* difference.

Another dynamic troubles serially judged competitions; let us call it "The Best Is Yet to Come Effect." Scores tend to get more extreme toward the end. Judges may be unsure how good or bad early competitors are and vote conservatively, reserving their strongest judgments for the final entrants. Later contestants, in turn, having seen what they are up against, may be motivated to perform at a higher level. Not uncommon are comments like that of the English gymnast Louis Smith: "If my main rival . . . goes through his routine and puts in a high score, it gives me the opportunity to think, 'Okay, maybe I need to try my harder routine.' " Athletes may intuit that an eye-catching move, strikingly different from what their immediate rival has done, will net them a higher score. Indeed, one analysis of gymnastics data, taking advantage of the different scores awarded for "difficulty" and "execution" (a system created after the notorious judging fiasco at the 2004 Olympics in Athens), finds what it calls a "difficulty bias." Even though the two metrics are supposed to be independent, the analysis found that when contestants try harder moves, their execution scores are "artificially inflated."

But a novel series of experiments by the German researchers Thomas Mussweiler and Lysann Damisch shows why judging bias, and not simply athletes rising to the occasion, may be behind score inflation. They begin by observing that athletes' scores tended to be higher "if the preceding gymnast presented a good rather than a flawed performance." This could simply be athletes adjusting: A gymnast coming on the heels of a terrible performance might decide to "play it safe" and get a respectably high score, rather than "going for broke."

Mussweiler and Damisch, however, argue that something else is going on. When we make comparison judgments, we instinctively look for similarities between things, or differences. Typically, we favor similarity—"one of the building blocks of human cognition," suggests Mussweiler—because sensing similarity is not only extremely useful, but quick and easy (children, after all, are not asked in puzzles to "spot the similarities"). You meet a new person, you immediately think how he or she reminds you of someone you know, not all the ways they are *unlike* someone you know. Even the search for differences tends to happen after this initial establishing of similarities. But this initial, often subconscious, decision (whether things feel more similar or more different) then goes on to profoundly influence how we feel about those things. When we perceive things to be similar, we tend toward "assimilation"—which will typically make us like something more: A good wine is lifted when it comes after a great wine. But if we emphasize differences among things to be judged, "contrast" will result. Judges will, in essence, be looking for things *not* to like.

In another experiment, Mussweiler and Damisch gathered a group of experienced German gymnastics judges and showed them clips of two low-vault routines. Judges were broken into two groups: One saw a high-quality routine, the other a low-quality routine. Then everyone saw a "moderate"—pretty good—routine. The groups were split another way: To one group of judges, the gymnasts in the two routines were both presented as "Australian." But another set of judges saw "Australian" gymnasts followed by "Canadian" gymnasts (in reality the same gymnasts in both clips). The researchers noted a curious effect: When both gymnasts were "Australian," the following gymnast benefited, scorewise, by following the good performance, but when he followed the "poor" performance, his score was actually brought down. Being Australian connected him, in the judges' mind, to the previous performer—good or bad. But when the second gymnast was thought to be "Canadian," the reverse pattern was found: Now the "Canadian" gymnast got a *lower* score when he followed a good "Australian" score—and better when he followed a poor one. In other words, the same performance was judged differently depending upon what came before—and how those things were connected by the judges. As much as by the strength of their routines, the gymnasts were being subtly compared by nationality, and they were either suffering or benefiting by the comparison.

The German gymnastic judges were judging even before they were judging by deciding how similar the two gymnasts were. Even if the fact of noticing the gymnasts' "different" nationalities was not intended as a qualitative judgment, merely making the observation seems to have influenced how the judges felt about the performance.

Humans seem to operate under a "similarity bias," a kind of presumptive desire that people we meet are more like us than not. When we think things are similar, they literally become more similar. In what is known as the "cheerleader effect," a person asked to rate the attractiveness of individuals gives them a higher score when they are in a group versus when they are alone. Any idiosyncrasies that, in isolation, might trigger someone's dislike seem, in a grouping, to be averaged out, or less noticeable. For similar reasons, people are rated as more attractive when they are seen in videos versus a static image—because the judgment is not based on one make-or-break image.

These effects do not show up only in contests. We are making comparisons all the time, and these influence how we feel about things, even ourselves. We seem to make comparisons even when we are not aware we are doing so. In another study by Mussweiler, students were asked "to reflect upon their athletic abilities" for one minute. As they did, images were subliminally flashed on a computer screen for about fifteen milliseconds. While the students did not recall seeing the images of Michael Jordan, Bill Clinton, or others who were shown, the answers they gave on their own athletic ability seemed directly influenced by whom they were unwittingly comparing themselves with. The more "extreme" the comparison—that is, Jordan—the worse they got. But a subconscious glimpse of someone like Bill Clinton seemed to turn them into better athletes. "Participants compared themselves with potential standards," wrote Mussweiler, "even if they were unaware of them."

What we are comparing things *with* matters. A study by Tversky offered subjects a choice of six dollars or an "elegant Cross pen" (he never mentions the value, but assume it's more than six dollars). Nearly a third of subjects opted for the pen, with the rest taking the cash. A second group could pick from the Cross pen, the cash, or a second pen that was "distinctly less attractive." Only 2 percent of the subjects wanted the cheaper pen. Suddenly, though, more people were clamoring for the Cross pen. The presence of the less attractive pen made the more attractive pen even more attractive. The reverse can happen as well. Research of actual speed-dating trials showed that potential daters (men, it turns out) became less interested in dating a woman, no matter how attractive she was perceived to be, when she followed a more attractive woman in the dating rounds.

The *way* we are making comparisons also matters. As mentioned earlier, when people are looking for the good things that distinguish each successive option in a list of choices, the later items fare better. But when they are making comparisons based on what is uniquely *bad* about each choice, suddenly the early option looks better.

One study presented subjects with a list of attributes of potential blind dates. When the second choice presented had positive qualities that were not shared by the first candidate, the subjects preferred the choice that came later. But when the second choice had *negative* qualities that were different from the first, they actually preferred the first. As the study's authors described it, qualities that are shared by the candidates are essentially recalled with equal clarity and thus cancel each other out. What is *different* about the second candidate suddenly stands out in memory. So what is uniquely good about the second candidate seems better than what is uniquely good about the first; conversely, the negative qualities of the second candidate seem worse than those of the first, so we reverse our preference.

As the authors of a Carnegie Mellon University study note, "Judging one experience can unduly influence our judgment of subsequent events and thus 'color' the entire sequence of experiences." What we might think of as our fairly hard-set preferences are often subtly manipulated on the fly, like some kind of "choose your own adventure" game.

Consider "the 11th Person Game." This is an "admittedly objectifying" thought exercise devised by the interaction designer Chris Noessel. The next time you are in a public place, point to a random doorway and ask a friend to choose one of the next ten people who walk through the door as a potential romantic partner. There are two rules: You cannot return to any previous person you passed up, and if, when the tenth person comes through the door, you have not chosen anyone, the eleventh becomes your de facto choice.

This is, as you might have noted, a serially judged competition; the fact that you cannot "go back" makes it different from most contests. In fact, as the psychological work on judged competitions shows, it is often hard for judges to "go back" and honestly reevaluate earlier candidates in the face of later ones. It gets even more difficult as the list grows longer and as each new entry "resets" the comparison standard.

In the beginning of the 11th Person Game, Noessel noted, players tend to robustly reject people. But over time, as the potential eleventh person looms, and choices begin to dwindle, players stop looking for flaws in each new person and start looking for "what's *right* about a given person." The slightly awkward grin becomes an entrancingly winning smile. A person's preference set, and search strategy, are suddenly reordered by the structure of choice. *Standards change.*

In Paris, Moormann was well aware of the potential pitfalls in making comparisons between cats, particularly among a host of entrants that might be, to the average eye, virtually indistinguishable. The first task is to group them into levels: good, very good, excellent. This is a natural "chunking" exercise that helps memory and discrimination. But merely grouping them might make them more similar to each other than they actually are. As Tversky notes, "Similarity serves as a basis for the classification of objects, but it is also influenced by the adopted classification." That is, the best "good" cat may not be that qualitatively far from the worst "excellent" cat, but each may be pulled "down" or "up" by being placed in a grouping with others.

What if there are a number of very good cats that are quite similar? "It is not very easy," Moormann said with a sigh. Cats are awarded weighted points for various features. The "subdimensions" of one cat, he has written, "are simultaneously compared with all the subdimensions of all the other cats within a group of cats." This is a "gigantic mental enterprise." Cat shows occur in real life, with cats that move, owners that kvetch, spectators who gawp, with all the bedlam of the show humming in the background. When one inspects cat after cat, "it seems likely the average judge cannot handle more than three dimensions simultaneously." Some judges, he suggested, might make choices on "the type of head alone."

Hovering over it all is the standard. This is the written description laying out, at formidable length, what each breed should actually look like. As Moormann says, judges are looking for universal qualities— "whether the cat is pleasing, whether the lines are good"—but each breed has its specific qualities. Throughout the afternoon, I paged through the breed standard book by Moormann's side. This is a curious document. There are achingly specific aesthetic prescriptions: The Chausie may have "some flecking or speckling" that "may occur on the stomach" but, it warns, "not to the degree of belly spots." With the Burmese, the guide admonishes, "there should be no evidence of obesity, paunchiness, weakness, or apathy." "Long, whippy tails" are bad for some cats, good for others.

The longer I paged through the breed book, the more the questions flowed. "The ideal Bombay," the guide notes, "has an unmistakable look of its own." But shouldn't every breed at a cat show? Otherwise, why bother with breeds? How does one actually judge a "sweet expression"?

"Don't believe everything that's written," Moormann warned me. "In the cat world, they love fantasy; they love stories." Moormann tells me that the "bird world"—yes, this apparent polymath has also judged birds—is "much more scientific." In the cat world, he said, "they love their frills and feathers." And anyway, he said, sternly, "The standard does not make the cat." But what makes the standard?

A simple, if not always so obvious, fact about cats is that they are a creation of human preference.

As soon as humans began to settle in the Fertile Crescent, some ten thousand years ago, mice and other vermin came calling. Wildcats came calling soon after, because where there were people, there were mice and rats. But humans wanted cats that were not too big (that is, dangerous). Here was our first selectively pressuring "like." As the writer Sue Hubbell has noted, rats got bigger in the company of men, but cats shrank.

Perhaps, some speculate, we liked the way they looked: the big round eyes, the large foreheads. But unlike dogs, which were bred for a variety of different tasks, cats already did what we wanted them to do—catch mice—with great efficiency (and, let us be honest, they probably did not have much inclination to take on any other tasks). And so the only selection pressures apart from size, as Leslie Lyons, a professor of veterinary medicine, notes, were aesthetic. Like looking through nature's version of the J. Crew catalog, we agonized over the color and length of the coat we desired.

Curiously, while a handful of different types of cats were long described, breeds only came to the fore with the nineteenth-century rise of the animal "fancy" in Victorian England. The word signaled that people were breeding animals not to serve some function but to their liking. From the first cat show, held at the Crystal Palace in 1871, a huge enterprise arose to create and determine ideal cat breeds. As Harrison William Weir, the artist, poultry breeder, and "father of the cat fancy," among other endowments, wrote in his 1889 book, *Our Cats and All About Them*, "Now that [the cat] is becoming 'a fancy' animal, there is no prophesying what forms, colours, markings, or other variations will be made by those who understand what can be done by careful, well-considered matching, and skilful selection."

But what made a good cat? What was careful, well-considered matching, and who decided, when not nature itself, what selection was skillful? Fanciers like Weir, sounding at times like interior decorators, laid out the aesthetic principles. For the "short-haired white cat," for example, he declared, "the eyes should be blue; green is a great defect; bright yellow is allowable . . . Orange gives a heavy appearance; but yellow will harmonise and look well with a gray-white." These "points," as they were called, carried "all the authority of a revelation," as the naturalist Walker Van Riper wryly observed.

With form essentially freed from function, breeders had a tabula rasa with a tail. The pedigreed animal, once more or less beneath notice, was a new lifestyle accessory exhibiting the anxious tendencies of the Victorians, with society in flux, to make granular class distinctions; animal breeding was a four-legged corollary of the "judicious mating" of humans called for by Francis Galton and other eugenicists (with dogs at times seeming to do double duty as proxies for human race theories). A dog could make the man, but man could also make the dog, with canines "up-bred" into class-appropriate companions. Take the bulldog. Far from noble sidekick, notes the historian Harriet Ritvo, it was darkly viewed as a fighting, "bullbaiting" dog with a "thirst for blood," "possessed of less sagacity" than the hounds. This formerly suspect breed could be genetically reformed, through careful breeding—even at the expense of its once functional traits—into a respectable member of polite canine and human society, the very hallmark of the English gentleman.

Then, as now, the animal fanciers argued over not only what made a certain animal a good example of breed X but what breed X actually was. In the case of the late nineteenth-century bulldog, as Ritvo writes, "almost any feature of the animal was open to debate." The "Dudley," or flesh-colored nose, was seen by some as the height of bulldogness. For others, it was an unbulldogly abomination.

The arguments were over human taste and had little to do with the bulldog. Hence the problem of trying to lay out, in a written standard, an animal's looks or essence. The judging organizations are well aware of the problems of standards, their guidebooks filled with cautionary advice. As a preface to the Cat Fanciers' Association show guidelines booklet declares, "The standard does not describe a living cat. It is an artistic ideal that is never completely attained."

Consider the Persian cat, one of the most striking examples of what happens when the shifting prerogatives of human taste are combined with the necessary vagaries of breed standards. The Persian is the Ur-animal in the fancy world. It was a Persian that took top honors at the Crystal Palace in 1871 at the first cat show. Queen Victoria herself owned a pair of blue Persians. One famous Persian, a chinchilla called Silver Lambkin, had an obituary in *The New York Times* ("in every country where cats are bred his progeny holds a leading position"). His remains are stored to this day in the British Museum.

But those Persians would not have been recognizable in Paris. To look at a Persian from the last century and one of today is to barely register the same animal. As Moormann told me, the whole cat had become "cobbier," cat-world talk for stocky. Its face is flatter, its nose much shortened, the whole package often squished into a small area, like an owl. It is not the image most of us would picture if asked to draw a cat. The worst of the lot, the so-called brachycephalic cats, are, as the *Journal of Feline Medicine and Surgery* admonishes, a "bastardisation of all the things that make cats special." Remarkably, these are not birth defects or aberrations but attributes that have been carefully selected throughout for generations of cats. And as much as the Persian has "undergone some remarkable changes," as Moormann wrote, the *"written standard has not changed much over time."*

So what happened? How did the cat in the flesh change so much more than the cat on paper? Talk to judges, and they struggle to explain it. "There are subtle changes," Vickie Fisher, the president of the International Cat Association, told me. "There's always this debate over whether breeders are leading the change, or is it what the judges are picking that leads to change?" Back when she was breeding Maine coons, "there were some cats that had come out with extremely tall ears. The standard says that the Maine coon is supposed to have a large ear." What is large? Ears are not measured to the millimeter. So big kept getting subtly bigger. Judges call it "overtyping"—taking a few characteristics of a breed to their extreme, to the detriment of the overall cat. Breeders can suffer "cattery blindness"; so enamored are they of their own cats that they fail to see how far they have strayed from the standard.

But if the standards per se were not encouraging the new-look Persians, what was? Was it their childlike, "Lorenzian" cuteness? Perhaps it was Lieberson's "ratchet effect" at work—an accidental mutation taking on a life of its own as a change in taste. Perhaps it was simple novelty. Louise Engberg, a Danish breeder of "traditional Persians," suggests that as these cats began to appear in show halls in force in the 1980s, "suddenly everyone wanted one." The fact that they were winning prizes, she says, implies that the "judges must have made quite a radical jump in the way they judge cats."

But cat breeds can change dramatically in a few generations. Why such radical change in a few decades, after a century of relative stasis? It could have been the continued influx of new breeds entering the show halls; the more breeds, Engberg told me, "the more people will say we need to distinguish our breeds compared to the others." As Vickie Fisher told me, the movement of people toward short-nosed Persians was not "something they do on purpose to hurt the cat. They just kind of keep going. They don't pull back."

In the language of Tversky, the anchor has shifted. The cat with the smushed face gradually becomes the "referent" against which other cats are judged. The first Persian with the shorter nose catches the eye of a judge and wins a prize; another breeder selects for a slightly shorter nose. The more the judges see of the new Persian, the more they get used to it, the more it no longer seems the new Persian.

Ironically, Persians have plummeted in popularity in recent years, as if all that extreme typing were too much a fleeting fashion trend. "A few years ago, at shows, 70 percent of cats were Persian," Moormann told me in Paris. "Now they are only perhaps 30 percent." Why? "It's the zeitgeist, what's in the mind. People didn't want to have this artificial thing anymore; they want to have more natural-looking cats." Persians, with their grooming regimens, among other things, are, in Fisher's words, "not for the faint of heart." One exception to this trend toward more natural cats, Moormann pointed out, is Russia. "In Russia, they love bold cats with strange ears or short legs. Very eccentric cats, not average. Because in Soviet times it was all average."

When I suggested to him that some of the cats, to my eyes at least, seem to have gravitated hopelessly far from those first enterprising mousers in the granary—far beyond the dictates of natural selection—he shrugged and said, "But what do you think about models in the fashion world? The gaps between the legs, where the upper leg is as thin as the lower leg. Do they look natural?"

The problems of standards are not limited to the excitable and noisome arenas of the animal fancy. Consider, for example, the seemingly sleepier world of soil judging. Admit it, you probably did not know there was a "world of soil judging." But soil judging is a common, and important, exercise used to assess the characteristics and quality of soil anytime it is used in great measure: to determine if a roadbed is sufficiently strong or if an agricultural plot is best for wheat or barley. At the collegiate level, there are teams, coaches, and even a national championship for soil judging; Virginia Tech and Kansas State University are the perennial powerhouses. A touch regrettably, to my mind, the contest is not known as the Dirt Bowl.

As James Shanteau, a retired professor of psychology at Kansas State University who has studied soil judges, among other types of experts, described it to me, sending soil samples to a national laboratory to be analyzed by machines is expensive and time-consuming. So a soil judge is brought in. Typically, the judge employs what is colloquially known as the "feel method"—sifting through the soil, patting it in his palm, spreading it around with water. The judge is trying to place it on the so-called soil triangle, a categorization of twelve soil types. Some judges, taking the concept of *terroir* to its limit, will actually put the soil in their mouths. "Not to taste it," Shanteau told me, "so much as to work it with their tongue and teeth, to feel for clay and sand."

You might similarly have seen a judge perusing an animal at a county fair and wondered just what he was looking at. The answer:

a lot. Previous studies of experts have noted that their decisions were made on the basis of one to six "dimensions" of information. Shanteau's research has found that livestock judges assessing gilts, or female pigs, use some *eleven* dimensions of information about the pigs, ranging from "ham thickness" to "freeness of gait." Crucially, unlike novices, they also know what information to leave *out*. And all this in a muddy ring of fidgety pigs. An attempt to create a computer model to mimic what judges do was foiled because, as he put it, "those damn pigs wouldn't hold still."

This is not to say judges are not prone to biases or irrelevant information. Shanteau was told by one livestock judge that certain judges seemed to like a curly tail on a pig. "Does a curly tail matter?" he asked. "He said, 'It just looks like what some people imagine a pig should look like.'" Some judges, he noted, admitted to finding "cuteness" in certain pigs. This brings to mind Edmund Burke's contention, in his essay, "Of the Sublime," that mere "fitness" is not sufficient for beauty. "On that principle," he wrote, "the wedge-like snout of a swine, with its tough cartilage at the end, the little sunk eyes, and the whole make of the head, so well adapted to its offices of digging and rooting, would be extremely beautiful."

While livestock judging, unlike the animal fancy, is theoretically not prone to shifts in taste—this is food, not fashion—the standard of the ideal pig has in fact shifted over the years as a result of human preferences. People now prefer much leaner pigs (to eat). The fattier hams seen in Shanteau's 1970s study are, as he put it, now "out of date," just as certain notions of desirable human shapes, as depicted in magazines, have fallen from favor over the years.

What makes a good judge? Confidence, for one. An expert, in Shanteau's view, is someone good at convincing others he or she is an expert. Good judges may make small errors, but they will "generally avoid large mistakes." When they encounter exceptions, experts are good at making "single-case deviations in their decision patterns." Novices, meanwhile, tend to stubbornly stick to rules, even when they are inappropriate.

The most important skill of a good judge, Shanteau told me, is extracting information. This, rather than some sage discriminatory ability, is the key to judging. Shanteau found that when novice judges were given detailed information about an animal, their judgments were virtually as good as the experts'. "The difference," he noted, "was that expert livestock judges could see patterns of information that novices could not."

As a simple example, I remember the astonishment I felt the first time a graphic designer pointed out to me the "vector," or arrow, in the FedEx logo (between the *E* and the *x*). I had never noticed it before; now I never fail to notice it. Was it always there, in my subconscious, making me think of the swiftness of FedEx? If an expert designer were to look at the logo, he could certainly tell me many things about its design, each broken down into established categories: the kerning (the space between the letters), the weight, the strokes.

We categorize things to help shape the world, but those categories in turn shape us; experts judge by criteria, but experts can, in effect, be judged *by* the criteria. The more we know, the more we categorize things; the more we can categorize things, the more we will know. The way an expert judge is different from you and me is that he sees and organizes the world—at least his particular part of it—differently.

Most of us operate most of the time at a fundamental threshold of abstraction that psychologists term the "basic level." When we perceive something, we tend to use these basic-level categories: *That store has a friendly cat. Did you see how fast that car was going? Would you like a glass of the red or the white?* But when you show a picture of a bird to the average person and then to an enthusiastic birder and ask them to identify it, chances are you will get two different answers: "a bird" and "a black-capped chickadee." The birder has gone to a "subordinate level" of classification. A judge would take this even further, examining the quality of the various points.

It is striking just how ingrained this way of looking at the world is. As the psychologists James Tanaka and Marjorie Taylor have shown, experts, in their area of expertise, do not seem to dwell much at the basic level. They can access subordinate knowledge *as fast as* basic categories. Veteran birders, for example, would know as many things that distinguished crows from robins as they would the things separating birds from dogs, and they could more quickly tell you a picture of a robin is not a sparrow than they can tell you it is not a *dog*.

Seeing the world informs their knowledge (and vice versa). But it is not enough. They need to talk about it.

SO YOU WANT TO BE AN EXPERT TASTER?
ON KNOWING WHAT'S ON THE TIP OF YOUR TONGUE

Quick, what does a carrot taste like?

Admit it, you probably had a hard time describing it. You might say it has a "bright" taste, though brightness per se is not an actual taste sensation. "Crunchy" might have crossed your mind, but that refers to texture. The color orange probably popped into your head. Again, this has nothing to do with its actual taste (and some carrots, of course, are not orange). You might say "vegetal," which could also describe many dozens of other . . . *vegetables.*

In the end, you may simply declare that it tastes "carroty" (and, just to reiterate the lessons of chapter 1, the *flavor* is carroty, not the taste—which is simply some proportion of sweet, salty, and so on). But this is not necessarily a cause for shame. For when one looks at the results of a number of studies in which expert panelists, trained in the sensory evaluation of carrots, have been asked to identify flavor attributes of carrots, sitting prominently on the list is *carroty.*

Sure, they go a bit better, adding descriptors like "piney" or "earthy" or "cloves." But even trained experts cannot seem to get around the idea that a carrot tastes like a carrot.

We have trouble talking about taste. Long before this was on the minds of people in the food industry, it vexed philosophers like John Locke. In his early *Essay Concerning Human Understanding,* after first noting how many smells "want names," he notes, "Nor are the different tastes, that by our palates we receive ideas of, much better provided with names. Sweet, bitter, sour, harsh and salt are almost all of the epithets we have to denominate that numberless variety of relishes."

At least some of this paucity, the historian of science Steven Shapin has argued, stems from the low regard with which taste was historically held. Taste was less an avenue for refined understanding of the pleasures of food than a mechanism for ensuring that what one was eating was palatable and safe.

There were always gourmands and food producers who had a more rarefied understanding of certain tastes, but in the twentieth century this became an applied science. As food became a global, industrialized, standardized product, with dizzying arrays of new products and flavors, and consumers were growing increasingly aware of concepts like *terroir* and provenance, methods were developed to bring a unified sensory understanding to food. So when a company sold an "apple-cinnamon oatmeal," there was some consensus on what "apple" meant. Not to mention that it would taste the same from coast to coast, from year to year.

While all the senses are deployed in sensory analysis, the end product in communicating those sensory experiences is, of course, language. The tongue rules taste, not simply via its taste buds. You cannot taste or smell precisely what someone else can taste or smell, but you can talk about it. One of the most popular techniques is known as "descriptive analysis," described by one textbook as "a sensory methodology that provides quantitative descriptions of products, based on the perceptions from a qualified group of subjects." Or, simply, groups of people sitting around trying to figure out what things taste like.

The result of this is any number of sensory "wheels" and lexicons, from whiskey to cheddar cheese. Things that might seem of a piece, like maple syrup, now have their own sensory wheels. Even carbonation has an entire dedicated lexicon, with scales for "bite, burn, and numbing." As one almond grower's report observed, sounding almost envious, "Although the sensory characteristics of peanuts are well documented, to date, no attempt had been made to quantify the appearance, aroma, flavor and textural characteristics of almonds." The aromatics of almonds, it turns out, range from "fresh cut lumber" to, rather defeatingly, "walnuts."

The ongoing quest to invent sensory language reaches back to another philosophical concept that troubled John Locke: namely, how to talk about the pineapple. The "royal" West Indies fruit had almost mythical status in England, its taste and appearance enticingly new in the late seventeenth century (a famous etching depicts the royal gardener John Rose grandly offering King Charles II the first pineapple grown in the country). People had not only not tasted anything like it before but never described anything like it before. What haunted the epistemologist Locke was the inability of words to convey what things actually tasted like. You needed the thing itself. The taster might compare pineapple to other things he had eaten, without coming any closer to its essence. "This is not giving us that idea by a definition," Locke wrote, "but exciting in us other simple ideas by their known names;

which will still be very different from the true taste of that fruit itself."
Indeed, Locke might have felt vindicated, centuries later, to see "fresh
pineapple" turn up in a *cheddar cheese* lexicon.

There are few entities in the world where the question of how things
taste, and what they taste like, looms larger than with the global flavoring giant McCormick. One day, I drove from my Brooklyn home to
suburban Baltimore to visit the company's headquarters and observe a
group of people at work who are, in essence, paid to taste.

As I pulled up, I detected a faint whiff of a spice that I could not quite
give a name to (John Locke, I feel your pain). When I met Marianne
Gillette, the company's vice president of applied research, she noted
that many old Baltimoreans, back when the company was based on the
waterfront, "associated the smell of Baltimore with McCormick."

Everyone "remembers the cinnamon," perhaps no surprise, because
not only is it a best-selling spice but, citing the company's internal
research on food and emotion, Gillette told me that "cinnamon is the
most loving spice." It is a virtual memory pathway—for many people,
one of the most potent smells of early childhood (I remember the oblong
white McCormick cinnamon tin in a way that I do not remember the
company's oregano). Although many of us may associate the McCormick
name with tins or bottles of spices, much of the company's business now
comes in providing "custom flavor solutions" for products higher up
the food chain. "We are in every aisle of the supermarket," Gillette told
me, and in any number of "quick-serve casual restaurants."

To visit the company's flavor laboratories is to see where the human
vagaries of flavor meet the certainties of hard science. As I spied a few
test tubes on a workbench, Silvia King, McCormick's white-coated
chief scientist, invited me to take a whiff. It smelled like tomato or,
more accurately, the smell that remains on your fingers after you touch
tomato leaves. "We had a customer come in who had a processed tomato
product," she told me, "that was really lacking in that fresh tomato
profile—where you pull it off the vine." And so, looking to add some
"top note"—the first thing you taste—McCormick's researchers have
at their disposal several thousands of molecules, each derived from natural compounds, to impart that fresh tomato flavor. These molecules

are added in ridiculously trace amounts. "This thiazole here," she said, pointing to a test tube, "one drop of that into an Olympic-size swimming pool would make that pool smell like a tomato plant."

To identify what is imparting that tomato flavor to tomato, the lab has any number of tools at its disposal. King pointed to a computer screen, across which bobbed jagged peaks. "This is a gas chromatogram; it's like a recipe to me. Every one of these peaks represents a specific compound." So you might blend the thiazole with dimethyl sulfide (which smells like creamed corn) or fennel ethyl alcohol (which smells like "roses or beer," King says) or isovaleric acids (chocolate and cheese). "Once you blend these," she said, "you can come up with a really wonderful top note," the very thing that often disappears as a tomato is cooked or ages. In the company's huge databases lurk the "molecular fingerprints that will distinguish Mexican from Israeli oregano."

The only problem with this machine knowledge of flavor is that humans are not machines. We do not taste something and provide, the way a refractometer would, a Brix number (the sugar content by percentage of weight in a liquid solution). Humans bring their own sensory and interpretive mechanisms to things. Seemingly minor changes in flavor have all kinds of ripple effects for humans, things machines would miss. Add a small amount of vanilla extract to low-fat milk, and the milk will suddenly seem, to the human taster, not only sweeter but creamier and thicker—even though vanilla extract does not actually change the sweetness, fat content, or viscosity.

Nailing down what a flavor actually means, to us, takes work. A customer will come to McCormick needing, as King noted, an avocado flavor. "They'll say, 'I don't even know where to start with developing this avocado flavor. I don't know whether I want a guacamole-type avocado or a freshly peeled avocado.'" The team will produce an entire range. At the consumer level, Gillette said, it gets even more confusing. "When a consumer says, 'I want avocado or guacamole,' they will have a very clear concept in their mind—which actually might not be avocado at all. It could be more like corn or the lime note in guacamole." Or an "anchor" guacamole they have every weekend at their favorite Mexican joint.

In a search for clarity, McCormick turns to what Gillette jokingly terms its "human chromatographs": trained sensory panelists. I joined

Jason Ridgway and Tess Aldredge, two of McCormick's senior sensory analysts, in a small room that faces, via a two-way mirror, a dimly red-lit room with a round table, around which a number of people were slowly nibbling pretzels from small paper cups. "They taste under red lights," Gillette had told me, "because if they taste two gravies and one is more brown than the other, our senses will say one is meatier and richer than the other." The absence of light and color makes the tasters' job harder, Aldredge said. "You don't get the bias of 'it's red, it's going to taste like strawberry.' You have to think it through. It's very taxing psychologically."

Ridgway flipped a switch, and audio from the other room filtered in, like a transmission from a distant spaceship. The panel's director was asking the panel about "persistence of crisp," which Ridgway defined for me as the "time to change in total quality during chewdown." A "persistence of crisp" scale was provided to the panelists, ranging from cornflakes all the way up to Pringles potato chips. He asked, "Is anybody else getting the burnt-like pieces?"

Then someone uttered the word "musty," which caught my ear. What does mustiness have to do with pretzels, and does anyone actually want a musty pretzel? "One thing to keep in mind when you hear terminology like musty or burnt," Ridgway told me, "is that they're describing the product. It's not a negative thing to have a musty or burnt note." Aldredge added, "Musty shows up in a lot of products. Often they'll describe these little water samples"—she pointed to one of the palate-cleansing paper cups—"as slightly musty." "They can usually tell when we need to change the filters on the filtration systems," said Ridgway. Even though mustiness does actually stem from a chemical compound—alpha-Fenchyl alcohol—Ridgway says a term like "musty"—or "wet dog" or "dirty socks"—is meant to be a bit more "user-friendly." He cautioned that "everybody has a slightly different interpretation of what musty is; you hear everything from a wet basement to old books." Aldredge chimed in, "Mine is hose water."

Words must be chosen carefully: The mere presence of a sensory descriptor ("fresh pineapple") may be enough to suggest its actual presence in the food (cheddar cheese), leading panelists to look for "phantom" attributes that are not really there, sending testers down a false path—or consumers down a path they may not want to travel. "We've done things before where somebody might say, 'I like that cheese,' and we go through and describe it, using all the descriptors, and all of a sudden they realize, 'Hey, this really does smell a lot like baby vomit.' They may not even use that cheese at home anymore." Every food is transformed. Onions have a "rubbery note." Mango exudes sulfur. "A really good papaya," says Gillette, "has a distinct aroma of garbage to it." (Note to self: If forced to eat garbage, think of papayas.)

Perhaps unsurprisingly, given the language on offer, the one question you will never hear asked in a sensory panel is the one we would probably first ask upon tasting: Do you like it? One problem is that expressing liking or disliking is liable to change the way sensory analysts experience the product. Also, expert tasters often tend to not *like* the same things as nonexpert tasters (that is, consumers). The title of one study, in *The Australian Journal of Dairy Technology*, says it all: "Cheese Grading Versus Consumer Acceptability: An Inevitable Discrepancy."

Introducing preference introduces noise. As the influential food scientist Harry Lawless puts it, "You would not ask a gas chromatograph or a pH meter whether it liked the product, so why ask your analytical descriptive panel?" If you ask panelists to identify whether product A or B has more salt, and then which one they prefer, what do you do when people guess the wrong way on the salt test? Is their hedonic judgment still valid? Then there is the problem that not everyone likes the same thing or likes it for the same reasons. An early version of McCormick's spice lexicon had a category for "off" notes, including "soapy" for cilantro. But casting soapy in this pejorative light rather ignores the idea that soapiness is part of the very *nature* of cilantro. Sensory lexicons go out of their way to avoid words that might connote quality or that may mean different things to different people. A lot of stereotypical "wine talk"—words like "well-rounded" or "chewy"—is not included in wine's professional sensory lexicon.

Another issue is that sensory testing does not happen in environments where food is actually consumed. Something that seems good enough in a small sample in a lab setting may be less appealing at the dinner table. You can break down the sensory profile of a soft drink in the lab, as Nancy Farace, McCormick's food insights manager, told me, but released into the wild, into consumers' hands, it may become a different beast. "How's the consumer going to drink it? Will they put it over ice? At thirty-two degrees? Will it be in a plastic cup, a glass cup, or in a can, or through a lid with a straw? What might they eat beforehand? Afterwards? It's not only knowing what they like but how and when they'll consume it." Simply asking people if they like something, as the Dutch food researcher E. P. Köster has pointed out, puts them suddenly on alert: They "taste more attentively and judge probably on different criteria than when they just eat it." On the other hand, asking average consumers to think more analytically may interfere with how they implicitly feel.

In short, in the food industry at least, you generally do not want to know *what* experts like (because most consumers probably won't like it), and you do not want to probe too deeply about *why* consumers like something (because they won't be able to explain it in useful terms). Take coffee. Bitterness is the essential thing that people like about coffee *as a sensory attribute*, as Moskowitz had told me, but you would never want to use the word to sell it. But if the ultimate goal is to sell things that most people will actually like, why bother with this rarefied sensory testing by people whose powers of discrimination are pitched at such a higher frequency? As Gillette described it, one reason is to calibrate sensory compounds with consumer taste. Instead of going to panels with fifty vanillas and trying to figure out which ones consumers might like, you can analyze the flavor profiles of the things they actually like and use that as a starting point for making new products.

Gillette had cautioned me that sensory experts were people whom "you didn't want to go to lunch with." And yet there we were, in a McCormick canteen, eating udon noodles with katzu and oregano, among other flavor-forward delicacies. As a trained panelist, she said, "you're really sensitive to aging and oil. An oil starts to go bad after a little bit; the consumer will be happily eating something that we would consider rancid, and wouldn't even notice it." Aldredge told me she will suddenly stop eating during a meal. "Your friends are like, 'Why did you stop eating?' You say, 'I really don't want to talk about it.' And then they're really interested."

The golden-tongued gourmet, or the flavoring industry "nose," with superhuman powers to divine dozens of discrete compounds lurking in things that to us seem an undifferentiated mass, has long been an alluring cultural figure. Brillat-Savarin, in *The Physiology of Taste*, talks of the "gourmands of Rome" who "could tell by the flavor whether fish was caught between the city bridges or lower down the river." In *Don Quixote*, Sancho Panza—himself possessing a "great natural instinct in judging wines," virtually a heritable trait in his family—tells a story of two of his relatives, challenged by villagers to describe the characteristics of a cask of wine: "The one tried it with the tip of his tongue, the other only smelled it; the first said the wine tasted of iron; the second said, it had rather a taste of goat's leather." The vintner protested his cask was clean. When it came time to empty the cask, a small key, with a small leather thong attached, came tumbling out.

But we should be wary of people reeling off ornate wine or coffee descriptions: Our ability to correctly identify particular odors in a complex, blended mixture, for example, begins to hit a "ceiling" at three. Beyond that, tests have shown, people become worse than chance at picking out correct aromas.

As for that "great natural instinct" of Sancho Panza, talk to sensory experts, and they will dismiss the idea of innate talent. As an aspirant master sommelier said in the 2013 documentary *Somm*, "A great samurai sword maker is someone who had a teacher. We think about this with wine and think that someone must be a natural. But we never think that someone is just a natural at making swords." "Honestly," Aldredge confessed, "I don't think I can taste better. I just know what I'm tasting and can describe it." Surely, there are individual differences in sensitivity, which often come into play on the panels. Tasters also need basic levels of ability, like being able to pass a "triangle test"; that is, which of these three things is not like the other two? But the real key to becoming an expert taster is not being born with a gifted tongue.

The secret—and it is no secret—is those things we have already discussed with our other experts. First, practice: McCormick's experts have roughly 150 hours of training before they get onto a panel. A sample question they are asked before being accepted is, "Are you willing to eat safe but unpleasant foods?" The importance of practice, versus some unwavering innate ability, has been shown in a number of studies in which experts, trained on one set of stimuli, are then given a new set. They do not do as well identifying and matching the new flavors. Or they simply transfer terms they know from another set, even when inappropriate.

Second, memory: To know that a pretzel has a roughly Ritz cracker–like "persistence of crisp" requires remembering the crispiness of a Ritz

cracker. To say a carrot has a hay-like flavor aromatic means remembering the smell of hay. Studies comparing expert with novice wine tasters
have generally found that what experts are best at is not the *absolute
detection* of odors in wines but the *recognition* of odors in wines. When
the odors were unfamiliar, experts and novices did almost equally well
at detecting their presence.

Perhaps most important, there is language. Going back to John
Locke, you could not use words to adequately understand how a pineapple tastes if you had never had one. Once you actually tasted the
pineapple, however, language could help you unlock what you were
actually tasting. Tasters sometimes talk about a kind of feedback loop
in which the more you taste, the more words you come up with, which
then unlocks more flavors. How much of the flavor of mint comes from
the word "minty" itself?

Language and memory are inexorably intertwined when it comes
to taste expertise. An Australian study tested wine experts and novices
on their ability to recall lists of wine words that "provided a consistent
description of a variety of wine." They were given sets of cards with
typical sensory descriptors for wines (alas, they were not offered the
actual wines). The Riesling, for example, had a "mineral and lime" palate, a "crisp with flowers" nose. Then the subjects were given shuffled
sets of sensory words, which no longer seemed to describe any one
wine. The experts were actually able to recall *fewer* wine words than
novices when the words were shuffled, much as a chess expert's superior
memory for chess positions seems to evaporate when the pieces are
random—not the familiar patterns seen in thousands of games.

Wine experts and sommeliers internalize a certain way of talking
about wine, generally based on a "taste grid" that lists a wine's qualities
in a very particular order—not unlike the familiar strategies employed
by a chess master. The *ordering* of these words becomes so dominant
in memory that the words themselves, when encountered outside those
familiar combinations, become less memorable. In any case, the words
are as important as tasting itself.

We might think of a wine-tasting panel as a group of people sitting
around, sniffing and aspirating their way through wines, then trying to
summon the mysterious secrets lurking within through colorful language. What is usually happening is rather the opposite. Wine experts
first consider a wine's category (for example, New Zealand sauvignon

blanc), summon a prototypical version of that wine, then look for things in the wine that match their memory of the prototype. It is far easier to recognize, say, the aroma of wine when one has a sense of what one is looking for. As the psychologist Sylvie Chollet and colleagues note, "think and sniff" is a better strategy for correctly identifying odors than "sniff and think."

Wine experts think *so* prototypically, in fact, that when you tamper with wine in interesting ways, it can backfire. When the sensory scientist Rose Marie Pangborn added flavorless red food coloring to white wine, it was wine experts—not novices—who suddenly declared it sweeter. "Possibly," noted Pangborn, "through their familiarity with sweet rosé wines." The wine experts' knowledge colored their taste, just as the substance colored the wine.

Maybe we want to ascribe natural talent to expert tasters because of the trouble we have, in tasting the very same products, "seeing" the things they are seeing. As the professor of philosophy Barry Smith notes, this discrepancy invites a dilemma: "Either the aromas and flavours of a wine are there for all to recognize, or there are flavours and aromas available only to those who enjoy particular taste sensations, who have special sensory equipment, as it were." By now, it should be clear that the answer is largely the former. Taste is less a gift than an outcome. It is less what you have than what you do with it.

Most of us do not do so much with it. In general, we skim across the surface of the sensory world, and taste is no different. The "acoustic ecologist" Murray Schafer once observed that to really hear, you needed to retrain the way your brain processed sound. His suggested training exercises ranged from closing one's eyes to help purge distractions to trying to craft an "onomatopoeic" name for a sound (an echo here of using language to try to describe flavors). But we typically consume food or drink with any number of distractions, with little or no language for what is going on in our mouths. Most of what we learn and remember about that food is "incidental," often beneath consciousness.

Samuel Renshaw, an Ohio State University psychologist, was known for creating a training system to help American soldiers during World War II more readily recognize enemy planes and ships. But he also worked with a distillery to improve its tasters' ability to detect variations in its products. Renshaw argued that most of us manage, in daily life, something "on the order of twenty percentile utilization of the sense modalities." Do we have a hidden reserve of discriminatory abilities, waiting to be deployed with the right training or under the right conditions?

In a fascinating Dutch study, subjects were asked to pick out the 1.4-percent-fat milk they usually favored from a sample of five milks with varying fat content. Few could do it reliably; all options seemed similar to their "own" milk. But when a different group was given the same milk, and this time asked to pick out their authentic "Dutch" milk from a group of what they were told were cheaper, lower-quality foreign imports, panelists suddenly became much better at choosing the 1.4 percent milk. People were suddenly *motivated* to detect differences (*How dare you replace my milk with this cheap foreign stuff!*). This emotional response "unlocked" implicit preferences that were there all along. The implication of this experiment is that our very own preferences are often hidden from us (*We are strangers to our taste*) and that simply asking us what we like may provide hardly a clue.

As I was talking over the sensory attributes of pretzels with the experts at McCormick, my attention somehow drifted to a can of Dr Pepper, one of a number of drinks offered on a nearby table. Like Locke with his pineapple, I realized that I did not have a good sense of what the flavor of Dr Pepper was, nor, admittedly, had I invested much thought in it. My thought was that it tastes "like Dr Pepper." How would I describe its various qualities to someone who had never had one? Clearly, the company uses this epistemological murk to its advantage, prominently advertising "23 flavors" right on the can. This invokes an appetizing mystery: What could those flavors be? Surely 23 is better than 11!

That mystery indeed informs the heritage of the brand. In the 1960s, the perception of Dr Pepper, notes Joseph Plummer, was riddled with misconceptions: It was medicinal or made from prune juice. But the company was able to turn the eccentricities of this brown not-tasting-of-cola drink into strengths. By the early 1970s, it was the country's fourth most popular soft drink. Not being able to identify a precise flavor can actually be a strength. As Howard Moskowitz had suggested to me, part of the popularity of Coca-Cola versus, say, an orange soda is its more complex flavor blend. Consumers tire of it less quickly than of an orange soda, which has a simpler, more recognizable profile (which might be "easier to like" on the first go-round). The more you can identify any one flavor, Moskowitz said, the more it sits in memory and thus is easier to remember.

As it happens, I am agnostic on Dr Pepper. It is not something I generally seek out, nor is it something I would reflexively avoid. Whatever my level of liking, it is a feeling for the thing *as a whole*, instead of an analytical distribution of various sensory and trigeminal attributes. My feelings may be partially informed by exposure. Dr Pepper has a southern regional identity, and not having been raised in the South, I have not had as many chances to consume it. But could it be a lack of appreciation as well? If I knew more about Dr Pepper, would I like it more?

It occurred to me: What better time than sitting with a bunch of sensory experts to have a taste test? "Let's train Tom on the aromatics of Dr Pepper," Gillette announced. I bring the glass to my nose. "What does it smell like to you?" Ridgway asked. "If you can't describe it, what does it remind you of?" There was something, but it evaded me. I could almost *feel* some frustrated synapse waiting to be fired that would connect my sensory machinery to my memory. Gillette, sensing my struggle, put her nose to the glass. "I smell something that isn't a beverage. It's something that I love to eat for dessert." An image shimmered at the edge of my mind. "It's always tough when you don't have the language first," Ridgway said, consoling me. Gillette gently asked me if she could help. "It reminds me of burgundy cherry ice cream. The vanillin, the creamy note, the black cherries."

It was as if a door had been opened. I smelled it again, and there it was, hanging like a sign right in front of me; how could I have missed it? I clearly knew the smell; this was no Lockean pineapple. Did I have some memory of what I thought it was, and did it take that terminology to bring forth the memory? Odor is famously talked about as a strongly evocative triggering mechanism for memory (particularly when the smell is unpleasant). But what triggers the memory for odors?

Science is rather divided on whether words (that is, "semantic mediation") are essential in triggering odor memories or whether smell memory fundamentally works on its own. Regardless, it struck me as curious that I could be having this clear sensation, smelling Dr Pepper, knowing that it was not Coca-Cola or 7UP but not really knowing what it was. How much of life itself comprises this sensory sleepwalking, these subconscious perceptions? How different is this sensation from hearing a piece of music from an unrecognizable genre or not being able to make out something in the distance with our eyes?

Paying too much attention could drive you crazy, I thought as we compared tasting notes. "I thought it was pruney," Aldredge said. Someone else countered, "I went nonfood—mulch." "Ah!" Gillette said, eyebrows raised. "There are some earthy notes," Aldredge said. "It's woody." A bit sheepishly, I proffered, "Some clove?" "Maybe," Ridgway responded evenly. In any case, no one in the room was going to nail all twenty-three flavors; remember the finding that people begin to peak after identifying three compounds. We were talking about flavor, using language to unlock our senses, forging new memories—and thus future tastes—in the process. As Gillette told me, "You will never experience Dr Pepper the same way again."

WHAT'S YOUR FAVORITE BEER? ON KNOWING WHAT TO LIKE

I was intrigued by the aesthetically minded, theoretically objective judgments on display at the cat show and, by contrast, the rigorous, detached sensory analysis of the "human instruments" at McCormick. These seemed to represent two sides of the human brain. I wondered what happens when you effectively combine these two pursuits; that is, when you try to make a qualitative judgment of something that you have put in your mouth.

And so I headed to Denver, Colorado, where, in the basement-level conference rooms of a large hotel, judging was under way for the Great American Beer Festival (GABF)—the Super Bowl of the American craft beer renaissance. There, in a vast "staging room," I found the festival's director, Chris Swersey, standing in the center of a sea of stouts and *saisons*, all precisely chilled to thirty-eight degrees, waiting to be poured, randomized, and dispatched to panels in the neighboring rooms. Speed was of the essence. "In twenty minutes' time, those samples will taste totally different," he said as he scanned the room.

As Swersey—middle-aged, goateed, and, like many of the beer people I seemed to meet, extremely affable and engaged—described it, the judging at GABF is a sort of "tweener." "We're not 100 percent subjective or 100 percent objective," he told me. A purely objective judging would hew strictly to the standards, with precise measures of IBUs (or International Bitterness Units) and "final gravity." This sounds like something astronauts experience, but in beers it refers to the liquid's density at fermentation, measured in "degrees Plato." As Garrett Oliver, the brewmaster of Brooklyn Brewery, had told me, beer people tend to talk like scientists—"here's our EBV, here's our IBU, our final gravity"—while the "wine guy is talking about rolling hills."

A purely subjective judging, by contrast, would see judges going down a list of a dozen beers and expressing liking. "You might give it a one because you love apricot," says Swersey, "or you hate it because you don't like apricot." Some judging styles are more pleasure based. In some beer competitions in England, for example, judges are asked questions like "Would you go out of your way to drink this beer?"*

The judging in Denver was held under the usual strict secrecy. Judges with mobile phones have been asked to leave. Swersey, going against usual GABF protocol, has allowed me to sit in and briefly observe—but not record or take notes on—the judging for the American-style stout category. The first thing he wants me to know is that beer judges do not spit. This is not because zythologists inherently lack willpower. "There are taste buds down below your Adam's apple that are highly attuned to hop components," Swersey told me. "It's proven in the research: You have to swallow it to get a full profile of that beer." Swallowing is only a small part of the whole process. Aroma, for Swersey, is the first step. "Aromas are very ethereal, they tend to disappear, and then you'll get a whole new suite later. You have to get on that beer fast and capture what you're smelling."

As we joined the stout panel and I began listening to their comments, it seemed like a more jocular and opinionated version of the McCormick sensory panel. There is similar descriptive language: "condensed milk," "solventy," "burnt vegetables," or, my favorite, "I wouldn't call it horse blanket." This is joined, however, by more expressive comments like "pretty amazing," "really clear," or, simply, "I just like that beer." Watching the panelists, I am reminded of something James Shanteau, the psychologist of expertise, had implied to me: Experts are people who have the same opinions as other experts. The panels here, Swersey

---

* This question to my mind needs one more piece of information: Just how far is "out of the way"?

said, are not about taste tyrants imposing their will but about finding carefully considered consensus on what beers best represent the particular style guidelines. "I don't really like conversations that go like this: 'Well, I was in Belgium last month, and I tasted this and this and this, and this doesn't taste like any of those.'"

While a beer competition might seem a world away from the Paris cat show, all the same issues are in play. There is the phenomenon of changing standards. Consider IPA, or India pale ale. Pale ales, as one of the stronger ales, are in general prized for their hoppy (that is, bitter) character. This in itself is a hallmark of beer connoisseurship. An interesting study by the Stanford University computer scientists Julian McAuley and Jure Leskovec examined review data on the popular Web site RateBeer.com. One of the ways you could distinguish novice reviewers from expert reviewers, they found, was that expert reviewers' opinions, as I have mentioned, tend toward concurrence. In certain genres of beers, however, expert and novice reviews almost *entirely* diverged. As they write, "Beginners give higher ratings to almost all lagers, while experts give higher ratings to almost all strong ales." And while no one really cares much for Bud Light on the site, experts *really* dislike it. Strong ales, apart from being an "acquired taste," indicate where you stand in relation to beer, the way the Velvet Underground became a totemic marker of one's musical taste.

The question of what an India pale ale is might seem settled. "In its heyday," Brooklyn's Oliver told me, "IPA was probably the most specific thing ever created; it was made to survive a sea voyage from England to India. It was always made dry, always bitter, always pale." But time, and the market, move on; to Oliver's distaste, there are now brews like the seemingly paradoxical Black IPA. In the staging room in Denver, Swersey poured me a glass of Mojo IPA, from Colorado's Boulder Beer. "This is a really hoppy IPA," says Swersey. "It's got Amarillo hops, which has a really intense grapefruit taste." There were also notes of spruce. "A lot of the same compounds in hop oil," he noted, "are identical to what you would have in a spruce tree." All this certainly seems to hew to the GABF standard for American-style India pale ale: "Hop aroma is high, exhibiting floral, fruity, citrus-like, piney, resinous, or sulfur-like American-variety hop characters."

But he suddenly snapped to quizzical attention. "They entered it as a strong pale ale," he says, referring to another GABF category, with less alcohol content. "They under-entered it." It was like putting a heavyweight boxer in the middleweight division. Perhaps, Swersey mused, Mojo IPA is actually in the American strong pale ale range (even if it has been marketed as an IPA). What is more likely is that the entire IPA landscape has shifted; everything got hoppier, more bitter. What was once a perfectly respectable IPA suddenly seems, by the rest of the entrants in the category, to be a pale imitation. "This beer is about seven or eight years old," he said. "IPAs may have grown up around them, past them."

Like the Persian cats, the product has gradually been getting more extreme, even if the same written standard still seems to apply. Consider one of the seminal American-style IPAs, Sierra Nevada Pale Ale, which was first brewed in the early 1980s and is now one of the country's most popular craft brews. "Back in the day," Swersey said, "it was a groundbreaking beer. It was unlike anything being made anywhere on earth. It really challenged people." While he says Sierra is still the beer that he, and other brewers he knows, "always keep in the fridge," it is "far out in the weeds" compared with Mojo; that is, it seems like pale ale with training wheels. Just by bittering units alone, the change is dramatic: Sierra Nevada has thirty-eight, while Mojo has seventy.

Categories set the entire landscape for liking. Even large, mainstream beers like Budweiser and Pabst Blue Ribbon, the less intensely flavored, more industrially produced brews that the craft movement essentially defines itself against, have their own category at GABF: American-style lager ("hop flavor is none to very low"; "corn, rice, or other grain or sugar adjuncts often used"). I found this a bit odd, as if the Sundance Film Festival had a category for "Big Hollywood Summer Action Flick." But it just reinforces the power of categories. Before you can determine whether something is good, you have to define good as *what?*

There are many people who would view something like Budweiser as not "real" beer. And there are many more people who actually drink Budweiser. The management professors David Choi and Martin Stack argue that the U.S. beer market has become "locked in a sub-optimal equilibrium in which most consumers are not familiar with the full range of what beer is and can be." Why? Prohibition, for one. People simply *forgot* the taste of beer. Post-Prohibition lagers, perhaps influenced by soft drinks, were higher in carbonation and made from gradually shrinking amounts of malt and hops. They literally lost their taste. The second factor was a post-Prohibition switch from draft beer to bottles and cans and a related insistence on serving beer "ice cold" (which "deadens" the taste). Over time, "consumers began to associate 'beer' with an increasingly narrow range of product characteristics." Why bother switching beers if the beer you were drinking was good enough, if it *was* beer? GABF, simply by having a category for this kind of beer, could get around the entire sticky question.

In beer (and in cats), I kept running into an endless loop of circularity. *What is a good beer? A good beer is one that best represents the standard. What makes the standard? Those things that people think make a beer good.* Repeat. And something else: *A good beer is one that best represents the standard. Then why did the standard change? Because people's thought of what a good beer was changed. Does that mean that what was once a good beer is no longer a good beer?*

Could there be a universally good beer—or cat? The philosopher Immanuel Kant, in his *Critique of Judgment*, suggested that our liking of merely "agreeable" things like wine (or beer or cats) was hopelessly subjective:

> A violet color is to one soft and lovely, to another dull and faded. One man likes the tone of wind instruments, another prefers that of strings. To quarrel over such points with the idea of condemning another's judgment as incorrect when it differs from our own, as if the opposition between the two judgments were logical, would be folly. With the agreeable, therefore, the axiom holds good: every one has his own taste (that of sense).

Taste judgment, Kant said, can only be "pure so far as its determining ground is tainted with no merely empirical delight." And so while the cat show or beer festival judges were, in one sense, acting in a "disinterested" Kantian fashion, suspending their own preferences for the sake of a larger set of criteria, the very fact that they had put criteria on the things they were judging, for Kant, rendered their judgments suspect. To fix these "rules"—"like all empirical rules, general only, not universal"—on the beauty of a human, a building, or a horse, argued Kant, is to "presuppose a concept of the end that determines what the thing should be, hence a concept of its perfection, and is thus merely adherent beauty." As the philosopher Matt Lawrence puts it, para-phrasing what Kant *might* have said about beer, "There is something about these beers themselves that makes them great." Not because of the reasons someone says they are great.

What Kant was trying to do, in his famously thorny and "forbid-ding" text, notes the Kant scholar Christian Wenzel, was to resolve the very dilemma I sensed was cropping up in the notion of shifting aesthetic standards: *Was taste subjective or objective?* "On the one hand," Wenzel notes, "the pleasure involved in a judgment of taste cannot be completely subjective. Otherwise, the claim that everyone should agree could never be justified; such a claim could not even arise and there would not be any quarrel in matters of taste."

So people cannot simply describe a cat or beer as good, for what would that mean, and how would we know which one was better? But "the grounds for pleasure in aesthetic contemplation cannot be com-pletely objective either," notes Wenzel, "because then quarrels in mat-ters of taste could be settled in a scientific fashion (as in physics)." A machine could tell you which beer was better. Taste—capital-*T* taste, the sort that conveys a judgment on what you are tasting—seems to occupy some hazy middle ground. What the apparatus of judging seems to do is to give people a way to talk about taste without really talking about taste, or at least anybody's *individual* taste.

So what is a good beer? I put the question to a small group of judges at the end of the festival's first day after they had endured many rounds of tasting. Appropriately—or curiously, perhaps—the conversation took place over beers, pilsners from Left Hand Brewing. "Judging takes a lot of concentration," Jamie Floyd, the tattooed, spiky-haired, and per-petually energetic owner of Ninkasi Brewing, based in Eugene, Oregon, told me. "It is good to have a nice clean pilsner in front of you."

What the judges first wanted me to know was that as analytical as they tried to be, at the end of the day they are humans, with human predilections. "We start out trying to be very objective, judging to these parameters of the style of criteria," said Brad Kraus, the rangy, cowboy-hat-wearing *maestro cervecero* at the Panamanian brewer La Rana Dorada. "But you have to be a little subjective, otherwise a machine could do this." A beer might hit all of the style guidelines, but was it actually a good beer? "Our brewery has an analytical lab and a sensory lab," added Floyd. "We have both of them—because lab equipment doesn't drink beer."

While Shanteau had told me one of the hallmarks of experts was convincing others they were experts, I sensed that the judges were surprisingly forthcoming in their own insecurity. I had noted that the setup of the stout judging panel had felt to me like a poker game: people grouped around a circular table trying to look as innocuous as possible as they studied what was in front of them (the beers are shuffled so facial gestures do not give away their "hand").

Fal Allen, brewmaster of Anderson Valley Brewing Company, bearded and with a scholarly mien, said judges often begin by pointing out flaws. This may be because flaws are detected first by the human sensory apparatus. But there is also the idea that it may be easier to point out flaws than to defend vaguely positive qualities. "I said that today—'I *like* this beer.' Someone said, 'Yeah, what do you like about it?' And I thought, 'Oh, now I am going to have to explain myself in front of these experts—am I going to say something stupid?' Sometimes it's easier to just pick out the bad things."

If there are any number of ways to be swayed at the judging table—by the beer you had before, by the temperature of the room or of the drink, by what every judge seems to be saying—in the real world the question of why we are liking a beer at any one moment is infinitely complex. Indeed, it may have little to do with the beer itself. Judges drink in a way that no one else does: anonymously, in relatively small amounts, paying attention only to what is being consumed, not for pleasure but with a purpose. Judges will eat a piece of chocolate or sniff their arms to "reset" their palates between brews; who does that in a bar? "When you're in a crowded bar, that beer can get away with a lot," Floyd said. "There's music, there's people you're attracted to, there's odors, there's bad karaoke. You could have a beer three or four times and have a pretty mellow impression of it. But then you're in a situation when you're really focusing on it, and you're like, 'What did I ever like about that beer?'"

The week before, I tell the judges, I had downed a dollar can of Pabst Blue Ribbon at a ramen restaurant in Brooklyn. I had probably not had a Pabst since college nor felt compelled to seek one out. But Pabst, through a rather accidental process, has enjoyed, beginning in the first decade of the twenty-first century, spectacular growth—in 2009, it posted a 25.9 percent increase in sales—so much so that its price a few years later in local bars was actually *rising*. Its popularity, as the writer Rob Walker has chronicled, seems to have been driven by a peculiar, law-of-supply-and-demand-subverting combination of low price, relative scarcity, and a discreet marketing campaign that had tried to seize upon the beer's perceived "authenticity" without alienating the longtime drinkers who lent it that authenticity. Its actual taste, at least judged by the thousands of people who have weighed in on RateBeer .com, is described in grudging, almost apologetic terms: "a decent lawn mower beer"; good "for standing in the crowd at a concert"; the "perfect college student brew, to drink while cranking out an essay." For the record, Pabst has actually won the American Light Lager category at GABF, but one judge told me, fairly snickering, "How could it not?"

But drinking the Pabst had left me wondering: What did it mean to drink a blander beer when there were so many others out there? Was I able to enjoy it "for what it was" by calibrating my top-down expectations accordingly? And how does this differ from the experience of a regular Pabst drinker who is suddenly served a craft beer, the likes of which he had never had? Is sensory pleasure only experienced in relation to knowledge, or could it flourish on its own? The most naive response is to think that the non-craft consumer would be immediately transported by the inherently superior taste, that he would suddenly think, "My God, why have I been drinking that other stuff all my life?"

One occasionally encounters the phrase "gateway beer" in the craft world. It is the beer that first "got you into" beer, a starter brew: not too extreme, perhaps a more robust version (with better ingredients) of something you might have already drunk. Once, this might have been Heineken; now maybe it is Sam Adams. Simply drinking a gateway beer, however, is unlikely to set one off on the road to connoisseurship.

Because the power of top-down conditioning will have primed him on what to expect, and thus like, in a beer, the drinker may simply be unable to enjoy a novel or strange brew *as* beer. Our senses do not respond well to violated expectations. "If you give someone a Guinness for the first time," says Fal Allen, "they're not going to be prepared for what that's going to be. They taste it and go, 'Whoa, what's going on?' You should say, 'It's not going to be like your beer. It's going to be chocolaty, and you should look for the espresso note.' When they taste it, they're more open to it." The presentation, Floyd added, must not be "about changing your life." Do not slam down the expensive Trappist ale and declare, as he puts it, *"I'm never going to see a Coors can in your house after this!* That's not really going to work out so well."

But what happens when the drinker passes through the gateway? In a discussion of the philosophical concept *qualia*—"the way things seem to us"—the philosopher Daniel Dennett speaks of two hypothetical coffee tasters working at Maxwell House. After six years' work, they secretly confess to each other that they no longer like the coffee. But they disagree on *why*. One says his standards have changed and that he is a better judge of coffee. He no longer likes the taste of Maxwell House. The other thinks something in his perceptual system has changed: The "coffee doesn't taste to me the way it used to." If it did, he would still like it. Dennett concludes that "we may not be able to settle the matter definitely," and perhaps, as with the idea of the "flavor object," there is something to both explanations: Some "internal brain image" of the coffee is interacting, across a number of neural networks, with the body's sensory receptors. How could one's standards not change if one's senses had changed (they get "more" from the coffee), and how could changing one's standards not change one's senses (to look for something "more")?

Whatever has happened to the coffee tasters, something changed. Which raises the question, per the gateway beer, of what happens when you go "back." When I drank the Pabst, did I enjoy it? If yes, was I enjoying it for the way it tasted now? Or was it knowing how much money I was saving; the curious hipster aura it possessed; or perhaps even feeling temporarily liberated from the *work* and weight of connoisseurship, of just indulging in the simpler tastes?

The brewmaster Garrett Oliver, a devoted gourmand, had told me during our talk that if someone had walked in bearing a bag of White Castle cheeseburgers, "I could demolish, like, ten of them. My opinion is not very high of White Castle cheeseburgers, but this does not alter the fact that when I was kid, this was one of the best things you could ever eat." But it will never taste as good as he remembers. As Dennett says, when we revisit childhood spaces (our bedroom, our backyard), they seem so much smaller. Our memory fails our current standard for what is big and what is small. You cannot drink that Pabst the way you once did, any more than you can currently inhabit your childhood room in the body and mind of the child you were.

But having gone through that gateway, is one just presented with an endless, Escher-style series of ever more gateways? Do people become happier because they are able to experience more kinds of beers, more kinds of pleasures, or do they risk a hedonic hangover? "In Oregon, 38 percent of all draft beer is craft," Floyd observed. "There's a lot of knowledge out there. There's also a lot of really unhappy beer lovers. They don't have anything nice to say anymore. The only reflection they have about beer now is about what isn't perfect to them anymore. I think sometimes this can happen: They become so biased about what is right that they lose focus about what they got excited by to begin with."

It is an open question as to who is happier: the person who only drinks one beer (even one that is judged to be merely adequate) and is barely aware of the beers he is missing, or the questing connoisseur who has drunk almost everything and might be aware that the thing he is drinking in the moment is not the best thing out there. Brad Kraus suggested a pragmatic, middle-ground strategy that seemed, in its humble way, to be a grand strategy for a happy life: "People often ask me, 'What's your favorite beer?' I don't have *a* favorite beer. I usually say it's the one in my hand. It's what sounded good to me."

TASTING NOTES

HOW TO LIKE

The picture of taste I have presented is hardly reassuring. We often do not seem to know what we like or why we like what we do. Our preferences are riddled with unconscious biases, easily swayed by contextual and social influences. There is less chance than we think that we will like tomorrow what we liked today and even less chance of remembering what led us to our previous likes. Even experts, as we have just seen, are hardly infallible guides to knowing what is truly good, to knowing their own feelings. Nothing could be more essential to identity than one's internal compass of liking—of food, of music, of art, of our brand of yogurt—and yet, throughout its almost constant operation, it sits largely outside reflection. In the course of our explorations, however, small themes have emerged, little signposts dotting a confusing, difficult path, offering encouragement and a bit of clarity. It is with these messages that I will end—a sort of "field guide to liking" in a world of infinite variety.

YOU WILL KNOW WHAT YOU LIKE OR DO NOT LIKE BEFORE YOU KNOW WHY. Our ability to express an "affective judgment" about something happens in the range of milliseconds. This is a great skill for a complex world, a filtering mechanism for efficiently navigating the crowded marketplace of life. But shortcuts can come at a price: We may miss what we might really prefer, we may discount something we will later come to love, we may be misattributing the source of our liking.

GET BEYOND "LIKE" AND "DISLIKE." In the world of sensory testing, the words "like" and "dislike" are discouraged. Why? Because they may throw off the very judgment of taste panelists. Liking and disliking can be top-down concepts that often get in the way of our actual experience of something. Asking whether you like something or not often puts a premature end to a much more interesting conversation.

DO YOU KNOW WHY YOU LIKE WHAT YOU LIKE? Remember the subjects at the country fair who seemed to have a decided preference for one of two seemingly identical ketchups? Their preference was unconscious, buried deep in childhood memory. We like to think our likes are authentic, but they may be covertly influenced by context (that bottle of Italian wine you bring home because it was the best thing you ever tasted) or tempered by expectation (people will like the Napa Valley wine more than the New Jersey wine, regardless of where *the wine is actually from*). One's individual tastes may simply reflect some larger cultural "frame" that has hardened into habit: As the researcher Evgeny Yakovlev has noted, for decades Russians had an overwhelming taste for vodka (which was relatively cheap and plentiful). Once market restrictions were lifted, however, beer consumption soared—*among younger consumers.* The old vodka drinkers? They still mostly drank vodka.

TALK ABOUT WHY YOU LIKE SOMETHING. Language can unlock liking. When we have a sensory experience, we might think it sufficient to let the senses do their work. "Words cannot describe" is a common refrain in online reviews. But if we like what we know, we only know what we remember, and we are more likely to remember hedonic events if we verbalize them. Caution: sometimes we may like something less for itself than because it is easier to talk about why we like it, over something we may actually prefer but whose qualities are more elusive.

WE LIKE THINGS MORE WHEN THEY CAN BE CATEGORIZED. Our pattern-matching brains are primed to categorize the world, and we seem to like things the more they resemble what we think they should. Studies have found that when subjects look at pictures of mixed-race people and are asked to judge their attractiveness, the answer depends on what *categories* are used; a Chinese-American man may be judged more attractive than men in general but *less* attractive than Chinese men. Things that are "hard to categorize" are hard to like—until we invent new categories. We like things more when we can categorize them, and categories can help us like things more, even things that aren't as good as we might like.

DO NOT TRUST THE EASY LIKE. As we crave fluency and mastery, we may immediately respond favorably to things that are "easy to get"—a simple but infectious pop riff, a piece of art whose meaning or style immediately registers, a sweet cocktail. But this very fluency may linger less in memory, and we may tire rapidly of the simple "stimulus." What seems harder to like at first—because it seems to require more mental bandwidth—may yield more long-term hedonic returns. There are few historical artists still relevant today who were widely liked, without any controversy, in the time they were working.

YOU MAY LIKE WHAT YOU SEE, BUT YOU ALSO SEE WHAT YOU LIKE. As much as we interpret the world through our senses, we prime our senses to interpret the world that we think should be out there.

LIKING IS LEARNING. There are very few inherent tastes. What is taken for a "natural" predilection is often culture, wrapped in biology's clothing.

WE LIKE WHAT WE EXPECT TO LIKE; WE LIKE WHAT WE REMEMBER. The novelist Julian Barnes, channeling Flaubert, called anticipation "the most reliable form of pleasure," for it cannot be dashed before it happens. Memory provides a similar safe haven; we rarely revise our remembered pleasures. Liking "in the moment" is often up for grabs, a burst of neural activity that could go either way.

**NOVELTY VERSUS FAMILIARITY, CONFORMITY VERSUS DISTINCTION, SIM-
PLICITY VERSUS COMPLEXITY.** These three oppositions, and the tension
that exists within each of the pairs, go a great way toward explaining our
liking, toward accounting for our tastes.

DISLIKES ARE HARDER TO SPOT BUT MORE POWERFUL. We live in a positive
world. *The Power of Negative Thinking* is not a best seller. Facebook does
not allow users to *not* like things. We do not look for "negative feedback."
As much as we seek out positive experiences, however, it is our dislikes that
register more powerfully. Our facial muscles work harder to express our
dislike of food, there are many more words for negative emotions than
for positive emotions, one negative review among a group of largely
positive reviews carries more weight than one positive among a group
of mostly negative reviews. Dislikes can reveal more about who you are
than likes.

ON ACCOUNTING FOR TASTE. Trying to explain, or understand, any one
person's particular tastes—including one's own—is always going to be a
maddeningly elusive and idiosyncratic enterprise. But the *way* we come
to have the tastes we do can often be understood through a set of psychological and social dynamics that function much the same, from the
grocery store to the art museum. The more interesting question is not
what we like, but *why* we like.

Notes

INTRODUCTION

WHAT'S YOUR FAVORITE COLOR (AND WHY DO YOU EVEN HAVE ONE)?

4   People buy fewer black cars: See Meghan R. Busse, et al., "Projection Bias in the Car and Housing Markets," *Working Paper 18212* (Washington, D.C.: National Bureau of Economic Research, July 2012).

4   In one elegantly constructed: Because the puppets did not "see" which food the infants had preferred, the researchers speculated, infants were preferring puppets who seemed to actually "hold" those tastes, not the puppets that were merely "expressing" those tastes so as to gain favor in some way. See Neha Mehajan and Karen Wynn, "Origins of 'Us' Versus 'Them': Prelinguistic Infants Prefer Similar Others," *Cognition* 124 (2012): 227–33. In another study, this effect disappeared when the puppets in question were shown to be "antisocial." J. Kiley Hamlin and Karen Wynn, "Who Knows What's Good to Eat? Infants Fail to Match the Food Preferences of Antisocial Others," *Cognitive Development* 27 (2012): 227–39.

4   Maddeningly, however: As Paul Rozin notes, "Surprisingly, parents, who share genes with their children and control most of the child's environment for the early years of life, do not transmit their food and other preferences very well to their children. Parent-child correlations are in the range of 0 to .30 for food or music preferences." Rozin, "From Trying to Understand Food Choice to Conditioned Taste Aversion and Back," http://w.american.edu/cas/psychology/cta/highlights/rozin_highlight.pdf.

5   "this delicate and aerial faculty": Edmund Burke, *A Philosophical Enquiry into the Sublime and Beautiful* (New York: Penguin, 2004), 63.

5   "No significant behavior": Gary Becker, *Accounting for Tastes* (Cambridge, Mass.: Harvard University Press), 49.

5   "explain everything": See Bryan Caplan, "Stigler-Becker Versus Myers-Briggs: Why Preference-Based Explanations Are Scientifically Meaningful and Empirically Important," https://ideas.repec.org/a/eee/jeborg/v50y2003i4p391-405.html#biblio.

5   But the Rocky Mountains: See Paul Albanese, "Introduction to the Symposium on Preference Formation," *Journal of Behavioral Economics* 17, no. 1 (1988): 1–5. Ernst Fehr and Karla Hoff also note that economists' traditional view—describing the preferences of individuals, and the society that they will create, and "that preferences remain the same regardless of the society that emerges"—is demonstrably false. See Fehr and Hoff, *Economic Journal* 121 (Nov. 2011): f396–f412.

5   Our tastes seem endlessly "adaptive": Elster, of course, is talking about more than

a taste for grapes. He writes, "The idea of sour grapes appears to me just as important for understanding individual behavior as for appraising schemes of social justice." Woven throughout his book is the implicit question of when people do what they really want or only what seems possible in the current constraints of their lives. See Elster, *Sour Grapes: Studies in the Subversion of Rationality* (Cambridge, U.K.: Cambridge University Press, 1983). The political scientist Michael Locke McLendon, in a worthwhile critique of Elster, suggests that Elster has mischaracterized the fox's response to not getting the grapes: "[Elster] claims that the fox readjusts his attitude towards the grapes. More accurately, he is readjusting the world to fit his failed preferences. The fox still wants grapes—that fact has not changed. Rather, he rejects the particular grapes on the trellis that he was unable to reach. Unable to consume the only available grapes, he falsely attributes to them traits they do not have, i.e., they are sour." See McLendon, "The Politics of Sour Grapes: Sartre, Elster, and Tocqueville on Emotions and Politics," http://ssrn.com/abstract=1460905 or http://dx.doi.org/10.2139/ssrn.1460905.

5   Where economists tend: As Dan Ariely and Michael Norton note, we might think we are choosing something because it is the best, but we may be drawing upon a memory of past choices, which now seem as if they were consciously made but might in fact not have been: "We suggest that rather than being driven by hedonic utility, behavior is based in part on observations of past actions, actions that have been influenced by essentially random situational factors—such as the weather—but that people interpret as reflective of their stable preferences." Ariely and Norton, "How Actions Create—Not Just Reveal—Preferences," *Trends in Cognitive Sciences* 12, no. 1 (Jan. 2008): 16.

5   Imagine the fox: Any number of studies have tried to sort out these dynamics, often by asking research subjects to rank a list of items, then choose their favorite, and then rerank the list. In theory, this could mean people liked an item *more* after they chose it (and *disliked* more what they didn't choose); in other words, the choice drove the preference. But in one study, researchers argued that in a "free choice" experiment, rankings will naturally spread even as attitudes remain "perfectly stable." They write, "While it may appear that participants became more fond of the higher ranked item after choosing it, in reality, participants were also 'more fond' of the higher ranked item before choosing it (so long as they eventually chose it). Thus, the spreading seen here, which would normally be mistaken for evidence of choice-induced attitude change, is better interpreted as evidence for the importance of choice information." See M. Keith Chen and Jane L. Risen, "How Choice Affects and Reflects Preferences: Revisiting the Free-Choice Paradigm," *Journal of Personal Social Psychology* 99, no. 4 (Oct. 2010): 573–94.

6   "An academic history": Stephen Bayley, *Taste: The Secret Meaning of Things* (New York: Pantheon, 1991), xviii.

6   "blue seven": See William E. Simon and Louis H. Primavera, "Investigation of the 'Blue Seven Phenomenon' in Elementary and Junior High School Children," *Psychological Reports* 31 (1972): 128–30. The finding was replicated in a number of other studies; see, for example, Julian Paciak and Robert Williams, "Note on the 'Blue-Seven Phenomenon' Among Male Senior High Students," *Psychological Reports* 35 (1974): 394.

6   "the sacred number": Louis Jacobs, "The Numbered Sequence as a Literary Device in the Babylonian Talmud," *Hebrew Annual Review* 7 (1983): 143.

6   Perhaps it is the way: The seminal research here was George Miller, "The Magical Number Seven, Plus or Minus Two: Some Limits on Our Capacity for Processing Information," *Psychological Review* 63, no. 2 (1956): 81–87.

7   And yet its influence: See, for example, Dave Munger, "Is 17 the 'Most Random' Number?," *Cognitive Daily* (blog), Feb. 5, 2007, http://scienceblogs.com/cognitive daily/2007/02/05/is-17-the-most-random-number/.

7   As for why my daughter: It is theorized that expressing preferences, and knowing how they might differ from other people's preferences, are key steps in a child's developing what psychologists call a "theory of mind," one part of which is empathy.

7   With a touch of alarm: Carol Zaremba Berg et al., "The Survey Form of the Leyton Obsessional Inventory-Child Version: Norms from an Epidemiological Study," *Journal of the American Academy of Child and Adolescent Psychiatry* 27, no. 6 (Nov. 1988): 759–63.

7   "public restroom at a California": See Nicholas Christenfeld, "Choices from Identical Options," *Psychological Science* 6, no. 1 (Jan. 1995). Ironically, this preference for the middle seems to make those the *least* clean stalls, at least according to one microbiologist, Dr. Charles Gerba, of the University of Arizona, known as Dr. Germ. See, for example, Elizabeth Landau, "Conquering the 'Ewww' Factor of the Public Potty," CNN, Dec. 9, 2008, http://www.cnn.com/2008/HEALTH /10/03/bathroom.hygiene/index.html?eref=rss_latest.

8   Has paper mounted: See, for example, "Ending the Over-Under Debate on Toilet Paper," NPR, http://www.npr.org/2015/03/19/393982199/ending-the-over -under-debate-on-toilet-paper.

8   As inconsequential as either: See Rick Kogan, *America's Mom: The Life, Lessons, and Legacy of Ann Landers* (New York: William Morrow, 2005), 163.

8   If people seem to prefer "bnick": As one report notes, "Typological research suggests that onsets with large sonority rises (e.g., blif) are preferred to onsets with smaller rises (e.g., bnif), which, in turn are preferred to sonority plateaus (e.g., bdif); the plateaus, in turn, are preferred to onsets with sonority falls (e.g., lbif)." This even though "the structure of the English lexicon offers English speakers little evidence for the sonority hierarchy." See Iris Berent et al., "What We Know About What We Have Never Heard: Evidence from Perceptual Illusions," *Cognition* 104 (2007): 590–631.

9   Why would artists' preferences: One finds this gap in almost every creative profession. One idea is that experts and laypeople disagree on what's good because of what criteria they are examining. In architecture, for example, one study noted that "architects and laypersons agreed that a meaningful building is an aesthetically good building . . . [b]ut the two groups used no physical cues in common as the basis for deciding which buildings are more (or less) meaningful." The authors of that study suggested a "cognitive reconciliation campaign" to bring this difference to light. See Robert Gifford et al., "Why Architects and Laypersons Judge Buildings Differently: Cognitive Properties and Physical Bases," *Journal of Architectural and Planning Research* 19, no. 2 (Summer 2002): 131–48.

9   Palmer queried a range: See Stephen Palmer and William Griscom, "Accounting for Taste: Individual Differences in Preference for Harmony," *Psychonomic Bulletin Review* 20, no. 3 (2013): 453–61.

10 Days after being: Teresa Farroni, Enrica Menon, and Mark H. Johnson, "Fac-

tors Influencing Newborns' Preference for Faces with Eye Contact," *Journal of Experimental Child Psychology* 95 no. 4 (2006): 298–308.

10 Since the dawn of psychology: Jastrow actually found in his study that women preferred red. See Joseph Jastrow, "The Popular Esthetics of Color," *Popular Science Monthly*, Jan. 1897. Jastrow cautioned that only a certain range of colors were presented and that people's choices might have been influenced by the arrangement of colors on the page. Still, a host of studies have largely found a consensus around blue (and for less liking of dark yellow). For an excellent survey on the work that has been done on human color preference, see A. Hurlbert and Y. Ling, "Understanding Colour Perception and Preference," in *Colour Design: Theories and Applications*, ed. Janet Best (Oxford: Woodhead, 2012), 129, 157. They caution, "Despite the common-sense appeal of these arguments, it is important to stress that neither the evolutionary nor the ontogenetic claim has been proven, and the extent to which preferences are hard-wired versus individually malleable is still an open question."

10 "general fussiness": Chloe Taylor et al., "Color Preferences in Infants and Adults Are Different," *Psychonomic Bulletin and Review* 20, no. 1 (Feb. 2013).

11 "It happens at the beach": See Nathan Heller, "The Cranky Wisdom of Peter Kaplan," *New Republic*, Sept. 14, 2012.

11 When Palmer and his colleagues: Karen Schloss, Rosa Poggesi, and Stephen Palmer, "Effects of University Affiliation and 'School Spirit' on Color Preferences: Berkeley Versus Stanford," *Psychonomic Bulletin Review* 18 (2011): 498–504.

11 Query Democrats and Republicans: Karen Schloss and Stephen Palmer, "The Politics of Color: Preferences for Republican Red Versus Democratic Blue," *Psychonomic Bulletin Review* 21, no. 2 (April 2014). As they note, the effect is not found on nonelection days. One reason might be that people actually normally associate Republicans with *blue* and Democrats with *red*. The media's use of Red and Blue America is rather recent. "When Republican Reagan swept the 1984 presidential elections," they write, "the election map coded Reagan victories in blue and was referred to as a 'suburban swimming pool.'"

12 Some have argued: The key proponent of this line of thinking is Itamar Simonson. He suggests preference construction is a sort of laboratory artifact and argues, "The literature on preference construction has been largely confined to local decisions and is less relevant to more enduring preferences." New innovations, like the Nintendo Wii, he argues, tap into preexisting, inherent preferences. The fact that people come to like something they initially disliked, he argues, is one "post-hoc indicator of inherent preferences." Simonson, "Will I Like a 'Medium' Pillow? Another Look at Constructed and Inherent Preferences," *Journal of Consumer Psychology* 18 (2008): 155–69. Critics have responded, however, that Simonson has set up an "unfalsifiable" condition, because we can never really know if someone who comes to like something she disliked at first merely adapted to something or liked it all along (and just didn't know it). See James Battman et al., "Preference Construction and Preference Stability: Putting the Pillow to Rest," *Journal of Consumer Psychology* 18 (2008): 170–74.

12 The idea that pink: For a thorough account, see Jo Paoletti, *Pink and Blue: Telling the Boys from the Girls in America* (Bloomington: Indiana University Press, 2013).

13 Just having a face: See Saeideh Bakshi, David A. Shamma, and Eric Gilbert, "Faces Engage Us: Photos with Faces Attract More Likes and Comments on

Instagram." *ACM: Proceedings of the SIGCHI Conference on Human Factors in Computing Systems* (2014). 965–74.

14 Are liking and disliking: The philosopher Karl Duncker notes that "the unpleasantness of a toothache and the pleasantness of a beautiful view are not likely to coexist—not so much because the two hedonic tones have opposite signs, but because the underlying experiences or attitudes are incomparable." See Duncker, "On Pleasure, Emotion, and Striving," *Philosophy and Phenomenological Research* 1, no. 4 (June 1941): 391–430.

14 In 2000, a team of Italian: C. Geroldi et al., "Pop Music and Frontotemporal Dementia," *Neurology* 55 (2000): 1935–36. In another case, in which the aesthetic transformation rather went the other way, a group of neuroscientists reported a patient whose liking for hard rock suddenly shifted—in the wake of a left temporal lobectomy—to a "preference for Celtic or Corsican polyphonic singing." The patient, they noted, "was surprised by his taste changes, did not find that they were the mere result of maturation, and complained about them." François Sellal et al., "Dramatic Changes in Artistic Preference After Left Temporal Lobectomy," *Epilepsy and Behavior* 4 (2003): 449–51.

14 It was not so much: See, for example, Daniel J. Graham, Simone Stockinger, and Helmut Leder, "An Island of Stability: Art Images and Natural Scenes—but Not Natural Faces—Show Consistent Esthetic Response in Alzheimer's-Related Dementia," *Frontiers in Psychology* 4 (March 2013), article 107. Curiously, the study found that people's recall of photographs of faces was far less stable than their preference for landscape and other paintings. The authors suggest that Alzheimer's patients, upon viewing faces, may be suffering "cognitive interference"—for example, a nagging thought that they have seen this photograph before; paintings, meanwhile, might "be evaluated more easily on basic esthetic grounds, with less interference of face detection and recognition systems."

14 In an experiment conducted: R. Haller et al., "The Influence of Early Experience with Vanillin on Food Preference Later in Life," *Chemical Senses* 24, no. 4 (1999): 465–67. The authors raise the interesting point that as "bottle feeding stops long before children speak," the experiment raises the idea that "olfactory memory" exists outside "verbal memory." We remember what we smell even before we know what the *what* is.

15 It is unlikely they made: Kevin Melchionne makes the interesting point that because "it is difficult to imagine doubting our immediate, sensual responses to food"—even if we might not be able to locate the precise reasons—we carry that confidence in our own judgment into fields like art, where we must certainly know what we like. See Melchionne, "On the Old Saw 'I Know Nothing About Art but I Know What I Like,'" *Journal of Aesthetics and Art Criticism* 68, no. 2 (Spring 2010): 131–40.

15 But the expert musicians: See Claudia Fritz et al., "Player Preferences Among New and Old Violins," *PNAS* 109, no. 3 (2012): 760–63. In Fritz's study, most players could not actually distinguish the old from the new instruments. That study was criticized because the testing was done in a hotel room. However, in a follow-up study whose locations include rehearsal spaces and a concert hall, more musicians preferred the new instruments. As Fritz cautions, there "is no way of knowing the extent to which our test instruments (old or new) are representative of their kind"—the same might be said about the musicians—"so results cannot

be projected to the larger population of fine violins." But it certainly raises the idea that what people love about an old Italian violin is that it *is* an old Italian violin, rather than its inherent sonic virtues. Fritz et al., "Soloist Evaluations of Six Old Italian and Six New Violins," *PNAS* 111, no. 20 (2014): 7224–29.

15 "adaptive unconscious": See Timothy Wilson, "Self-Knowledge and the Adaptive Unconscious," in *Neuroscience and the Human Person: New Perspectives on Human Activities,* Pontifical Academy of Sciences, Scripta Varia 121 (Vatican City, 2013).

15 Following his example: One designer created a book, equipped with facial recognition software, that would not open until the prospective reader's face was completely neutral; that is, there was no prejudging going on. See Alison Flood, "The Book That Judges You by the Cover," *Books* (blog), *Guardian,* Feb. 2, 2015, http://www.theguardian.com/global/booksblog/2015/feb/02/book-judges-you -by-your-cover-moore-thijs-biersteker.

15 "the archetype of all taste": Pierre Bourdieu, *Distinction: A Social Critique of the Judgment of Taste* (London: Routledge, 1986), 79.

CHAPTER 1
WHAT WOULD YOU LIKE?

18 "with such other worthy": See Paul Rozin, "Preadaptation and the Puzzles and Properties of Pleasure," in *Well-Being: Foundations of Hedonic Psychology,* ed. Daniel Kahneman, Edward Diener, and Norbert Schwarz (New York: Russell Sage Foundation, 1999), 114.

18 In some experiments: Curt P. Richter, "Experimentally Produced Reactions to Food Poisoning in Wild and Domesticated Rats," *Annals of the New York Academy of Science* 56 (1953): 225–39. It should be noted that no one has probably done more to understand rat behavior than Richter. As one account noted, "From 1919 to 1977, Richter conducted a steady stream of research projects on psychobiological phenomena of the rat, including spontaneous activity, biological clocks, physiologic effects of adrenalectomy, self-selection of nutrients, poisoning, stress, and domestication." See Mark A. Suckow, Steven H. Weisbroth, and Craig L. Franklin, eds., *The Laboratory Rat* (New York: Academic Press, 2005), 14.

18 We are particularly alert: See, for example, Léri Morin-Audebrand et al., "The Role of Novelty Detection in Food Memory," *Acta Psychologica* 139 (2012): 233–38. As the authors note, "People may spend a long time finding the ten differences between two similar pictures in visual puzzles, but will usually immediately notice the slightest differences in the odor, flavor, and mouthfeel of foods, although they cannot describe them."

18 This alarm is most well tuned: As the prominent psychologist Wilhelm Wundt described it, more than a century ago, "gradually substitute for a sweet sensation one of sour or bitter, keeping the intensity constant," and "it will be observed that, for equal intensities, sour and, more especially, bitter produce a much stronger feeling than sweet." See Wilhelm Max Wundt, *Outlines of Psychology,* accessed Oct. 14, 2013, http://psychclassics.yorku.ca/Wundt/Outlines/sec7.htm.

18 We start getting *really* choosy: See, for example, Gillian Harris, "Development of Taste and Food Preferences in Children," *Current Opinion in Clinical Nutrition and Metabolic Care* 3, no. 3 (May 2008): 315–19.

18 Even our desire for salt: B. J. Cowart, G. K. Beauchamp, and J. A. Mennella, "De-

velopment of Taste and Smell in the Neonate," in *Fetal and Neonatal Physiology*, 3rd ed., vol. 2, ed. R. A. Polin, W. W. Fox, and S. H. Abman (Philadelphia: W. B. Saunders, 2004), 1819–27.

19   those English burghs with "wich": This detail comes from Robert P. Erickson, "A Study of the Science of Taste: On the Origins and Influence of the Core Ideas," *Behavioral and Brain Sciences* 31 (2008): 59–105.

19   Even anencephalic babies: J. E. Steiner, "The Gustofacial Response: Observation on Normal and Anencephalic Newborn Infants," in *Symposium on Oral Sensation and Perception—IV (Development in the Fetus and Infant)*, ed. J. F. Bosma (Bethesda, Md.: NIH-DHEW, 1973), 254–78.

19   No one living really dislikes: Another interesting indicator of how much we treasure sweetness is that it seems, at least according to one study, that we can more accurately remember the sweetness of a meal than, say, its texture. See Léri Morin-Audebrand et al., "Different Sensory Aspects of a Food Are Not Remembered with Equal Acuity," *Food Quality and Preference* 20 (2009): 92–99.

19   Cilantro, for some: Nicholas Eriksson et al., "A Genetic Variant near Olfactory Receptor Genes Influences Cilantro Preference," *Flavour* 1, no. 22 (2012), accessed Nov. 1, 2013, http://www.flavourjournal.com/content/pdf/2044-7248-1-22.pdf.

19   The ability of humans: See JinLiang Xue and Gary D. Dial, "Raising Intact Male Pigs for Meat: Detecting and Preventing Boar Taint," *Swine Health and Production* 5, no. 4 (1997): 151–58. As a testament to the variety of sensory experiences humans can often have, boar taint, the authors note, has been compared to a huge range of other scents, both good and bad: "The smell and/or taste of boar-tainted meat has been described variously as an 'off' or 'boar' odor; onion-like, perspiration-like, or urine-like; like perfume, wood, musk, or 'Ivory' soap; sweet, fruity, ammonia-like, and animal-like; and fecal or bitter."

19   Just because you find: As Jane Wardle and Lucy Cooke write about the famed "supertaster" aversion to the chemical compound known as PROP, "Despite the attractiveness of the idea that variations in taste sensitivities could underlie food dislikes, the weight of the evidence is that PROP taster status has only limited influence on food preferences in everyday life." See Wardle and Cook, "Genetic and Environmental Determinants of Children's Food Preferences," supplement, *British Journal of Nutrition* 99, no. S1 (2000): S15–S21.

20   "It is striking": Martin Yeomans, "Development of Human Learned Flavor Likes and Dislikes," in *Obesity Prevention: The Role of Brain and Society on Individual Behavior*, ed. Laurette Dubé et al. (New York: Academic Press, 2010), 164.

20   Studies show that most of us: See Peter H. Gleick, *Bottled and Sold: The Story Behind Our Obsession with Bottled Water* (New York: Island Press, 2010), 81.

20   Eggplant, after all: See "Plant Guide," U.S. Department of Agriculture, accessed Nov. 1, 2013, http://plants.usda.gov/plantguide/pdf/pg_some.pdf.

20   Then again, tomatoes: And thankfully, as one researcher notes, tomatoes or potatoes or other ilk from the genus *Solanum* seem unlikely to actually kill us: "Fatalities from solanine poisoning are not well documented in the modern medical literature." Donald G. Barceloux, "Potatoes, Tomatoes, and Solanine Toxicity (*Solanum tuberosum* L., *Solanum lycopersicum* L.)," *Disease-a-Month* 55, no. 6 (June 2009): 391–402.

20   She is certainly not: In Gabriel García Márquez's novel *Love in the Time of Cholera*,

we learn that the protagonist Fermina Daza "had despised eggplants ever since she was a little girl, even before she had tasted them, because it always seemed to her that they were the color of poison." García Márquez, *Love in the Time of Cholera* (New York: Vintage, 2007), 208. And indeed, Fermina does grow to like eggplants.

20 "most disliked" vegetable: *Japan Today*, Sept. 4, 2001, accessed Oct. 14, 2013, http://www.japantoday.com/category/food/view/eggplant-most-hated-vegetable -among-kids.

20 "People like to be": Quoted in Harry T. Lawless, *Sensory Evaluation of Food* (New York: Springer, 2010), 260.

21 The Cornell University researcher: Brian Wansink and Jeffery Sobal, "Mindless Eating: The 200 Daily Food Decisions We Overlook," *Environment and Behavior* 39, no. 1 (2007): 106–23.

21 we like the same food less: Brian Wansink et al., "Dining in the Dark: How Uncertainty Influences Food Acceptance in the Absence of Light," *Food Quality and Preference* 24, no. 1 (2012): 209–12.

22 Research has shown: Massimiliano Zampini and Charles Spence, "The Role of Auditory Cues in Modulating the Perceived Crispness and Staleness of Potato Chips," *Journal of Sensory Studies* 19, no. 5 (Oct. 2004): 347–63.

22 high-frequency "crispiness": In food "rheology" circles, the word "crispy" is a very specific thing, different from the lower-pitched, longer-lasting sounds of "crunchiness." Notes one study, "Crispy foods generate high pitched sounds with frequencies higher than 5 kHz, crunchy foods yield low pitched sounds with a characteristic peak on frequency range of 1.25–2 kHz." See Mayyawadee Saeleaw and Gerhard Schleining, "A Review: Crispness in Dry Foods and Quality Measurements Based on Acoustic–Mechanical Destructive Techniques," *Journal of Food Engineering* 105, no. 3 (2011): 387–99.

22 People have, for example, reported: There are many studies to this effect, but see, for example, Cynthia DuBose et al., "Effects of Colorants and Flavorants on Identification, Perceived Flavor Intensity, and Hedonic Quality of Fruit-Flavored Beverages and Cake," *Journal of Food Science* 45 (1980): 1393–99.

22 When trained panelists: See Lance G. Philips et al., "The Influence of Nonfat Dry Milk on the Sensory Properties, Viscosity, and Color of Lowfat Milks," *Journal of Dairy Science* 78, no. 10 (Oct. 1995): 2113–18.

22 Flipping the switch: This story is reported in Herbert Mieselman and Halliday McFie, *Food Acceptance and Consumption* (New York: Springer, 1996), 13. The study it refers to is J. Wheatley, "Putting Color into Marketing," *Marketing*, Oct. 23–29, 1973, 67.

22 "In virtually all analyses": Carolyn Korsmeyer, *Making Sense of Taste: Food and Philosophy* (Ithaca, N.Y.: Cornell University Press, 2014), 51.

23 In Zellner's plating study: Curiously, the researchers found that people seemed to feel the same about the string beans, one of the foods on offer, regardless of how they were presented. In a line that resonates with parents everywhere, they write, "There might be something special about vegetables that makes it difficult to change how much people like them." Debra Zellner et al., "It Tastes as Good as It Looks! The Effect of Food Presentation on Liking for the Flavor of Food," *Appetite* 77 (June 2014): 31–35.

23 "What is the adaptive": Rozin, "Preadaptation and the Puzzles and Properties of Pleasure," 16.

23 "function to promote": Paul Rozin, J. Haidt, and C. R. McCauley, "Disgust," in *Handbook of Emotions*, ed. M. Lewis and J. M. Haviland-Jones (New York: Guilford Press, 2000), 638.

23 This particular face: See H. A. Chapman et al., "In Bad Taste: Evidence for the Oral Origins of Moral Disgust," *Science* 323, no. 5918 (2009): 1222–26.

23 and we use more facial muscles: Tsuyoshi Horio, "EMG Activities of Facial and Chewing Muscles in Human Adults in Response to Taste Stimuli," *Perceptual and Motor Skills* 97 (2003): 289–98.

24 Instances of disgusting behavior: Ibid., 644.

24 "Choices depend on taste": W. M. Gorman, "Tastes, Habits, and Choice," *International Economic Review* 8, no. 2 (June 1967): 218.

24 "innately appealing": See Sam Sifton, "Always Be Crisping," *New York Times*, Sept. 13, 2012.

24 "likely to evoke the sense": John S. Allen, *The Omnivorous Mind: Our Evolving Relationship with Food* (Cambridge, Mass.: Harvard University Press, 2012), 36.

24 The more tempting the language: See Esther K. Papies, "Tempting Food Words Activate Eating Simulations," *Frontiers in Psychology* 4 (2013), doi:10.3389/fpsyg .2013.00838.

24 "An item won't be on": Tyler Cowen, *An Economist Gets Lunch: New Rules for Everyday Foodies* (New York: Penguin, 2012), 71.

25 The mere fact of having a menu: See D. Bernstein, M. Ottenfeld, and C. L. Witte, "A Study of Consumer Attitudes Regarding Variability of Menu Offerings in the Context of an Upscale Seafood Restaurant," *Journal of Foodservice Business Research* 11, no. 4 (2008): 398–411.

25 And while the anticipation: Lauren A. Leotti and Mauricio R. Delgado, "The Inherent Reward of Choice," *Psychological Science* 22, no. 10 (2011): 1310–18.

25 "memories are the building blocks": Daniel T. Gilbert and Timothy Wilson, "Prospection: Experiencing the Future," *Science*, Sept. 7, 2007, 1351–54. As they note, "Mental simulation is the means by which the brain discovers what it already knows. When faced with decisions about future events, the cortex generates simulations, briefly tricking subcortical systems into believing that those events are unfolding in the present and then taking note of the feelings these systems produce." It is as if we rehearse in the moment the future pleasure (or displeasure) to come.

25 "The present is never our end": Blaise Pascal, *The Thoughts, Letters, and Opuscules of Blaise Pascal* (New York: Hurd and Houghton, 1869), 194.

26 When people in one study: Daniel Kahneman and Jackie Snell, "Predicting a Changing Taste: Do People Know What They Will Like?," *Journal of Behavioral Decision Making* 5, no. 3 (Sept. 1992): 187–200.

26 "The correlation between": Debra A. Zellner et al., "Conditioned Enhancement of Humans' Liking for Flavor by Pairing with Sweetness," *Learning and Motivation* 14 (1983): 338–50.

26 We also seem to crave: This has been called "diversification bias." Daniel Read and George Loewenstein have theorized various reasons why we may be biased toward more variety than we actually want when we make decisions, some involv-

ing "bias," others not. In the latter camp, they note, "people seek variety because they are risk averse and uncertain about their preferences. Choosing variety reduces the likelihood of repeatedly consuming something undesirable." Variety also helps us find new favorites. But among the "biased" explanations is the idea that people "subjectively shrink the interconsumption interval" when making a choice; for example, when presented with the chance of consuming one's favorite ice cream every day for a week, the scenario may sound as if that were a lot of ice cream consumption. But a day lasts a long time (and ice cream is pleasant, after all). "Yet satiation is fleeting, and our preferences typically return to their preconsumption level within a short time." Read and Loewenstein, "Diversification Bias: Explaining the Discrepancy in Variety Seeking Between Combined and Separated Choices," *Journal of Experimental Psychology: Applied* 1, no. 1 (1995): 34–49.

26 In one experiment: See E. Robinson, J. Blissett, and S. Higgs, "Changing Memory of Food Enjoyment to Increase Food Liking, Choice, and Intake," *British Journal of Nutrition* 108, no. 8 (2012): 1505–10.

27 Buyer's remorse: See Yan Zhang, "Buyer's Remorse: When Evaluation Is Affect-Based Before You Choose but Deliberation-Based Afterwards" (Ph.D. diss., University of Chicago, Booth School of Business, 2009).

27 Even amnesiacs: Matthew D. Lieberman et al., "Do Amnesics Exhibit Cognitive Dissonance Reduction? The Role of Explicit Memory and Attention in Attitude Change," *Psychological Science*, 12, no. 2 (March 2001): 135–40.

27 The same effect, interestingly: See Geraldine Coppin et al., "I'm No Longer Torn After Choice: How Explicit Choices Implicitly Shape Preference of Odors," *Psychological Science* 21 (2010): 489–93. As they write, "We demonstrated the existence of postchoice preference changes not only when choices were remembered, but also, critically, when choices were forgotten."

27 Even when people were making: Tali Sharot et al., "How Choice Reveals and Shapes Expected Hedonic Outcome," *Journal of Neuroscience*, March 25, 2009, 3760–65. The researchers note that subjects might have had some preference for a vacation destination before they made their choice but that "these differences may not have been large enough prechoice to be captured behaviorally using standard ratings." But, they note, "postchoice differences in preferences became large enough to be observed using the same rating scale. The critical finding is that after a decision was made, the difference in caudate nucleus activity associated with the selected, versus the rejected, option was further enhanced." For another study, which involved an increase in liking for a CD after it was chosen (associated with specific brain activity), see Jungang Qin et al., "How Choice Modifies Preference: Neural Correlates of Choice Justification," *NeuroImage* 55 (2011): 240–46.

27 In a follow-up study: The authors point out that they were trying, in this study, to counter a methodological critique that has been made against arguments that preference can come after choice: "The core argument here is that people's preferences cannot be measured perfectly, and are subject to rating noise. As participants gain experience with the rating scale they will provide more accurate ratings such that post-choice shifts in ratings simply reflect the unmasking of the participants' initial preferences (which can be predicted by their choices) rather than reflecting any changes in preference induced by choice." In this study,

however, preferences were actually entirely detached from the decision-making process. See Tali Sharot et al., "Do Decisions Shape Preference? Evidence from Blind Choice," *Psychological Science* 9 (2010): 1231–35.

28 Some even suggest: See Carlos Alós-Ferrer et al., "Choices and Preferences: Evidence from Implicit Choices and Response Times," *Journal of Experimental Social Psychology* 48, no. 6 (Nov. 2012): 1336–42.

29 In studies Zellner has done: See Debra Z. Zellner et al., "Protection for the Good: Subcategorization Reduces Hedonic Contrast," *Appetite* 38 (2002): 175–80. Zellner notes, "Notice the subjects had plenty of room in the rating scale to indicate that the test stimuli were less good than the context (good) stimuli without indicating that they disliked them."

29 A more palatable opening: See Martin Yeomans, "Palatability and the Microstructure of Feeding in Humans: The Appetizer Effect," *Appetite* 27 (1996): 119–33. In another study, it was noted that the mere *sight* of a palatable meal (versus a less palatable meal) was enough to increase the subjects' "rated desire to eat." See Andrew J. Hill et al., "Hunger and Palatability: Tracking Ratings of Subjective Experience Before, During, and After the Consumption of Preferred and Less Preferred Food," *Appetite* 5 (1984): 361–71.

29 The peak of our sudden disliking: "For all sensory variables measured and for all foods consumed, the greatest decline in pleasantness occurred for the eaten food 2 min after consumption." See Marion Heterington, Barbara J. Rolls, and Victoria J. Burley, "The Time Course of Sensory-Specific Satiety," *Appetite* 12 (1989): 57–68.

30 "The pleasantness of foods": Barbara J. Rolls et al., "How Sensory Properties of Foods Affect Human Feeding Behavior," *Physiological Behavior* 29 (1982): 409–17.

30 In monkeys the mere *sight:* The drop-off was much less for foods that had not been eaten, even after satiation. Hugo D. Critchley and Edmund T. Rolls, "Hunger and Satiety Modify the Olfactory and Visual Neurons in the Primate Orbitofrontal Cortex," *Journal of Neurophysiology* 75, no. 4 (April 1996): 1673–86.

30 Scientists have speculated: See, for example, Edmund T. Rolls, "Multisensory Neuronal Convergence of Taste, Somatosensory, Visual, Olfactory, and Auditory Inputs," in *The Handbook of Multisensory Processes*, ed. Gemma Calvert, Charles Spence, and Barry E. Stein (Cambridge, Mass.: MIT Press, 2004), 319.

30 "There were no failures": See Clara M. Davis, "Results of the Self-Selection of Diets by Young Children," *Canadian Medical Association Journal*, Sept. 1939, 257–61. For an excellent account of the context and impact of Davis's work, see Stephen Strauss, "Clara M. Davis and the Wisdom of Letting Children Choose Their Own Diets," *Canadian Medical Association Journal*, Nov. 7, 2006, 1199–201. Strauss notes that Davis had planned a follow-up experiment that would measure what would happen if infants could pick from less healthy, processed foods: "But alas, it was not to be: 'The depression dashed this hope,' she laconically remarked, after a lack of funding forced the original experiment itself to end in 1931."

30 Sensory-specific satiety: F. Zampollo et al., "Food Plating Preferences of Children: The Importance of Presentation on Desire for Diversity," *Acta Paediatrica* 101 (2012): 61–66. That same study noted that children seemed to desire the maximum number—seven—of food items and colors.

31 When people were offered: Barbara J. Rolls, Edward A. Rowe, and Edmund T. Rolls, "How Sensory Properties of Foods Affect Human Feeding Behavior," *Ap-*

petite 12 (1989): 57–68. Interestingly, the researchers also conducted an experiment to see if the "shape" of food would affect sensory-specific satiety, using pasta ("bow ties," "hoops," and "spaghetti"). They reported that "there was a larger decrease in the pleasantness of the taste of the shape of the pasta eaten . . . [t]han of the other shapes of the pasta which were not eaten."

31   In a potato chip study: Andrea Maier, Zata Vickers, and J. Jeffrey Inman, "Sensory-Specific Satiety, Its Crossovers, and Subsequent Choice of Potato Chip Flavors," *Appetite* 49 (2007): 419–28.

31   In the so-called ice cream effect: Robert J. Hyde and Steven A. Witherly, "Dynamic Contrast: A Sensory Contribution to Palatability," *Appetite* 21 (1993): 1–16.

31   the so-called dessert effect: As Elizabeth Capaldi notes, "Our habit of eating dessert at the end of a meal will increase preference for the sweet taste of the dessert because the postingestive consequences of the meal are more closely associated with the flavor of the dessert than the flavor of the meal." See Capaldi, "Conditioned Food Preferences," in *Psychology of Learning and Motivation*, ed. Douglas Medin (San Diego: Academic Press, 1992), 9.

31   "A few bites": Elizabeth Rode, Paul Rozin, and Paula Durlach, "Experience and Remembered Pleasure for Meals: Duration Neglect but Minimal Peak, End (Recency) or Primacy Effects," *Appetite* 49 (2007): 18–29.

31   Our memory for meals: Ibid.

33   "desiccated vegetables": William C. Davis, *A Taste for War: The Culinary History of the Blue and the Gray* (Mechanicsburg, Pa.: Stackpole Books, 2003), 22.

34   Tell people a coffee is bitter: This effect may only work when the intrinsic experiences align with the extrinsic information. In one fascinating study, subjects were given samples of wine they were told was sour due to an off year (while some weren't given any information about its potential quality). Some subjects were merely given the wine; others were given the wine spiked with a dose of "miracle fruit," which turns the sour into sweet. People who tasted the wine without the miracle fruit (but with the "sour" information) liked it less than those who simply drank the wine without any taste information. Those who tasted the miracle fruit version and were told it would taste sour actually liked the wine more than those who were not told what to expect. The authors write, "In the face of expecting to taste potentially sour elements, but having a disrupted ability to do so, the wine was rated as tasting better than in the absence of such a contrast with an extrinsic taste signal." In other words, people were not merely blindly swayed by the information that it would be sour when it in fact *could not be*. See Ab Litt and Baba Shiv, "Manipulating Basic Taste Perception to Explore How Product Information Affects Experience," *Journal of Consumer Psychology* 22, no. 1 (Jan. 2012): 55–66.

35   The opposite can happen: See Issidoros Sarinopoulos et al., "Brain Mechanisms of Expectation Associated with Insula and Amygdala Response to Aversive Taste: Implications for Placebo," *Brain, Behavior, and Immunity* 20, no. 2 (March 2006): 120–32.

35   Tell subjects that an orange juice: See Gerard J. Connors et al., "Extension of the Taste-Test Analogue as an Unobtrusive Measure of Preference for Alcohol," *Behavioral Research and Therapy* 16 (1978): 289–91. The authors note, "When subjects were asked to estimate how much alcohol they had consumed during the

two taste-tests, the average estimation was 3.31 oz; individual values ranged from 1 to 10 oz."

35　People will still like it: See Joel Wolfson and Naomi S. Oshinsky, "Food Names and Acceptability," *The Journal of Advertising Research* 6 (1961): 21–23.

35　In one well-known study: Martin R. Yeomans et al., "The Role of Expectancy in Sensory and Hedonic Evaluation: The Case of Smoked Salmon Ice-Cream," *Food Quality and Preference* 19, no. 6 (Sept. 2008): 565–73.

35　"If we say something": Melissa Clark, "The Best in the Box," *New York Times*, Feb. 5, 2003.

35　"novel foods": Armand Cardello et al., "Role of Consumer Expectancies in the Acceptance of Novel Foods," *Journal of Food Science* 50 (1985): 1707–14.

37　Three months after: See Wei Xiao, "The Competitive and Welfare Effects of New Product Introduction: The Case of Crystal Pepsi" (Food Marketing Policy Center, Research Report No. 112, University of Connecticut, Nov. 2008).

37　A blind taste test: Larry Brown, "A New Generation: Pepsi Offers Clear Choices," *Seattle Times*, Jan. 13, 1993.

37　"taste enough like Pepsi": David Novak, "It Tasted Great in the Lab," *Conference Board Review*, http://tcbreview.com/tcbr-quick-insights/it-tasted-great-in-the-lab.html.

37　"principal use": Lawrence Garber, Eva Hyatt, and Richard Starr, "The Effects of Food Color on Perceived Flavor," *Journal of Marketing Theory and Practice* 8 (2003): 59–72.

37　The program itself: For a good history of food research at Natick and its predecessor agencies, see Herbert L. Meiselman and Howard G. Schutz, "History of Food Acceptance Research in the U.S. Army," *Appetite* 40 (2003): 199–216.

38　"11-point scale": See, for example, Warren D. Smith, "Rating Scale Research to Scale Voting," http://www.rangevoting.org/RateScaleResearch.html. Original source is D. R. Peryam and F. J. Pilgrim, "Hedonic Scale Method of Measuring Food Preferences," *Food Technology*, Sept. 1957, 9–14.

38　"Perhaps surprisingly": G. J. Pickering, "Optimizing the Sensory Characteristics and Acceptance of Canned Cat Food: Use of a Human Taste Panel," *Journal of Animal Physiology and Animal Nutrition* 93, no. 1 (2009): 52–60.

38　Other methods, like polygraphs: See Meiselman and Schutz, "History of Food Acceptance Research in the U.S. Army."

38　The number eight: This is a problem that other, more complex methods, like "magnitude estimation scales," have tried to factor.

38　As work by Timothy Wilson: Timothy Wilson et al., "Introspecting About Reasons Can Reduce Post-choice Satisfaction," *Personal Social Psychology Bulletin* 18, no. 3 (June 1993): 331–39.

39　There is just one problem: See Richard Popper and Daniel R. Kroll, "Just-About-Right Scales in Consumer Research," *Chemosense* 7, no. 3 (June 2005). As the authors note, other scales, such as those that measure for "intensity" of a certain attribute, often have less bias, even though the attributes being measured are the same. "The difference between the two scale types is that in answering JAR questions respondents need to consider how products differ from an ideal, which may focus them on reasons why they like or dislike a product, something that intensity scales may not."

39 Ask them ahead of time: It is as if, as Cardello once wrote, "our stated preferences for foods reflect a quintessential or idealized image or memory trace of the food, and that actual preparations of the food item are never as good or as bad as this mental image." See A. V. Cardello and O. Maller, "Relationship Between Food Preferences and Food Acceptance Ratings," *Journal of Food Science* 47 (1982): 1553–57.

39 "Even foods that are extremely": Lyle V. Jones, David B. Peryam, and L. L. Thurstone, "Development of a Scale for Measuring Soldiers' Food Preferences" (paper presented at the Fourteenth Annual Meeting of the Institute of Food Technologists, Los Angeles, June 29, 1954).

40 The thing most liked: See, for example, Seo-Jin Chung and Zata Vickers, "Influence of Sweetness on the Sensory-Specific Satiety and Long-Term Acceptability of Tea," *Food Quality and Preference* 18 (2007): 256–64. In this study, they found that subjects' view of the ideal sweetness of tea changed over time. "Liking ratings for the low sweet tea increased over the 19 days of the test, becoming equal to the optimally sweetened tea in the latter half of the study." In another study, Vickers and colleagues found that while a very sweet yogurt received the highest test scores, less of the high-sweet yogurt was actually eaten. Our likes are not always the surest, or only, guide to our preferences. See Z. Vickers, E. Holton, and J. Wang, "Effect of Ideal-Relative Sweetness on Yogurt Consumption," *Food Quality and Preference* 12 (2001): 521–26.

40 We begin to pick things: See Rebecca K. Ratner, Barbara E. Kahn, and Daniel Kahneman, "Choosing Less-Preferred Experiences for the Sake of Variety," *Journal of Consumer Research* 26, no. 1 (June 1999): 1–15.

40 "Would it be so terrible": See Tyler Cowen, "But We Just Had Indian Food Yesterday!," *Marginal Revolution*, Oct. 16, 2013, http://marginalrevolution.com /marginalrevolution/2013/10/but-we-just-had-indian-food-yesterday.html.

40 "variety amnesia": See Jeff Galak and Joseph P. Redden, "Variety Amnesia: Recalling Past Variety Can Accelerate Recovery from Satiation," *Journal of Consumer Research* 36 (Dec. 2009), accessed Nov. 1, 2013, http://papers.ssrn.com /sol3/papers.cfm?abstract_id=1344541. Per Cowen's dilemma, they suggest, "The current findings likely provide more actionable advice to consumers fighting satiation. The recommendation is straightforward: If consumers wish to keep enjoying their favorite experiences, then they should simply think of all the other related experiences they have recently had. For example, the next time you find yourself in the all too common situation of not wanting to eat the same thing for lunch, try to recall all of the other things you have eaten since yesterday's lunch. Our findings suggest this will make your current lunch taste just a little bit better."

41 People eating in an ethnic restaurant: Meiselman and Schutz, "History of Food Acceptance Research in the U.S. Army."

41 The most adventurous gourmands: E. P. Köster, "The Psychology of Food Choice: Some Often Encountered Fallacies," *Food Quality and Preference* 14 (2003): 359–73. In a correspondence, Köster elaborated: "My guess was that at the brink of day eating is not our primary concern other than to satisfy needs. Day planning and organizing activity are more important." There is also the case, he notes, that some people seem essentially content to eat the same thing day after day, something he once thought not likely. "This illusion was disturbed by two

exceptional experiences. The first one was in a little Indian village in Surinam where people ate cassava every day for lack of other things and seemed quite satisfied in doing so. They would introduce variety when they could get it, however. More perplexing was my experience in Nepal, where the people eat a rice dish called *Bat* every day. The only variation is that they eat it with cucumber in the summer and with cauliflower in the winter. *Bat* is indeed a delicious dish very well spiced and with an exquisite sensory complexity. I lived for about two weeks with a family and to my surprise I loved it still. They obviously did too, because when I invited them to a restaurant in Kathmandu, they chose one that offered exactly the same dish as the one we had at home. It taught me that variety seeking can not be necessary when there is sufficient variety and complexity in the dish."

43   Terpenes triggering receptors: Massimiliano Zampini and Charles Spence make this point in "Assessing the Role of Visual and Auditory Cues in Multisensory Perception of Flavor," in *The Neural Bases of Multisensory Processes*, ed. M. M. Murray and M. T. Wallace (Boca Raton, Fla.: CRC Press, 2012), accessed Oct. 28, 2013, http://www.ncbi.nlm.nih.gov/books/NBK92852/#ch37_r118.

43   How we perceive something: Paul Rozin, " 'Taste-Smell Confusions' and the Duality of the Olfactory Sense," *Perception and Psychophysics* 31 (1983): 397–401.

43   "reading is a longer": The Woolf quotation comes via Katerina Koutsantoni, *Virginia Woolf's Common Reader* (London: Ashgate, 2013), 71.

43   What we like is sometimes: As one well-known study found, people's preference for Coca-Cola over Pepsi in a taste test was influenced by having access to brand information. Samuel McClure et al., "Neural Correlates of Behavioral Preference for Culturally Familiar Drinks," *Neuron* 44 (2004): 379–87.

44   "The same cognitive": See Astrid Poelman et al., "The Influence of Information About Organic Production and Fair Trade on Preferences for and Perception of Pineapple," *Food Quality and Preference* 19, no. 1 (Jan. 2008): 114–21. The authors noted an interesting effect. "When the subjects are considered as a uniform group, the individual differences indicating different outcome of underlying cognitive processes will be kept hidden." However, "when subjects were grouped according to their affective attitudes towards organic or fair trade products, perception differed as a result of the information provided. Subjects with a positive attitude towards organic or fair trade products perceived products to have a stronger sensory impact in the presence of such information than in its absence. Similarly, subjects with a negative attitude towards organic or fair trade products perceived products to have a weaker sensory impact in the presence of such information than in its absence."

44   The power of this conditioning: See, for example, Kevin P. Myers and Margaret C. Whitney, "Rats' Learned Preferences for Flavors Encountered Early or Late in a Meal Paired with the Postingestive Effects of Glucose," *Physiology and Behavior* 102, no. 5 (March 2011): 466–74.

45   In her study, people who downed: See M. L. Pelchat and G. M. Carfagno, "GI Glucose Enhances 'Mere' Exposure in Humans," *Appetite* 54 (2010): 669.

45   One way to avoid the treatment: Graciela V. Andresen, Leann L. Birch, and Patricia A. Johnson, "The Scapegoat Effect on Food Aversions After Chemotherapy," *Cancer* 66, no. 7 (1990): 1649–53.

45   "Mere repeated exposure": R. B. Zajonc, "Attitudinal Effects of Mere Exposure," *Journal of Personality and Social Psychology* 9, no. 2, pt. 2 (June 1968): 1–27.

45   In one typical study: Leann L. Birch and Diane Wolfe Marlin, "I Don't Like It; I Never Tried It: Effects of Exposure on Two-Year-Old Children's Food Preferences," *Appetite* 3, no. 4 (Dec. 1982): 353–60.

45   Try it: Or, as the food writer Jeffrey Steingarten put it, "after repeatedly sampling ten of the sixty varieties of kimchi, the national pickle of Korea, kimchi has become my national pickle, too." Steingarten, *The Man Who Ate Everything* (New York: Alfred A. Knopf, 1997), 4.

45   They often abandon efforts: See B. R. Carruth, P. J. Ziegler, and S. I. Barr, "Prevalence of Picky Eaters Among Infants and Toddlers and Their Caregivers' Decisions About Offering a New Food," *Journal of the American Dietetic Association* 104 (2004): 57–64.

45   In an English study: A. Bingham, R. Hurling, and J. Stocks, "Acquisition of Liking for Spinach Products," *Food Quality and Preference* 16, no. 5 (July 2005): 461–69.

46   People liked peas: But what *about* those spinach dislikers? Is mere exposure a form of liking, or does it merely reflect "weaker distaste"? The psychologist Christian Crandall set out to answer this in an innovative experiment at a salmon cannery in Alaska. Rather than introduce something unfamiliar, he introduced, in a fairly controlled setting, something already liked, though novel to the factory: doughnuts. The longer doughnuts were in the factory break room, the more of them people ate. Considering other explanations, Crandall suggests that sheer boredom might have led cannery workers to eat more sweets, although parallel consumption of other desserts did not rise during this time. One wonders, however, if there was also some novelty effect at work, and whether doughnut consumption would have itself stabilized and even dropped over time. Or perhaps there is just something inherently likable—even addictive— about doughnuts. See Crandall, "The Liking of Foods as a Result of Exposure: Eating Doughnuts in Alaska," *Journal of Social Psychology* 125, no. 2 (1995): 187–94.

46   In one study, people began: Lisa Methven, Elodie Langreney, and John Prescott, "Changes in Liking for a No Added Salt Soup as a Function of Exposure," *Food Quality and Preference* 26, no. 2 (Dec. 2012): 135–40.

46   the soup was not labeled: See D. G. Liem, N. Toraman Aydin, and E. H. Zandstra, "Effects of Health Labels on Expected and Actual Taste Perception of Soup," *Food Quality and Preference* 25, no. 2 (Sept. 2012): 192–97. Although, as Fredrik Fernquist and Lena Ekelund have noted, the type of food seems to determine whether health information has an effect on hedonic liking. Earlier studies include cases where health aspects do not affect liking, suggesting that food which is already considered healthy is not affected by information about, for example, fat content. Fernquist and Ekelund, "Credence and the Effect on Consumer Liking of Food—a Review," *Food Quality and Preference*, in press, manuscript accessed online on Nov. 1, 2013.

46   In another experiment: Richard J. Stevenson and Martin R. Yeomans, "Does Exposure Enhance Liking for the Chilli Burn?," *Appetite* 24, no. 2 (1995): 107–20. The authors note that "no subject referred specifically to liking or preference in describing the purpose of the experiment. However, some subjects thought that the experiment concerned some form of sensory adaptation to the chilli burn." One wonders if this in itself could predispose the subjects to "like" the chili more

the hotter it got, to please the researchers or show their own bravery. But before and after the trial, subjects drank a tomato juice mixture with capsaicin added, and they reported no increased liking for that.

46 "Some people would answer": George Orwell, *As I Please: 1944–1945* (Boston: David R. Godine, 2000), 42.

46 Chances are your mother did: Julie A. Mennella, Coren P. Jagnow, and Gary K. Beauchamp, "Prenatal and Postnatal Flavor Learning by Human Infants," *Pediatrics* 107, no. 6 (June 2001), accessed Nov. 1, 2013, http://www.ncbi.nlm.nih.gov /pmc/articles/PMC1351272/. The authors note, "The flavor of a food includes, among other sensory stimuli, the oral sensation of taste and the retronasal sensation of smell. It has been suggested that relative to taste, where hedonic tone and liking are more hard-wired, liking for olfactory components of flavor is largely determined by individual experience."

46 Trained sensory panelists: See J. A. Mennella, A. Johnson, and G. K. Beauchamp, "Garlic Ingestion by Pregnant Women Alters the Odor of Amniotic Fluid," *Chemical Senses* 20 (1995): 207–9.

46 Out of the womb: As adults, our reactions are not quite so important but still significant enough that in one experiment, face-reading software was able to tell when subjects were drinking an orange juice they said they did not like. It had less luck with the juices we *liked*. See Lukas Danner et al., "Make a Face! Implicit and Explicit Measurement of Facial Expressions Elicited by Orange Juices Using Face Reading Technology," *Food Quality and Preference* 32, pt. B (March 2014): 167–72, http://dx.doi.org/10.1016/j.foodqual.2013.01.004.

46 Making faces is part: One study found that only disliking food triggered "microexpressions of negative emotions," particularly on the first exposure. See René A. De Wijk, "Autonomic Nervous System Responses on and Facial Expressions to the Sight, Smell, and Taste of Liked and Disliked Foods," *Food Quality and Preference* 26, no. 2 (2012): 196–203.

46 Simply seeing other people: Particularly if the food in question is perceived to be healthful. In a study by Morgan Poor, subjects rated chocolate higher when they saw images of just the chocolate versus someone *eating* the chocolate; with apples, the reverse was true. Morgan Poor, Adam Duhachek, and H. Shanker Krishnan, "How Images of Other Consumers Influence Subsequent Taste Perceptions," *Journal of Marketing* 77, no. 6 (Nov. 2013): 124–39.

46 "Babies who refused tomato juice": Sibylle K. Escalona, "Feeding Disturbances in Very Young Children," *American Journal of Orthopsychiatry* 15, no. 1 (Jan. 1945): 76–80.

46 In a study of preschoolers: L. L. Birch, "Effect of Peer Models' Food Choices and Eating Behaviors on Preschoolers' Food Preferences," *Child Development* 51 (1980): 489–96.

47 "The French eat horses": See Gillian Tett, "The Science Interview: Jared Diamond," *Financial Times Magazine*, Oct. 11, 2013.

47 As with any food: See the excellent essay by Kari Weil, "They Eat Horses, Don't They? Hippophagy and Frenchness," *Gastronomica* 7, no. 2 (Spring 2007).

47 "The sweet taste of sucrose": John Prescott, *Taste Matters* (London: Reaktion Books, 2012), 31.

48 "That was twenty years ago": As Small notes, "When an odor is experienced with a taste, the odor later comes to smell more like the taste with which it was expe-

rienced." The suntan lotion virtually *becomes* Malibu. See Dana Small and Barry Green, "A Proposed Model of a Flavor Modality," in Murray and Wallace, *Neural Bases of Multisensory Processes.*

48   "a distributed circuit": See ibid.

48   In one experiment: Ivan E. de Araújo et al., "Metabolic Regulation of Brain Response to Food Cues," *Current Biology* 23, no. 10 (May 2013): 878–83.

48   Kent Berridge, a neuroscientist: Mike J. F. Robinson and Kent Berridge, "Instant Transformation of Learned Repulsion," *Current Biology* 23, no. 4 (2013): 282–89. The authors note that in previous work, it was "not clear whether an instant transformation is powerful enough to reverse intense learned repulsion (such as to a CS for Dead Sea concentrations of 9% NaCl) into instant strong desire. Our results show that both do happen: a CS instantly powerful enough to reverse cue value from strongly negative to strongly positive."

49   "mesolimbic circuits of 'wanting'": Kent Berridge, "Wanting and Liking: Observations from the Neuroscience and Psychology Laboratory," *Inquiry* (Oslo) 52, no. 4 (2009): 378.

50   The idea of finding: As one neuroscientist has noted, "Not a single area implicated in pleasure in the human literature has failed to be implicated in aversive processing as well." The quotation is by Siri Leknes, in Morten L. Kringelbach and Kent C. Berridge, *Pleasures of the Brain* (New York: Oxford University Press, 2010), 15.

CHAPTER 2
THE FAULT IS NOT IN OUR STARS, BUT IN OURSELVES

53   And yet their own creators: For a good discussion of the work involved in the Netflix optimization prize, and Netflix's evolution of rating systems, see Clive Thompson, "If You Liked This, You're Sure to Love This," *New York Times Magazine*, Nov. 23, 2008.

55   the "cheap talk" problem: See Raymond Fisman and Edward Miguel, *Economic Gangsters: Corruption, Violence, and the Poverty of Nations* (Princeton, N.J.: Princeton University Press, 2008).

56   So where Netflix once relied: For instance, John Riedl, who headed GroupLens at the University of Minnesota and created an early system to help people filter through the increasing torrent of Usenet articles, based on their ratings, told *The New Yorker:* "What you tell us about what you like is more predictive of what you like in the future than anything else we've tried . . . It seems almost dumb to say it, but you tell that to marketers sometimes and they look at you puzzled." Riedl himself sensed some of the limitations of ratings-based systems, including how to get people to actually rate things. "Some researchers have proposed compensation systems that reward users for entering ratings. While the economic consequences of this solution are interesting, we wonder whether compensation would be necessary if ratings could be captured without any effort on the part of the user. We believe an ideal solution is to improve the user interface to acquire *implicit* ratings by watching user behaviors. Implicit ratings include measures of interest such as whether the user read an article and, if so, how much time the user spent reading it. Our initial studies show that we can obtain substantially more ratings by using implicit ratings and that predictions based on time spent

reading are nearly as accurate as predictions based on explicit numerical ratings." See Joseph A. Konstan et al., "Grouplens: Applying Collaborative Filtering to Usenet News," *Communications of the ACM* 40 (1997): 77–87.

57 "We find that upward mobility": Erving Goffman, *The Presentation of Self in Everyday Life* (New York: Anchor, 1959), 37.

57 "I'm actually a quite different person": I found the Horvath quotation in Hartmut Rosa, *Social Acceleration: A New Theory of Modernity* (New York: Columbia University Press, 2013), 24.

57 "an offensive strategy": Robert Trivers and William von Hippel, "The Evolution and Psychology of Self-Deception," *Behavioral and Brain Sciences* 34, no. 1 (2011): 1–56.

57 It wants to recommend things: Which may or may not be the things you like. In a paper written before he joined Netflix, Amatriain noted that "modeling user preferences on the basis of implicit feedback has a major limitation: the underlying assumption is that the amount of time that users spend accessing a given content is directly proportional to how much they like it." Xavier Amatriain et al., "I Like It . . . I Like It Not: Evaluating User Noise in Recommender Systems," *UMAP: Proceedings of the 17th International Conference on User Modeling, Adaptation, and Personalization* (2009), 247–58.

58 "contraction bias": See E. C. Poulton, *Bias in Quantifying Judgments* (London: Taylor and Francis, 1989), 172.

58 "integer bias": See, for example, "A Better Way to Rate Films," *Bad Films Are Bad* (blog), http://goodfil.ms/blog/posts/2011/10/07/a-better-way-to-rate-films/.

58 "A great many people": Francis Newman, "Short Stories of 1925," *New York Times*, Feb. 7, 1926.

59 While we might take this: Chinese online movie reviews, to take one example, seem to be kinder, and more evenly distributed than their U.S. equivalents, perhaps, it has been suggested, because of a tendency toward consensus seeking in Chinese society and a subdued expression of likes and dislikes. See Nooi Sian Koh, Nan Hu, and Eric K. Clemons, "Do Online Reviews Reflect a Product's True Perceived Quality? An Investigation of Online Movie Reviews Across Cultures," *Electronic Commerce Research and Applications* 9, no. 5 (Sept.–Oct. 2010): 374–84. The authors note, "Western reviews are much more likely to be extreme over time, while Chinese reviews tend to have a much more bell-shaped distribution and newer additional posts are much more likely to be closer to the mean rather than more extreme."

59 "Users are increasingly rating": See Yedua Koren, "Collaborative Filtering with Temporal Dynamics," *Communications of the ACM* 53, no. 4 (April 2010): 89–97.

59 Ask someone to re-rate a movie: Dan Cosley et al., "Is Seeing Believing? How Recommender System Interfaces Affect Users' Opinions," *Proceedings of the SIGCHI Conference on Human Factors in Computing Systems* (New York: ACM, 2003), 585–92.

59 People seem to rate things differently: See "Statistics Can Find You a Movie, Part 2," Web site article from AT&T Labs, http://www.research.att.com/articles/featured_stories/2010_05/201005_netflix2_article.html?fbid=IH3z2Gar6-b.

61 Perhaps as a concession: The noise goes on and on. Netflix engineers, for example, must also wade through seemingly conflicting taste signals from the same user. The initial problem, the "household" account where everyone's taste—from

kids' movies to romantic comedies to action flicks—was mashed up, was easily solved by adding separate "profiles" for family members. But what about when a single person's account seems to oscillate all over the place? Netflix calls these "moods." "You might be in a horror mood because your cousin is visiting and he loves horror," Yellin said. Is that a "true" signal? How long should that signal last?

63   "a piece of praise": The discussion of Harvey Sacks comes from Camilla Vásquez's interesting study of the nature of complaints, "Complaints Online: The Case of *TripAdvisor*," *Journal of Pragmatics* 43 (2011): 1707–17. As she notes, "There is no doubt that complaints develop differently in an online forum, where people do not 'know' one another in the same way they do in face-to-face interactions. As was illustrated, the differences in participant structure allowed online complaints to be simultaneously direct and indirect. With respect to other features of complaints, Heinemann and Traverso (2009) also claim that in face-to-face interactions, complaints require delicacy and implicitness because they make the complainant vulnerable, and that therefore, explicit 'complaint-devices' like extreme case formulations, idiomatic expressions, and negative observations 'only surface in extraordinary situations.'"

63   "The difficulty of distinguishing": See George Akerlof, *An Economic Theorist's Book of Tales* (New York: Cambridge University Press, 1984), 22.

64   "The customers are seldom local": George Akerlof, "The Market for 'Lemons': Quality Uncertainty and the Market Mechanism," *Quarterly Journal of Economics* 84, no. 5 (Dec. 1963): 941–73.

64   "higher relative share": Judith Chevalier and Austan Goolsbee, "Measuring Prices and Price Competition Online: Amazon.com and BarnesandNoble.com," *Quantitative Market and Economics* 1 (2003): 203–22. While Amazon is not particularly forthcoming with its data—it refused my request for an interview—the authors were able to extrapolate data by using differences in review and ranking at Amazon's and Barnes & Noble's Web sites. "Of course, data limitations force our analysis to differ somewhat from the ideal experiment, as we discuss later. However, we observe the same books, their customer reviews, and a proxy for each book's market share at each site."

64   Hotels were either responding: Pádraig Cunningham et al., "Does TripAdvisor Make Hotels Better?," *Technical Report UCD-CSI-2010-06*, Dec. 2010.

65   When all "known information": This description of the efficient market hypothesis is drawn from Burton G. Malkiel, "The Efficient Market Hypothesis and Its Critics" (CEPS, working paper 91, April 2003).

66   "The excising of the expert review": Suzanne Moore, "What Does the TripAdvisor Furore Teach Us About Critics?," *Guardian*, Feb. 12, 2012.

66   "scattered about the world": José Ortega y Gasset, *The Revolt of the Masses* (New York: W. W. Norton, 1994), 13.

67   "Anybody who believes Yelp": The Reichl quotation is from Russ Parsons, "Ruth Reichl on Conde Nast, Gourmet Live, and Online Reviews," *Los Angeles Times*, Feb. 11, 2013. http://articles.latimes.com/2013/feb/11/news/la-dd-ruth-reichl-conde-nast-gourmet-live-online-reviews-20130211.

67   Slippery though it may be: See Balázs Kovács, Glenn R. Carroll, and David W. Lehman, "Authenticity and Consumer Value Ratings: Empirical Tests from the Restaurant Domain," *Organization Science* 25, no. 2 (2014): 458–78. The authors

created an index of keywords by which they attempted to quantify (on a scale from 1 to 100) the notion of "authentic"—with authentic itself generating a 95, "scam" netting a 4, and "decent," as you might expect from such a middling word, sitting rather in the middle, at 51.

67   "because there is little": See Judith Donath, "Signals, Cues, and Meaning" (un-published paper), http://smg.media.mit.edu/papers/Donath/SignalsTruthDesign /SignalsCuesAndMeaning.pdf.

67   Even as it aggregates: After filtering out reviews for various reasons, including those suspected of being fraudulent (which seems to also exclude many honest, but hyper-enthusiastic, five-star reviews).

68   But have the online review sites: For an interesting discussion of TripAdvisor and the idea of trust and authority, see Ingrid Jeacle and Chris Carter, "In TripAdvi-sor We Trust: Rankings, Calculative Regimes, and Abstract Systems," *Accounting, Organizations, and Society* 36, nos. 4–5 (2011): 293–309.

68   In fact, Groupon users: See John W. Byers, Michael Mitzenmacher, and Geor-gios Zervas, "The Groupon Effect on Yelp Ratings: A Root Cause Analysis," in *Proceedings of the 13th ACM Conference on Electronic Commerce* (New York: ACM, 2012), 248–65.

69   "Work increasingly isn't": Paul Myerscough, "Short Cuts," *London Review of Books*, Jan. 3, 2013.

69   Nearly one-fourth of Yelp reviews: Susan Seligson, "Yelp Reviews: Can You Trust Them?," *BU Today*, Nov. 4, 2013.

70   A group of Cornell University researchers: See "Finding Deceptive Opinion Spam by Any Stretch of the Imagination," *Proceedings of the 49th Annual Meeting of the Association for Computational Linguistics* (2011), 309–19.

70   When people lie: As Matthew L. Newman and his colleagues point out, "When people are attempting to construct a false story, we argue that simple, concrete actions are easier to string together than false evaluations. Unpublished data from our labs have shown a negative relationship between cognitive complexity and the use of motion verbs (e.g., walk, move, go). Thus, if deceptive communications are less cognitively complex, liars should use more motion verbs and fewer exclusive words." See Newman et al., "Lying Words: Predicting Deception from Linguis-tic Styles," *Personal and Social Psychology Bulletin* 29, no. 5 (May 2003): 665–75.

70   Curiously, the researchers noted: Myle Ott, Claire Cardie, and Jeffrey T. Han-cock, "Negative Deceptive Opinion Spam," *Proceedings of the 2013 Conference of the North American Chapter of the Association for Computational Linguistics: Human Language Technologies* (Atlanta, June 9–14, 2013), 497–501.

70   When I ran my imagined: It did, however, flag my use of the rather vague word "place."

70   At one online retailer: See Jessica Love, "Good Customers, Bad Reviews," Kel-loggInsight, Aug. 5, 2013, http://insight.kellogg.northwestern.edu/article/good _customers_bad_reviews/.

71   "brag and moan phenomenon": See Christopher S. Leberknight, Soumay Sen, and Mung Chiang, "On the Volatility of Online Ratings: An Empirical Study" (10th Workshop on E-business, Shanghai, 2011).

71   "artificially high baseline": Byers, Mitzenmacher, and Zervas, "Groupon Effect on Yelp Ratings."

71   when a similar property: See Georgios Zervas, Davide Proserpio, and John Byers, "A First Look at Online Reputation on Airbnb, Where Every Stay Is Above Average" (Jan. 28, 2015), http://ssrn.com/abstract=2554500.

71   Similarly, on eBay: See Judith A. Chevalier and Dina Mayzlin, "The Effect of Word of Mouth on Online Book Sales" (NBER, working paper 10148, National Bureau of Economic Research, Cambridge, Mass., Dec. 2003).

71   "minimum service standard": Geoffrey Fowler, "On the Internet, Everyone's a Critic but They're Not Very Critical," *Wall Street Journal*, Oct. 5, 2009.

71   "Seems like when it comes": "Five Stars Dominate Ratings," YouTube blog, http://youtube-global.blogspot.com/2009/09/five-stars-dominate-ratings.html.

72   The most helpful reviews: See Pei-yu Chen, Samita Dhanasobhon, and Michael D. Smith, "All Reviews Are Not Created Equal: The Disaggregate Impact of Reviews and Reviewers at Amazon.com," May 2008, http://papers.ssrn.com/sol3/papers.cfm?abstract_id=918083.

72   On Amazon, reviews: Ibid.

72   When the performance is over: Computer scientists have tried to model the so-called standing ovation problem. One model posits a rather simple formula: "Each audience member uses a majority rule heuristic—if a majority of the people that she sees are standing, she stands, if not she sits." There are a number of variables to consider, however: Is the audience composed mostly of groups of friends? How much of the audience can an audience member actually see? Is there a time lag in which various audience members decide to stand? The standing ovation—and its extreme reverse, the cacophony of boos—are expressions of taste en masse and in real time but are seemingly open to conformity or social learning effects. See John H. Miller and Scott E. Page, "The Standing Ovation Problem," *Complexity* 9, no. 5 (May-June 2004): 8–16.

73   "We tend to herd": Sinan Aral, "The Problem with Online Ratings," *MIT Sloan Management Review*, Dec. 19, 2013.

74   "The more ratings amassed": David Godes and José Silva, "Sequential and Temporal Dynamics of Online Opinion," *Marketing Science* 31, no. 3 (2012): 448–73.

74   As the HP Labs: Fang Wu and Bernardo Huberman, "Opinion Formation Under Costly Expression," *ACM Transactions on Intelligent Systems and Technology* 1, no. 1, article 5 (Oct. 2010): 1–13.

74   Rationally, there is none: See Nan Hu, Noi Sian Koh, and Karempudi Srinivas Reddy, "Ratings Lead You to the Product, Reviews Help You Clinch It? The Mediating Role of Online Review Sentiments on Product Sales," *Decision Support Systems* 57 (2014): 42–53. As the authors note, reviews voted most helpful, or that are simply most recent, have an impact on sales that is "much larger than the average impact of all reviews." Amazon, of course, structures its user interface to feature these two variables, which certainly drives some if not all of the effect; a user cannot search, for example, for "least helpful reviews."

74   "don't-believe-the-hype effect": The authors note that even "if consumers corrected for the review bias, we would still observe monotonically rising or declining curves (because the very first reviews would still be biased), but the undershooting pattern in ratings would never appear because consumers would not make purchase mistakes." *Information Systems Research* 19, no. 4 (2008): 456–74.

75   When a review mentions: See Ye Hu and Xinxin Li, "Context-Dependent Prod-

uct Evaluations: An Empirical Analysis of Internet Book Reviews," *Journal of Interactive Marketing* 25 (2011): 123–33.

75   Context takes over: "When book quality is held constant," as the researchers Ye Hu and Xinxin Li found in an Amazon study, "newly posted reviews tend to disagree with existing reviews." This happens more for long-tail products (a reviewer can make more of an impact); when the previous reviews are more similar (a smoother ocean on which to make waves); when the number of previous reviews goes up (more context to react to); and when reviews actually mention previous reviews. To show that it was not merely a statistical artifact, Hu and Li randomized the reviews and found the negative trend no longer applied. "The actual order in which these reviews are written," they concluded, "indeed matters." See Hu and Li, "Context-Dependent Product Evaluations: An Empirical Analysis of Internet Book Reviews," *Journal of Interactive Marketing* 25, no. 3 (2010): 123–33.

76   "Tastes (i.e., manifested preferences)": Bourdieu, *Distinction*, 49.

76   "paradox of publicity": Balázs Kovács and Amanda J. Sharkey, "The Paradox of Publicity: How Awards Can Negatively Affect the Evaluation of Quality," *Administrative Science Quarterly* 59, no. 1 (2014).

76   Once the book was adorned: This also, the authors point out, rules out a simple regression to the mean explanation.

77   "As the band gets bigger": The Steve Albini quotation comes from Neil McDonald, "Fire Fighting: Steve Albini Interviewed," *The Quietus*, Sept. 2, 2013.

77   "Slightly negative reviews": Cristian Danescu-Niculescu-Mizil et al., "How Opinions Are Received by Online Communities: A Case Study on Amazon.com Helpfulness Votes," *ACM: Proceedings of the 18th International Conference on World Wide Web* (2009), 141–50.

77   Unlike with windshield wipers: As Shahana Sen and Dawn Lerman note, "A consumer looking for a hedonic product will be more committed and more able to refute negative information, than one looking for a utilitarian product." Sen and Lerman, "Why Are You Telling Me This? An Examination into Negative Consumer Reviews on the Web," *Journal of Interactive Marketing* 21, no. 4 (Autumn 2007).

78   "Taste is a merciless betrayer": Bayley, *Taste*, 5.

78   "The less a choice": Sheenya Iyengar, *The Art of Choosing* (New York: Twelve, 2010), 103.

78   It makes one wonder: Wrote Bourdieu, "Tastes are first and foremost distastes, provoked by horror or visceral intolerance ('sick-making') of the tastes of others." Bourdieu, *Distinction*, 49.

79   Indeed, when people in one study: Sen and Lerman write, "When consumers say negative things about utilitarian goods," fellow consumers seem to "believe that these comments were more likely to be based on the reviewer's true experiences," whereas, with hedonic goods, "consumers may be more likely to feel that reasons unrelated to the product's quality influenced the reviewer, and they were guided by internal or personal reasons." Why these sentiments themselves should be any less *authentic* when talking about a book or a vacuum cleaner is an interesting question, but it seems that we just do not trust other people's taste experiences the way we trust their experiences with other kinds of products. Sen and Lerman, "Why Are You Telling Me This?"

79   A "content analysis" of movie reviews: See Stephen Spiller and Helen Belogo-
     lova, "Discrepant Beliefs About Quality and Taste" (Feb. 4, 2014), http://public
     -prod-acquia.gsb.stanford.edu/sites/default/files/documents/mktg_03_14_
     Spiller.pdf.

79   In nearly half of moviegoer reviews: See Anidia Chakravarty, Yong Liu, and Tri-
     bid Mazumdar, "The Differential Effects of Online World-of-Mouth and Critics'
     Reviews on Pre-release Movie Evaluation," *Journal of Interactive Marketing* 24,
     no. 3 (2010): 185–97. The study found, interestingly, that "frequent moviegoers"
     were more influenced by critics' reviews, while "infrequent moviegoers" were
     more influenced by word of mouth.

79   Books are savaged: Hannah Johnson, "One-Star Ratings for Book on Amazon
     Without Kindle Version," *Wall Street Journal*, Jan. 18, 2010. By the time of this
     writing, curiously, a Kindle version was in place, and the significant number of
     one-star reviews shifted to more politically minded protests.

CHAPTER 3

HOW PREDICTABLE IS OUR TASTE?

82   "way to give you recommendations": The quotation comes from MathBabe.org,
     http://mathbabe.org/2012/10/18/columbia-data-science-course-week-7-hunch
     -com-recommendation-engines-svd-alternating-least-squares-convexity-filter
     -bubbles/.

84   "A quietly radical promise": Devin Leonard, "What You Want: Flickr Creator
     Spins Addictive New Web Service," *Wired*, Aug. 2010.

84   "signifies union": Georg Simmel, "Fashion," *International Quarterly* 10 (Oct.
     1904): 130–55. Reprinted in *American Journal of Sociology* 62, no. 6 (May 1957):
     541–58.

84   "everyone felt that they": See Jennifer Tsien, *The Bad Taste of Others* (Philadel-
     phia: University of Pennsylvania Press, 2012), 3. Tsien argues that in France, in
     particular, taste served as a kind of nation-building strategy: "The aspiration to
     establish France as the new world leader in matters of culture underlies many of
     the calls to crush examples of bad taste in their midst. In order to accomplish their
     goal, eighteenth-century critics needed not only to set the standard of good taste
     but also to assume the authority to pass judgment."

84   As more people had more money: As the sociologist Omar Lizardo notes, in the
     "consumer revolution" of the eighteenth century, "upwardly mobile merchant
     classes and aspiring middle classes developed what appears to be an insatiable
     appetite for consumer goods, resulting in an aestheticization of previously 'func-
     tional' objects among the rising middle classes and the development of an incipi-
     ent taste for innovative cultural productions and cultural objects." See Lizardo,
     "The Question of Culture Consumption and Stratification Revisited," *Sociologica*
     2 (2008): 1–31.

85   "burning everything you have got": See Charles Harvey, Jon Press, and Mairi
     Maclean, "William Morris, Cultural Leadership, and the Dynamics of Taste,"
     Business History Review 85, no. 2 (Summer 2011).

85   "People who are hoping": *Punch*, Dec. 23, 1925, http://www.middlebrow-network
     .com/.

85 "Copernican revolution": See Keijo Rahkonen, "Bourdieu and Nietzsche: Taste as a Struggle," in Susen and Turner, *Legacy of Pierre Bourdieu*, 126.

85 "social subjects, classified": Bourdieu, *Distinction*, 6.

86 were not two different people: The novelist Ben Lerner makes this a wonderful joke in his excellent novel *Leaving the Atocha Station*.

86 "Taste is the basis": Bourdieu, *Distinction*, 6.

86 "The science of taste": Ibid., 7.

86 If Hunch.com had a pop Bourdieu feel: In one paper, Liu analyzed the profiles of users of MySpace, a place where subtle, Bourdieu-like "taste performances" were displayed. See Hugo Liu, "Social Network Profiles as Taste Performances," *Journal of Computer-Mediated Communication* 13 (2008): 252–75. Incidentally, Matthew Ogle, a former engineer at Last.fm, told me, "MySpace is where you pretend to be into something, but at Last.fm we really knew what you played." Interview, April 17, 2014. And for an account of how one's publicly displayed "taste performances" might actually help shift one's internal taste preferences, see Benjamin K. Johnson and Brandon Van Der Heide, "Can Sharing Affect Liking? Online Taste Performances, Feedback, and Subsequent Media Preferences," *Computers in Human Behavior* 46 (2015): 181–90.

87 Subsequent scholarship had cast doubt: See, for example, Peter Jackson, *Food Words: Essays in Culinary Culture* (London: Bloomsbury, 2013), 220.

87 Traditional taste signifiers: Charlene Elliott notes two interesting strands in contemporary culture. "One is the inscription of 'connoisseur' status upon objects previously outside the realm of connoisseurship; and the second is the 'democratization' of objects previously located squarely within the realm of connoisseurship." In other words, even as once more rarefied tastes become more available to everyday consumption, once everyday activities become subjected to more rarefied analysis. See Elliott, "Considering the Connoisseur: Probing the Language of Taste," *Canadian Review of American Studies* 36, no. 2 (2006): 229–36.

87 When an executive: For an excellent discussion of the dynamics of counter-signaling, see Nick Feltovich, Richmond Harbaugh, and Ted To, "Too Cool for School? Signaling and Countersignaling," *RAND Journal of Economics* 33, no. 4 (Winter 2002): 630–49.

87 The anxious positioning: An attempt that typically fails, according to one study, which found that "humblebraggers" were less liked than braggers, who were presumably being more honest. See Ovul Sezer, Francesca Gina, and Michael I. Norton, "Humblebragging: A Distinct—and Ineffective—Self-Presentation Strategy" (Harvard Business School, working paper 15-080).

87 "Our song has just come on": The example comes from Harris Wittels, *Humblebrag: The Art of False Modesty* (New York: Grand Central, 2012).

88 "People in our studies": Caroline McCarthy, "Hunch Homes In on Who You Are," *CNET*, March 29, 2010.

88 "My own taste reflects": Carl Wilson, *Let's Talk About Love* (New York: Bloomsbury, 2014), 78.

89 Rather, I was associating: One problem with the presence of all this information online is that seemingly huge, anonymous swaths of data can be linked, without too much trouble, to people's individual-level behavior. As much as it is a security flaw, it is also a reminder of our predictability. See Joseph A. Calandrino et al.,

"'You Might Also Like': Privacy Risks of Collaborative Filtering," *2011 IEEE Symposium on Security and Privacy*, May 22–25, 2011, 231–46. The authors, as it happens, included Hunch.com (among others, such as Last.fm and Amazon.com) in their analysis, noting that "when optimized for accuracy, our algorithm infers a third of the test users' secret answers to Hunch questions with no error." The inference is made by observing "temporal changes in the public outputs of a recommender system." And when researchers in the U.K. analyzed "relatively basic levels of human behavior"—for example, publicly available Facebook "likes"— they were able to predict, at levels much higher than chance, whether people were male or female, gay or straight, Christian or Muslim. The reasons behind some observed correlations, they allowed, were oblique: "There is no obvious connection between Curly Fries and high intelligence." Michal Kosinski, David Stillwell, and Thore Graepel, "Private Traits and Attributes Are Predictable from Digital Records of Human Behavior," *PNAS* 110, no. 15 (2013): 5802–5.

89   "Nothing more clearly affirms": Bourdieu, *Distinction*, 18.

90   People's music preferences: See Peter J. Rentfrow and Samuel D. Gosling, "Message in a Ballad: The Role of Preferences in Interpersonal Perception," *Psychological Science* 17, no. 3 (2006): 236–42.

90   A person's clothes reveal: This idea comes from Richard R. Wilk, "A Critique of Desire: Distaste and Dislike in Consumer Behavior," http://www.indiana.edu/~wanthro/disgust.htm. Wilk writes, "The different social signals sent by consumption and non-consumption also help to explain why, in mass consumer society, dislikes are key in creating explicit boundaries between the individual and other people, in creating a sense of unique identity. Our dislikes and aversions are known to friends and relatives, while our likes are publicly stated in our conspicuous choices of clothes, cars, houses and other goods. Likes might therefore often take conformist, categorical forms that signal membership and consensus, while dislikes set boundaries and build distinctive personal interior identities." In the world of the Internet, likes are what you broadcast on your Facebook page; dislikes might be conveyed via Snapchat.

91   "Clearly no one really believes": Roger Scruton, "Judging Architecture," in *Design and Aesthetics: A Reader*, ed. Mo Dodson and Jerry Palmer (London: Routledge, 2003), 13.

91   The closer people are: Wrote Bourdieu, "Explicit aesthetic choices are in fact often constituted in opposition to the choices of the groups closest in social space with whom the competition is most direct and most immediate." Bourdieu, *Distinction*, 53.

91   One study, which plotted: See Mike Savage and Modesto Gayo-Cal, "Against the Omnivore: Assemblages of Contemporary Musical Taste in the United Kingdom" (CRESC, working paper 72, University of Manchester, Nov. 2009).

91   "The horrors of popular kitsch": Bourdieu, *Distinction*, 62.

92   They may in fact do the opposite: See Kevin Lewis, Marco Gonzalez, and Jason Kaufman, "Social Selection and Peer Influence in an Online Social Network," *PNAS* 109, no. 1 (2012): 68–72. As the authors write, "Our findings suggest that friends tend to share some tastes not because they influence one another, but because this similarity was part of the reason they became and remained friends in the first place." The one music genre they found that seemed to "spread" among Facebook friends was classical/jazz, less, they surmised, due to some inherent

viral likability for the genre than because of its "unique value as a high-status cultural signal."

94 humans can recognize a genre: Namely, 250 milliseconds. See Robert O. Gjerdingen and David Perrot, "Scanning the Dial: The Rapid Recognition of Music Genres," *Journal of New Music Research* 37, no. 2 (2008): 93–100.

94 Genres, to paraphrase the music critic: See Simon Frith's excellent *Performing Rites: On the Value of Popular Music* (Cambridge, Mass.: Harvard University Press, 1996), particularly the "Genre Rules" chapter.

95 "At Sony records": The Lucinda Williams anecdote is taken from Madeleine Schwartz's interview in *The Believer*, reprinted in *Confidence, or the Appearance of Confidence: The Best of "Believer" Music Interviews*, ed. Vendela Vida and Ross Simonini (San Francisco: Believer Books, 2014), 472.

95 Her song "Passionate Kisses": And the fact that Carpenter was even played on country radio stations was a bit of categorical confusion. As the radio consultant Sean Ross told me, "She was promoted to country radio because there was no place for female singer-songwriters. If she had come along four years later when Shawn Colvin and Sheryl Crow were having hits, she would have been a pop artist."

95 In one Bourdieu-style exercise: Their political affiliations were gleaned from Facebook "likes."

96 "One can hear famous pieces": The quotation comes from Evan Eisenberg's excellent book, *The Recording Angel: Music, Records, and Culture from Aristotle to Zappa* (New Haven, Conn.: Yale University Press, 2005), 45.

96 "The appreciation of classical music": Richard A. Peterson, "Problems in Comparative Research: The Example of Omnivorousness," *Poetics* 33, nos. 5–6 (2005): 257–82.

97 "There's just too much music": Nitsuh Abebe, "The Palmer Problem," Pitchfork .com, March 25, 2011.

97 The old highbrows: This idea comes from the sociologist Omar Lizardo, who argues that "omnivorousness is likely to be most unambiguously manifested as a horizontal boundary-drawing resource distinguishing the culturally advantaged from other proximate but distinct class fractions." See Lizardo, "Reconceptualizing and Theorizing 'Omnivorousness': Genetic and Relational Mechanisms," *Sociological Theory* 30, no. 4 (2012): 263–82.

97 "liking the same things differently": Bourdieu, *Distinction*, 279.

97 In places like the personals section: In a study of personal ads in *The New York Review of Books*, the sociologist Roger Kern notes that one thing missing from the personals, which is important in Bourdieu's work on "symbolic exclusion," is dislikes. "Perhaps the persistent use of negatives in describing one's self," he writes, "is perceived by the ad writers that they are snobbish, contrary, and/or hostile." He also identified an emphasis on varied cultural activities, which support "the conceptualization of a mastery of a wide range of cultural forms as a valuable personal resource marking high status." Kern, "Boundaries in Use: The Deployment of Personal Resources by the Upper Middle Class," *Poetics* 25, nos. 2–3 (1997): 177–93.

97 One struggles to imagine: As John Seabrook notes, of the phenomenon he calls "Nobrow": "In the old high-low world, you got status points for consistency in your cultural preferences, but in Nobrow you get points for choices that cut

across categories: you're a snowboarder who listens to classical music, drinks Coke, and loves Quentin Tarantino; you're a preppy who likes rap; you're a chop-socky B-movie fan who prefers Frusen Glädjè to Häagen-Dazs, or a World Cup soccer fan who wears FUBU and likes opera." From "Nobrow Culture: Why It's Become So Hard to Know What You Like," *New Yorker,* Sept. 20, 1999.

98 "musical forms consume people": Noah Mark, "Birds of a Feather Sing Together," *Social Forces* 77, no. 2 (Dec. 1998): 453–85.

98 By one analysis: See "The Death of the Long Tail," *Music Industry Blog,* March 4, 2014, http://musicindustryblog.wordpress.com/2014/03/04/the-death-of-the-long-tail/. The report's author argues that the sheer variety of digital music has only intensified the winner-take-all effect: "In fact digital music services have actually intensified the Superstar concentration, not lessened it. The top 1% account for 75% of CD revenues but 79% of subscription revenue. This counter intuitive trend is driven by two key factors: a) smaller amount of 'front end' display for digital services—especially on mobile devices—and b) by consumers being overwhelmed by a *Tyranny of Choice* in which excessive choice actually hinders discovery."

99 "proto-utopian carnival community": As Douglas Holt notes, this may be one of the most common forms of distinction. "Awareness of class differences in taste at the grounded level of preferences for and distaste toward particular cultural objects and practices need not take the form of lower class deference nor upper class disdain," he writes. "In fact, it is *more typical* that those with lesser cultural capital resources are dismissive of, or antagonistic towards, the objects and practices of those with greater cultural capital resources" (italics added). See Holt, "Distinction in America? Recovering Bourdieu's Theory of Taste from Its Critics," *Poetics* 25, nos. 2–3 (1997): 93–120.

100 "People's image of the classification": Bourdieu, *Distinction,* 473.

100 "you can be a juggalo": Kent Russell, "American Juggalo," *n+1,* no. 12 (Fall 2011): 29–55.

100 "the more serious kind": See Theodor Geiger, "A Radio Test of Musical Taste," *Public Opinion Quarterly* 14, no. 3 (Autumn 1950): 453–60.

101 The larger question is: How does the way music is represented—by genre or otherwise—influence our feelings toward it? How often are we telling a sociologist, when he comes calling with a survey, what we like, versus simply what we know? In his essay "The Philosopher and the Sociologist," Jacques Rancière accused Bourdieu of "transforming the test of musical taste into a test of knowledge." The sociologist "will judge musical tastes *without having anyone hear music.*" Respondents, guessing at the nature of the inquiry, answer accordingly. Rancière, *The Philosopher and His Poor* (Durham, N.C.: Duke University Press, 2004), 187.

101 In one study, people liked: From an experiment described by Paul Randolph Farnsworth in his book *Musical Taste* (Stanford, Calif.: Stanford University Press, 1950), 64.

101 Tell people that Hitler: See M. G. Rigg, "Favorable Versus Unfavorable Propaganda in the Enjoyment of Music," *Journal of Experimental Psychology* 38, no. 1 (1948): 78–81.

101 He once served subjects: Paul Rozin, Linda Millman, and Carol Nemeroff, "Op-

eration of the Laws of Sympathetic Magic in Disgust and Other Domains," *Journal of Personality and Social Psychology* 50, no. 4 (1986): 703–12.

102 There is a huge body of literature: In a meta-analysis of exposure studies, Robert Bornstein found that the "exposure-affect relationship is robust and reliable." Bornstein, "Exposure and Affect: Overview and Meta-analysis of Research, 1968–1987," *Psychological Bulletin* 106, no. 2 (1989): 265–89.

103 We translate this ease of processing: The fluency effect does not actually require repeated exposure to work: People, for example, seem to judge statements as more true when they are presented in easier-to-read colors. See Rolf Reber and Norbert Schwarz, "Effects of Perceptual Fluency on Judgments of Truth," *Consciousness and Cognition* 8, no. 3 (1999): 338–42. The authors note, "One may worry, however, that participants in the moderately visible presentation condition may simply have judged some statements as 'false' because they were unable to read them." Pilot testing, however, revealed that not to be the case.

103 "I've seen that triangle": Elizabeth Hellmuth Margulis, "One More Time," *Aeon Magazine*, March 7, 2014, http://aeon.co/magazine/culture/why-we-love-repetition-in-music/.

103 People in studies have tended: See Piotr Winkielman et al., "Prototypes Are Attractive Because They Are Easy on the Mind," *Psychological Science* 17, no. 9 (2006): 799–806. In another study, Winkielman and colleagues examined an apparent contradiction: "On the one hand, composite stimuli (averages) should be easy to process, because they represent a good summary of the perceiver's previous experience (i.e., a category prototype). On the other hand, composite stimuli should be difficult to process, because they are maximally ambiguous with regard to the original faces composing them." They noted an example of this in images of mixed-race faces, which some studies had found to be judged more attractive than others, while some studies had found the opposite effects. They suggest the discrepancy is explained by what category the images are judged by; for example, a Chinese-American man will be judged less attractive than other "Chinese" faces but perhaps more attractive than male faces in general. They note, "That is, mixed-race individuals should elicit more positivity when race is less salient and, ironically, attention to racial background could, via the disfluency it engenders, reduce positive feelings towards them." They also stress that "motivational factors"—for example, how one feels about race—could play a part in their findings. See Winkielman et al., "Easy on the Eyes, or Hard to Categorize: Classification Difficulty Decreases the Appeal of Facial Blends," *Journal of Experimental Social Psychology* 50 (Jan. 2014): 175–83.

103 birds or cars or shapes: J. B. Halberstadt and G. Rhodes, "It's Not Just Average Faces That Are Attractive: Computer-Manipulated Averageness Makes Birds, Fish, and Automobiles Attractive," *Psychonomic Bulletin and Review* 10 (2003): 149–56.

103 "A first encountered stimulus": Mario Pandelaere et al., "Madonna or Don McLean: The Effect of Order of Exposure on Relative Liking," *Journal of Consumer Psychology* 10, no. 4 (2010): 442–51. A similar "first is strongest" effect has been found in brain-imaging studies in which subjects were exposed to an odor that was paired with a visual object; that association generated more brain activity than when the odor was later paired with another object. The first smell is the one

we remember. See Andreas Keller, "Odor Memories: The First Sniff Counts," *Current Biology* 19, no. 21 (2009): 988–89.

103 The problem with that analysis: Robert Zajonc, "Mere Exposure: A Gateway to the Subliminal," *Current Directions in Psychological Science* 10, no. 6 (Dec. 2001): 224–28.

104 "The first time he played it": The acid house story is drawn from Tim Lawrence's interesting article, "Acid—Can You Jack?," retrieved from the Web site DJHistory.com; and also from Bob Stanley's excellent history of pop music, *Yeah! Yeah! Yeah! The Story of Pop Music from Bill Haley to Beyoncé* (New York: W. W. Norton, 2014), 466.

104 especially the things we disliked: As one journal article notes, "While the mere exposure effect robustly leads to more liking for stimuli that are novel and neutral in connotation, this research suggests that with initially negative attitudes repeated exposure may strengthen these negative affective reactions." See Richard J. Crisp, Russell R. C. Hutter, and Bryony Young, "When Mere Exposure Leads to Less Liking," *British Journal of Psychology* 100 (2009): 133–49.

104 There is no exact formula: See, for example, Daniel Berlyne, "Novelty, Complexity, and Hedonic Value," *Perception and Psychophysics* 8 (1970): 279–86.

105 When the Beatles' catalog is arranged: Adrian North and David Hargreaves, *The Social and Applied Psychology of Music* (New York: Oxford University Press, 2008), 83.

105 "As the condiment becomes stronger": Howard R. Moskowitz, "Engineering Out Food Boredom: A Product Development Approach That Combines Home Use Tests and Time-Preference Analysis," *Food Quality and Preference* 11, no. 6 (Nov. 2000): 445–56.

105 If, as Moskowitz argued: From a conversation with the author, but see also Moskowitz, "Engineering Out Food Boredom."

105 colas were popular because: In blind taste tests, people have often preferred Pepsi. One study argues that when consumers drink the two beverages blind and then are asked to analyze why they liked each one, they rely on established heuristics for things like soda, one of which might be "sweeter is better." As they write, "The greater ease of participants in verbalizing their positive reasons for Pepsi than for Coke indicates that the former cola possesses characteristics that provide a more plausible basis for experienced pleasantness." It is, in essence, easier to talk about why we might like Pepsi than why we might prefer Coke. Theoretically, that processing fluency, rather than the beverage itself, might explain our liking. See Ayumi Yamada et al., "The Effect of an Analytical Appreciation of Colas on Consumer Beverage Choice," *Food Quality and Preference* 34 (June 2014): 1–4.

105 Music scholars have even used: P. A. Bush and K. G. Pease, "Pop Records and Connotative Satiation: Test of Jakobovits' Theory," *Psychological Reports* 23 (1968): 871–75. The study about which they used the word "satiation" is Leon Jakobovits, "Studies of Fads: I. The 'Hit Parade,'" *Psychological Reports* 18 (1966): 443–50. Bush and Pease argued that Jakobovits's observed pattern was more complicated than he presented and might have represented a statistical artifact: "We suggest that the use of change in mean ratings in the kind of situation presented here may be unrealistic. Consideration of changes in the distribution of ratings and changes in ratings of individuals may be necessary to give a picture of the effects of repeated presentation of 'pop' records which is not misleading." Jako-

bovits, for his part, noted that the disliking engendered by overexposure could be corrected over time. "Therefore, one would expect that a song, which enjoyed high popularity and received extensive massed exposure, should be able to be 'revived' after some time and that this second popularity should be higher than that for another song, which was not as highly popular during its first life span." There are many examples of this; to name one, the use of Journey's "Don't Stop Believin'" in *The Sopranos*, *Glee*, and *The X Factor* among other shows, which resurrected its popularity; in the U.K., the song actually charted higher in 2010 than upon its initial 1981 release.

105   "a vast amount of brain space": Michael Pollan, *The Omnivore's Dilemma* (New York: Penguin, 2006), 4.

106   So we fall back on exposure: The causal chain between liking and familiarity and preference can get convoluted. As one experiment on familiarity and musical choice concluded, "The results also confirm that liking does not drive the strong relationship between familiarity and preference. In fact, familiarity predicts choice above and beyond liking, has a stronger direct effect on choice than does liking, and in some tests has even more explanatory power than does liking." See Morgan K. Ward, Joseph K. Goodman, and Julie R. Irwin, "The Same Old Song: The Power of Familiarity in Music Choice," *Marketing Letters* 25 (May 2013): 1–11.

106   It saves us time: The music critic Alex Ross, in wondering why modern audiences seemed more resistant to modern classical music—where they embraced more innovation in other fields—hints at the effect of exposure and familiarity when he writes, "Rather, modern composers have fallen victim to a long-smouldering indifference that is intimately linked to classical music's idolatrous relationship with the past. Even before 1900, people were attending concerts in the expectation that they would be massaged by the lovely sounds of bygone days. ('New works do not succeed in Leipzig,' a critic said of the premiere of Brahms's First Piano Concerto in 1859.)" What is good in classical music has been what has been familiar—for a few hundred years. Ross, "Why Do We Hate Modern Classical Music?," *Guardian*, Nov. 28, 2010.

106   It would be strange: But this raises a question. Were Holbrook and Schindler, as Rancière had accused Bourdieu, simply issuing a kind of musical recall test, quizzing people more on what they knew than what they liked? Given enough exposure to "Sledgehammer," would an older person not come to prefer it to "Smoke Rings"? How could younger people prefer the Mills Brothers' tune when there is in fact little chance they have ever heard it?

106   although the long-held idea: See, for example, Karsten Steinhauer, Erin J. White, and John E. Drury, "Temporal Dynamics of Late Second Language Acquisition: Evidence from Event-Related Brain Potentials," *Second Language Research* 25, no. 1 (2009): 13–41. See also Stefanie Nickels, Bertram Opitz, and Karsten Steinhauer, "ERPs Show That Classroom-Instructed Late Second Language Learners Rely on the Same Prosodic Cues in Syntactic Parsing as Native Speakers," *Neuroscience Letters* 557, pt. B (Dec. 17, 2013): 107–11.

107   "taste freeze": This phrase comes courtesy of Brian Whitman at the Echo Nest.

107   "The events and changes": Howard Schuman and Jacqueline Scott, "Generations and Collective Memories," *American Sociological Review* 54, no. 3 (1989): 359–81.

107   By this analysis: The Minutemen's Mike Watt, in the documentary *We Jam Econo*,

neatly encapsulated the idea of generational determinism: "You can't help when you were born, and what you are into. Some people were born before, some after, some during." People take it for granted that the "during" was their coming of musical age.

108   He had wrestled with the problem: "The idea that all music is equal and deserves equal rights is somehow fundamentally a democratic idea; as is the corresponding idea that the public, and not some small cadre of experts, is the best judge of musical quality," wrote Zapuder on his blog. "But the fact that some music not only attracts more listeners, but also seems to mean more to more people over a longer period of time, indicates that there is actually something fundamentally unequal about music as well." *Play Listen Repeat* (blog), Pandora, Feb. 25, 2009, http://blog.pandora.com/2009/02/25/imagine_that_yo/.

CHAPTER 4
HOW DO WE KNOW WHAT WE LIKE?

113   "while someone is eating": W. H. Auden, *Collected Poems* (New York: Vintage Books, 1991), 177. For a fascinating essay on the contemporary events that inspired Auden's comments on the sixteenth-century painting, see Alexander Nemerov, "The Flight of Form: Auden, Bruegel, and the Turn to Abstraction in the 1940s," *Critical Inquiry* 31, no. 4 (Summer 2005): 780–810.

114   for we get a measurable neural charge: See Andrew Parker, "Revealing Rembrandt," *Frontiers in Neuroscience*, April 21, 2014, doi:10.3389/fnins.2014.00076.

114   "The question of 'liking' Nauman": Peter Schjeldahl, "The Trouble with Nauman," in *Bruce Nauman*, ed. Robert C. Morgan (Baltimore: Johns Hopkins University Press, 2002), 100.

114   "which the senses find pleasing": Immanuel Kant, *The Critique of Judgment*, in *Basic Writings of Kant* (New York: Modern Library, 2001), 295.

114   "Art is first of all": Clement Greenberg, "The State of Art Criticism," in *Twentieth Century Theories of Art*, ed. James Thompson (Ottawa: Carleton University Press, 1990), 102.

114   It not only informs: For a good discussion, see Eric Anderson, Erika H. Siegel, and Lisa Feldman Barrett, "What You Feel Influences What You See: The Role of Affective Feelings in Resolving Binocular Rivalry," *Journal of Experimental Social Psychology* 47, no. 4 (2011): 856–60.

115   "we live in two worlds": See Eric Kandel, *The Age of Insight* (New York: Alfred A. Knopf, 2012), 284.

115   "the bucket theory": The reference comes from Alan Musgrave, *Common Sense, Science, and Scepticism* (Cambridge, U.K.: Cambridge University Press, 1993), 62.

115   Indeed, our memory of how we felt: Zajonc, in one experiment, exposed people to one-millisecond flashes of "random polygons," then asked subjects how much they liked them and whether they recognized them. When they saw a polygon more than once, they liked it, even though they were usually unable to remember, at a level above chance, which ones they had actually seen. See W. R. Kunst-Wilson and R. B. Zajonc, "Affective Discrimination of Stimuli That Cannot Be Recognized," *Science* 207, no. 4430 (1980): 557–80.

116   Similarly, if you like contemporary art: See Rémi Radel and Corentin Clément-Guillotin, "Evidence of Motivational Influences in Early Visual Perception: Hun-

ger Modulates Conscious Access," *Psychological Science* 23, no. 3 (March 2013): 232–34.

116   "I make a distinction": Edwin Denby, *Dance Writings and Poetry* (New Haven, Conn.: Yale University Press, 1998), 259.

116   "empyrean air": The phrase belongs to William Hazlitt, "Picture-Galleries in England," in *The Collected Works of William Hazlitt* (London: J. M. Dent, 1903), 7.

116   "way of seeing": See Svetlana Alpers, "The Museum as a Way of Seeing," in *Exhibiting Cultures*, ed. Ivan Karp and Steven D. Lavine (Washington, D.C.: Smithsonian Institution Press, 1991), 26.

116   fire extinguishers: See, for example, Karen Archey, "Christopher Williams's 'For Example: Dix-Huit Leçons sur la Société Industrielle (Revision 19),'" *Art Agenda*, Dec. 11, 2014, http://www.art-agenda.com/reviews/christopher-williams%E2%80 %99s-%E2%80%9Cfor-example-dix-huit-lecons-sur-la-societe-industrielle -revision-19%E2%80%9D/.

117   "must *create* his own experience": John Dewey, *Art as Experience* (New York: Perigee, 2005), 54.

117   "It fixed me like a statue": Thomas Jefferson, *The Papers of Thomas Jefferson*, ed. J. P. Boyd (Princeton, N.J.: Princeton University Press, 1955), 11:187.

117   "I came to recognize": Richard Wollheim, *Painting as an Art* (Princeton, N.J.: Princeton University Press, 1987), 8.

117   No one really knows: Ladislav Kesner makes the point that while we can empirically know people are having only a "fleeting encounter with a museum object," it is "impossible to articulate the opposite—to define comprehensively, let alone in empirically measurable terms, the satisfactory perceptual activity vis-à-vis a museum object." Kesner, "The Role of Cognitive Competence in the Art Museum Experience," *Museum Management and Curatorship* 21, no. 1 (2006): 4–19.

117   "This casual visitor": Edward S. Robinson, "The Behavior of the Museum Visitor," *Publications of the American Association of Museums*, n.s., 5 (1928).

117   "The fact is that": Jeffrey K. Smith and Lisa F. Wolf, "Museum Visitor Preferences and Intentions in Constructing Aesthetic Experience," *Poetics* 24, nos. 2–4 (1996): 222.

118   In a less scientific study: Philip Hensher, "We Know What We Like, and It's Not Modern Art," *Daily Mail*, March 12, 2011, http://www.dailymail.co.uk/news /article-1365672/Modern-art-How-gallery-visitors-viewed-work-Damien-Hirst -Tracy-Emin-5-seconds.html.

118   "an intelligent man": Benjamin Ives Gilman, "Museum Fatigue," *Scientific Monthly*, Jan. 1916, 62–74.

118   The density of sheer sensory input: See Alessandro Bollo et al., "Analysis of Visitor Behavior Inside the Museum: An Empirical Study," http://neumann.hec.ca /aimac2005/PDF_Text/BolloA_DalPozzoloL.pdf.

119   "walking past works of art": This phrase comes from Philip Fisher, via John Walsh, "Paintings, Tears, Lights, and Seats," *Antioch Review* 61, no. 4 (Autumn 2003): 767–82.

119   more coffee and chairs: See James M. Bradburne, "Charm and Chairs: The Future of Museums," *Journal of Museum Education* 26, no. 3 (Fall 2001): 3–9.

119   "According to averages": Robinson, "Behavior of the Museum Visitor."

119   trying to see as much: The museum researcher Stephen Bitgood argues that visitors are driven by a "value ratio, aiming to reap the largest benefit or satisfaction

per investment of time and money." See Bitgood, "An Analysis of Visitor Circulation: Movement Patterns and the General Value Principle," *Curator* 49, no. 4 (2006): 463–75; and Bitgood, "An Overview of the Attention-Value Model," in *Attention and Value: Keys to Understanding Museum Visitors* (Walnut Creek, Calif.: Left Coast Press, 2013).

119   Research suggests: For a fascinating, micro-level video analysis of how people stand in front of paintings in museums, see Dirk Vom Lehn, "Configuring Standpoints: Aligning Perspectives in Art Exhibitions," *Bulletin Suisse de Linguistique Appliquée*, no. 96 (2012): 69–90.

119   People may look more: The museum researcher Beverly Serrell, looking at a number of museums, including the American Museum of Natural History, found that the one with the lowest "sweep rate"—square footage divided by time spent by visitors—was a small museum in Alaska. One reason was self-selection: The people who came all the way to Homer, Alaska, really wanted to see the show. See Serrell, "Paying More Attention to Paying Attention," Informal Science, March 15, 2010, http://informalscience.org/perspectives/blog/paying-more-attention-to-paying -attention.

120·   In an experiment in a Swiss museum: See Martin Tröndle et al., "The Effects of Curatorial Arrangements," *Museum Management and Curatorship* 29, no. 2 (2014): 140–73.

120   Curiously, other studies: See Jeffrey Smith, *The Museum Effect: How Museums, Libraries, and Cultural Institutions Educate and Civilize Society* (Lanham, Md.: Rowman & Littlefield, 2014), 34.

120   Even when people visit in groups: See ibid., 22. Smith calls the behavior "visit together, look alone."

120   the more people do talk: See Martin Tröndle et al., "A Museum for the Twenty-First Century: The Influence of 'Sociality' on Art Reception in Museum Space," *Museum Management and Curatorship* 27, no. 5 (2012): 461–86.

120   "Don't make large down payments": See Jay Rounds, "Strategies for the Curiosity-Driven Museum Visitor," *Curator* 47, no. 4 (Oct. 2007): 404.

121   In as little as fifty: See, for example, Paolo Viviani and Christelle Aymoz, "Colour, Form, and Movement Are Not Perceived Simultaneously," *Vision Research* 41, no. 22 (Oct. 2001): 2909–18. Semir Zeki raises the interesting idea that the primacy of color in visual processing might affect our aesthetic evaluation: "It is plausible, and interesting, to suppose that combinations that satisfy some more primitive significant configuration, and are found to be more aesthetically pleasing, may be processing more rapidly than those which, not coming as close to satisfying a significant configuration, are found to be less satisfying aesthetically." See Semir Zeki and Tomohiro Ishizu, "The 'Visual Shock' of Francis Bacon: An Essay in Neuroesthetics," *Frontiers in Human Neuroscience* 7 (Dec. 2013): 9.

121   young woman's face: For an interesting account of how subjects in paintings, like Vermeer's girl, came to be usually looking "at us," see Olivier Morin, "How Portraits Turned Their Eyes upon Us: Visual Preferences and Demographic Change in Cultural Evolution," *Evolution in Human Behavior* 34, no. 3 (2013): 222–29. In some cultures, he notes, the direct gaze is discouraged, but "in traditions where gaze direction is left free to vary, so that we find both averted and direct-gaze portraits, the latter style should enjoy more success and, over time, become the default option."

121   rove more freely: See Davide Massaro et al., "When Art Moves the Eyes: A Be-
        havioral and Eye-Tracking Study," *PLoS ONE* 7, no. 5 (2012): 1–12. How we
        look at individual faces is also an interesting mixture of top-down and bottom-up.
        When we look at famous faces, for example, we look less at the eyes and other
        upper areas—typically so important for identification—probably because we al-
        ready recognize the person and we are just looking elsewhere to confirm our
        hypothesis. See Jason J. S. Barton et al., "Information Processing During Face
        Recognition: The Effects of Familiarity, Inversion, and Morphing on Scanning
        Fixations," *Perception* 35, no. 8 (2006): 1089–105.

121   Judged by eye tracking: See Paul Locher, "The Structural Framework of Pictorial
        Balance," *Perception* 25, no. 12 (1996): 1419–36.

121   As for the frame: This would be for the good; he noted that the frame, "instead
        of attracting attention to itself," limits "itself to concentrating attention and mak-
        ing it spill onto the picture." Neither painting nor wall but a hermetic barrier
        between the two, it was meant to be invisible everywhere except when it did not
        have a painting inside it. See José Ortega y Gasset, "Meditations on the Frame,"
        Perspecta 26 (1990): 185–90.

121   studies routinely demonstrate: See, among others, C. F. Nodine, P. J. Locher,
        and E. A. Krupinski, "The Role of Formal Art Training on the Perception and
        Aesthetic Judgment of Art Compositions," *Leonardo* 26, no. 3 (1993): 219–27.

121   "The appreciation of the aesthetic worth": H. J. Eysenck, "The Experimental
        Study of the 'Good Gestalt'—a New Approach," *Psychological Review* 49, no. 4
        (July 1942): 351. Thanks to Paul Locher for the quotation.

122   In one of Locher's studies: Paul J. Locher, "The Aesthetic Experience with Visual
        Art 'at First Glance,'" in *Investigations into the Phenomenology and the Ontology of
        the Work of Art: What Are Artworks and How Do We Experience Them?*, ed. Peer F.
        Bundgaard and Frederik Stjernfelt (New York: Springer, 2015).

122   "What do you see": See Abigail Housen, "Eye of the Beholder: Research, Theory,
        and Practice" (paper presented at the conference "Aesthetic and Art Education: A
        Transdisciplinary Approach," Sept. 27–29, 1999, Lisbon, Portugal).

122   "old friend": See "Aesthetic Development," Visual Thinking Strategies, http://
        www.vtshome.org/research/aesthetic-development.

122   As many art historians have noted: Kenneth C. Lindsay and Bernard Huppe
        note, for example, "We must search through masses of detail in order to find the
        iconographical center." Lindsay and Huppe, "Meaning and Method in Brueghel's
        Painting," *Journal of Aesthetics and Art Criticism* 14, no. 3 (March 1956): 376–86.

122   "For most decisions": Robert Zajonc, "Feeling and Thinking: Closing the De-
        bate over the Independence of Affect," in *Feeling and Thinking: The Role of Affect
        in Social Cognition*, ed. Joseph P. Forgas (New York: Cambridge University Press,
        2000).

123   You are more likely: See Andrew P. Bayliss et al., "Affective Evaluations of Ob-
        jects Are Influenced by Observed Gaze Direction and Emotional Expression,"
        Cognition 104, no. 3 (Sept. 2007): 644–53. For another study, which actually used
        paintings as the target stimulus, see Clementine Bry et al., "Eye'm Lovin' It! The
        Role of Gazing Awareness in Mimetic Desires," *Journal of Experimental Social
        Psychology* 47, no. 5 (Sept. 2011): 987–93.

123   Even that creepy look: See Carole Henry, "How Visitors Relate to Museum Ex-
        periences: An Analysis of Positive and Negative Emotions," *Journal of Aesthetic*

Education 34, no. 2 (Summer 2000): 99–106. She reports in one study an uncomfortable exchange between a visitor and a guard: "The student's museum experience was no longer focused on the art but instead reflected an embarrassing incident."

123   "Affect often persists": Zajonc, "Feeling and Thinking," 157.

123   As the critic Clement Greenberg quipped: The quotation comes from Thierry de Duve, *Clement Greenberg Between the Lines* (Chicago: University of Chicago Press, 2010), 19.

123   "I think you need to give": See George Plimpton, "The Art of the Matter," *New Yorker*, June 10, 2012.

123   Our ability to so quickly: As a curator once told the professor of psychology Mihaly Csikszentmihalyi, "Paintings give the illusion that you can see them in one second." Or less! The apparent ease of our viewing—the painting is just laid out flat there for us, and there is nothing telling us what we are not getting—combined with quick and instinctive feelings of affect, helps explain why it is not uncommon to find, in surveys of visitors, a pervading sentiment that people are "waiting": waiting for a painting to blow them away, waiting to "get the message" of a painting. Mihaly Csikszentmihalyi and Rick E. Robinson, *The Art of Seeing: An Interpretation of the Aesthetic Encounter* (Malibu, Calif.: J. Paul Getty Museum and the Getty Center for Education in the Arts, 1990), 147.

123   "find my first impression": Kenneth Clark, *Looking at Pictures* (London: John Murray, 1960), 16.

123   One museum study found: See "Interpretation at the Minneapolis Institute of Arts: Policy and Practice," http://www.museum-ed.org/wp-content/uploads /2010/08/mia_interpretation_museum-ed.pdf.

124   which, as research has shown: In one well-known study, the psychologist Alfred Yarbus had viewers—equipped with a primitive eye-tracking device—look at a painting (Ilya Efimovich Repin's *Unexpected Return*, which shows a soldier returning from Siberian exile), and then asked them questions like the following: How long had he been away? What is the socioeconomic condition of the family? Depending on the question asked, viewers' gaze patterns were quite different. It is not difficult to draw a comparison to the information that labels might provide and how that would direct viewer attention. See Yarbus, *Eye Movements and Vision*, trans. Basil Haigh (New York: Plenum Press, 1967). Also, for a good summary of Yarbus's research, see Sasha Archibald, "Ways of Seeing," *Cabinet*, no. 30 (Summer 2008), http://www.cabinetmagazine.org/issues/30/archibald.php.

124   "decide how much time": Hensher, "We Know What We Like, and It's Not Modern Art."

124   That abstract by de Kooning: This example was provided to me by Pablo Tinio, in his paper "From Artistic Creation to Aesthetic Reception: The Mirror Model of Art," *Psychology of Aesthetics, Creativity, and the Arts*, 7, no. 3 (2013): 265–75.

124   We get caught: See David Brieber et al., "Art in Time and Space: Context Modulates the Relation Between Art Experience and Viewing Time," *PloS ONE* 9, no. 6 (June 2014): 1–8.

125   Elsewhere in the Prado: See Mary Tompkins Lewis, "The Power, and Art, of Painting," *Wall Street Journal*, Sept. 25, 2009.

125   "exotic and dangerous character": Michael Baxandall, *Painting and Experience in Fifteenth Century Italy* (Oxford: Oxford University Press, 1988), 11.

125   In a study of visitors: See Jeffrey K. Smith and Pablo P. L. Tinio, "Audibly Engaged: Talking the Walk," in *Digital Technologies and the Museum Experience: Handheld Guides and Other Media*, ed. Loïc Tallon and Kevin Walker (New York: AltaMira Press, 2008), 75.

125   "a lot of people": Ludwig Wittgenstein, *Lectures and Conversations on Aesthetics, Psychology, and Religious Belief* (Berkeley: University of California Press, 2007), 3.

126   "Even when contemplating": Alain de Botton, *Art as Therapy* (London: Phaidon Press, 2013), 170.

126   Hence the anxieties: Ayumi Yamada, "Appreciating Art Verbally: Verbalization Can Make a Work of Art Be Both Undeservedly Loved and Unjustly Maligned," *Journal of Experimental Social Psychology* 45, no. 5 (2009): 1140–43.

126   As one museum consultant: The curator Ingrid Schaffner notes that wall labels in contemporary art can "say what the small museum won't tell," that is, "it's okay that you don't find this pleasing, it wasn't made to be." See Schaffner, "Wall Labels," in *What Makes a Great Exhibition?*, ed. Paula Marincola (London: Reaktion Books, 2007), 154–69.

128   "how unconsciously many people": Harlow Gale, "On the Psychology of Advertising," *Psychological Studies*, July 1900, 39–69.

128   "one of the most interesting": *Art-Journal* 11 (1872): 37.

129   "Certainly, compared with its rival": *New York Times*, Nov. 12, 1871.

129   Hardly anyone replied: See Erika Michael, *Hans Holbein the Younger: A Guide to Research* (New York: Routledge, 2013), 327.

129   "antique appearance": Fechner collected the results of his study in the document *Bericht über das auf der Dresdner Holbein-Ausstellung ausgelegte Album* (Leipzig: Breitkopf und Härtel, 1872). Thanks to Sophie Duvernoy for translation assistance.

129   Fechner's work, which became known: See, for example, Jay Hetrick, "Aisthesis in Radical Empiricism: Gustav Fechner's Psychophysics and Experimental Aesthetics," *Proceedings of the European Society for Aesthetics* 3 (2011): 139–53.

129   "Everybody knows that he": The Fechner quotation is referenced in J. E. V. Temme, "Fechner's Primary School Revisited: Towards a Social Psychology of Taste," *Poetics* 21, no. 6 (1993): 463–79.

130   Critics noted that his studies: Subsequent studies have found various forms of statistical bias; for example, while there might be a weak "population wide" preference for a certain rectangle, when you drilled down to the individual level, people had quite strong—and quite varied—preferences. See I. C. McManus, "Beauty Is Instinctive Feeling: Experimenting on Aesthetics and Art," in *The Aesthetic Mind: Philosophy and Psychology*, ed. Elisabeth Schellekens and Peter Goldie (Oxford: Oxford University Press, 2011), 179. McManus writes, "Some people do like rectangles, but there is no special status for the Golden Section rectangle."

130   And how did you know people: This point comes from Richard Padovan: "The general preference for figures between a square and a half and a square and three quarters could equally be due simply to the subjects' familiarity with similar shapes in such everyday things as playing cards, window panes, books, and paintings." See Padovan, *Proportion: Science, Philosophy, Architecture* (London: Taylor and Francis, 1999), 312.

130   After Fechner, many have objected: The philosopher Rudolf Arnheim, for example, charged that by making it a matter of "preference," the practitioners of experimental aesthetics "neglected everything that distinguishes the pleasure

generated for a work of art from the pleasure generated by a dish of ice cream." Fechner's studies of rectangles, even if they seemed to reveal some preferences, could tell *what* people liked; they could not tell *why*. Most studies, Arnheim charged, "tell us deplorably little about what people see when they look at an aesthetic object, what they mean by saying that they like or dislike it, and why they prefer the objects they prefer." See Arnheim, "The Other Gustav Theodor Fechner," in *New Essays on the Psychology of Art* (Berkeley: University of California Press, 1986), 45. Even one of the field's most prominent advocates, the psychologist Daniel Berlyne, who picked up the experimental aesthetics torch in the early 1970s, observed that "experimental aesthetics has had a long but not particularly distinguished history." Berlyne, *Studies in the New Experimental Aesthetics* (Washington, D.C.: Hemisphere Publishing, 1974), 5.

130 Artists, Zeki has argued: As with Fechner, there are suggestions that neuroaesthetics tries to reduce the complexity of art to simple metrics, like "beauty," whose relevance in contemporary art is suspect. For example, an interesting study of gallery visitors who were hooked up to a device that measured galvanic skin responses, heart rate, and other physiological measures while people looked at paintings found that a work like Andy Warhol's *Campbell's Soup Cans*, while rating low on "aesthetic value," nevertheless generated higher-than-average physical responses. "We assume that the reason is the work's broad popularity and that the encounter with the 'original' may cause these strong effects." See Martin Tröndle and Wolfgang Tschacher, "The Physiology of Phenomenology: The Effects of Artworks," *Empirical Studies of the Arts* 30, no. 1 (2012): 79–117. Another critique is that the findings of neuroaesthetics are too obvious. For example, the art critic Blake Gopnik wrote, "To discover that kinetic art is an art of motion, and that it triggers motion sensors in the visual cortex, or that the Fauves were colorists, and (guess what) made art that especially triggers color sensors, . . . adds almost nothing that wasn't already obvious about these movements." Quoted in Arthur P. Shimamura and Stephen E. Palmer, eds., *Aesthetic Science: Connecting Minds, Brains, and Experience* (New York: Oxford University Press, 2013), 145. Neuroaesthetics, others have argued, "may be killing your soul." Philip Ball, "Neuroaesthetics Is Killing Your Soul," *Nature*, March 22, 2003.

130 "exploring the potential": See George Walden, "Beware the Fausts of Neuroscience," *Standpoint*, April 2012, http://www.standpointmag.co.uk/node/4367/full.

130 So Mondrian, for example: Writes Zeki, "When we view one of Mondrian's abstract paintings in which the emphasis is on lines . . . large numbers of cells in charted visual areas of our brains will be activated and responding vigorously, providing a line of given orientation falls on the part of the field that a cell with a preference for that orientation 'looks at.'" See Semir Zeki, *Inner Vision: An Exploration of Art and the Brain* (Oxford: Oxford University Press, 1999), 114. Interestingly, it may not matter how you look at a painting by Mondrian to excite the right effect. One study found that his work *Composition* was preferred more in three other orientations than the original way it was meant to be displayed (although subjects were much better at guessing the proper orientation of other modern paintings). See George Mather, "Aesthetic Judgment of Orientation in Modern Art," *i-Perception* 3, no. 1 (2012): 18–24. Another study took a number of Mondrian images and rendered their lines as oblique, rather than horizontal and vertical (using "lozenge"-shaped frames to avoid a corrupting influence of the

frame's orientation). Here people much preferred the original paintings (though as always there could be a familiarity effect—people know what Mondrians are supposed to look like). See Richard Latto, "Do We Like What We See?," in *Multidisciplinary Approaches to Visual Representations and Interpretations*, ed. Grant Malcolm (Amsterdam: Elsevier, 2004), 343–56.

130 It is not unthinkable: See Zaira Cattaneo et al., "The World Can Look Better: Enhancing Beauty Experience with Brain Stimulation," *Social Cognitive and Affective Neuroscience* 9, no. 11 (2014): 1713–21. Interestingly, similar effects have been found with food. In one trial, an "electrode-equipped spoon," which comes with lights as well, was used to "augment the perceived intensity of the flavor." See Aviva Rutkin, "Food Bland? Electric Spoon Zaps Taste into Every Bite," *New Scientist*, Oct. 31, 2014.

131 We even seem able: See Joel S. Winston et al., "Brain Systems for Assessing Facial Attractiveness," *Neuropsychologia* 45 (2007): 195–206. As the researchers note, "Indeed it appears that actually attending to facial attractiveness appears to diminish activity in at least some reward-related areas. One possible interpretation of these results is that the reward value (or perhaps aesthetic value) of a visual stimulus is diminished when trying to evaluate it. Clearly further behavioural and neuroimaging research is needed to elucidate this seemingly paradoxical effect."

131 When people look at painted: See Dahlia Zaidel, *Neuropsychology of Art: Neurological, Cognitive and Evolutionary Perspectives* (New York: Psychology Press, 2013), 167.

132 "visual shock": See Zeki and Ishizu, "'Visual Shock' of Francis Bacon."

132 "to *something unusual*": Michael Peppiatt, *Francis Bacon: Anatomy of an Enigma* (London: Weidenfeld & Nicolson, 1996), 153.

132 "It is unnatural": For an elaboration, see Dahlia Zaidel and Marjan Hessamian, "Asymmetry and Symmetry in the Beauty of Human Faces," *Symmetry* 2, no. 1 (2010): 136–49.

132 The left side of the face: See, for example, H. A. Sackeim and R. C. Gur, "Lateral Asymmetry in Intensity of Emotional Expression," *Neuropsychologia* 16 (1978): 473–82.

132 Artists, indeed, might have sensed: See I. C. McManus, "Turning the Left Cheek," in *Consciousness Regained: Chapters in the Development of Mind*, ed. Nicholas Humphrey (Oxford: Oxford University Press, 1983), 138–42. James Schirillo has questioned the innate nature of this preference. "In modern society," he writes, "the right side of a woman's face is typically judged to be more attractive by both men and women alike." So during the era of painters like Rembrandt, people might have actually preferred right-cheeked portraits but deferred instead to social norms (the right cheek, he suggests, might express "prowess, dominance and status," which might have been deemed threatening in female subjects. See Schirillo, "Hemispheric Asymmetries and Gender Influence Rembrandt's Portrait Orientations," *Neuropsychologia* 38, no. 12 (Oct. 2000): 1593–606.

133 "He uses the technique": Zeki makes this point in more detail in "The Woodhull Lecture: Visual Art and the Visual Brain," reprinted in *Exploring the Universe: Essays on Science and Technology*, ed. P. Day (London: Oxford University Press, 1997), 37.

133 What is more interesting: See Richard P. Taylor et al., "Perceptual and Physiological Responses to Jackson Pollock's Fractals," *Frontiers in Human Neuroscience*, June 22, 2011, 11. It could be, the authors suggest, that we find Pollock's

"high D" fractal work so compelling because our eyes are in essence trying to find the more familiar fractal forms or solving a kind of puzzle. Maybe Pollock himself became so familiar with fractals that he began to gravitate to more complex forms (and as we became more familiar with Pollock, so did we).

133   But research has shown: See Connon Diemand-Yauman, Daniel M. Oppenheimer, and Erikka B. Vaughan, "Fortune Favors the Bold (and the Italicized): Effects of Disfluency on Educational Outcomes," *Cognition* 118, no. 1 (Jan. 2011): 111–15. The authors note, "Importantly, disfluency can function as a cue that one may not have mastery over material." In art, this attempt toward "mastery" might be what keeps you thinking about, what keeps you coming back to, a piece.

134   "their aesthetic beauty": See Hans Richter, *Dada: Art and Anti-art* (London: Thames and Hudson, 1965), 207–8.

134   "nothing that meets the eye": Arthur Danto, *The Abuse of Beauty* (New York: Open Court, 2003), 17.

134   You can parse the validity: See Lea Höfel and Thomas Jacobsen, "Electrophysiological Indices of Processing Aesthetics: Spontaneous or Intentional Processes?," *International Journal of Psychophysiology* 65, no. 1 (July 2007): 20–31. The authors write, "The early frontocentral ERP effect, taken to reflect impression formation in an aesthetic judgment task for the assessment of not beautiful patterns, was not obtained in the present study. It thus appears to require the intention to assess the aesthetic value of the stimuli as well as to decide on an aesthetic judgment. Neither viewing nor contemplating the stimulus material evoked an ERP signature indicating processes that differentiate between beautiful and not beautiful patterns." Which suggests an interesting idea: That we do not "know" how we feel about something aesthetically until we are actually forced to think about it. This study, it should be noted, used abstract graphic forms, not actual artworks. As Helmut Leder and Pablo Tinio note, "The question of whether cortical structures that respond to artworks are the same as those that respond to everyday objects remains unresolved and open for examination." See Tinio and Leder, "The Means to Art's End: Styles, Creative Devices, and the Challenge of Art," in *Neuroscience of Creativity*, ed. Oshin Vartanian, Adam S. Bristol, and James C. Kaufman (Cambridge, Mass.: MIT Press, 2013), 273–98.

134   "I just paint things": The quotation comes via Victor Bockris, *Warhol: The Biography* (New York: Da Capo Press, 2009), 148.

134   Art is what the art world: Arthur Danto, *Journal of Philosophy* 61, no. 19 (1964): 571–84. The notion of what makes a piece of conceptual art art is where, Danto wrote, "we enter a domain of conceptual inquiry where native speakers are poor guides: *they* are lost themselves."

134   This flip tautology: In an interesting study held at Switzerland's St. Gallen Fine Arts Museum, a "site specific" intervention—a series of small tagged comments in marker on the museum's pristine walls—by the artist Nedko Solakov was used as the "stimulus" to learn whether visitors considered the art to be, in essence, art. Even after various experimental manipulations that explained the context of the show, its rationale, and so on, only a bare majority considered the work "art." See Martin Tröndle, Volker Kirchberg, and Wolfgang Tschacher, "Is This Art? An Experimental Study on Visitors' Judgement of Contemporary Art," *Cultural Sociology*, April 7, 2014, http://cus.sagepub.com/content/early/2014/04/07/1749975513507243.full.pdf. On the other hand, a neuroimaging study found

that when subjects viewed images they were told were from a prestigious museum, and other objects that were said to be computer generated, differing brain
activations (and higher aesthetic ratings) were noted for the "museum" paintings
than for the others. See Ulrich Kirk et al., "Modulation of Aesthetic Value by
Semantic Context: An fMRI Study," *NeuroImage* 44 (2009): 1125–32.

134   As Edward Vessel: Edward Vessel, Irving Biederman, and Mark Cohen, "How
Opiate Activity May Determine Spontaneous Visual Selection" (paper presented
at the Third Annual Vision Sciences Society meeting, Sarasota, Fla., 2003).

135   In one study: In the tricky world of art, of course, people may prefer an Ed Rus-
cha picture of a parking lot to a landscape painting.

135   "universal language": See Hannah Brinkmann et al., "Abstract Art as a Universal
Language?," *Leonardo* 47, no. 3 (June 2014): 256–57.

135   People seem to prefer things: When viewers in one study were shown abstract
artworks, their liking for the works increased with a title that seemed semanti-
cally related (liking declined when the title did not seem to correspond to the
painting). See Benno Belke et al., "Cognitive Fluency: High-Level Processing
Dynamics in Art Appreciation," *Psychology of Aesthetics, Creativity, and the Arts* 4,
no. 4 (Nov. 2010): 214–22. See also Helmut Leder et al., "Entitling Art: Influence of Title Information on Understanding and Appreciation of Paintings," *Acta
Psychologia* 121, no. 2 (2006): 176–98.

135   After people are shown photographs: A. S. Cowen, M. M. Chun, and B. A. Kuhl,
"Neural Portraits of Perception: Reconstructing Face Images from Evoked Brain
Activity," *NeuroImage*, July 1, 2014, 12–22. See also Kerri Smith, "Brain Decoding: Reading Minds," *Nature*, Oct. 23, 2013; and Larry Greenemeier, "Decoding
the Brain," *Scientific American*, Nov./Dec. 2014.

136   "an immersion so complete": Dewey, *Art as Experience*, 288.

137   In the early 1990s: See James E. Cutting, "Gustave Caillebotte, French Impressionism, and Mere Exposure," *Psychonomic Bulletin and Review* 10, no. 2 (2003):
319–43.

138   In a final experiment: See ibid.

139   Caillebotte himself was "rediscovered": Wrote one art historian, "It is almost as
if we had to wait a century to perceive properly the mysteries of the humdrum
recorded by Caillebotte." Morton Shackleford, *Gustave Caillebotte: The Painter's
Eye* (Chicago: University of Chicago Press, 2015), 19.

139   "roughly match Kinkade's subject matter": Aaron Meskin et al., "Mere Exposure
to Bad Art," *British Journal of Aesthetics* 53, no. 2 (2013): 139–64.

140   "classic is a book": See Robert McCrum, "The 100 Best Novels: An Introduction," *Guardian*, Sept. 22, 2013, http://www.theguardian.com/books/2013/sep
/22/100-best-novels-robert-mccrum.

140   "desire to feel": Alexis Boylan, in Alexis Boylan, ed., *Thomas Kinkade: The Artist in
the Mall* (Durham, N.C.: Duke University Press, 2011), 13.

140   his glowing windows: Kinkade once said, "I paint glowing windows because
glowing windows say home to me." And, per Kundera's formulation, they must
say home to you and the rest of the world as well. The quotation comes from
Michael Clapper, "Thomas Kinkade's Romantic Landscape," *American Art* 20,
no. 2 (Summer 2006): 76–99.

140   "The meaning of a great work": Clark, *Looking at Pictures*, 15.

141   In an age of anxious social mobility: For an excellent study of the period, see

Jeremy Black, *Culture in Eighteenth-Century England: A Subject for Taste* (London: Bloomsbury, 2006).

141   more indicative of one's own character: As David Marshall notes, "As the criteria for judging works of art shifted from conformity to classical rules to the power of art to shape the subjective experience of readers and beholders, unprecedented demands were placed on the experience of art." See Marshall, *The Frame of Art: Fictions of Aesthetic Experience, 1750–1815* (Baltimore: Johns Hopkins University Press, 2005), 6.

141   "notoriously difficult": A not infrequent characterization, but this one in particular comes from George Dickie.

141   Kant argues that things: Zeki, for instance, ran an experiment to determine whether people found certain mathematical equations more beautiful. But how could you ever find someone who had never seen a single mathematical formula? See Semir Zeki et al., "The Experience of Mathematical Beauty and Its Neural Correlates," *Frontiers in Human Neuroscience*, Feb. 13, 2014, 1–12, http://journal .frontiersin.org/Journal/10.3389/fnhum.2014.00068/full. Zeki raises the interesting point that even if people who did not understand the equations per se, but still found them beautiful (more so than others): "It leads to the capital question of whether beauty, even in so abstract an area as mathematics, is a pointer to what is true in nature, both within our nature and in the world in which we have evolved." One imagines an experiment, for example, in which laypeople were given true and false mathematical equations; if the ones they thought were more beautiful turned out to be the true ones, there might be something to the idea of beauty and truth. Expert mathematicians, of course, would already be able to tell if they were true or false, and that would confound their aesthetic judgment.

141   "All of this activity": See Denis Dutton, "The Experience of Art Is Paradise Regained: Kant on Free and Dependent Beauty," *British Journal of Aesthetics* 34, no. 3 (1994): 226–39.

141   Even knowing it was a shell: In Kant's view, we could look at a picture of a never-before-seen cluster of objects in space, have no preconception of it, nothing to even refer it to—and find beauty in it. In the real world, astronomers enhance the images with "false color" and other techniques to make the images look more like our concept of what beautiful objects in space should look like. See Lisa K. Smith et al., "Aesthetics and Astronomy: Studying the Public's Perception and Understanding of Imagery from Space," *Science Communication* 33, no. 2 (June 2011): 201–38. See also Anya Ventura, "Pretty Pictures: The Use of False Color in Images of Deep Space," in *Invisible Culture*, issue 19, Oct. 29, 2013, http://ivc.lib.rochester.edu/portfolio/pretty-pictures-the-use-of-false-color-in -images-of-deep-space/. As the author notes, "Although the public is encouraged to interpret these images as landscapes—photographic dispatches from the outer limits—we have no referent by which to judge the authenticity of these topographies, no physical mirror of understanding."

141   "a pure judgment of taste": Immanuel Kant, *Critique of Judgment*, in *The Bloomsbury Anthology of Aesthetics*, ed. Joseph J. Tanke and Colin McQuilian (London: A. C. Black, 2012), 256.

142   Whereas he was once "underrated": See Peter Jones, "Hume's Aesthetics Reassessed," *Philosophical Quarterly* 26, no. 102 (1976): 56.

142   Although he was said to have: For example, Hume's "judgment of poets and play-

wrights was notably bad." See Timothy M. Costelloe, "Hume's Aesthetics: The Literature and Directions for Research," *Hume Studies* 30, no. 1 (April 2004): 88.

142 "The great variety of taste": See David Hume, "Of the Standard of Taste," in *Selected Essays*, ed. Stephen Copley and Andrew Edgar (Oxford: Oxford University Press, 2008), 133.

142 "Men of the most confined knowledge": As one study noted, rather despairingly, "The literature concerning visual arts preferences is often contradictory and confusing . . . the findings of one study frequently contradict another, and none have concerned themselves with why two apparently similar children (age, sex, socio-economic status) respond differently to the same artwork." Pauline J. Ahmad, "Visual Art Preference Studies: A Review of Contradictions," *Visual Arts Research* 11, no. 2 (Fall 1985): 104.

143 for it was only recently: In some ways, they were still not separated: Hume himself, as a member of a trade society, had overseen the judging of a "discourse on Taste" that featured not only "the belles lettres and the sciences" but "porter" and "strong ale." See Ernest Campbell Mossner, *The Life of David Hume* (Oxford: Oxford University Press, 2001), 283. The winner of the competition was Alexander Gerard's "Essay on Taste."

143 "confounds the genuine sentiment": Hume, "Of the Standard of Taste," 144.

143 Did he, in saying: As the philosopher Peter Kivy notes, the question of whether something was a good piece of art was now replaced with whether someone was a good critic, and who was to decide that? How did you know if you yourself had sufficient capacity for appreciation, and if you did not, how could you tell *who* had it? See Kivy, "Hume's Standard of Taste: Breaking the Circle," *British Journal of Aesthetics* 7, no. 1 (1967): 57–66. There is also a problem of metacognition. As George Dickie notes, "The problem with Hume's view here is that a person who lacks delicate taste cannot easily come to know that another person has it." See Dickie, *The Century of Taste* (Oxford: Oxford University Press, 1996), 134.

143 "abandon their own prejudices": See Michelle Mason, "Moral Prejudice and Aesthetic Deformity: Rereading Hume's 'Of the Standard of Taste,' " *Journal of Aesthetics and Art Criticism* 59, no. 1 (Winter 2001): 60. She raises a larger problem, what she calls the "moral prejudice dilemma." If a work of art—say something generated by the Nazi regime—goes against the moral convictions of a critic, the critic must disregard his moral objections (she says Hume calls this a "perversion of sentiments"), or if he takes a moral stand against the artwork, he risks failing the "freedom from prejudice" standard of the ideal critic. She argues Hume sides with the moralists in the end. And what about a critic's "delicacy of taste"— was there an optimal range in his sensory apparatus? So-called supertasters, with their heightened discriminatory powers, would seem super-ideal critics. But they often dislike foods that most of us like. Does that make them good or bad judges? Frances Raven raises this point in an interesting essay, "Are Supertasters Good Candidates for Being Humean Ideal Critics?," *Contemporary Aesthetics*, http://www.contempaesthetics.org/newvolume/pages/article.php?articleID=282. Perhaps most provocatively, Jerrold Levinson wonders why we should actually follow the aesthetic judgment of ideal critics: "Why should one be moved by the fact that such and such things are preferred by ideal critics, if one is not oneself?" If you are already aesthetically gratified by, say, Thomas Kinkade, why should you care if critics say he is not a great artist? Sure, you could go and learn about all

the better painters that are out there, spending all that time in earnest aesthetic apprenticeship, learning to (one hopes) like what ideal critics like. "Granted," Levinson notes, "this would allow one to register the qualities of and be gratified by works that one was blind to and unmoved by before." But is all that *worth* it—all that time, energy, not to mention the "foregone pleasures of what has already come to appreciate," when you could simply stick with what you already know and like? See Jerrold Levinson, "Hume's Standard of Taste: The Real Problem," *Journal of Aesthetics and Art Criticism* 60, no. 3 (Summer 2002): 227–37.

143   "instead of fixing": From the *Critical Review* 3 (1757): 213, quoted in Kivy, "Hume's Standard of Taste," 65.

143   As the professor of philosophy: James Shelley, "Hume's Double Standard of Taste," *Journal of Aesthetics and Art Criticism* 52, no. 4 (Autumn 1994): 437–45.

144   Kinkade may be in: See Boylan, *Thomas Kinkade*, 1.

144   but the work of Maxfield Parrish: See, for example, "Maxfield Parrish: The Gertrude Vanderbilt Whitney Murals," http://www.tylermuseum.org/MaxfieldParrish.aspx.

144   Good luck finding him: Interestingly, the critical take on Maxfield Parrish is still evolving; see, for example, Edward J. Sozanski, "Taking Maxfield Parrish Seriously," Philly.com, June 9, 1999, http://articles.philly.com/1999-06-09/entertainment/25498843_1_maxfield-parrish-fine-arts-currier-gallery.

146   "You can hate something": See Plimpton, "Art of the Matter." Or, as another MOBA curator said, "If someone says 'turn around and look at that,' you don't know whether it's good or bad—either way, people want to share it." This quotation comes from a MOBA video presentation accessed at http://vimeo.com/11917386.

146   "that are almost identical": Semir Zeki and John Paul Romaya, "Neural Correlates of Hate," *PLoS ONE* 3, no. 10 (Oct. 2008): 4.

146   "formless, incoherent": Kendall Walton, "Categories of Art," *Philosophical Review* 79, no. 3 (1970): 334–67. Thanks to Jonathan Neufeld for recommending this paper.

146   There is a bit of a causal loop: See Rachel Smallman and Neal J. Roese, "Preference Invites Categorization," *Psychological Science* 19, no. 12 (2008): 1228–32.

147   My favorite record store: In what has been suggestively called the "mere categorization" effect, simply having categories, "even when those categories do not provide information about the options in the assortment," seems to make consumers feel better about the things they choose. C. Mogilner, T. Rudnick, and S. S. Iyengar, "The Mere Categorization Effect: How the Presence of Categories Increases Choosers' Perceptions of Assortment Variety and Outcome Satisfaction," *Journal of Consumer Research* 35, no. 2 (2008): 202–15.

147   When we do not like something: A study looking at the differences between architects' preferences and those of laypeople noted, "As consumers develop into connoisseurs they take account of new attributes in product evaluation, thereby changing their overall preferences; for example, a wine connoisseur will detect and attach importance to attributes of a wine that are not apparent to non-connoisseurs. This model suggests that non-connoisseurs have a simpler decision model, such as 'pitched roof = good, flat roof = bad.' *The short time taken by users* to complete the visual preferences survey may support this hypothesis" (italics added). See William Fawcett, Ian Ellingham, and Stephen Platt, "Reconciling the

Architectural Preferences of Architects and the Public: The Ordered Preference Model," *Environment and Behavior* 40, no. 5 (2008): 599–618.

147 Liking seems to require: See Rachel Smallman, Brittney Becker, and Neal J. Roese, "Preferences for Expressing Preferences: People Prefer Finer Evaluative Distinctions for Liked Than Disliked Objects," *Journal of Experimental Social Psychology* 52 (May 2014): 25–31.

147 "collective roots": From Simon Frith's excellent essay, "What Is Bad Music?," in *Bad Music: The Music We Love to Hate*, ed. Christopher Washburne and Maiken Derno (New York: Psychology Press, 2004), 17.

148 "transgressions of rule or order": Liking the bad upsets this argument, as well as many of the traditional theories of hedonic appreciation. The traditional model of exposure, per the Kinkade study, is that we will come to like the good more, and the less good less, upon repeated exposures. What happens, though, when you spend day after day with the works in the Museum of Bad Art, which are prized for their badness? If you start to like something, are you liking it more *as* bad? Or have you committed, in your initial enthusiasm, an error of judgment, per Hume—maybe what you thought was bad might actually be good or, more confusingly, not bad? And if you begin, over time, to like it less *for* its badness, does that mean it is starting to get, in your estimation at least, *good?*

148 "seriousness that fails": Susan Sontag, *Against Interpretation, and Other Essays* (New York: Picador, 2001), 283.

148 "are rough and tumble": See Erik Piepenburg, "Wild Rides to Inner Space," *New York Times*, Aug. 28, 2014.

149 Irony is an emotional dead end: Although you can of course end up loving what you set out to watch with ironic disdain, as in, for example, the case of many so-called bronies—older male followers of the colorful cartoon series *My Little Pony*. As one participant noted, "We were going to make fun of it, but instead everybody got hooked." See Una LaMarche, "Pony Up Haters: How 4chan Gave Birth to the Haters," *Observer*, Aug. 3, 2011, http://betabeat.com/2011/08/pony-up-haters-how-4chan-gave-birth-to-the-bronies/#ixzz3MGiPbXdS.

149 "bad good": As the design critic Stephen Bayley once opined, "Bad, it turns out, can be better than good and is always better than bad good, but good bad is perhaps the best of all (certainly the most entertaining)." Stephen Bayley, "Books We Hate to Love," *Los Angeles Times*, March 3, 2006.

149 "dwelling with delight": Samuel Johnson, *The Works of Samuel Johnson* (London: Talboys and Wheeler; and W. Pickering, 1825), 50.

149 implicating women: In the eighteenth century, novels, read widely by women, were viewed roughly with the derision of reality television. See Ana Vogrincic, "The Novel-Reading Panic in 18th Century in England: An Outline of an Early Moral Media Panic," *Medijska istraživanja* 14, no. 2 (2008): 103–23.

149 "I listen to it in secret": Quotation retrieved via "Guilty Pleasures: Nicholas McGegan's Symphonic Sweet Tooth," NPR, March 16, 2011, http://www.npr.org/blogs/deceptivecadence/2011/03/14/134543756/guilty-pleasures-nicholas-mcgegans-symphonic-sweet-tooth.

150 In one study, subjects were offered: HaeEun Chun, Vanessa M. Patrick, and Deborah J. MacInnis, "Making Prudent vs. Impulsive Choices: The Role of Anticipated Shame and Guilt on Consumer Self-Control," *Advances in Consumer Research* 34 (Jan. 2007): 715–19.

150 Merely triggering feelings: See Vanessa M. Patrick, HaeEun Helen Chun, and Deborah MacInnis, "Affective Forecasting and Self-Control: Why Anticipating Pride Wins over Anticipating Shame in a Self-Regulation Context," *Journal of Consumer Psychology* 19, no. 3 (2009): 537–45.

150 "In futurity events": Samuel Johnson, *The Works of Samuel Johnson*, ed. Samuel Johnson and Arthur Murphy (London: H. C. Carey and I. Lea, 1825), 310.

150 One proposed difference: For a thorough account of the differences between shame and guilt, see Jeff Elison, "Shame and Guilt: A Hundred Years of Apples and Oranges," *New Ideas in Psychology* 23, no. 1 (2005): 5–32.

150 "affective-cognitive hybrid": Ibid.

150 To assuage guilt: For a good discussion of the dynamics of guilt, see Roy F. Baumeister, Arlene M. Stillwell, and Todd F. Heatherton, "Guilt: An Interpersonal Approach," *Psychological Bulletin* 115, no. 2 (1994): 243–67.

150 We consume some bit of culture: As Charles Allan McCoy and Roscoe C. Scarborough note, in an excellent discussion of guilty pleasure consumption, people who watch bad television as a guilty pleasure must simultaneously "consume" and "condemn"; "they do not completely resolve the normative contradiction, but instead suffer through it." To defuse things, they excuse and apologize for "their viewing habits as a bit of mindless, ultimately harmless, fun that is ultimately beyond their control to resist watching." See McCoy and Scarborough, "Watching 'Bad' Television: Ironic Consumption, Camp, and Guilty Pleasures," *Poetics* 47 (Dec. 2014), http://dx.doi.org/10.1016/j.poetic.2014.10.003.

150 You would only call something: There have been arguments "against" the concept of guilty pleasures, and when people start talking about things like "guilty pleasure cocktails," I can sympathize. But these tend to be arguments "from above," in the skyboxes of cultural capital, where the phrase is most often used and where it is most loaded.

CHAPTER 5
WHY (AND HOW) TASTES CHANGE

152 "far-fetched": See Michael Seymour, *Babylon: Legend, History, and the Ancient City* (New York: I. B. Tauris, 2014), 178.

152 "painting of great merit": See John Ruskin, *The Complete Works of John Ruskin* (Philadelphia: Reuwee, Wattley & Walsh, 1891), 25: 181.

153 "richness and archaeology": The quotation is drawn from an excellent essay by Sophie Gilmartin, "For Sale in London, Paris, and Babylon: Edwin Long's *The Babylonian Marriage Market*" (2008), http://pure.rhul.ac.uk/portal/en/publications /for-sale-in-london-paris-and-babylon-edwin-longs-the-babylonian-marriage -market(a2cebodf-8eee-475f-bd1c-e9fa133cb49b).html.

153 It even spoke slyly: *The Art Journal*, in its obituary of Holloway, noted, "Those who were fortunate enough to send to auction pictures he fancied benefited no doubt largely from his princely mode of procedure . . . and those whose productions he acquired may possibly have to regret the inflated prices which for the moment their works assumed." The quotation comes via Geraldine Norman, "Victorian Values, Modern Taste," *Independent*, Nov. 14, 1993.

153 Indeed, the auctioneer: See Shireen Huda, *Pedigree and Panache: A History of the Art Auction in Australia* (Canberra: ANU E Press, 2008), 19.

153 "were dispiritingly low": Philip Hook, *The Ultimate Trophy: How the Impressionist Painting Conquered the World* (Munich: Prestel, 2012), 36.

153 Renoir's *La Loge:* Philip Hook, "The Lure of Impressionism for the Newly Rich," *Financial Times,* Jan. 30, 2009.

153 "The garish color": Hook, *Ultimate Trophy,* 53.

153 There is always the chance: Indeed, as Ken Johnson noted in 2009, reviewing a show of Victorian paintings, including the rarely traveled *Babylonian Marriage Market,* "Disdained, derided and dismissed by Modernist art critics from Roger Fry to Clement Greenberg, Victorian painting staged a comeback in the Postmodern era. Its novelistic storytelling, florid symbolism and polished, academic technique appealed to art lovers bored by the pure abstraction and abstruse conceptualism of the 1960s and '70s." See Johnson, "Social Commentary on Canvas: Dickensian Take on the Real World," *New York Times,* June 18, 2009.

154 "Authority or prejudice": David Hume, "Of the Standard of Taste," in *The Philosophical Works of David Hume,* vol. 3 (New York: Little, Brown, 1854), 255.

154 "People behave as if": See George Loewenstein and Erik Angner, "Predicting and Indulging Changing Preferences," in *Time and Decision: Economic and Psychological Perspectives of Intertemporal Choice,* ed. George Loewenstein, Daniel Read, and Roy F. Baumeister (New York: Russell Sage Foundation, 2003), 372.

155 By the time we get home: Rebates also go unclaimed because companies have traditionally made it hard to claim them. See Katy McLaughlin, "Claiming That Holiday Rebate: Is It Really Worth the Headache?," *Wall Street Journal,* Dec. 3, 2002, http://www.wsj.com/articles/SB103885749443602015 3.

155 It is what keeps tattoo removal: Of course, some people have found strategies for reconciling the permanence of tattoos. As Eric Madfis and Tammi Arford write, "Some tattooed people become aware that almost every tattoo will be subject to infinite interpretations and misinterpretations by people who view the image. Even these varied meanings associated with whatever image one chooses are ultimately likely to change, as are the values and desires of the individual tattoo recipient. Accordingly, some people are able to transcend these dilemmas by placing value on esthetic beauty over concrete symbolic meaning and, whenever possible, understanding tattoos as markers of the past rather than indicators of stable identity." See Madfis and Arford, "The Dilemmas of Embodied Symbolic Representation: Regret in Contemporary American Tattoo Narratives," *Social Science Journal* 50, no. 4 (Dec. 2013): 547–56.

155 "watershed moment": See Jordi Quoidbach, Daniel T. Gilbert, and Timothy Wilson, "The End of History Illusion," *Science,* Jan. 4, 2003, 96–98.

156 "a field of ugliness": Oscar Wilde, "The Philosophy of Dress," *New-York Tribune,* April 19, 1885, 9. Thanks to the Web site www.oscarwirican.com for supplying the reference.

156 "We like what we are used to": Quoted in Sara Ahmed, *The Promise of Happiness* (Durham, N.C.: Duke University Press, 2010), 79.

157 "are taught to want new things": Quoted in Nathan Rosenberg, *Exploring the Black Box: Technology, Economics, and History* (New York: Cambridge University Press, 1994), 57.

157 "a lot of times": Chunka Mui, "Five Dangerous Lessons to Learn from Steve Jobs," *Forbes,* Oct. 17, 2011, http://www.forbes.com/sites/chunkamui/2011/10/17/five-dangerous-lessons-to-learn-from-steve-jobs/.

157 "a completely new category": Mat Honan, "Remembering the Apple Newton's Prophetic Failure and Lasting Impact," *Wired*, Aug. 5, 2013.

157 "resistance to the unfamiliar": Raymond Loewy, *Never Leave Well Enough Alone* (Baltimore: Johns Hopkins University Press, 2002), 277.

157 "If beer went on tasting": See Daniel C. Dennett, "Quining Qualia," in *Consciousness in Contemporary Science*, ed. A. J. Marcel and E. Bisiach (Oxford University Press, 1988), reprinted in *Mind and Cognition: A Reader*, ed. William G. Lycan (Cambridge, Mass.: MIT Press, 1990), 60.

158 Looking back, we can find it: Take the archetypal case of Nick Drake, the English folksinger who died of an overdose in 1974 after a short, brilliant, and cosmically unsuccessful career (and who later became far more popular). It is often suggested he was "ahead of his time." But Joe Boyd, his producer and stalwart torchbearer, has argued that Drake's music was of its time; it was recorded then; it bears certain contemporary influences. He suggested that something else might be at work. "In a way its failure at the time has been part of its success now," he said. Rather than being musically unanchored from the period in which it was made, Boyd argued, it was "culturally unanchored." It was not showing up on the soundtrack of endless baby boomer films, it was not endlessly played by parents of his future fans, it was not played on "classic" radio stations. "It's free to be adapted and embraced by people from other generations and people who just come upon it," Boyd said. "It doesn't say 'I'm from the 60s.' It just says, 'I'm Nick Drake.'" It was not new, but it was *novel*.

158 Mittie or Virgie: See BabyNameWizard.com, http://www.babynamewizard.com /archives/2011/6/the-antique-name-illusion-in-search-of-the-next-ava-and -isabella.

158 "it took a couple of years": See Matt Tyrnauer, "Architecture in the Age of Gehry," *Vanity Fair*, Aug. 2010, http://www.vanityfair.com/culture/2010/08/architecture -survey-201008.

158 "maybe we only ever learn": The Wigley quotation is taken from Joachim Bessing, "Mark Wigley," *032c* (Summer 2007): 55.

158 "less complex": See Kimberly Devlin and Jack L. Nasar, "The Beauty and the Beast: Some Preliminary Comparisons of 'High' Versus 'Popular' Residential Architecture and Public Versus Architect Judgments of Same," *Journal of Environmental Psychology* 9, no. 4 (Dec. 1989): 333–44.

159 "Utzon's breathtaking building": Jonathan Glancey, "Sydney Opera House: 'An Architectural Marvel,'" BBC.com, July 11, 2013, http://www.bbc.com/culture /story/20130711-design-classic-down-under.

160 "non-concerted emergent collective phenomenon": See Jonathan Touboul, "The Hipster Effect: When Anticonformists All Look the Same," *arXiv*, Oct. 29, 2014.

160 "disaligned with the majority": See Jeff Guo, "The Mathematician Who Proved Why Hipsters All Look Alike," *Washington Post*, Nov. 11, 2014.

160 "The quest for distinctiveness": See Paul Smaldino and Joshua Epstein, "Social Conformity Despite Individual Preferences for Distinctiveness," *Royal Society Open Science* 2 (2015): 14037, http://dx.doi.org/10.1098/rsos.140437.

160 "The social being": Gabriel Tarde, *The Laws of Imitation* (New York: Henry Holt, 1903), 12. Elihu Katz suggests that one reason Tarde may be overlooked today is that a word like "imitation" is out of fashion. "It sounds altogether too mechanis-

tic and unthinking, although it may well be that [Tarde] had 'influence'—a better word—in mind." See Katz, "Rediscovering Gabriel Tarde," *Political Communication* 23, no. 3 (2006): 263–70.

161 As the anthropologist: See Joseph Henrich, "A Cultural Species: Why a Theory of Culture Is Required to Build a Science of Human Behavior," http://www2 .psych.ubc.ca/~henrich/Website/Papers/HenrichCultureFinal.pdf.

161 "We take our medicine": Peter J. Richerson and Robert Boyd, *Not by Genes Alone: How Culture Transformed Human Evolution* (Chicago: University of Chicago Press, 2004), 11.

161 My favorite example: Catherine Hobaiter and Richard W. Byrne, "Able-Bodied Wild Chimpanzees Imitate a Motor Procedure Used by a Disabled Individual to Overcome Handicap," *PLoS ONE* 5, no. 8 (Aug. 2010).

162 One day in 2010: See Edwin J. V. van Leeuwen, Katherine A. Cronin, and Daniel B. M. Haun, "A Group-Specific Arbitrary Tradition in Chimpanzees (*Pan troglodytes*)," *Animal Cognition* 17, no. 6 (2014): 1421–25.

162 "tended to re-create": Victoria Horner and Andrew Whiten, "Causal Knowledge and Imitation/Emulation Switching in Chimpanzees (*Pan troglodytes*) and Children (*Homo sapiens*)," *Animal Cognition* 8, no. 3 (2005): 164–81. See also Daniel Haun, Yvonne Rekers, and Michael Tomasello, "Children Conform to the Behavior of Peers; Other Great Apes Stick with What They Know," *Psychological Science* 25, no. 12 (2014): 2160–67.

163 "they are independent": As Georg Simmel wrote, "Fashion is merely a product of social demands . . . This is clearly proved by the fact that very frequently not the slightest reason can be found for the creations of fashion from the standpoint of an objective, aesthetic, or other expediency." See Simmel, "Fashion," 544.

163 "The modes of furniture": Adam Smith, *The Theory of Moral Sentiments* (London: Cambridge University Press, 2002), 228.

163 In a study conducted: Curiously, the children reported having no memory of which model was watched and which one was not, as if they had picked up the cue subconsciously. See Maciej Chudek et al., "Prestige-Biased Cultural Learning: Bystander's Differential Attention to Potential Models Influences Children's Learning," *Evolution and Human Behavior* 33, no. 1 (2012): 46–56.

163 "When environmental cues": See Joe Henrich and Robert Boyd, "The Evolution of Conformist Transmission and the Emergence of Between-Group Differences," *Evolution and Human Behavior* 19, no. 4 (1998): 215–41.

164 "arrival of the fittest": The quotation is taken from an excellent article by Philip Ball, "The Strange Inevitability of Evolution," *Nautilus*, Jan. 8, 2015.

164 The artist or innovator: Gabriel Tarde, the fin-de-siècle French economist who was one of the first to compare innovation with evolution, described the innovator as a "madman . . . leading sleepwalkers." The quotation comes from Faridah Djellal and Faïz Gallouj, "The Laws of Imitation and Invention: Gabriel Tarde and the Evolutionary Economics of Innovation" (March 2014), https://halshs.archives -ouvertes.fr/halshs-00960607.

164 People want to feel: See, for instance, Michael Lynn and C. R. Snyder, "Uniqueness Seeking," in *Handbook of Positive Psychology*, ed. C. R. Snyder and Shane Lopez (New York: Oxford University Press, 2002), 395–410.

165 "Differences of opinion": Thanks to Robert Sapolsky for this example.

165   Under a theory called: See Dan Ariely and Jonathan Levav, "Sequential Choice in Group Settings: Taking the Road Less Traveled and Less Enjoyed," *Journal of Consumer Research* 27, no. 3 (Dec. 2000): 279–90.

165   The psychologists Matthew Hornsey: Matthew Hornsey and Jolanda Jetten, "The Individual Within the Group: Balancing the Need to Belong with the Need to Be Different," *Personality and Social Psychology Review* 8, no. 3 (Aug. 2004): 248–64.

165   In a study of people with body piercings: Jolanda Jetten et al., "Rebels with a Cause: Group Identification as a Response to Perceived Discrimination from the Mainstream," *Personality and Social Psychology Bulletin* 27, no. 9 (2001): 1204–13.

165   "normcore": For an excellent analysis of the trend, see Eugenia Williamson, "The Revolution Will Probably Wear Mom Jeans," *Baffler*, no. 27 (2015).

165   antifashion trend: As Elihu Katz has noted, "There are unlabeled fads or fashions." Labels give shape to inchoate activities and help them build upon themselves. "It is usually through the label," writes Katz, "that the fashion acquires fame—even beyond its consumer audience." Rolf Myersohn and Elihu Katz, "Notes on a Natural History of Fads," *American Journal of Sociology* 62, no. 6 (1957): 594–601.

165   Normcore was more conceptual art: See Richard Benson, "Normcore: How a Spoof Marketing Term Grew into a Fashion Phenomenon," *Guardian*, Dec. 17, 2014.

165   "If obedience to fashion": Simmel, "Fashion," 549.

166   "this might help explain": See Richard Wilk, "Loving People, Hating What They Eat: Marginal Foods and Social Boundaries," in *Reimagining Marginalized Foods: Global Processes, Local Places*, ed. Elizabeth Finnis (Tucson: University of Arizona Press, 2002), 17.

166   "is saying someone hasn't got it": Mullan raised this point during a discussion of taste on the BBC program *In Our Time*, http://www.bbc.co.uk/programmes /b0082dzm.

166   "Most movements in art": E. H. Gombrich, *News and Form: Studies in the Art of the Renaissance* (London: Phaidon Press, 1966), 88.

166   What our tastes "say about us": At least one study has proposed that mimicking a previously disliked person led to no increase in liking for that person; mimicking someone *already liked*, however, led to more liking of that person. See Mariëlle Stel et al., "Mimicking Disliked Others: Effects of *A Priori* Liking on the Mimicking-Liking Link," *European Journal of Social Psychology* 40, no. 5 (2010): 867–80.

167   "counter-imitate": The concept and the word come from Gabriel Tarde, but I was pointed to it by Djellal and Gallouj in their paper, "Laws of Imitation and Invention."

167   When someone knows: This formulation is laid out in Herbert Hamilton, "Dimensions of Self-Designated Opinion Leadership and Their Correlates," *Public Opinion Quarterly* 35, no. 2 (1971): 266–74.

167   This conquered the language: For a good account, see Britt Peterson, "Linguists Are Like, 'Get Used to It!,'" *Boston Globe*, Jan. 25, 2015.

167   "poverty and degradation": Daniel Luzer, "How Lobster Got Fancy," *Pacific Standard*, June 7, 2013.

167   Then there is the nettlesome problem: Marjorie Perloff makes this point in a

good essay on taste, inspired by Raymond Williams's famous *Keywords* text. See Perloff, "Taste," *English Studies in Canada* 3, no. 4 (Dec. 2004): 50–55.

167 Groups "transmit" tastes: In a famous study the psychologist Henri Tajfel conducted in the 1970s, a group of schoolboys was asked about their preferences for a series of abstract, unlabeled paintings by two "foreign painters." The boys were then grouped as "Klee" or "Kandinsky" fans. There was a catch, however. The groups they were placed into had nothing to do with the paintings they actually preferred. But here they were, lumped together as Klee or Kandinsky fans and now asked to distribute a certain number of "points"—a standard exercise in psychology—between the two groups, in ways that could benefit their own group or stress overall equity. What happened? The Klee subjects consistently gave more "points" to their own group—even when they could have thrown some points to the Kandinsky camp without hurting their own profits. Tajfel, who called this the "minimal group paradigm," was trying to show how "out group" discrimination and "in-group" favoritism could blossom under the flimsiest of pretexts. What could be more flimsy, Tajfel noted, than invented preferences toward "artists they had never heard of"? See Tajfel et al., "Social Categorization and Intergroup Behavior," *European Journal of Social Psychology* 1, no. 2 (1971): 149–78.

167 Small, seemingly trivial: The sociologist Michael Macy and colleagues note: "When reverberated through the 'echo chamber' of interaction with similar alters, even very small within-individual biases can serve as coordinating mechanisms that catalyze network autocorrelation in large populations. A similar coordinating role can be played by opinion leaders with broad influence, even if this influence is far weaker than that of peers. It takes only a very small 'nudge,' whether from 'within' or 'above,' to tip a large population into a self-reinforcing dynamic that can carve deep cultural fissures into the demographic landscape." See Daniel DellaPosta, Yongren Shi, and Michael Macy, "Why Do Liberals Drink Lattes?" *American Journal of Sociology* 120, no. 5 (March 2015): 1473-1511.

168 He conforms to the group: As one group of researchers notes, "Conformity has the interesting theoretical property that it reduces behavioral variation within population while potentially increasing variation among populations." See C. Efferson et al., "Conformists and Mavericks: The Empirics of Frequency-Dependent Cultural Transmission," *Evolution and Human Behavior* 29, no. 1 (2008): 56–64.

168 "loud and distinctive": See Bruce E. Byers, Kara L. Belinsky, and R. Alexander Bentley, "Independent Cultural Evolution of Two Song Traditions in the Chestnut-Sided Warbler," *American Naturalist* 176, no. 4 (Oct. 2010).

169 In the fashion of: As R. F. Lachlan and colleagues notes, it is likely that "every individual learns a cultural trait slightly inaccurately, but only the cumulative effect of many such inaccurate learning events leads to the generation of a trait that is perceived as different from the original." Lachlan et al., "The Evolution of Conformity-Enforcing Behaviour in Cultural Communication Systems," *Animal Behavior* 68 (2004): 561–70.

169 The songs that disappear first: "When they are rare, and copying is random," Byers told me, "the rarest thing is mostly likely to disappear." This makes sense, but he stressed we should not underestimate the randomness of it: "If just by chance in one generation only eight birds copy it, instead of ten, then

next, just by chance, six birds, suddenly it is now rare, subject to extinction by chance."

169   Memes that thrive: This is not the whole story, of course. One study of Twitter hashtag adoption found that a hashtag that was more frequently retweeted early on ended up being eclipsed by a rival hashtag, which seemed to pull ahead on the strength of "replies" on Twitter, signaling not only some kind of deeper engagement but some sense among users that the initially faster-rising tweet was perhaps a bit faddish. See Yu-Ru Lin et al., "#Bigbirds Never Die: Understanding Social Dynamics of Emergent Hashtags," *arXiv*, 1301.7144v1, March 28, 2013. With bird memes, there are also particular characteristics, beyond exposure and frequency, that seem to promulgate success (like "longer duration, great amplitude modulation and higher mean frequency"). See, for example, Myron Baker and David Gammon, "Vocal Memes in Natural Populations of Chickadees: Why Do Some Memes Persist and Others Go Extinct?," *Animal Behaviour* 75, no. 1 (2008): 279–89.

170   "The more frequent a verb": This example comes from Erez Aiden and Jean-Baptiste Michel's fascinating book, *Uncharted: Big Data as a Lens on Human Culture* (New York: Riverhead, 2013), 36.

170   "Thrived" thrived because people: And, they note, because of a remarkable Proto-Germanic invention, the "-ed" suffix, circa 500–250 B.C.

170   Music is filled with moments: For an interesting argument about the role of "accidents" in pop music, see Charles Kronengold, "Accidents, Hooks, Theory," *Popular Music* 24, no. 3 (2005): 381–97.

171   And so in a couple of decades: For an interesting account of Goree Carter and the recording of "Rock Awhile" (which the rock historian Robert Palmer cites as the first rock-and-roll song—not Ike Turner's "Rocket 88"—with distorted guitars a key criteria), see John Nova Lomax, "Roll Over, Ike Turner," *Texas Monthly*, Dec. 2014. For a good timeline of key moments in guitar distortion, see Dave Hunter, "Who Called the Fuzz? Early Milestones in Distorted Guitars," accessed via the Web site of the guitar manufacturer Gibson: http://www2.gibson.com /News-Lifestyle/Features/en-us/who-called-the-fuzz-714.aspx.

171   "complete accident": See Jann Wenner, "Pete Townshend Talks Mods, Recording, and Smashing Guitars," *Rolling Stone*, Sept. 14, 1968.

171   "To discover something": Pierre Bourdieu, *Sociology in Question* (New York: Sage, 1993), 109.

171   "predicted that the vast majority": J. Stephen Lansing and Murray P. Cox, "The Domain of the Replicators," *Current Anthropology* 52, no. 1 (Feb. 2011): 105–25.

172   This was what R. Alexander Bentley: Harold Herzog, R. Alexander Bentley, and Matthew Hahn, "Random Drift and Large Shifts in Popularity of Dog Breeds," *Proceedings of the Royal Society B: Biological Sciences*, Aug. 7, 2004, 353–56.

172   A study that looked at positive breed: See Stefano Ghirlanda et al., "Fashion vs. Function in Cultural Evolution: The Case of Dog Breed Popularity," *PLoS ONE* 8, no. 9 (2013): 1–6.

172   Harold Herzog, a co-author of Bentley's: Harold Herzog, "Forty-Two Thousand and One Dalmatians: Fads, Social Contagion, and Dog Breed Popularity," *Society and Animals* 14, no. 4 (2006): 383–97.

172   The bigger the box office: See Stefano Ghirlanda, Alberto Acerbi, and Harold

Herzog, "Dog Movie Stars and Dog Breed Popularity: A Case Study in Media Influence on Choice," *PLoS ONE* 9, no. 9 (2014). Note the authors, "These data suggest that movies featuring dogs tend to use breeds whose popularity had been increasing for some time."

172   "fabulous rise in poodle popularity": See "Fads: The Poodle Dethroned," *Time*, Feb. 23, 1962.

173   "rogue waves": I wrote about this in "When Good Waves Go Rogue," *Nautilus*, July 31, 2014. As with fashion trends, certain places are particularly suited for the formation of rogue waves, but there is essentially no way to predict the emergence of the wave itself.

174   "It costs no more": See Stanley Lieberson's landmark book, *A Matter of Taste: How Names, Fashions, and Culture Change* (New Haven, Conn.: Yale University Press, 2000), 25.

175   One statistical analysis: Jonah Berger et al., "From Karen to Katie: Using Baby Names to Understand Cultural Evolution," *Psychological Science*, Oct. 2012, 1067–73.

175   A study of naming patterns: Ibid.

175   This is not so different: See Alan T. Sorenson, "Bestseller Lists and Product Variety," *Journal of Industrial Economics* 55, no. 4 (Dec. 2007): 738.

176   "the qualities inherent": See H. Leibenstein, "Bandwagon, Snob, and Veblen Effects in the Theory of Consumers' Demand," *Quarterly Journal of Economics* 64, no. 2 (May 1950): 183–207. Leibenstein refers to three phenomena of "non-additive demand": The "bandwagon effect," in which demand goes up for something that other people are consuming; the "snob effect," by which demand goes down for something that other people are consuming; and the "Veblen effect," after Thorstein Veblen, in which consumer demand is increased because a good has a higher price.

176   As one study showed: See Marianne Bertrand and Senhil Mullainathan, "Are Emily and Greg More Employable Than Lakisha and Jamal? A Field Experiment on Labor Market Discrimination" (NBER, working paper 9873, July 2003). The researchers note that while names can reflect social background as well as race ("African American babies named Kenya or Jamal are affiliated with much higher mothers' education than African American babies named Latonya or Leroy"), they did not find that this actually affected callbacks: "In summary, this test suggests little evidence that social background drives the extent of discrimination."

176   another analysis found: See Petra Moser, "Taste-Based Discrimination: Empirical Evidence from a Shock to Preferences During WWI" (Stanford Institute for Economic Policy Research, discussion paper 08-019, 2009).

176   Names that appear to be neutrally: This example comes from Lansing and Cox, "Domain of the Replicators."

178   Hit songs, meanwhile: See "A World of Hits," *Economist*, Nov. 26, 2009. As the magazine notes, "A recent analysis by *Billboard*, a trade magazine, found a similar trend in America. There, sales had declined across the board, but the hits were holding up best. Albums ranked between 300 and 400 suffered the greatest proportionate losses." As *Billboard* noted of the skew between the top-performing tracks and those out on the long tail, "In any given week, the top 200 digital tracks account for nearly one in four track purchases. To put that in context, Amazon

.com's MP3 store currently lists 9.99 million tracks. So, the top 200 tracks represent only 0.002% of what a large download store stocks." Glenn Peoples, "Tracking the Hits Along the Musical Long Tail," *Billboard*, May 11, 2009.

178   The curving long tail chart: Anita Elberse notes that in the wake of the transition to digital music the long tail has gotten longer and flatter: "Although today's hits may no longer reach the sales volumes typical of the pre-piracy era, an ever smaller set of top titles continues to account for a large chunk of the overall demand for music." Elberse, "Should You Invest in the Long Tail?," *Harvard Business Review*, July 2008.

178   "lesser known alternative": William McPhee, *Formal Theories of Mass Behavior* (New York: Free Press of Glencoe, 1963), 136.

178   Through sheer statistical distribution: McPhee's theory was supported by the findings of a study by the marketing professor Anita Elberse, who examined behavior at online music and movie sites: "Even for consumers who regularly choose the most obscure products, hit products typically constitute the lion's share of their choices." See Elberse, "A Taste for Obscurity: An Individual-Level Examination of 'Long Tail' Consumption" (Harvard Business School, working paper 08-008, Aug. 2007). For an analysis of the principle applied to consumer brands, see also Andrew Ehrenberg and Gerald Goodhardt, "Double Jeopardy Revisited, Again," *Marketing Research* (Spring 2002): 40–42. Other research has suggested that "long tail" consumption is not driven by people who overwhelmingly seek out the obscure; rather, "everyone is a bit eccentric," choosing "niche products at least some of the time." For example, some 85 percent of Netflix users have "ventured into the tail." See Sharad Goel et al., "Anatomy of the Long Tail: Ordinary People with Extraordinary Tastes," *WSDM'10*, Feb. 4–6, 2010.

179   Knowing what other listeners: In a later study, Watts and Salganik tried to force the issue, by actually manipulating the order of songs' perceived popularity. While this caused a short-term lift in the popularity of actually unpopular songs, they question "whether these dynamics would have led to permanent effects on the popularity of the songs, or whether the observed effects were merely transitory." Duncan Watts and Matthew Salganik, "Leading the Herd Astray: An Experimental Study of Self-Fulfilling Prophecies in an Artificial Cultural Market," *Social Psychology Quarterly* 71 (Dec. 2008): 338–55.

179   "When individual decisions": See Matthew Salganik, Peter Sheridan Dodds, and Duncan J. Watts, "Experimental Study of Inequality and Unpredictability in an Artificial Cultural Market," *Science*, Feb. 10, 2006, 855.

179   In 2013, it was estimated: See "The Death of the Long Tail," www.midiaconsulting .com.

180   Molanphy suggests that if radio: And, by contrast, things that were less popular would suffer. When, in 1991, the SoundScan "point of sale" system was introduced, which brought new granularity and accuracy to the reporting of record sales, *Billboard* noted that forty-five albums, many by "developing artists," "fell off the chart altogether." See Geoff Mayfield, "A Decade Ago, SoundScan Burst onto the Scene," *Billboard*, June 2, 2001.

181   "the world had suddenly": Ortega, *Revolt of the Masses*, 38. For a good discussion of the various models of linguistic diffusion, see John Nerbonne, "Measuring the Diffusion of Linguistic Change," *Philosophical Transactions B* 370, no. 1666 (April 2015).

181   There are said to be: This estimate comes from Eric D. Beinhocker, *The Origin of Wealth: Evolution, Complexity, and the Radical Remaking of Economics* (Cambridge, Mass.: Harvard University Press, 2006), 9.

182   studies suggest social media: Take, for example, a number of studies that have found correlations between Facebook usage and self-esteem. "Given that 10 million new photographs are uploaded to Facebook every hour (Mayer-Schönberger & Cukier, 2013), Facebook provides women with a medium for frequently engaging in appearance-related social comparisons, and can therefore potentially contribute to body image concerns among young women." See Jasmine Fardouly et al., "Social Comparisons on Social Media: The Impact of Facebook on Young Women's Body Image Concerns and Mood," *Body Image* 13 (March 2015): 38–45.

182   "frenzy": Carol Pogash, "During Bakery Break-In, Only Recipes Are Taken," *New York Times*, March 6, 2015.

182   "lexical innovation": The historian Irving Allen writes, "The new culture of urbanism included lexical culture. Some of it was slang that expressed new social categories, new forms of social inequality, new relationships, new technologies, new ways of life, and other ruptures of tradition." See Allen, *The City in Slang* (New York: Oxford University Press, 1995), 5.

182   It spreads outward: See, for example, Emile Alirol et al., "Urbanisation and Infectious Diseases in a Globalised World," *Lancet: Infectious Diseases* 11, no. 2 (Feb. 2011): 131–41.

182   "composite result of what": Leonard Bloomfield, *Language* (New York: Holt, Rinehart and Winston, 1933), 46.

182   Media, ever more global: See Bates L. Hoffer, "Language Borrowing and Language Diffusion: An Overview," *Intercultural Communication Studies* 11, no. 4 (2002). See also Ben Olah, "English Loanwords in Japanese: Effects, Attitudes, and Usage as a Means of Improving Spoken English Ability," http://www.u-bunkyo.ac.jp/center/library/image/kyukiyo9_177-188.pdf.

183   New Yorkers, already physically exposed: See, for example, Allison Stadd, "Guess What the World's Most Active Twitter City Is?," *Social Times* (blog), *Adweek*, Jan. 2, 2013, http://www.adweek.com/socialtimes/most-active-twitter-city/475006.

183   "Living and working online": See R. Alexander Bentley and Matthew W. Hann, "Is There a 'Neutral Theory of Anthropology'?," from comments in Lansing and Cox, "Domain of the Replicators," 118.

183   Whatever the direction: Jan Lorenz et al., "How Social Influence Can Undermine the Wisdom of Crowd Effect," *PNAS* 108, no. 22 (2011). As the authors note, "Presumably, herding is even more pronounced for opinions or attitudes for which no predefined correct answers exist." This can certainly be applied to new fashions, new art, new music. As Mark Buchanan notes, James Surowiecki's influential book, *The Wisdom of Crowds*, noted—in a message that seems to be often overlooked—that for crowds to be wise, people have to judge independently of one another; only "unbiased" estimates will average into accurate estimates.

183   They take less information: If we think about the *Billboard* charts in this way, the more people see other people liking hit songs, the more they will listen to those same songs, the less frequently they will range outside that narrow band of songs to listen to others, and, via a sort of "confidence bias," the more convinced they will be that those hits must be what is best to listen to.

CHAPTER 6
BEER, CATS, AND DIRT

186   "forgets that there is no objective": Peter Paul Moormann, "On the Psychology of Judging Cats," Rolandus Union International, http://rolandus.org/eng/library/judging/moormano3.html.

187   A Belgian study: Filip Boen et al., "The Impact of Open Feedback on Conformity Among Judges in Rope Skipping," *Psychology of Sport and Exercise* 7, no. 6 (Nov. 2006): 577–90.

188   classical music competitions: See Herbert Glejser and Bruno Heyndels, "Efficiency and Inefficiency in the Ranking in Competitions: The Case of the Queen Elisabeth Music Contest," *Journal of Cultural Economics* 25, no. 2 (May 2001): 109–29.

188   synchronized swim meets: See Vietta Wilson, "Objectivity and Effect of Order of Appearance in Judging of Synchronized Swimming Meets," *Perceptual and Motor Skills* 44, no. 1 (Feb. 1977): 295–98.

188   "Judges," she concluded: Wändi Bruine de Bruin, "Save the Last Dance for Me: Unwanted Serial Position Effects in Jury Evaluations," *Acta Psychologica* 8, no. 3 (March 2005): 245–60.

188   Nothing comes before or after: For a review see S. R. Schmidt, "Distinctiveness and Memory: A Theoretical and Empirical Review," in *Learning and Memory: A Comprehensive Reference*, ed. John H. Byrne (Oxford: Academic Press, 2008), 125–44.

189   "direction of comparison effect": See Amos Tversky, "Features of Similarity," *Psychological Review* 84, no. 4 (July 1977): 327–52. See also Susan Powell Mantel and Frank R. Kardes, "The Role of Direction of Comparison, Attribute-Based Processing, and Attitude-Based Processing on Consumer Preference," *Journal of Consumer Research* 25 (March 1999): 335–52.

189   Judges need to be looking: As Bruine de Bruin writes, "Jury members may have noticed that the first figure skater made an impressive pirouette, the second an extraordinary double axel, and the third a breathtaking choreography." So while skater 8 might have made an equally good pirouette as skater 7, the amazing double axel that only skater 8 performed draws an inordinate amount of attention. Even here, memory is implicated, because judges, seduced by what skater 8 did that was different from skater 7, have perhaps by now forgotten what skater 7 *did* that was different from skater 8. See Bruine de Bruin, "Save the Last Dance for Me."

189   "If my main rival": Laurie Whitwell, "Smith Playing Russian Roulette as Gymnast Will Wait Until Last Minute to Decide Which Routine to Perform on Pommelhorse," *Daily Mail*, Aug. 3, 2012.

189   "difficulty bias": See Hillary N. Morgan and Kurt W. Totthoff, "The Harder the Task, the Higher the Score: Findings of a Difficulty Bias," *Economic Inquiry* 52, no. 3 (July 2014): 1014–26.

189   "if the preceding gymnast": Lysann Damisch, Thomas Mussweiler, and Henning Plessner, "Olympic Medals as Fruits of Comparison? Assimilation and Contrast in Sequential Performance Judgments," *Journal of Experimental Psychology: Applied* 12, no. 3 (2006): 166–78.

189   "one of the building": Thomas Mussweiler, "Same or Different? How Similarity

versus Dissimilarity Focus Shapes Social Information Processing," in Jeffrey W. Sherman, Bertram Gawronski, and Yaacov Trope, eds., *Dual-Process Theories of the Social Mind* (New York: Guilford Press, 2014), 328–39.

190 Judges will, in essence: In another experiment, Mussweiler and Damisch asked people to spot differences or similarities between two sets of pictures. Then they were shown two filmed clips of ski jumps and asked to estimate lengths. Those "primed" to look for similarities in the photographs thought the ski jumps were closer in length than did the people who had looked for differences. These sorts of similarities or differences can be rather minor: When people are first shown a picture of an unattractive "target" person, research has shown, they generally judge themselves to be more attractive. Show them an attractive person first, and they do not get that same beauty boost. But when they learn they share the same birthday as the attractive target, they feel better about their own attractiveness, as if they have "assimilated" some of the target's good looks. Jonathan Brown et al., "When Gulliver Travels: Social Context, Psychological Closeness, and Self-Appraisals," *Journal of Personality and Social Psychology* 62, no. 5 (1992): 717–27.

190 Now the "Canadian" gymnast: This raises the interesting idea that a judge need not even be from the same country as an athlete for a form of "nationalistic" bias to occur.

190 Even if the fact of noticing: As Ravi Dhar and colleagues note, "It is likely that consumers judge similarity or dissimilarity when they come across new products in reference to what they already own. For example, individuals may evaluate the similarity of a new house being built to their own house. Such judgments of similarity are often made without simultaneously making a preference or evaluative judgment."

191 In what is known as the "cheerleader effect": As the psychologists Drew Walker and Edward Vul note, the group setting "biases their percepts of individual items to be more like the group average." Walker and Vul, "Hierarchical Encoding Makes Individuals in a Group Seem More Attractive," *Psychological Science* 25, no. 1 (Jan. 2014): 230–35.

191 For similar reasons: R. Post et al., "The Frozen Face Effect: Why Static Photographs May Not Do You Justice," *Frontiers in Psychology* 3 (2012), doi:10.3389 /fpsyg.2012.19122.

191 "Participants compared themselves": See Thomas Mussweiler, Katja Rüter, and Kai Epstude, "The Man Who Wasn't There: Subliminal Social Comparison Standards Influence Self-Evaluation," *Journal of Experimental Social Psychology* 40, no. 5 (2004): 689–96. Similar results were achieved on measures like aggression; people judged themselves more aggressive when they "saw" an image of Arnold Schwarzenegger versus the "German pop-singer Nena." Ravi Dhar, Stephen M. Nowlis, and Steven J. Sherman, "Comparison Effects on Preference Construction," *Journal of Consumer Research* 26, no. 3 (Dec. 1999): 293–306.

191 Research of actual speed-dating trials: Saurabh Bhargava and Ray Fisman, "Contrast Effects in Sequential Decisions: Evidence from Speed Dating" (Columbia Business School, 2012). Curiously, the authors note, "while both male and female dating decisions are determined by contemporaneous target attractiveness, only male evaluators are sensitive to prior target attractiveness. For males, the contrastive influence of recent target attractiveness is 31 percent as large as the influence of current target attractiveness."

192   One study presented subjects: David A. Houston, Steven J. Sherman, and Sara M. Baker, "The Influence of Unique Features and Direction of Comparison on Preferences," *Journal of Experimental Social Psychology* 25, no. 2 (1989): 121–41.

192   "Judging one experience": See Tanuka Ghoshal et al., "Uncovering the Coexistence of Assimilation and Contrast Effects in Hedonic Sequences" (Tepper School of Business, paper 1395, 2012), http://repository.cmu.edu/tepper/1395.

193   A person's preference set: More discussion of Chris Noessel's 11th Person Game can be found at Christopher Noessel, "Is Serial Presentation a Problem in the Circuit?," *Sci-Fi Interfaces*, Oct. 4, 2013, http://scifiinterfaces.wordpress.com /2013/10/04/is-serial-presentation-a-problem-in-the-circuit/. It is interesting to think how this game might be manipulated: If a perceived-to-be-undesirable candidate were sent through the doorway first, one imagines a person would subsequently make a faster choice; having seen the "worst," the person would recalibrate his notion of the best. Sending an extremely desirable person through the door first might prolong one's decision, as if one had raised one's own internal bar (not to mention the player will be more choosy in trying to pick someone who approaches the ideal set by the first candidate).

193   "Similarity serves as a basis": See Amos Tversky, *Preference, Belief, and Similarity: Selected Writings* (Cambridge, Mass.: MIT Press, 2004), 34.

193   "are simultaneously compared": Moormann, "On the Psychology of Judging Cats."

194   "The ideal Bombay": The breed standards are available via the Web site of the Cat Fancier's Association, http://www.cfainc.org/.

194   "Don't believe everything": Take, for instance, the description that TICA (or the International Cat Association, one of the world's two largest breeding councils) gives to the Donskoy: "The Donskoy is in a class of its own. It is a highly intelligent, beautiful loving cat that looks directly into your eyes and seems to penetrate your very soul." That is probably the most sober sentence in the entire description of this cat, which is also compared to "extra terrestrials coming from the outer universe." But even the official standard lays it on pretty thick: "The Donskoy is a very intriguing, unique, soft-hearted and social cat of medium size with soft hairless wrinkled skin that feels hot and velvety to the touch." Can soft hearts, I ponder at the judge's table, be selected for genetically?

194   As the writer Sue Hubbell: See Sue Hubbell's wonderful book *Shrinking the Cat* (New York: Mariner Books, 2002).

194   But unlike dogs: As Carlos A. Driscoll and colleagues point out, "Unlike dogs, which exhibit a huge range of sizes, shapes and temperaments, house cats are relatively homogeneous, differing mostly in the characteristics of their coats. The reason for the relative lack of variability in cats is simple: humans have long bred dogs to assist with particular tasks, such as hunting or sled pulling, but cats, which lack any inclination for performing most tasks that would be useful to humans, experienced no such selective breeding pressures." See Driscoll et al., "The Evolution of House Cats," *Scientific American*, June 2009.

195   "Now that [the cat]": Harrison William Weir, *Our Cats and All About Them* (London: Fancier's Gazette Limited, 1892), 84, http://www.gutenberg.org/files /35450/35450-h/35450-h.htm.

195   "all the authority": See Walker Van Riper, "Aesthetic Notions in Animal Breeding," *Quarterly Review of Biology* 7, no. 1 (March 1932): 84–92.

195   tabula rasa with a tail: "Persevering fanciers might derive interest and amusement from trying to breed out-of-the-common specimens," wrote Frances Simpson in *The Book of the Cat*. "A black-and-white spotted like a Dalmatian hound, or a cat marked with zebra stripes, could doubtless be produced in time by careful and judicious selection." Fanciers invoked artistic principles of beauty but admitted they were sometimes prone to fashion on four legs. "At present in England the very dark smokes are the rage," Simpson noted, "but in America the light ones are more sought after." Simpson, *The Book of the Cat* (New York: Cassell, 1903), 236. Some suspected a certain arbitrariness at play. One commentator of the period, writing about the dog fancy, suggested there was nothing logical in why "a small eye shall be a merit in one breed (toy terrier) and a defect in another (King Charles spaniel)." *The Dog: Its Varieties and Management in Health and Disease* (London: Frederick Warne, 1873), 87.

195   "judicious mating": The twinning of these enterprises reached its apogee in the "Fitter Families" movement, a eugenics campaign that briefly swept through county fairs in the United States in the early twentieth century. A regular feature was the livestock-style judging of humans. "While the stock judges are testing the Holsteins, Jerseys, and White-faces in the stock pavilion," as one official noted, "we are testing the Joneses, Smiths, and the Johnsons." There, nestled among the "Milch Goat" and "Pet Stock" categories, were troops of families being measured on any number of things, including a mental agility test and dental exams. See Laura L. Lovett, "Fitter Families for Future Firesides: Florence Sherbon and Popular Eugenics," *Public Historian* 29, no. 3 (2007): 69–85. As a curious bit of historical trivia, one of the judges at a competition administering the "anthropomorphic structural assessment" was none other than James Naismith, the father of basketball.

195   with dogs at times: On the eve of the twentieth century, a breeders' group formed near Stuttgart, notes the historian Aaron Skabelund. Their goal was to transform a local sheepdog into the vaunted "German shepherd," a "primeval Germanic dog," a "warlike proud German" that was eminently loyal and, in an eerie echo of what was to come, racially pure. See Skabelund, "Breeding Racism: The Imperial Battlefields of the 'German' Shepherd Dog," *Society and Animals* 16 (2008): 354–71. Notes Skabelund, "People do not often recognize or forget that animal breeds, like human races, are contingent, constantly changing, culturally constructed categories that are inextricably interconnected to state formation, class structures, and national identities."

195   Take the bulldog: As the historian Harriet Ritvo writes about the Victorian dog fancy and the rise of London's canine population, "Any other kind of dog might compromise its owner's social status." See Ritvo, "Pride and Pedigree: The Evolution of the Victorian Dog Fancy," *Victorian Studies* 28, no. 2 (1986): 227–53.

196   "The standard does not describe": From the Cat Fanciers' Association "Show Standards," http://www.cfainc.org/Portals/0/documents/forms/14-15standards .pdf. This discrepancy between the standard and the reality can lead into philosophical thickets. Take the question of trying to establish the artistic ideal for a new breed. How do you know it is the perfect cat when you have never seen that type of cat before? As Vickie Fisher, president of TICA, told me, the first step is to answer the question, why is it a breed? Fisher points to the Munchkin, a relatively

new breed, based on a genetic mutation, that TICA, not without controversy, introduced in the 1990s. "The short-legged mutation came about," she said, "so the idea was, let's make a breed. But what we saw at first in the creation—and we still see a lot of this now—is that one trait does not a breed make." In other words, the Munchkin people were leaning an awful lot on those short legs.

196 "in every country where cats": *New York Times*, Dec. 21, 1906.

196 It is not the image: Louise Engberg, a Danish breeder of what she calls "classic Persians," has a simple test for distinguishing the Persians of yore from today's. Take a piece of paper and align it along the bottom of the eyes. "You should not be able to see the nose leather beneath the eye rim," she told me. On most modern cats, you can.

196 "bastardisation of all the things": While the Cat Fanciers' Association notes that "today's Persian is a living, playing, purring result of more than 150 years of loving, astute breeding," at their most extreme, these brachycephalic (or short-headed) cats are riddled with health problems. As described by the *Journal of Feline Medicine and Surgery*, these range from "stridulous breathing and possibly obstructive sleep apnea" to a brain "crammed into the wrong-size cranial vault." See Richard Malik, Andy Sparkes, and Claire Bessant, "Brachycephalia—a Bastardisation of What Makes Cats Special," *Journal of Feline Medicine and Surgery* 11, no. 11 (2009): 889–90.

197 Was it their childlike: The *Journal of Feline Medicine and Surgery* notes that the cats invoke the childlike qualities of the Lorenz theory of beauty: "An infant's face with full curves is associated with purity, sincerity, honesty and vulnerability. This immediately provokes a protective instinct in us." See Claudia Schlueter et al., "Brachycephalic Feline Noses: CT and Anatomic Study of the Relationship Between Head Conformation and the Nasolacrimal Drainage System," *Journal of Feline Medicine and Surgery* 11, no. 11 (2009): 891–900.

199 "On that principle": Burke, *Philosophical Enquiry into the Sublime and Beautiful*, 134.

199 just as certain notions of desirable: See, for example, David M. Garner et al., "Cultural Expectations of Thinness in Women," *Psychological Reports* 47, no. 2 (1980): 483–91. Looking at *Playboy* centerfolds, among other sources, the authors note that particularly in the 1970s "there has appeared to be a shift in the idealized female shape from the voluptuous, curved figure to the angular, lean look of today." Curiously, a later study found that "the trend [found by Garner et al.] of increasing thinness among the Playmates has stabilized and may have actually begun to reverse itself." See Mia Foley Sypeck et al., "Cultural Representations of Thinness in Women, Redux: Playboy Magazine's Depiction of Beauty from 1979 to 1999," *Body Image* 3, no. 3 (Sept. 2006): 229–35.

200 As the psychologists: See James W. Tanaka and Marjorie Taylor, "Object Categories and Expertise: Is the Basic Level in the Eye of the Beholder?," *Cognitive Psychology* 23, no. 3 (1991): 457–82.

201 But even trained experts: See L. A. Gills et al., "Sensory Profiles of Carrot (*Daucus carota* L.) Cultivars Grown in Georgia," *HortScience* 34, no. 2 (1999): 625–28.

201 "Nor are the different tastes": John Locke, *An Essay Concerning Human Understanding* (London: T. Tegg, 1836), 35.

202 "a sensory methodology": Herbert Stone et al., eds., *Sensory Evaluation Practices* (New York: Academic Press, 2012), 202.

202   "bite, burn, and numbing": See Steven J. Harper and Mina R. McDaniel, "Carbonated Water Lexicon: Temperature and CO_2 Level Influence on Descriptive Ratings," *Journal of Food Science* 58, no. 4 (1993): 893–98.

202   "Although the sensory characteristics": See Janine Beucler et al., "Development of a Sensory Lexicon for Almonds," http://www.almonds.com/sites/default/files /content/Sensory%20Lexicon.pdf.

202   "This is not giving us": See John Locke, *The Philosophical Works of John Locke* (London: George Ball & Sons, 1892), 2: 20.

204   Humans bring their own: The idea of devising some flavor based purely on a gas chromatograph brings to mind the line from *The Matrix* in which the character Mouse says, "Maybe they [the machines] couldn't figure out what to make chicken taste like, which is why chicken tastes like everything."

204   Add a small amount of vanilla: This example comes from Harry T. Lawless and Hildegarde Heymann, *Sensory Evaluation of Food: Principles and Practices* (New York: Springer, 2010), 216.

205   Words must be chosen carefully: See Herbert Stone and Joel Sidel, *Sensory Evaluation Practices* (New York: Academic Press, 2010), 210.

206   If you ask panelists: "There is no good solution," writes Lawless, "to the question of what to do with preference judgments from correct versus incorrect panelists in the discrimination tests." See Lawless and Heymann, *Sensory Evaluation of Food*, 306.

206   A lot of stereotypical "wine talk": F. J. Prial, "Wine Talk," *New York Times*, May 29, 1985.

207   "taste more attentively": E. P. Köster, "Diversity in the Determinants of Food Choice: A Psychological Perspective," *Food Quality and Preference* 20, no. 2 (2009): 70–82.

207   "gourmands of Rome": Jean Anthelme Brillat-Savarin, *The Physiology of Taste; or, Meditations on Transcendental Gastronomy* (New York: Alfred A. Knopf, 2009), 55. Brillat-Savarin also argued that humans had the most developed taste apparatus, though his logic is somewhat perfunctory: "Man, king of all nature by divine right, and for whose benefit the earth has been covered and peopled, must perforce be armed with an organ which can put him in contact with all that is toothsome among his subjects."

208   But we should be wary: See Harry T. Lawless, "Descriptive Analysis of Complex Odors: Reality, Model, or Illusion?," *Food Quality and Preference* 10, nos. 4–5 (1999): 325–32.

208   The importance of practice: See Sylvie Chollet, Dominique Valentin, and Hervé Abdi, "Do Trained Assessors Generalize Their Knowledge to New Stimuli?," *Food Quality and Preference* 16 (2005): 13–23. In the study, a number of panelists were trained on a number of beers and then given new beers to which new flavors were added. As the authors note, "Trained assessors did not use different terms to describe learned and unlearned beers. Rather they tended to apply the aroma descriptors they have learned during training to all beers even if these terms were not a priori appropriate. This result suggests that while trained assessors are able to provide efficient descriptions for new beers, they are not able to identify new aromas in beer."

209   Studies comparing expert: See Dominique Valentin et al., "Expertise and Memory

for Beers and Beer Olfactory Compounds," *Food Quality and Preference* 18, no. 5 (2007): 776–85.

209 much as a chess expert's superior memory: See, for example, Yanfei Gong, K. Anders Ericsson, and Jerad H. Moxley, "Recall of Briefly Presented Chess Positions and Its Relation to Chess Skill," *PLoS ONE* 10, no. 3 (2015).

209 Wine experts and sommeliers: "Wine expertise," the study's authors concluded, "which is seemingly based on perceptual ability, is similar to a number of other expertise domains in relying heavily on knowledge." A. L. Hughson and R. A. Boakes, "The Knowing Nose: The Role of Knowledge in Wine Expertise," *Food Quality and Preference* 13, no. 7 (2002): 463–72.

209 Wine experts first consider: For an account of the prototypicality of wine expert language, see Frederic Brochet and Denis Dubourdieu, "Wine Descriptive Language Supports Cognitive Specificity of Chemical Senses," *Brain and Language* 77, no. 2 (2001): 187–96.

210 "think and sniff": Chollet, Valentin, and Abdi, "Do Trained Assessors Generalize Their Knowledge to New Stimuli?"

210 Wine experts think *so* prototypically: Experts in general are, it has been suggested, susceptible to the so-called *Einstellung* effect: that is, when they depend so rigidly on their expertise, it blinds them to new information or to different solutions. For a good survey, as well as an experiment involving chess players, see Merim Bilalić, Peter McLeod, and Fernand Gobet, "Inflexibility of Experts—Reality or Myth? Quantifying the Einstellung Effect in Chess Masters," *Cognitive Psychology* 56, no. 2 (March 2008): 73–102.

210 "Possibly," noted Pangborn: Rose M. Pangborn, Harold W. Berg, and Brenda Hansen, "The Influence of Color on Discrimination of Sweetness in Dry Table-Wine," *American Journal of Psychology* 76, no. 3 (Sept. 1963): 492–95.

210 The wine experts' knowledge: See also Wendy V. Parr, Geoffrey White, and David Heatherbell, "The Nose Knows: Influence of Colour on Perception of Wine Aroma," *Journal of Wine Research* 14, nos. 2–3 (2003): 79–101.

210 "Either the aromas and flavours": Barry Smith, *Questions of Taste: The Philosophy of Wine* (New York: Oxford University Press, 2009), 67.

210 It is less what you have: As the wine critic Mike Steinberger notes, "Some people are better at judging wines than others, but based on what I've learned, the reasons for this are more likely to be found in the brain than in either the nose or the mouth." Steinberger, "Do You Want to Be a Supertaster?," *Slate*, June 22, 2007, accessed Dec. 17, 2013, http://www.slate.com/articles/life/drink/2007/06/do_you_want_to_be_a_supertaster.2.html.

210 The "acoustic ecologist": The description of Schafer's work comes from Trevor Cox, *Sonic Wonderland: A Scientific Odyssey of Sound* (London: Bodley Head, 2014), prologue.

210 "on the order of twenty": See David G. Wittels, "You're Not as Smart as You Could Be," *Saturday Evening Post*, April 17, 1948.

211 In a fascinating Dutch study: K. Kjaerulff, "Comparing Affective and Cognitive Aspects of Sensory Tests—Are Affective Tests More Sensitive?" (master's thesis, Royal Veterinary and Agricultural University, Copenhagen, Denmark, 2002). Referenced in Köster, "Psychology of Food Choice."

211 This emotional response: In another fascinating experiment, Danish milk consumers were better able to discern among milks when they were asked to pick

between their own "Danish" milk and some "foreign" milk about which subjects had been told an "upsetting, untrue, story" versus when they were asked to perform a more analytical sensory analysis of the milks. See Lise Wolf Frandsen et al., "Subtle Differences in Milk: Comparison of an Analytical and an Affective Test," *Food Quality and Preference* 14, nos. 5–6 (July–Sept. 2003): 515–26.

211   By the early 1970s: Joseph T. Plummer, "How Personality Makes a Difference," *Journal of Advertising Research* 40, no. 6 (2000): 79–84. Curiously, as Dr Pepper became ever more popular, moving into third place, its sales soon began to reverse. As Plummer notes, "We had inadvertently walked away from Dr Pepper's major strength—its unique brand personality. That was what really set it apart for certain consumers as an alternative to Coke and Pepsi and fruit flavors."

212   Odor is famously talked about: See Keller, "Odor Memories," as well as Yaara Yeshurun et al., "The Privileged Brain Representation of First Olfactory Associations," *Current Biology* 19, no. 21 (2009): 1869–74.

212   Science is rather divided: For a discussion, see Vanessa Danthiir et al., "What the Nose Knows: Olfaction and Cognitive Abilities," *Intelligence* 29, no. 4 (July–Aug. 2001): 337–61.

213   "You will never experience": A few weeks after the panel, I conducted my own blind taste test using a few sodas I thought were most similar to Dr Pepper—Dr. Brown's black cherry and Moxie, the regional New England soda favored by Calvin Coolidge. Perhaps these were poor choices, but I was struck by how quickly I was able to pick out Dr Pepper, now aided by the language provided to me at the panel. Dr. Brown's black cherry has a hint of the same cherryness, but it is a much simpler, sweeter, syrupy sort of cherry. Moxie is similar to Dr Pepper in that it is a complex blend of flavors, but it is rather different, with more of a medicinal flavor that reminded me of a (slightly flat) cola.

216   "locked in a sub-optimal equilibrium": David Y. Choi and Martin H. Stack, "The All-American Beer: A Case of Inferior Standard (Taste) Prevailing?," *Business Horizons* 48, no. 1 (2005): 79–86.

217   "A violet color": Kant, *Critique of Judgment*, 301.

218   "There is something about these beers": Matt Lawrence, *Philosophy on Tap: Pint-Sized Puzzles for the Pub Philosopher* (New York: John Wiley & Sons, 2011), 45.

218   "On the one hand": Christian Helmut Wenzel, *An Introduction to Kant's Aesthetics: Core Concepts and Problems* (New York: John Wiley & Sons, 2008), 11.

219   But Pabst, through a rather accidental process: Steve Annear, "Are Hipsters Driving Up the Cost of Pabst Blue Ribbon at Bars?," *Boston Magazine*, May 13, 2013, accessed Jan. 15, 2014, http://www.bostonmagazine.com/news/blog/2013/05/23/pabst-blue-ribbon-price-hipsters/.

221   "coffee doesn't taste to me": Dennett, "Quining Qualia," in Lycan, *Mind and Cognition*, 390.

CONCLUSION
TASTING NOTES

224   people will like the Napa Valley wine: Robert Ashton, " 'Nothing Good Ever Came from New Jersey': Expectations and the Sensory Perception of Wines," *Journal of Wine Economics* 9, no. 3 (Dec. 2014): 304–19.

224   As the researcher: Evgeny Yakovlev, "USSR Babies: Who Drinks Vodka in Rus-

sia" (Center for Economic and Financial Research, working paper wo198, Nov. 2012).

225 Studies have found that when subjects: See Winkielman et al., "Easy on the Eyes, or Hard to Categorize."

226 Our facial muscles work harder: See Paul Rozin and Edward B. Royzman, "Negativity Bias, Negativity Dominance, and Contagion," *Personality and Social Psychology Review* 5, no. 4 (2001): 296–320.

Index

Tom Vanderbilt has written for many publications, including *The New York Times Magazine*, *WSJ Magazine*, *Popular Science*, the *Financial Times*, *Smithsonian*, and the *London Review of Books*. He is a contributing editor of *Wired* (U.K.), *Outside*, and *Artforum*. He is author of *Traffic: Why We Drive the Way We Do (and What It Says About Us)* and *Survival City: Adventures Among the Ruins of Atomic America*. He has appeared on a wide range of television and radio programs, including the *Today* show, the BBC's World Service, and NPR's *Fresh Air*. He has been a visiting scholar at NYU's Rudin Center for Transportation Policy and Management, a research fellow at the Canadian Centre for Architecture, a fellow at the Design Trust for Public Space, and a winner of the Warhol Foundation Arts Writers grant, among other honors. He lives in Brooklyn, New York, with his wife and daughter.

A NOTE ON THE TYPE

This book was set in Janson, a typeface long thought to have been made by the Dutchman Anton Janson, who was a practicing typefounder in Leipzig during the years 1668–1687. However, it has been conclusively demonstrated that these types are actually the work of Nicholas Kis (1650–1702), a Hungarian, who most probably learned his trade from the master Dutch typefounder Dirk Voskens. The type is an excellent example of the influential and sturdy Dutch types that prevailed in England up to the time William Caslon (1692–1766) developed his own incomparable designs from them.

Typeset by Scribe,
Philadelphia, Pennsylvania

Printed and bound by Berryville Graphics,
Berryville, Virginia

Designed by Soonyoung Kwon